matt

MDL003@mcdaniel.

Family Lineage
Organization and
Social Change in
Ming and Qing Fujian

Family Lineage Organization and Social Change in Ming and Qing Fujian

ZHENG ZHENMAN

Translated by Michael Szonyi
with the Assistance of Kenneth Dean and David Wakefield

University of Hawai'i Press
Honolulu

Originally published in Chinese by the Hunan Educational Press in 1992
Printed in the United States of America

01   02   03   04   05   06   6   5   4   3   2   1

Library of Congress Cataloging-in-Publication Data

Cheng, Chen-man.
[Ming Ch'ing Fu-chien chia tsu tsu chih yu she hui pien ch'ien. English]
Family lineage organization and social change in Ming and Qing Fujian / Zheng
Zhenman ; translated by Michael Szonyi, with the assistance of Kenneth Dean
and David Wakefield.
p.   cm.
ISBN 0–8248–2333–8 (alk. paper)
1. Family—China—Fujian Sheng.   2. Fujian Sheng (China)—Social conditions.
I. Title.

HQ684.Z9 F843 2001
306.85'0951'245—dc21   00–061604

Designed by Kenneth Miyamoto
Printed by The Maple-Vail Book Manufacturing Group

Contents

Illustrations

Ming and Qing Reign Periods

Ming

Hongwu	1368–1398
Jianwen	1399–1402
Yongle	1403–1424
Hongxi	1425
Xuande	1426–1435
Zhengtong	1436–1449
Jingtai	1450–1456
Tianshun	1457–1464
Chenghua	1465–1487
Hongzhi	1488–1505
Zhengde	1506–1521
Jiajing	1522–1566
Longqing	1567–1572
Wanli	1573–1619
Taichang	1620
Tianqi	1621–1627
Chongzhen	1628–1644

Qing

Shunzhi	1644–1661
Kangxi	1662–1722
Yongzheng	1723–1734
Qianlong	1735–1795
Jiaqing	1796–1820
Daoguang	1821–1850
Xianfeng	1851–1861
Tongzhi	1862–1874
Guangxu	1875–1907
Xuantong	1908–1911

Terms for Measures
and Money

A bewildering range of local terms for weights and measures appear in these texts, and it is not always possible to find a modern equivalent. Moreover, the meaning of the terms, and the ratios of correspondence between them also varied greatly according to time and place. All of the figures below should be treated as approximations.

AREA:
1 *mu* = 7,260 square feet or 0.14 acre
1 *mu* = 10 *fen* = 100 *li* = 1,000 *hao* = 10,000 *si*
100 *mu* = 1 *qing*

Because these ratios did not vary, measures of area in the text have been converted into decimal units of *mu* and *qing*. The situation is made more complex because plot sizes in Fujian were often expressed in terms of a measure of volume corresponding to the amount of seed that should be planted.

CAPACITY:
1 picul (*shi/dan*) = 67 liters or 99 quarts
1 picul = 4 baskets (*luo*) = 10 pecks (*dou*) = 17 boxes (*tong*) = 100 pints (*sheng*)

WEIGHT:
1 picul (*shi/dan*) = 133 lbs
1 picul = 100 catty (*jin*) = 16 taels (*liang*)

LENGTH:
1 *li* = 1/3 mile
1 *zhang* = 3.581 meters or 12 feet 6 inches
1 *zhang* = 10 *chi*

MONEY:
Value is expressed in three main ways in texts translated here.
1. In terms of silver:

    1 tael (*liang*) = 37.8 grams of silver
    1 tael = 10 mace (*qian*) = 10 candareen (*fen*)

2. In terms of silver coin:

    1 silver dollar (*yuan*) = 10 *jiao*

Many types of silver dollars were in use in Ming, Qing, and Republican China. Two of the most common terms used were the big silver dollar (*da yuan*) and the foreign silver dollar (*yang yuan*).

3. In terms of copper coin (*wen*)

Translator's Preface

The important and complex role of agnatic kinship in the history of Chinese local society must have been impressed on Zheng Zhenman since his youth in a village in Putian, where stately ancestral halls and rows of huge courtyard-style family dwellings have survived the turmoil of the Maoist period. In *Family Lineage Organization and Social Change in Ming and Qing Fujian*, Zheng outlines a new model of the history of agnatic kinship in Chinese history. He begins by building a typology of household and lineage organizations and a structural model for the relationship between the two. Next, he considers the internal development cycles of households and lineages in different historical contexts, elucidating the impact of geographical and historical factors on the development of the Chinese lineage. He then links the emergence of lineage society to broader trends in Chinese economic, political, and cultural history.

Zheng's work will strike Western readers by its strong empirical basis, and its use of rich and complex local documents, particularly genealogies, and also contracts of land sale and household division, stone inscriptions, official documents, and the writings of local elites. These sources provide a candid and little-known commoner's perspective on the crucial issues of everyday life that intrigue the social historian: how did families or lineage organizations avoid taxes, corvee labor, or military conscription? How did a family prevent dissolution, given the principle of partible inheritance? How did individuals, households, and lineages respond to the growing commercialization of the Chinese economy from the mid-Ming to Qing dynasties? Was capitalism incompatible with the Chinese lineage, or did the lineage possess the flexibility to transform itself into an efficient economic investment organization? The wealth of source materials gathered over the course

1

of ten years of fieldwork and translated here permits new and more comprehensive answers to these questions, and provides a broader historical context for research by modern anthropologists. The use of these types of materials for historical research also presents new methodological challenges that will be of interest to historians not just of China but also of other societies.

In the late 1970s, Zheng was a member of one of the first cohorts to return to the universities after the Cultural Revolution, studying history at Xiamen University, where Fu Yiling and Yang Guozhen were teaching the collection and analysis of local documents. Their students would later spread throughout the universities of southern China and lead a profound rethinking of many aspects of Ming and Qing social and economic history. In the 1980s, Zheng Zhenman traveled widely throughout Fujian, gathering documents and writing about some central issues in the history of the Ming and Qing: the processes and institutions of local society; the relationship between local society and the state, and the relationships between economics, ideology or norms, and behavior. His ideas were first introduced in the pages of the journal *Chinese Social and Economic History Research*, published by the history department at Xiamen, where Zheng continues to teach. *Family Lineage Organization and Social Change in Ming and Qing Fujian*, which originated as Zheng's 1989 doctoral thesis and was published in 1992, is a synthesis and further development of this historical project. It relies on new sources and comes to new conclusions about society in the late imperial period and, perhaps most importantly, offers readers a contemporary Chinese perspective on central issues in Chinese history.

The Scholarly Context: Chinese and Western Scholarship on Household and Lineage

Zheng Zhenman is a product of a different intellectual tradition from that which informs most Western-language work on the Chinese household and lineage, and it is therefore useful both to set his work in its own context and to discuss briefly its relation to the Western-language literature. Previous scholarship on household structure in European history bears directly on work in Chinese anthropology and demography, and on Zheng's own work on household structure in Fujian history. One of the central concerns in European historical demography has been to identify the long-term trends in household structure. Peter Laslett's introduction to the influential 1972 collection *Household and Family in Past Time* sets many of the parameters of the debate. Laslett criticizes what he considers to be the widely held assumptions that households in past times were universally large and complicated, and that the broad historical trend over the past few centuries has been from large and complex to small and simple households. He argues that, in most societies at most times, the norm has always been the small nuclear family household. He also disagrees with the assumption that the size and character of the household are an expression of values or beliefs. Rather, he believes they result from economic or legal factors such as the inheritance system.[1] Lutz Berkner challenges Laslett's findings in a number of ways. First, he critiques the isolation of the inheritance system as an independent variable, arguing that the system itself may simply be the product of economic and, above all, demographic factors. He also notes that, as a given household structure may also be thought of as a phase in the domestic cycle, the proportion of households with that structure in any community may reflect merely the length of time for which that phase of the domestic cycle persists relative to other phases. Thus, even though a community may have few complex households at any given time, this does not mean that most households do not pass through a complex phase at some time or another. The critical factor determining this question is demographic. For Berkner, demographic factors are key in shaping the household development cycle.[2]

A comparable debate runs through the scholarship on Chinese demographic history. Olga Lang long ago argued that, while the multiple-family household was held as the ideal in traditional China, only the wealthy could achieve this ideal in practice.[3] Unfortunately, there is little data from Chinese history that would allow empirical exploration of the domestic cycle and enable scholars to confirm or refute Lang's claim. Arthur Wolf's work on population registers from the period of the Japanese occupation of Taiwan suggests that many men, not just the wealthy, lived part of their lives in a large multiple-family household. In other words, rich and poor families followed a similar development cycle. It was the relative proportion spent in each phase of the cycle that varied with economic position. Nonetheless, "Chinese farm families were potentially large everywhere and actually large wherever material conditions were somewhat better than miserable."[4] More recent demographic work, some of it done by Chinese scholars, has refined Wolf's arguments. Liu Ts'ui-jung argues that many men could potentially have lived part of their lives in complex households, but sheer demographics meant that such households were not prevalent, because members of the senior generation tended to die before or not long after they became grandfathers or great grand-fathers.[5] Zhao Zhongwei's work on genealogies leads to similar con-clusions: many men could potentially have lived in a common house-hold with their grandfathers, but few could have lived together with their great grandfathers.[6] But the work of James Lee and Cameron Campbell, who have used Banner records to study the domestic cycle and household formation in northeastern Liaodong in the Qing, sug-gests that most households were multiple-family households, and that household structure changed only rarely. Simpler households tended to be more volatile, for the simpler the household, the more likely it was to deteriorate or even disappear when the status of a single member changed. By contrast, even after a multiple family divided, the members of the original household were likely to continue to live in newly formed multiple households. As a result, the multiple-family household was "perennial" in Qing Liaodong.[7]

Rather than taking a stand on the simplistic question of what type of household structure predominated, Zheng Zhenman also points to the importance of devoting attention to the household development cycle in understanding the lived experience of household members. For Zheng, demographic, material, legal, and cultural factors all shape the household development cycle. He considers the inheritance system, specifically the timing of household division and its effects, to be par-ticularly important; so too are cultural factors, such as the idealization of filial piety. He does wade into the debate over directly relating the size and complexity of household structure to wealth. In the complex economy of Ming and Qing Fujian, diversification of labor within the household made sense for the poor as well as for the rich and could lead even the poorest of families to maintain or attempt to maintain a single household for generations.

* * *

Western readers may find Zheng's definitions of the terms for the types of household structure confusing, for they differ from the standard ter-minology of the field. Rather than trying to force Zheng's typology into the language of Western scholars, I have elected in this translation to retain his own language. Table 1.1 presents an equivalency table relating Zheng's terminology to that of Peter Laslett and Arthur Wolf.

Table 1.1. Equivalency Chart of Household Structure Terminology

Terminology/Author	Basic Unit of Analysis	Laslett	Wolf	Zheng
		Conjugal Family Unit	Nuclear Unit	Conjugal Unit Family (*peiou de jiating*)
Household consisting of no basic units	single individual	solitary	solitaire	
	two or more individuals but no basic unit	no family	subelementary family	incomplete family (*bu wanzheng jiating*)
Household consisting of one basic unit	one basic unit	simple family a.k.a. nuclear family or elementary family	elementary family	small family (*xiao jiating*) a.k.a. nuclear family (*hexin jiating*)
	one basic unit plus others	extended family	augmented elementary family	
Household consisting of two or more basic units	generic term for household of two or more basic units	multiple family household (joint household in some other sources)		large family (*da jiating*)
	two basic units, one consisting of parents and the other of a second basic unit in lower generation	stem family	stem family	stem family (*zhugan jiating*)
	more than two basic units, one consisting of parents and the other of a second basic unit in lower generation, plus other basic units in lower generation		grand family	lineal family (*zhixi jiating*)
	two or more basic units linked by filial linkage to a conjugal unit no longer present	frérèche	frérèche	joint family (*lianhe jiating*)

One important difference to keep in mind is that Zheng's classification system rests on a fundamental distinction between the household with only one conjugal unit, which he labels the small household, and the household with more than one, which he labels the large household. This distinction is stressed much less in the typologies of Laslett and Wolf.

Zheng Zhenman's work tries to bridge the gap between studies of the household and studies of the lineage by building a logical link between the two. He argues that the lineage first emerged out of the particular characteristics of the process of household division in Fujian, namely, that certain rights and responsibilities are not divided in that process but continue to be held collectively. Turning from the scholarship on the household to that on the larger kinship group requires that we consider briefly not just two, but three distinct traditions. Though there are few direct links between Zheng's thought and late imperial writings on lineage organization, these writings do influence his text, in that they shape the vocabulary of his sources. Thus one set of terms that appears frequently in this work is the great and lesser descent-line (da zong, xiao zong), which are references to the system of descent-line inheritance in antiquity. The *Liji* (Book of ritual) describes two types of descent-lines (zong). The great descent-line is a single line of descent, continuing indefinitely, of eldest sons of eldest sons going back to a feudal lord. In antiquity, certain prerogatives were attached to the great descent-line, including the permanent maintenance of sacrifice to the founding ancestor. A younger son became the focus of a lesser descent line, which lasted only four generations, after which ancestral sacrifice ceased.[8] There is no way of knowing how accurately this system describes early Zhou kinship practices, but beginning in the eleventh century some neo-Confucian scholars proposed that it should be revived, and in the Ming and Qing discourse on ancestral worship the descent-line system was often used as a reference to which current practice could be compared.[9] Similarly, the *Zhouli* (Rituals of the Zhou) and other ancient classics prescribe that ancestral tablets should be arranged on an altar with odd-numbered generations on one side and even-numbered generations on the other, an arrangement known as *zhaomu* order, and one that people in Ming and Qing times sought to emulate.

Scholarship on the Chinese lineage in the People's Republic of China has focused mostly on its political functions. In his famous "Report on an Investigation into the Peasant Movement in Hunan," Mao had identified lineage authority as one of the four types of political authority oppressing peasants in traditional China, the others being political, religious, and patriarchal.[10] Seen largely as a tool by which the landlord class obscured class contradictions and oppressed the masses, the lineage was an important target for criticism. In an article that appeared just before the Cultural Revolution put an end to most scholarly endeavors, Zuo Yunpeng attempted to trace the historical origins of lineage authority. He identified the Tang–Song period as the crucial transition, when feudal property relations were undermined and an emergent landlord class made use of lineage ideology and lineage collective property to dominate the rest of society.[11] After the Cultural Revolution, Li Wenzhi continued the effort to link lineage development to larger social changes, both ideological and material. He stressed the rise of the gentry class, and its efforts to use lineage organization to strengthen rural solidarity. In an important intervention, Xu Yangjie noted that household and lineage both grow out of a common moral order but are very distinct in their practical manifestation, that is, in their material form. For example, households are characterized by collective ownership of property and organization of labor, whereas lineages are not.[12] Zheng Zhenman's arguments are in part an effort to deal with the contradictions he detects in drawing this sharp distinction. He finds that collective ownership of property and organization of labor may also be characteristics of lineage organization.

*　*　*

Zheng Zhenman began his studies in history under Fu Yiling, and Fu's ideas on diverse subjects strongly inform this project. In an important article that first appeared in 1963, Fu laid out his position in the debate on the failure of capitalism to develop in China. For Fu, the explanation lay in the complex system of control that had been evolved by the feudal ruling classes to govern the people and suppress any threat to their control of land. Fu's interpretation of the system owed much to Mao's analysis of the problems in Chinese society prior to the revolution. He divided the four types of political authority identified in the Hunan report into two categories: the public, which encompassed the first type of authority, that of the state; and the private, which encompassed the remaining three types, lineage, religious, and patriarchal authority.[13]

The specific role of the lineage was explored in another essay from the early 1960s, based on a paper Fu had written in 1946 but had much revised to reflect his growing understanding of Marxist, and Maoist, ideas about history. Here Fu considered the territorial expression of the lineage, developing the influential formulation of the lineage village, or territorial lineage (*xiangzu*): "The landlord class ruled the peasants not only through an authoritarian and bureaucratic structure, but also by means of a more subtle method, which was to use the influence of the territorial lineage, a remnant of the [ancient] clan system, to moderate the intensification of social and class contradictions, and effectively control the peasants."[14] The body of the paper then went on to examine the various ways in which the territorial lineage exercised power in late imperial Chinese society. The utility of Fu's notion of lineage village, which made possible a much more nuanced understanding of the role of the lineage in local society, is demonstrated in a collection of essays on Fujian local history by him, Yang Guozhen, and their students at Xiamen University. Mori Masao has intelligently related the term to the Japanese formulation of *kyōdōtai*.[15]

Zheng Zhenman would disagree with Fu's interpretation of the origins of the lineage in Fujian in the clan system of antiquity, reinforced by the need for participants in successive waves of migration into South China to organize for defensive purposes. But the notion of the lineage village that exercises control in highly flexible ways within a particular cultural context strongly influenced Zheng's own research. In fact, the very title of this book could be read as a reflection of Zheng's desire to extend Fu's ideas. Fu developed the notion of the lineage and its relationship with territorial organization (*xiangzu*); here, Zheng wishes to show that the analysis of the lineage must also be pushed into the relationship of the lineage with the household (*jiazu*).

The other major scholarly influence on Zheng's work has been recent Taiwanese anthropology. Indeed, his basic typology of lineage organization is adapted from the writings of Tang Meijun.[16] Other anthropologists of Taiwan, in particular Zhuang Yingzhang and Chen Qi'nan, have explored the history of lineage organization in great detail and discovered what some consider to be the product of Taiwan's unique historical circumstances in the development of kinship-based organizations suited to the early immigrant period. The difficulty for an individual migrant of ensuring continuity of ancestral sacrifice, the endemic violence among migrants from different regions of China and between migrants and aboriginal groups, the particularities of large-scale land reclamation, and other factors contributed to extremely flexible organizational forms, many based on the principle of share investment, which seem quite different from lineages on the mainland.[17] Convinced that the structural features of Taiwanese society are essentially those of Chinese society, Zheng has tried in this work to develop a unified model that can encompass the historical experiences of both mainland Fujian and Taiwan. In the sections of the work that deal specifically with Taiwan in Chapters 2 and 4, Zheng's goal is to demonstrate that the data from Taiwan can be interpreted according to his model. His category of contractual lineage, in particular, is adapted from the work of Taiwanese anthropology but is intended to explain organizations on both sides of the Taiwan Straits.

Study of the Chinese lineage in the West has been informed by two traditions, social history and social anthropology.[18] Western studies of the Chinese lineage continue to be strongly influenced by the work of Maurice Freedman, who argued on the basis of the limited sources available to him that the Chinese lineage was essentially an inheritance group characterized by lineage corporate property, and that its development therefore was rooted in issues of control and allocation of resources.[19] Western social historians have been most interested in the lineage for its role in social mobility, elite power and resources, and the dynamics of local society.[20] Zheng Zhenman approaches the question from a very different angle than most authors writing in English. Working with sources that until very recently were largely unavailable to Western historians, he attempts to demonstrate that the lineage emerged as a dominant social institution in Fujian after the Song, spreading because of economic, political, and ideological developments, but also notes that, even within Fujian, regional factors led to highly divergent trajectories of lineage development. Nevertheless, there are numerous points of congruity between Zheng's work and that of Western social historians and anthropologists. For example, the notion that "elites pursue strategies of lineage formation to protect family resources from division through partible inheritance" resonates strongly with Zheng's arguments about the formation of inheritance lineages, though he differs in seeing lineage formation as a strategy that made sense for all families, not just elite ones.[21] Zheng's findings also invite comparison with the work of Patricia Ebrey and Kai-wing Chow on the changing discourses and practices of ritual since the Song.[22] Working entirely on the basis of the writings of literati from Fujian, Zheng identifies similar processes of reinterpretation of the classical texts to suit contemporary needs to those discussed by Ebrey and Chow.

Zheng's terminology of the lineage, like his terminology of the household, is rather different from that found in much of the English language scholarly literature. The standard definition of the term "lineage" in Western literature on China is a group the members of which share common descent, share ownership in collective assets like property, engage in corporate activities, and are conscious of themselves as a group.[23] Recent anthropological work, particularly Myron Cohen's study of North China, has challenged the focus on property as the criteria for lineage organization.[24] For Zheng, too, none of these four criteria is strictly necessary for the existence of a lineage. He uses the Chinese terms *zu* and *jiazu*, both translated here as lineage, to mean a very broadly defined organizational entity, whose members either share, or claim to share, descent from a common ancestor. It is an organization which may share ownership in collective assets, but need not, and may on the other hand share collective responsibilities or duties. The term does not imply solidarity or corporate structure.[25] Another key difference in Zheng's terminology is that the term "lineage" in English is usually considered an exclusive ascription—that is, a person may belong to one and only one lineage. The only possible exception in the English-language scholarship is that a person may belong to a local residential lineage and also to what is called variously a higher-order lineage or a clan, that is, an "umbrella organization that ties together several patrilineally related localized lineages," or an "organization composed of lineages or descent groups [in which] the agnatic links between these constituent units are extremely remote and most likely fictionalized."[26] Zheng would not agree with the analytical distinction between lineages and higher-order lineages or clans, but considers all of these to be lineages of different types.[27] He also denies the privileging of one form over another; both are lineages, just different kinds of lineages. Zheng's definition of lineage is thus broader than that with which most Western readers will be familiar. At times it can also be narrower. The Chinese terms *fang*, *zhi*, or *pai*, usually translated as lineage segment or branch—that is, all the descendants of a single member of a lineage, whether or not these have formally organized or divided themselves—are for Zheng themselves types of lineage organizations. Since the key criterion for a lineage is simply claimed descent from a common ancestor, lineage membership is not

exclusive. An individual can be simultaneously a member of an infi-
nite number of lineage organizations, some within the village, others
extending beyond the limits of the prefecture or even the province.

Moreover, for Zheng, the term "lineage" is even more flexible
than this. When persons who claim descent from a common ancestor
organize themselves for whatever purpose, the organization that results
is a lineage organization. Voluntary associations, or *hui*, may be formed
by certain members of a lineage for various purposes, including religious and economic ones. These organizations are themselves lineage
organizations, though their membership includes not all the members
of an existing lineage but only some. Membership in these associations
can often be inherited, which make them tend toward institutional-
ization over time, but since all those who inherit a share in the membership of an association do so on the basis of descent from a
common ancestor, association membership itself becomes a type of
lineage organization. Zheng distinguishes three main types of lineage
organization: inheritance lineages, based primarily on ties of inheritance through kinship; lineages based primarily on internal relations
of power and subordination, and contractual lineages based primarily
on ties of common interest. This formulation, based on Lewis Morgan's
classification of society, first appears in the literature on the Chinese
lineage in the work of Tang Meijun, but is used rather differently by
Zheng.

The lineage is at its most flexible in Zheng's formulation of the
lineage village or territorial lineage (*xiangzu*), to which he returns at
the end of the work. Here, he argues that lineage organization provided the model that underlay all other organizations within late imperial Chinese society. Political factions, secret societies, native-place
associations and guilds, as well as local militias and joint stock investment corporations, were all constructed out of, or according to the
principles of, lineage organization.[28] Thus the lineage can transcend
any definition based on formal principles, and indeed, the lineage
organizational form has shaped organizations that do not even share
the essential criterion of shared descent. Zheng's interest, which he
shares with Fu Yiling, in the existence and historical elaboration of
such areas of associational activity, independent of state interference,
ties their work into the debates on civil society and the public sphere
in modern China that have been influential in Western studies of Chinese history over the last decade.[29] Zheng's book can provide support for both sides of the debate, for it demonstrates that there was

indeed a complex structure of civil organizations formed outside of the state, but also that this structure was linked to the state in complex ways and served functions in society so different from what Jurgen Habermas described as the public sphere as to make that use of the European term to describe Chinese society highly problematic.

The Geographic Context: A Brief History of Fujian

The history of the southeastern coastal province of Fujian has been shaped by the broad patterns of Chinese history, and also by important local particularities. This history is relatively accessible to the nonspecialist, with many recent works in Western languages.[30] For most of the Qing dynasty, the province included the island of Taiwan. The mainland portion of the province is mostly mountainous, with four large coastal plains in which are located the major political and economic centers. Communication with the rest of China has traditionally been by sea or across difficult mountain passes. Han Chinese migrants began to enter the region in the Han dynasty, displacing and absorbing the indigenous population. Hans Bielenstein has outlined the spread of Han settlement, which accelerated through the first millennium.[31] After the collapse of the Tang, the short-lived independent Min kingdom was established in Fujian by recent migrants, a story told by Edward Schafer.[32] By the Song, Fujian had become a major economic center, and Quanzhou was one of the greatest ports in the world. Shiba Yoshinobu has discussed Fujian's relations with the rest of China in the Song, and Hugh Clark the effects of commercial development on the region itself.[33] The great Song neo-Confucian synthesizer Zhu Xi spent much of his life in Fujian, which was also the native place of many of his students and other important figures in this movement.

From the Song onward, international trade was crucial to the well-being of the province, in particular its southern region. For the Ming and Qing period with which this work is mainly concerned, William Skinner's description of the major economic macrocycles of Fujian, part of his larger project to differentiate the economic cycles of China's different macroregions, provides a useful point of departure. According to Skinner, a period of economic expansion centered on Quanzhou lasted until the early fourteenth century, after which Ming prohibitions on trade led to a long-term depression. Contemporary sources blamed economic decline in this period on the raids and banditry of Japanese pirates (*wokou*; Japanese *wakō*), but historians today believe that many, perhaps most, of these pirates were actually Chinese merchants whose livelihood was threatened by Ming restrictions on trade.[34] Growth was renewed in the sixteenth century, in part by increased trade with Europeans. Then, in the early Qing, the coastal region was beset by a partial evacuation imposed by the state to cut off ties to the forces of the Ming loyalist Zheng Chenggong, also known as Koxinga. Skinner claims that the economy of Fujian in the seventeenth century performed poorly, not only because of the evacuation, which was later repealed, but also by renewed trade restrictions and growing demographic pressures.[35] But Ng Chin-keong has convincingly challenged Skinner's claim that prosperity did not return until the opening of Xiamen as a treaty port in 1840, arguing that coastal trade and the opening up of Taiwan actually led to an economic upswing that lasted through the mid-Qing.[36] Skinner's analysis also ignores the intensification of economic activity in the mountainous interior of the province.

Geographic factors have worked against cultural and economic homogenization, and considerable diversity persists among the different regions of the province, which remains home to a number of mutually unintelligible dialects. Zheng divides the province into three broad areas: the coastal regions of the south and east, the north and western interior, and Taiwan. But it is possible to make some generalizations across the mainland portions of the province as a whole. Sources from the Song through to the twentieth century describe Fujian in terms of low ratios of arable land to population, which has encouraged commercialization and given rise to a range of social tensions, including food riots in urban areas, violent interlineage feuding in rural areas, and rebellions by impoverished miners and tenants in the mountains. At the time, the shortage of arable land was seen as the main factor driving many local people to become involved in trade. Modern scholars are divided as to whether the main causes of rising commercialization were the demographic constraints, the position taken by Fu Yiling, or the lure of economic opportunities, an argument made by Evelyn Rawski.[37] The high demand for land, economic and social reasons favoring land over other investments, and large amounts of surplus merchant capital gave rise to one of the peculiarities of Fujian: the practice of divided or multiple landownership, a phenomenon that appears frequently in the documents used in this book. Multiple ownership arose when the right to cultivate land was sold but other rights of ownership and certain obligations were retained by the seller, creating a system where various people had invested in and held various rights to the same plot of land. The causes of multiple land-ownership in Taiwan were somewhat different, with early migrants contracting with the state and indigenous inhabitants to reclaim large tracts of land for settled agriculture, then selling rights to reclaim and cultivate to another stratum of owners, who then leased the land to tenants. A wide variety of terms was in local use to characterize these divided ownership rights, and it is not always clear in isolated documents to what exact right a given term refers. The work of Yang Guozhen has explored how the terms were used in different parts of Fujian.[38]

Another long-term trend in the history of coastal Fujian has been the importance of overseas trade and emigration. Fu Yiling argues that this trade was transformed in the sixteenth century, as Chinese merchants moved into the trade that had previously been dominated by Japanese, Arabs, and others, and as the trade shifted from luxuries to bulk goods. Many merchants adopted sons to engage in trade on their behalf, granting them considerable responsibility in exchange for some of the risks of overseas trade. Trade also stimulated emigration—both to Taiwan, which became a prefecture of Fujian province in 1683, and to Southeast Asia, where colonial powers actively encouraged Chinese immigration. Emigrants chose to leave their homes for reasons that included overpopulation and shortage of land. These same factors led to the internal colonization of the highlands of Fujian's interior, where the exploitation of resources such as timber contributed to the broader trend of commercialization. Kenneth Dean's work has shown that the development of local cult networks structured by the Daoist liturgical framework is also an important part of the social history of Fujian in the Ming and Qing, and this is a topic which Zheng Zhenman himself is now exploring.[39] The other striking aspect of local social history has been the development of lineage society, the focus of this work. The most visible symbol of lineage society is the lineage ancestral hall. Free-standing, dedicated ancestral halls spread in Fujian from the mid-Ming onward. These halls were often used for sacrifice to distant ancestors—that is, ancestors beyond the mourning grades. Local lineages often maintained traditions about their earliest ancestor who had migrated to Fujian from North China and the first ancestor who had settled in their current home. Such founding ancestors often occupied pride of place in the ancestral hall.[40] Part of Zheng's task in this book is to explain how this situation came about.

Summary and Notes on the Translation

Zheng's model of family and lineage organization is elaborated over the course of the book. The first chapter outlines his basic analytical framework, which he believes provides the basis for a more comprehensive understanding of lineage organization in Ming–Qing Fujian, by making possible an analysis of the historical causes of different lineage forms, their developmental processes, and their discrete functions. Chapter 2 focuses on the structural features of cycles of household development. Zheng argues that, in what he calls the state of tension between the subsistence and commercial economy that obtained in Fujian in the late imperial period, occupational diversification and specialization was the most sensible strategy for all, and this favored the growth of complex households. Zheng is thus concerned here with issues such as the effects of the domestic cycle on household wealth and the division of labor within the household. On the other hand, tensions within the household as well as taxation policies favored division of the household with each passing generation. The practice of household division thus restricted the development of large households, guiding family structure into a cyclical pattern of alternating large and small household phases.

Chapter 3 introduces Zheng's typology of three main types of lineage organization: inheritance, control-subordination, and contractual. An inheritance lineage, the most basic type, formed when a household divided and was a response to the tensions created by the practice of household division. Thus Zheng identifies an essential link between household development and lineage development. Lineage society generally developed first by the spread and formation of inheritance lineages and second by evolving into mixed formations of control-subordination and contractual lineages, which were lineages formed on the principle of territorial control or common interest, respectively. The overall line of lineage development in Ming–Qing Fujian was thus from inheritance lineages to control-subordination and contractual lineages. Chapter 4 refines this model by considering the effects of particular historical conditions and environmental factors on lineage development. In the relatively stable and commercially less developed region of northeastern Fujian, inheritance lineages often grew very large before transforming into control-subordination or contractual lineages. In coastal Fujian, however, with its much higher level of commercialization, control-subordination lineages predominated and inheritance lineages were comparatively less well developed. In the immigrant society of Qing Taiwan, it was contractual lineages that dominated. In Chapter 5, Zheng links the spread of lineage society to larger themes in Chinese cultural, political, and economic history, exploring the popularization of lineage ideology, the increasing autonomy of local society, and the development of cooperative economic relations. Chapter 6 is a conclusion that elaborates on the theoretical significance of the work. Zheng sees lineage organization in the Ming-Qing period as a multilayered, multipurpose structure that served as the basis of organization and control at the most basic level of society. The flexibility of lineage organization also allowed it to serve as the foundation and the model for all other social organizations in late imperial China. This point brings Zheng's conclusions back to Fu Yiling's conception of the lineage village. Understanding Ming-Qing lineage organization serves to illuminate the complex structure and particular characteristics of traditional Chinese society and deepens our understanding of Chinese history.

*   *   *

This translation is essentially complete, with the major exception of the review of the scholarly literature in Chapter 1 of the original. I felt that it was more useful to locate Zheng's work in a larger context including work in Chinese anthropology and social history and European social and demographic history, and have tried to do so in this preface. A number of shorter cuts have been made for other reasons. Passages in the original that were duplicated elsewhere in the work have been removed, as have two lengthy tables. I have abbreviated several very lengthy citations in order to highlight the relevant passages and moved other citations to the Notes. I have also excised most of the formulaic polite or self-deprecating phrases conventionally used by Chinese scholars. The conventions regarding scholarly apparatus are rather different for historians in the People's Republic of China than for those working in the West. Providing references only to *juan*, and not to specific page numbers, is one of these conventions. For many of the sources used in this work it would be hard to do otherwise. Zheng has consulted many genealogies that survive only in the hands of local villagers. Such genealogies are often badly decayed and irregularly numbered; moreover, it is impossible to consult them without actually visiting these villages, and so page references would be of limited use. In preparing the Notes and the Bibliography, I have simply included all the details provided in the original. I have followed Zheng's syntax for providing the titles of genealogies, which retains any geographic terms in the title of the work and indicates which of these terms refer to counties or larger geographic units by enclosing them in parentheses. This should help readers get some sense of the origin of particular sources. Where possible, I have consulted original sources for the translation of citations, and this has led to some discrepancies with the Chinese original of Zheng's book. For the sake of readability, all Chinese titles have been converted according to the system used in Charles Hucker's *Dictionary of Official Titles in Imperial China*. Where possible, dates have been converted to the Western calendar. For ease of reading, ages have been converted from *sui* to years, but because Chinese reckoned their age according to the passage of the New Year, not their own actual birthday, ages given in the text may be overstated by one year. Names of prominent people have been standardized according to the name by which the person is commonly known. Thus the Song neo-Confucian Zhu Xi appears only as such, and not by his other names or titles, such as Master Wen, Zhu Yuanhui, or Zhu Zhonghui. I have not tried to translate personal names, with the exception of those names which consist of ordinal numbers, as in Ancestor Shiqi (Seventeen). Explanatory comments on the translation appear as footnotes enclosed in square brackets.

Several colleagues contributed to the translation of *Family Lineage Organization and Social Change in Ming and Qing Fujian*. The late David Wakefield conceived the project and found the funds to bring Zheng Zhenman to North America for several months in 1997. I made a preliminary translation of the entire work with Zheng Zhenman's assistance in 1997 and revised the manuscript in 1999. Kenneth Dean, Zheng's longtime collaborator, was responsible for the initial contact with the University of Hawai'i Press and has supported the project throughout. Richard Bachand prepared the maps. My research assistants, Belinda Huang, Dong Bo, and Blaine Chiasson, helped with the preparation of the tables and proofreading of the manuscript. My thanks to all of them. I am also indebted to Sharon Yamamoto, Masako Ikeda, and Patricia Crosby of the University of Hawai'i Press and to Barbara Folsom for her expert copy-editing. I am of course responsible for any errors in the translation.

Source: Zhongguo Lishi dituji; vol. 8; Plates 42-43; Beijing: Ditu chubanshe, 1987

Map 1. Fujian Province in the Qing Dynasty

FUNING DEPARTMENT
1. Funing Department Seat
2. Xiapu
3. Fuding
4. Shouning
5. Fu'an
6. Ningde

FUZHOU PREFECTURE
7. Fuzhou Prefectural Seat
8. Minxian
9. Houguan
10. Pingnan
11. Gutian
12. Luoyuan
13. Lianjiang
14. Changle
15. Fuqing
16. Yongfu
17. Minqing

JIANNING PREFECTURE
18. Jianning Prefectural Seat
19. Chong'an
20. Pucheng
21. Zhenghe
22. Jian'an
23. Ouning
24. Jianyang
25. Songxi

LONGYAN DEPARTMENT
26. Longyan Department Seat
27. Ningyang
28. Zhangping

QUANZHOU PREFECTURE
29. Quanzhou Prefectural Seat
30. Hui'an
31. Nan'an
32. Tong'an
33. Jinjiang
34. Anxi
35. Maxiang Subprefecture

SHAOWU PREFECTURE
36. Shaowu Prefectural Seat
37. Guangze
38. Taining
39. Jianning

TINGZHOU PREFECTURE
40. Tingzhou Prefectural Seat
41. Changting
42. Ninghua
43. Qingliu
44. Guihua
45. Liancheng
46. Shanghang
47. Wuping
48. Yongding

XINGHUA PREFECTURE
49. Xinghua Prefectural Seat
50. Putian
51. Xianyou

YANPING PREFECTURE
52. Yanping Prefectural Seat
53. Jiangle
54. Nanping
55. Yong'an
56. Shaxian
57. Shunchang
58. Youxi

YONGCHUN DEPARTMENT
59. Yongchun Department Seat
60. Dehua
61. Datian

ZHANGZHOU PREFECTURE
62. Zhangzhou Prefectural Seat
63. Longxi
64. Zhangpu
65. Nanjing
66. Changtai
67. Pinghe
68. Zhao'an
69. Haicheng
70. Yunxiao Subprefecture

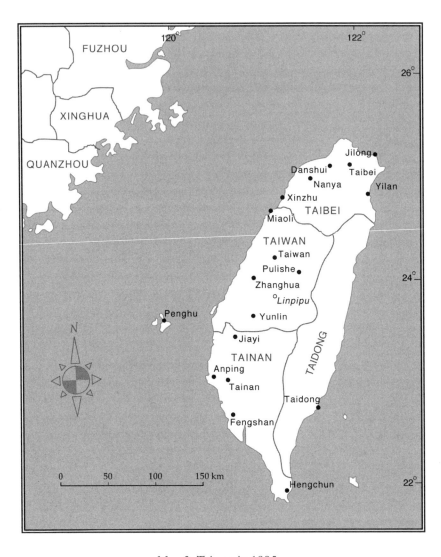

FUZHOU

XINGHUA

QUANZHOU

120°

122°

26°

Jilong

Danshui
Nanya
Taibei

Yilan

Xinzhu

TAIBEI

Miaoli

TAIWAN

Taiwan

Pulishe

24°

Zhanghua

°Linpipu

Penghu

Yunlin

TAIDONG

Jiayi

TAINAN

Anping

Tainan

Taidong

Fengshan

0   50   100   150 km

22°

Hengchun

N

Map 2. Taiwan in 1885

1
Introduction

This work is a study of family and lineage organization in Fujian and Taiwan in the Ming–Qing period. It discusses the fundamental structure of traditional Chinese society and the trends in its historical development. This is an area of research in which Chinese and foreign scholars have shown great interest and scholars past and present have made significant contributions and achieved considerable results. The ideas in this work have benefited in many ways from the pioneering work of previous scholars, but I have also tried to present new ideas of my own. Most research in the Chinese historical world has stressed the political nature of family lineage organization and adopted the viewpoint of class analysis. The formation of this scholarly tradition is perhaps linked to the Chinese Communist Party's practice of political struggle. In his famous "Report of an Investigation into the Peasant Movement in Hunan," Mao Zedong wrote that, in modern China, "the system [of the lineage], ranging from the central and branch ancestral temples to the head of the household," comprises the lineage system of authority, represented by the ancestral hall and the lineage head, which is one of the four main systems of authority that oppress the Chinese people.[1] Because it was seen as hindering class differentiation and oppressing the masses, "feudal family lineage organization" became an important target of criticism and a symbol of struggle during the revolution. Marxist historians in the People's Republic, looking for historical explanations for the longevity of Chinese feudal society, have continued to criticize feudal family lineage ideology and sought to demonstrate the connections between family lineage organization, the feudal system of landownership, and autocratic government. . . .[2]

Since 1983, as part of the National Social Sciences Plan Key Project

"Research into the Social and Economic History of Fujian in the Ming and Qing," my colleagues and I have conducted extensive investigation into social and economic history throughout Fujian, gathering and analyzing many historical documents including genealogies, contracts, sacrificial property registers, and documents of family division. We have discovered that family lineage organization in Ming–Qing Fujian was the most systematized form of organization in local society, playing critical roles in the fields of politics, economics, and culture, among others. Therefore, careful study of the structure and functions of family lineage organization is essential to fully explaining the social and economic history of the period. Under the direction of my teachers Fu Yiling and Yang Guozhen, I conducted some preliminary investigation into this topic and published several specialized essays, the common theme of which was the position and function of family lineage organization in the structure of traditional Chinese society. This is also the main theme and starting point of this work.

The characteristics of family lineage organization in Ming and Qing Fujian were extremely complex and varied. In terms of external appearance, family lineage organization ranged from large and powerful lineages that built ancestral halls, compiled lineage genealogies, and owned considerable property, to small, weak lineages with neither halls nor genealogies and with little property, and to all manner of households, small and large, whose members lived and owned property in common. In terms of scale of development, family lineage organization ranged from dispersed lineages that transcended county, prefectural, and even provincial boundaries, to residentially concentrated lineages comprising the population of a single village or several villages, and to solitary migrant or sojourning households. The ties that could link the members of a family or lineage together included pure kinship relations such as marriage and descent, forms of manipulated kinship such as adoption of a relative, or "transferring posterity" (*guoji*) adoption, adoption of non-kin, and also other kinds of relationships based on common locality or common interest.[3] In a single period, within a single locality and within a single family lineage, these different forms could coexist and intermingle. At different times, in different places, and at different stages in the development of a single family or lineage organization, the characteristics of the organization were constantly changing. Thus it would be extremely difficult to explore all the various forms of family lineage organization completely and systematically.

Family lineage organization in Ming and Qing Fujian had very extensive social functions. In the political realm, family lineage organization merged with the taxation and service levy *(lijia)* and local security *(baojia)* systems and gradually became the fundamental organization of political authority, responsible for such important tasks as the maintenance of local order, administration of justice, property registration, and the allocation of tax and service levy responsibilities.[4] In the economic realm, family lineage organizations were not only the basic social units for production and consumption but also played an important role in such aspects of economic reproduction as irrigation, transportation, marketing, commerce, and social welfare. In the cultural realm, family lineage organizations were responsible for hiring teachers and arranging education, promoting candidates for the examination system, conducting all kinds of religious ritual, and organizing various forms of popular culture. Family lineage organizations were an important force in promoting morality and maintaining the traditional value system. It would not be an exaggeration to say that in the local society of Ming and Qing Fujian there were no social functions which could not potentially be performed by families or lineages. This is not to argue that a single family lineage organization always performed all these functions, or that the social functions of every family lineage organization were identical. Quite to the contrary, responsibility for various social functions was always divided between numerous family lineage organizations organized at different levels, with each family lineage organization undertaking one or several functions. Particular social functions were usually associated with particular levels of family lineage organization. If we wish to discuss the social functions of family lineage organization in general, therefore, it is necessary to consider the multiple levels and functions of organizations within the larger structure.

In terms of structure and functions, then, family lineage organization in the Ming and Qing was extremely complex, and family lineage organization could take hundreds of possible forms. It would be impossible to analyze each of these different forms in detail and demonstrate a specific example for each. How then is such a complex social and historical phenomenon to be analyzed? I believe that, given the objectives of social history, we ought to focus on analyzing the social relationships among family lineage members and the principles shaping their behavior. This is the basic criterion that distinguishes the different types of family lineage organization, and also reflects the fundamental characteristics of the process of family lineage development. With this in mind, this book begins with a discussion of the social relationships among family lineage members, and the particular principles shaping their behavior, in order to develop a typology of family lineage organizations. On this basis, I next consider the relationship between the different types and their developmental trends in order to construct a diachronic model of family lineage structure. The social functions of family lineage organization were largely determined by the social relationships among the members, so these functions are also discussed. The structure and functions of family lineage organization were also conditioned by the immediate local historical context and social environment. To demonstrate the effects of the context on the development of families and lineages, and the relationship between family lineage organization and broader changes in society, this work also surveys the history of Fujian and Taiwan in the Ming and Qing.

Previous scholars have constructed different definitions of and typologies for family lineage organization and suggested a number of explanatory systems to justify these approaches. To avoid misunderstandings, I begin with a brief discussion of my own ideas and the logic of my arguments. I use the term "family lineage organization" *(jiazu zuzhi)* to refer to two social forms: the family and the lineage. By "family" *(jia)*, I mean a group living together and owning property in common, linked by genuine or fictive kinship relations. By "lineage" *(zu)*, I mean a group whose members live and own property separately, but who form a group that is linked by genuine or fictive consanguinal relations and that claims descent from a common ancestor. I believe that considering the family and lineage in traditional Chinese society together within a single analytic framework has important theoretical significance. This is not just because both share certain of the characteristics of kinship groups but, more important, because their structure and functions are mutually interdependent, so their logical relationship cannot be ignored. Engels wrote that "the social organization under which the people of a particular historical epoch and a particular country live is determined by both kinds of production: by the stage of development of labour on the one hand and of the family on the other."[5] This means that people must construct forms of social organization that are appropriate to their particular form of family development. Lineage organization is a social organization constructed directly above the family, so it naturally is also deeply shaped by family development. From a functionalist perspective; family and lineage might be described as the first and second lines of defense of the individual respectively.[6] Thus, the significance of the lineage is that it directly supplements functions of the family and performs functions the family fails to perform, which is to say that the lineage plays the role of the "designated heir" of the family. The various social relations within the family, such as marriage relations, consanguinal relations, and adoption relations, as well as the inheritance relations that grow out of them, have a powerful influence on the constitution and development of the lineage. Therefore, historical investigation of the form of the traditional family is the logical starting point for the historical study of the lineage. Because previous scholarship has neglected the logical relationship between the household and the lineage, it has not been able to explain the internal causes for the development of the lineage, and thus the explanation of the social functions of the lineage has remained incomplete. This is one of the central theoretical problems I hope to address in this work.

My typology of family structure and lineage organization is based primarily on the nature of the links between family and lineage members, the basic social relationships that shape and restrain the members of the family and lineage. Within a family, aside from economic relations—that is, living together and owning property in common—there may also be different kinds of social relations, such as marriage, consanguinity, and adoption. Because real consanguinal relations or fictive consanguinal relations created by adoption characterize the social relations of virtually all households, they are not a suitable criterion for a typology of household structure. Previous scholars have generally relied instead on marriage relations as the main criterion distinguishing different forms of family. According to this criterion, the traditional family can be divided into three forms: the large family, a household comprising two or more conjugal units; the small family, a household containing only a single conjugal unit; and the incomplete family, a household in which there is no conjugal unit.

The members of a lineage are nominally linked by a shared descent-line and a common ancestor, in other words, real or fictive consanguinal relations. But in practice the social relations that shape and restrain them need not consist just of consanguinal relations, but may also include ties of common locality and common interest. I therefore divide lineage organization into three types. The first is the inheritance lineage *(jichengshi zongzu),* in which consanguinal relations are the basic unifying links. The second is the control-subordination lineage *(yifushi zongzu),* in which the basic unifying links are ties of common locality. The third is the contractual lineage *(hetongshi zongzu),* in which the basic unifying links are those of common interest. This typology is expressed graphically in Figure 1.1.

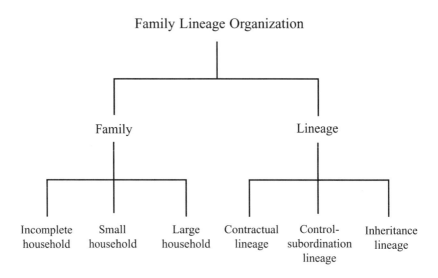

Figure 1.1. Basic Typology of Family Lineage Organization

Of course, like any typology, this is an essentialized typology. In practice, the different types of family lineage organization were not independent, coexclusive, and static, but mutually dependent, interconnected, and constantly developing and changing. To develop a general picture of the structure and functions of family lineage organization, therefore, it is necessary not only to distinguish between the different types of family lineage organization but also to consider their organic relationship and attempt to grasp the structure and functions of family lineage organization in general. The documents I have collected suggest that within a single highly developed family lineage system, all six forms of family lineage organization could coexist simultaneously. The basic structure of their relationship is illustrated in Figure 1.2

In the chart, single lines indicate relationships of inclusion, while double lines indicate simultaneous coexistence. The relationships of inclusion and connection linking the different forms of family lineage organization make for a highly complicated multilevel system, but

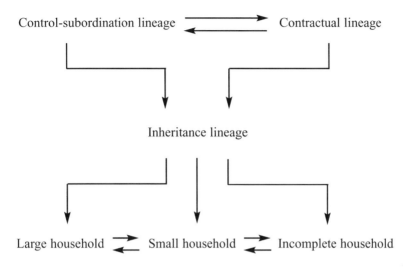

Figure 1.2. Relationship between Different Family Lineage Forms

one in which the different levels can still be clearly distinguished. The different levels of family lineage organization are interlocking in structure and complementary in function, forming a system that embodies marriage relations, consanguinal relations, and ties of common locality and common interest within an organic, unified whole. The individual member of the family lineage belongs not only to specific components but also to the larger system. Thus, we can grasp the general characteristics of the family lineage system only if we consider the interrelationship between the different types of family lineage organizations.

From the perspective of historical development, each of the different forms of family lineage organization had the potential to transmute into another form, and these transformations together make up the development cycle of the system. Under normal circumstances, every family lineage begins with a common founding ancestor. When this ancestor marries and has children, a small family and later a large family is created. When division of the household estate takes place, an inheritance lineage begins to form. After several generations of natural growth, the consanguinal relations between the members of this lineage grow ever weaker and are gradually replaced by ties of common locality or interest. The inheritance lineage accordingly gives way to a control-subordination or contractual lineage. This process is reflected graphically in Figure 1.3

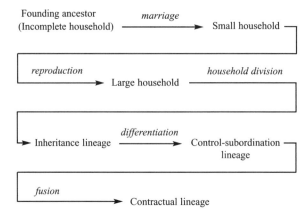

Figure 1.3. Family Lineage Development Process

In the chart, the different forms of family lineage organization represent different stages in the development of a family lineage. Marriage, reproduction, household division, differentiation, and fusion are the processes that link the different stages. The formation and development of family lineage organization is a gradual, continual process that follows a definite order. The long-term trend is the transformation of the more basic stages of family lineage organization as they successively give rise to higher stages. This is the key to the continuous development of family lineage organization. Moreover, the higher stages in this process also give rise to the more basic stages, creating a cyclical pattern, which explains the coexistence of the numerous levels of family lineage organization. This is expressed graphically in Figure 1.4.

In this chart, the vertical lines represent the transformation from more basic stages to higher stages; the horizontal lines, the return from the higher stages back to the more basic stages. The former represent the potential for change within a given family lineage organization; the latter represent the inclusiveness of a given family lineage organization. This shows that the process of family lineage organization development follows a fixed pattern of accretion. Therefore, only if the different forms of family lineage organization are located in a historical continuum is it possible to illustrate their development trends and fully understand the entire process of family lineage development.

Of course, this is only an idealized model. In practice, the development of a family lineage might skip some stages, moving directly from more basic stages to higher stages. For example, the lineage organiza-

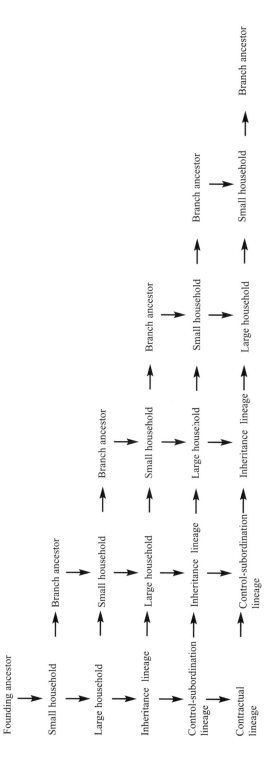

Figure 1.4. Model of Family Lineage Organization Forms and Development

tions of early Taiwanese immigrant society did not generally begin as
inheritance lineages that developed on the basis of natural population growth, but rather as contractual lineages, which were formed
by the fusion of several large, small, or incomplete families whose
consanguinal relations were unclear. In periods of high social instability in the aftermath of war and turmoil, or in locales with high
social mobility, this phenomenon would have been common. But in
more stable contexts, the development of family lineage organization
generally moved through the six different stages, from the more basic
to the higher stages in succession. This makes it possible to avoid becoming confused by the disorder and complexities of the phenomena,
and to provide a rational explanation for the development of family
lineage organization.

*   *   *

The discussion of the links between household structure, lineage organization, the historical environment and social change in Ming and
Qing Fujian and Taiwan in the body of this work follows the internal
logic of family lineage organization development. Chapter 2 looks at
the practice of household division to discuss the basic patterns and
long-term development cycle of household structure. Chapter 3 inves-
tigates the different forms of lineage organization in order to analyze
their basic structure and functions. Chapter 4 considers the process of
development of lineage organization in three areas—mountainous
northwestern Fujian, coastal southeastern Fujian, and Qing Taiwan
—discussing the effects of the social environment on lineage development in each. Chapter 5 discusses the relationship between family
lineage organization and social developments in Ming and Qing
society from the perspectives of lineage ideology, political control, and
property relations. Chapter 6 presents a general summary of the
arguments made in the book and also adds some brief remarks on
certain themes that are not directly covered in the work, in the interest
of promoting discussion. I believe that the analytic framework developed in this study is valid both synchronically and diachronically,
and permits a systematic explanation of the basic forms of family
lineage organization, the trends in their development, and their relationship with the sociohistorical environment. Naturally, it remains
to be seen if this goal can be attained.

2
Family Structure and the Household Development Cycle

Most previous scholarship on family structure in traditional China has concentrated on identifying the predominant type of family to the neglect of the domestic cycle.[1] In traditional Chinese society, the prevalence of household division strongly affected the development cycle of the family. In studying family structure in traditional Chinese society, therefore, investigating the circumstances and timing of division is central to understanding the family development cycle. For example, if it is typically the case that the family is large immediately prior to division, and small subsequent to division, then the basic development cycle is a cyclical fluctuation between small and large family phases. This assumption can be tested through the study of documents of household division and other genealogical materials. This chapter explores the practices of household division in order to discuss the family development cycle in Ming and Qing Fujian and the particular characteristics of family structure in Qing Taiwan.

The Limits on Family Expansion

In circumstances where the family estate is divided in every generation, the limits on family expansion are determined by the timing and circumstances of the division. If at the time of division the parents are living and none of the sons is married, or if the parents are dead and only one son is married, then the maximum size to which the family develops is a nuclear family. If the parents are living and one of the sons has already married, then the maximum is a stem family. If the parents are living and two or more of the sons are already married, then the maximum is a lineal family. If the parents are dead and two or more sons are already married, then the maximum is a joint family.

31

In the first of these four patterns, the maximum is a small family, and in the other three the maximum is a large family. Clearly, the potential of any family to develop into a large family depends mainly on whether or not the parents are living and the sons are married at the time of household division.

Since the Tang dynasty, descendants were forbidden by law to register separately or to divide their property so long as their parents or grandparents were alive, or while mourning was being observed on their behalf.[2] This would suggest that the most common family structure prior to household division must have been the large family in which father and sons lived together and owned their property in common. In fact, this law was honored more in the breach than the observance, and certainly did not guarantee the existence of large families. From as early as the Song, in order to avoid onerous service levy obligations, which were assessed according to the number of individuals registered in a household, families often registered fathers and sons under separate household registrations, and even tried to marry off widows and orphans in order to downgrade their registration status. Because local officials assumed that more families in their jurisdiction meant higher tax receipts, they showed little initiative in ensuring that the division of the household and its property complied with the law.[3] The timing and circumstances of household division among the populace were thus determined not by official laws and regulations but in response to the specific historical context.

The documentary evidence suggests that family structure in Fujian in the early Ming was typically quite simple. It was common for fathers and their sons, or two or more brothers, to be registered separately and to own their property separately. This may have been connected with the unstable political conditions of the time. According to the genealogy of the He lineage of Quanzhou:

> Our ancestor Jingzhi moved again to [Quanzhou]. His sons were Tianqing, Tianzhi, Tianrun, Xinzu, Xinfu, Xinge, and Xinqi. Tianqing was registered as an official. Since he was unable to prepare defenses against the turmoil caused by Saipuding Alimike, he begged leave to retire and returned home. Afraid of bringing disaster on the whole family, he boarded a ship and took to the sea. He came to east of the Temple of Favourable Relief *(shunji gong)* in Tong'an and dwelled there. Before he had even settled down, because of the matter of capturing the deserters of E Lizhi, he was arrested in order to fulfill service obligations. He tried to use his title to force [his brothers] to replace him. Tianzhi and Tianrun fled back to Jinjiang. Xinzu, Xinfu,

Xinge, and Xinqi had no choice . . . but to conceal and change their names and flee to Nanxi in Zhangpu County, Zhangzhou.[4]

Soon after the wars of the Yuan–Ming transition, the people of Fujian faced the incursions of pirates known as *wokou*.[5] The He brothers once again scattered to avoid military conscription to deal with the pirate threat. "When the Ming was established, brothers Xinzu and Xinfu had quite a lot of property in Zhangpu. In 1376, the anti-pirate defense intensified. From every [family] with two adult males *(ding)*, one was conscripted, and from every [family with] three, two were conscripted. It was impossible for our relatives to avoid being dispersed and scattered."[6] The genealogy explains:

> In 1376, the danger on the borders intensified. The military was ex-
> panded in order to defend against pirates. Three men were con-
> scripted [from our family]. . . . So Xinge and Xinqi fled in succession
> to Hecang. In 1379, conscription was extremely severe. At that time,
> in the early years of the dynasty, the law was extremely strict, and the
> guilty found it difficult to gain amnesty. Xinge fled again to Hedi.
> Xinqi died. His son was named Zen. He was unable to avoid [being
> conscripted in order] to fulfill the obligation of his uncle He Zongzhi.[7]

These records demonstrate that, in the periods of turmoil of the late Yuan and early Ming, it was extremely difficult for a large family to develop normally.

So as to ensure there would be sufficient numbers of military fam-ilies and salt-producing households, early Ming policy encouraged the populace to establish separate household registrations. Objectively, this too impeded the development of large families. A Quanzhou genealogy records:

> At the beginning of the dynasty the registers were revised and fixed.
> Concerned that too many families would register as commoners, the
> officials took extraordinary measures to support families registered as
> military and salt-producing households, in order that the people would
> not object to being [registered as] military families and would be
> pleased to be [registered as] salt-producing families. [This ancestor]
> went to the county seat and reported that he had three sons, and that
> he desired to have each one registered separately. So each of the three
> sons was given a household registration, and was registered separately
> as a salt-producing family.[8]

Usually, though, this practice of dividing a single family into multiple registrations was the result not of choice but compulsion. Military households, in particular, often originated from conscription or crim-inal punishment. He Qiaoyuan commented:

There are about one-third as many military households as commoner
households, and the number of individuals is about half the number in
[households] with commoner registration. Why is it that there are half
as many [people registered in] military households as in commoner
households? It is because in the early period of the dynasty there was
concern that the number of military registered [households] was insufficient. One out of every three adult males was conscripted. Criminals
were often registered [as military households], such that fathers could
not avoid being separated from their sons, and brothers from brothers.[9]

It was difficult for those conscripted into military households to avoid
division of the family estate. A genealogy from Jianyang County contains the following account by one Li Tong:

I was accused by Huang Ting of trying to evade rich household status,
so I was conscripted into the Central Guard Battalion of the Nanjing
Regency under Hundred Family Head Zhao Heng. . . . My eldest son,
Zhantong, and my daughter Funu remained in the ancestral home,
and I took my second son, Zhanda, with me to the garrison to fulfill
the conscription requirements. In the Xuande period (1426–1435),
because some soldiers were intimidated and fled, the garrison despatched me to arrest deserters in Yanping and Jianning. Zhanda and I
were granted a pass to return to our old home, where we stayed for
four months. We respectfully invited our relatives and friends to discuss things. It was agreed that the land previously [acquired] and
the family implements should be divided equally among grandsons
Chongfu, Shunyi, Yong, Dang, and Tai.[10]

Although the Li did not formally divide their estate until the Xuande
period, because Li Tong and his second son had already lived in Nanjing for an extended period while fulfilling their military obligations,
the original large family had effectively already disintegrated. Had it
not been for the collective ownership of property, not even this limited
version of a large family would have persisted.

The attacks on rich families and heavy *lijia* obligations of the early
Ming state also posed a serious challenge to the development of large
families, for it forced many people to accelerate household division.
This too made the development of large families most difficult. A document from a genealogy from Chong'an County records:

In 1370, my elder brother Jingzhao and I [Yuan Shouba] first divided
the ancestral estate. I yielded all the family property to my brother. I
did not yet have a son, and the laws of the new dynasty were extremely strict. I was happy just to gain temporary security. . . . After
that, I had my son, Wusun, and purchased in succession lands earning
a total of 2,000 piculs *(dan)* rent. . . . In 1382, rich families were ordered

to go to the capital. Unfortunately, my family was deliberately reported as a rich family with three or more adult males by Subcanton *(li)* head Song Lin and others.[11] An official was sent to prod me; I had no choice but to go. The land [registered] under my family was considerable and the taxes heavy, and my son was still too young to fulfill the [tax and service] obligations. I truly worried that this might be beyond our abilities.[12] I reflected on the situation in this way: I had to go and live in the capital, but I was also resentful and wished to levy an accusation against the partiality of Song Lin and the others. So I told my son, Wusun: "It will soon be time for reporting land holdings and tax obligations for the [compilation of] the Yellow Registers. Why not take advantage of this opportunity and register as much of the lower quality land as possible under someone else's name, thereby freeing ourselves from the registration as ward *(tu)* chief and *li* head under the name of Yuan Jin, and retaining only the tax responsibilities of the single household in the name Yuan Cheng, in order to ensure our safety. Otherwise, our land and tax burden will still be the greatest in the *li*, and we will once again have to fulfill the service levy duties of the ward chief for the next ten years. This would surely cost us our property and our lives." Wusun appreciated what I had said and agreed. So land earning over one thousand piculs rent that belonged to our family was registered under the name of Li Ceng and others of Sangui Subcanton and elsewhere. The tax responsibilities associated with the household under the name of Yuan Jin were transferred away so that not even the smallest measure remained. Besides the land that was registered under other families, we retained high-quality land earning 950 piculs rent. In that year, I went to the capital and got an investigator to bring an accusation against Song Lin at the Ministry of Works. The suit was transferred to the Ministry of Punishments for investigation and the truth came out. Song Lin and eight others were sentenced to conscription. That fall I returned home, and had another son named Tiesun. . . .

With reluctance, in 1388, we informed the ancestors: Of the land originally belonging to us plus the land purchased from Zhang Ba and others, earning a total of 1,100 piculs rent, 450 piculs' worth will be given to my son Wusun to earn the rent and manage; another 450 piculs to my son Tiesun to earn the rent and manage; 50 piculs to my wife née Li and our ailing daughter Qiniang to earn the rent and manage; 50 piculs to my concubine and our ailing son Binsun to earn the rent and manage. . . . I will collect the rent of over 100 piculs on the remaining land in order to maintain me in my old age, but I will not be liable for tax.[13] Later, this property will serve to meet collective expenses, and is [to be managed] in rotation by the two branches [descended from] Wusun and Tiesun.[14]

In 1388, when Yuan Shouba divided his family estate, his sons were not yet adult, so the family must have been nuclear in structure. After household division, the sons were divided into their own families, which must have been incomplete families. Why, then, did Yuan Shouba decide "with reluctance" to divide his estate? Clearly, his goal was to use household division in order to downgrade his family's registration, so as to avoid registration as a prosperous family and the resulting service levy obligations of *li* head. In another case from the same period, it is recorded of Zhou Ziyuan of Jianyang that his "granary had surplus grain, and his storehouse surplus wealth." Although his sons were still young, he hurriedly divided his family estate, so that "each managed his own share, devoted himself to his own affairs, and did not interfere with one another."[15] These examples suffice to demonstrate that when tax and service levy responsibilities were unevenly distributed, commoners with no special tax exemptions found it extremely difficult to maintain a large family of several generations living together.

By the mid-Ming, the evolution of the household registration system and changes to the taxation system led to the gradual stabilization of the development of large families in Fujian. We see this in the history of the Kang lineage of Taoyuan in Yongchun County:

We do not know who the distant ancestors of our lineage are. But the family has passed down the plaque [recording] household and field registration of one Zhenfu, registered as a commoner in Ganhua Subcanton in Anxi County, dated 1370. He had [a son named] Kunbao. It is also recorded that he had an unmarried younger brother, from whom he became separated when he fled from unrest. There was only [Kunbao's descendant] Mengcong, who struggled through in Yong-[chun]. . . . Until 1465, he continued to live at Jindou Luqiu. Investigation shows that at that time he must have been sixty-three, his eldest son Fucheng thirty-three, his second son Furui twenty-seven, and his third son Fuqing twenty-three. It is not known how old his eldest grandson Kuanyang was; second grandson Guanyang was just six years old, and third grandson Gongbao had just been born in that year. . . . They moved again to Hongshan and entrusted [to someone else the property] remaining at Shi'ercheng. In 1472, Fucheng first entered the registration of the households [under *li* head] Chen Gui, taking on the household registration of Chen Focheng, whose family was extinguished [i.e., he had died without descendants], and taking over responsibility for land in the *jia* that earned 120 piculs rent. At the same time, [properties associated with] the registration of [*jia* head] Huang Bosun, whose family was extinguished, consisting of land at Mei'an and mountain lands behind the abandoned monastery at Yuannei, were also obtained as a result.[16]

Clearly, by the time this document was written, household registration had become a mere formality, and people were able to move about freely and substitute for one another's registrations. The *lijia* organization had thus become basically a tax allocation unit, a development discussed in more detail in Chapter 5. When the relative tax and service levy obligations due from each registered household became fixed, and no longer bore any direct relationship to the size or property of that family, these obligations no longer threatened the development of large families. Prior to Mengcong's death in the mid-fifteenth century, the Kang were a lineal family. In 1471, when they registered for tax payment, they had not yet divided their estate, so the family was probably a joint one in which the basic conjugal units were those of the three brothers of the second generation. On the death of the eldest brother, Fucheng, in 1481, the household estate was divided. The original large family did not completely disintegrate, but rather divided into a nuclear family headed by the late Fuqing's son Kuanyang—that is, a member of the third generation—and a joint family headed by the two surviving brothers of the second generation, Furui and FuQing. Their document of household division reads:

> Now we have together discussed and agreed to divide evenly the previously acquired land. One plot located at Hongshan Weian as well as one fishpond, and also mountain land in front of and behind Shanmu, are given to nephew Kuanyang to manage and control. One plot located at the ruins of the abandoned monastery at Hongshan as well as the large fishpond at the gate, and also mountain land in front of and behind Shanmu are given to Furui and Fuqing to manage and control. Each is to build his own residence. . . . [These properties] are to be passed down to the descendants in perpetuity, to manage and fulfill the tax and service levy obligations. They must not encroach on or contest the boundaries of the plots.[17]

At around the same time as these developments in the Kang family, a large family with several generations living together was growing among the Liu of Liu'an village in Yongchun. According to their genealogy, Zhongzi of the eighth generation, who lived in the late fourteenth and early fifteenth centuries, was "hardworking and thrifty in the running of the family. He ate his meals together with his younger brother, continuing to do so without interruption until the end of his life. Together they built the ancestral home and purchased land earning more than two hundred piculs in rent." Zhongzi's son Jiqing "and his cousin Jizong ate their meals together, and together purchased con-

siderable property and three houses." Jiqing's son Shibo, who lived in
the late fifteenth and early sixteenth centuries, "and his uncle Jizong
together purchased over one hundred *mu* of land and four residences."
Only after the time of Jizong and Shibo did this large family, which
had endured for over a hundred years and already consisted of multiple
internal segments, divide its family estate.[18]

The development of large families after the mid-Ming can also
be linked to the prevalence of adoption. In his *Family Injunctions,*
Lin Xiyuan, a literatus from Tong'an, wrote: "In this family, previous generations consisted of only a few males, so adopted sons
were sometimes entered into the registers so they could help fulfill
the family's [service levy responsibilities]."[19] Though such adoptees,
known as Righteous Sons *(yizi),* were nominally distinguished from
blood sons, they were not identical to ordinary bondservants who
were labeled with the same term. Rather, they were a distinct category of family lineage member. A biography in the genealogy of the
Luo of Longshan in Hui'an records: "All the ancestral property at
Yuntou has been distributed to the adopted sons to manage and control, and they have been given our surname, and together recorded in
the household registration. This demonstrates that they are considered the same [as our own sons] in our hearts."[20] Prior to household
division, adopted sons and blood sons could thus live together and
own property in common.

In the late Ming, commercial development in coastal Fujian made
the adoption of sons a widespread social practice. He Qiaoyuan's
seventeenth-century *Min Shu* records: "Haicheng enjoys the fruits of
foreign trade. Those who engage in it take to the seas to increase
their capital. They may take orphans and abandoned children and raise
them as if they were their own sons. When they have grown up they
send them abroad to engage in trade, without worrying themselves
whether they live or die."[21] The *Haicheng County Gazetteer* of 1632
makes a similar point: "Some people bear daughters but do not raise
them; some take other people's sons as their own, and do not consider
muddling the descent-line to be shameful. Those raised in merchant
families are sent off with capital in all different directions, traveling
in difficult circumstances, rising and falling in the rough seas, risk-
ing their lives at any time from the wind and waves, while [the merchants'] own sons reap the benefits in safety."[22] The educated elite of
the time approved of this practice. As Cai Qing wrote in a letter to Li
Zongyi: "Borrowing capital from others and commanding one's reli-

able brothers or adopted sons to engage in trade and earn profits definitely does not threaten righteousness."[23] The practice of adoption naturally increased family size and could thus also lead to an extension of the limits of the family development cycle.

The relationship between an adopted son and the adopting father's family is suggested by the will of Li Jiaren of Shaowu, dating from the mid-eighteenth century.

> The maker of this deed of property division, Jiaren, in previous years raised an adopted son, whose father Ji Yingsong was from Ninghua County of Tingzhou Prefecture, but lived temporarily at Shuangsu village, Kanxia, Shaowu County. [Ji Yingsong] had a son named Xianghui, who was only nine years old. In 1698, because his family was poor, he had no choice but to rely on middlemen Ou Mei of Shuangsu, Zhang Yinai of Kangxia, and Chen Zishi of this town, who introduced him to me, Li Jiaren of sector [du] 33, to raise [the boy] as an adopted son. At that time, in the presence of the middlemen as witnesses, Yingsong received my gift of three taels. The child's name was changed to Li Hongcheng. Henceforth he was to obey me, exert his labor, and work for me. Now I have already raised him to maturity and found him a wife, and he has had three sons.... Each son has been sent to school for three years, and their food and clothing have been provided for them. It can be said that I have exerted much spirit and devoted much energy to them. Now Hongcheng is fifty-seven years old. His three sons have all reached maturity, and ought to split up and live independently. But my wealth is limited, so with the agreement of the members of the lineage and in accordance with the law, I now give paddy lands which I have acquired myself worth one hundred *ping*[24] to my adopted son Hongcheng to inherit....
>
> If in the future Hongcheng and his sons should make unanticipated plans and abandon this land, they must obey the decisions of my descendants, and may not independently sell this land off to others. If such a thing comes to pass, my descendants are to immediately recover the land that has been given [to Hongcheng]. Hongcheng and his sons may not bully them and seize the land.[25]

This document shows that Hongcheng and his sons comprised a large family, living together and owning property in common. According to the genealogy, Li Jiaren had only one birth son. Had he not adopted Hongcheng, his family would have been able to develop at best into a stem family. But when Hongcheng was adopted, the scale of the family expanded, and it became possible for it to develop into a lineal family.

Even more significantly, the prevalence of the practice of adoption created the possibility for some small families with no descendants to develop into large families. For example, according to a 1709 will from Houguan County:

> The maker of this document of household division is Lin Lichang. My wife, née Yu, originally of sector 9, had come to my house for ten years and had not given birth to a child. [At the time] I was almost forty. My younger brother had not yet taken a wife, and because our family was poor I could not afford to take another. I reflected that of the three kinds of unfilial behavior, the worst is to have no descendants. In accordance with my father's instructions, I adopted a newborn infant of the Dong surname of Gekou. . . . He was newly born, just three days old, and named Wushi. He suffered because his mother had no milk, but day and night we fed him by hand, caring for all his needs. He has fortunately now reached twenty-five years of age, and has taken a wife née Huang. Further benefiting from the assistance of Heaven, he has had a grandson and two granddaughters. Even if the son is considered to be adopted,[26] one could not say further that the grandson is adopted. Now I am ill and will soon die. In accord with reason and in the presence of all the relatives, I bestow all of the property that is my lot to Wushi to control and manage. The younger brothers and nephews of the lineage should not engage in wishful thinking and contest this [decision], claiming that they are my designated heir or making some such excuse.[27]

In Qing Fujian, many lineages forbade the adoption of nonconsanguinal kin and permitted only a close relative to be designated the heir of a man with no son. This policy was aimed at preventing "muddling the descent-line" *(luanzong)* and property belonging to the lineage from falling into the hands of outsiders. In practice, the designation of a close relative to serve as heir took place only once a man was elderly, or even after his death. The designated heir could thus easily be controlled by his birth parents and could not be counted on to devote himself to the interests of the family from which he inherited. As a result, many people without descendants preferred adoption from outside the lineage *(minglingzi)* over adoption of a relative *(guoji)*. By the late Qing, some lineages could not avoid acknowledging this fact and assumed less restrictive attitudes toward adoption. In the Guangxu period, the genealogy of the Peng of Hongshan in Jinjiang records that "adopting sons of a different surname was forbidden by our old genealogy. But the large families in the nearby area all do this. Through imitation, this has already become a common practice in our lineage, and the descendants who have been raised by these adopted sons are indeed numerous. For all of them to be excluded from the genealogy would make for all sorts of problems and would be extremely difficult to implement. Having acted with laxity in the beginning, to impose great strictness at the end would not be judicious. In this case the text [of the rule] should be changed and new rules implemented. In all cases where an adopted son of another surname serves as posterity, then the term adopted son *(yangzi)* should be written [in the genealogy]."[28] Within this lineage, the proportion of adopted sons was clearly significant. In considering the development of large families in Ming and Qing Fujian, therefore, the important effects of widespread adoption cannot be ignored.

*   *   *

In mainland Fujian in the Qing, the common practice was to delay household division until each member of the second generation had married. Therefore the most common structure of families immediately prior to household division was either lineal or joint. Division rarely took place before this stage and special circumstances were usually involved. One example is found in the 1864 document of household division of the Chen of Fuzhou:

> I have heard that the virtuous man of great wealth damages his determination, and the foolish man of great wealth compounds his transgressions. Why then should I want to leave a large estate to my descendants? Owing to the protection I have received from my ancestors, and the favor of the nation, the excess from my meager salary has been the basis for our maintenance. Now I have returned to my old home to recover from illness. I can't bear inconvenience and trouble. Rather than keeping the whole family together and allowing them to live wastefully at will, would it not be better to have them split up, so each will understand what it means to live within one's means? Now I take the property that I originally inherited from my ancestors, and that which I have successively acquired myself, and aside from some to be set aside as corporate property, divide the rest among you, my sons, who are [known as the] Shi, Shu, and Li branches. Because the Shi branch is more numerous than the others, I have specially given a double share. The sons in the Shu and Li branches have not yet married, so each of them is given just one share. Now although each of you has your own property . . . do not let money hurt your warm relations; do not let the distinction between sons of the principal wife and sons of concubines lead to dislike and suspicion; do not let pride and selfishness generate hatred. Do not allow laziness and indolence, rather be hardworking and frugal. If the brothers treat one another with friendship and love, the family will be full of warm feelings. How could others then find ways to bully us?[29]

The author of this contract, the man responsible for the division, was an official on leave. Prior to the division, only one of his three sons was married, so clearly this was a stem family. The Chen family estate was extremely wealthy; it included a pawnshop and a paper warehouse together worth several tens of thousands taels, and a large amount of land. What caused the disintegration of this family? The preface suggests that there were two basic reasons: first, the author's desire to avoid "inconvenience and trouble," and second, his wish to have his sons "understand what it means to live within one's means." The economy of the family was extremely complex, and it appears that the three sons were not entirely or equally reliable. This was the main reason given for the division of the estate. Moreover, the father's warning not to "let the distinction between sons of the principal wife and sons of concubines lead to dislike and suspicion" suggests that one or two of the sons had been born to a concubine, which no doubt meant that there were profound contradictions within the large family prior to division. We can speculate that, if the father found managing the family caused "inconvenience and trouble" while he was present in the home, it would be even more difficult to maintain life as a large family once he left to take up office. Thus, the internal contradictions in the families of rich and powerful officials could be more serious and complex than those in ordinary families.

*   *   *

Some scholars believe that in Chinese history the large family in which multiple generations lived together "was only possible for an extremely small number of official families, which placed great stress on the ethics of filiality and had great landholding wealth. Both the original stimulus of education and the sustaining power of economic [factors] were necessary conditions. This was not something most people could easily accomplish."[30] This view has a certain logic to it, but it does not apply in every case. Chen Zhiping and I have conducted fieldwork on a large family of five generations living together in Dongtou village in Pucheng County. Prior to land reform this family had no fixed assets and relied instead primarily on renting mountain land, making paper and charcoal, and cutting firewood to make a living. The family belonged to the shed people *(pengmin)* whose socioeconomic position was extremely low. It was precisely because the family was so impoverished and isolated that its members were forced into long-term economic cooperation in order to survive.[31]

Among documents of household division from Ming and Qing Fujian one finds many cases of large families with very little property. For example, a document of household division from Minqing County, dated 1714, shows that at the time of division the family had only enough land to "give to our mother to pay the costs of her needle and thread. After one hundred years, this land should be converted into sacrificial property." The sons inherited only "a site for the construction of houses, which is to be divided into three equal shares."[32] According to the household division document of a Fang surname family of Pucheng, dated 1855, aside from a very small amount of land which served as the "retirement estate for our father and mother," the three sons had only their dwelling and family implements "to draw lots for and divide evenly amongst themselves."[33]

The large family to which the father of Lin Zexu belonged is a typical example. The document of division of his family reads:

> My father was a Government Student but never received a higher degree. He had five sons, none of whom had his own property, and the members of the family were extremely numerous. For more than ten years . . . my father sojourned and studied in Shandong, Henan, and other provinces. My mother arranged a marriage for eldest brother Zhiyan to a woman née Xie. Not long after, our grandmother died. Our mother née Hu also died. Fifth brother Tianyu also died young. When father had just returned from his studies, he arranged a marriage for second elder brother Meng'ang to a woman née Zheng. Because we had considerable debts and the interest was piling up, we sold our dwelling in order to repay our debts. The next year, my father also died. Our family had not an inch of land, or a half *mu* of fields. Since there was no property to be divided, we did not draw up a formal document of division. The four brothers split up to make their own living and live off their own efforts.[34]

Even though his family had already been bankrupted, so long as Lin Zexu's grandfather remained alive, determined efforts were still made to maintain the style of life of a large family. Later, even though the four brothers split up and earned their livings separately, and the large family had effectively disintegrated, the economic ties between the brothers were not cut off completely:

> When my eldest brother Zhiyan died, I bore all the expenses of the coffin, the mourning clothes, the funeral, and the burial. Because his son Yuanqing was my blood nephew, the affines and agnates urged me to provide for him a monthly allowance for a fixed number of years, and a document was drawn up to this effect. I included in this

document the phrase "there was no property to be divided, and therefore we did not draw up a formal document of division," in order to prevent conflict in the future. The affines and agnates all made their mark on the document to verify it.[35]

Among close relatives, the mutual obligation to provide support was unavoidable. This was the moral basis for the long-term survival of the large family.

*   *   *

The spread of large families in Qing Fujian was driven not only by a cultural tradition that idealized filiality and fraternity but also in response to the economic structure of the period. The labor market of Fujian was underdeveloped in the Qing, and production involved an obvious natural division of labor in which the family was the basic unit of both production and consumption. A solitary male—that is, an incomplete family—would have found it very difficult to create a niche for himself in society, establishing a family and a livelihood solely through his own efforts. To ensure that household division did not lead to the creation of incomplete families, it had to be delayed until every member of the second generation had already married. Therefore it was most often lineal or joint families which underwent division.

From another perspective, given the stalemate between the subsistence and the commercial economies, maintaining a large family on a considerable scale facilitated the expansion of financial resources and improved the family's economic structure by creating opportunities to participate in both economies. In relatively large families in Qing Fujian, labor was typically diversified into several occupations, with family members organically integrating scholarship, agriculture, handicraft and industrial production, and commerce within a single family economy. This point is demonstrated in several biographies in the *Genealogy of the Fanyang Zou Lineage* of Changting County.

> [Zou Jianying] had five sons. Hengci was the eldest. While still a youth who had not yet been capped, he went with his uncle to Hubei and lived in the Jingzhou official *yamen*, where he could constantly receive his uncle's training and instruction. Later he obtained an official position. Huanci was the second son. His abilities were outstanding, so Educational Commissioner Peng entered him into the county school. Xuanci was the third son. Strong and in the prime of life, he personally worked in the fields. Langci was the fourth son. He was humble but determined and clever. He remained behind closed doors and engaged in self-cultivation. Qiuci was the fifth son. He traveled

long distances until he staggered, engaging in commerce in Guangdong. Each of them worked hard at his own affairs; none was lazy. . . .

[Zou Kongmao's] grandfather entrusted him with handling the administration of the family. . . . He took charge of the more than thirty individuals living in the single residence, some of whom worked in agriculture, others in scholarship, and others in commerce. All of them obeyed the will of the senior generation. He had them all work hard in their own occupations, so that they would not be distracted by amusements. Over a period of several dozen years . . . there was nothing that was not well arranged.

[Zou Dazhen] studied Confucianism but did not succeed in the examinations. In middle age, he traveled to Suzhou to do business. . . . He had five sons, some of whom studied, some worked in the fields, and some were merchants. All were excellent sons.

[Zou Jizu] had seven sons. He sent the smarter ones to school and the honest ones to work in the fields. He had the more capable ones work hard, and the less capable try to hang on stubbornly to what they had. . . . He did not inherit much property from the ancestors, nor was there much savings. But he was a diligent manager, and he gradually became wealthy.

[Zou Jiyun] abandoned his studies and engaged in commerce. . . . All the printing blocks that were produced, and the fields that were successively purchased were a result of his diligence. Later, the family grew very numerous, so he and his brothers divided [the estate]. The property he had established was all divided evenly, and without partiality.[36]

The Zou lived in the remote mountains of western Fujian. In the Qing they became wealthy in the printing and bookselling businesses. In terms of occupational structure, though, they were never able to escape completely the limitations of the subsistence economy, but sought instead to maintain a combination of scholarship, agriculture, industrial production, and commerce within the family and lineage. During the same period, there were many cases of this sort of occupationally diversified large family among the Ma lineage of the same region. What explains the development of this kind of occupationally diversified family structure? I believe the answer lies in the persistence of the subsistence economy. In Qing Fujian, overpopulation and the shortage of arable land made it objectively difficult for the natural subsistence economy to be sustained, while on the other hand low productivity inhibited the full development of a commercial economy. In this deadlock of a semisubsistence and semicommercial economy, a certain social division of labor existed but full specialization was still impossible. As a result, occupational diversification of labor within the family was seen as the ideal strategy.

It might appear that the development of the large family depended on sufficient economic resources, and this has frequently led to the misunderstanding that only the very wealthy were able to maintain the lifestyle of a large family. In fact, a flourishing family economy might be not the cause of the development of a large family, but rather its result. Many wealthy large families in Qing Fujian had developed out of relative impoverishment. For example, a document of household division from Taining County, dated 1809, explains:

> My grandfather moved here with nothing. . . . When I was just over ten years old I abandoned my studies for the examinations and turned to learn about agriculture. When I was still young I started to assist a money changer in his business. . . . In this way, I obtained a house by giving a mortgage, opened my own shop, found myself a wife, and continued to add to my property. My two younger brothers followed my instructions, and labored diligently with the same heart. Things have gone on like this for many years. During this time, we registered our family for tax payment, my two brothers married, and we have been able to perform ourselves and in the appropriate order all the major rituals called for in the *Rites,* one after the other. In this way, we Ouyang have become a prominent family in Shanyi.[37]

The development process of the Ouyang family into a large family was simultaneously the process of their rise to wealth. Before the large family disintegrated, "the sons and nephews had all been given a room and made their own name [i.e., had married]," and possessed a great deal of "land, houses, rental shops," and other property. But because "in recent times their conduct has been different, and the various expenses considerable and troublesome, it has become difficult to manage things in common," so they eventually had no choice but to divide the family.

The document of household division of the Gu of Guangze, dated 1831, contains a preface written by another member of their lineage that describes the family's path to riches from the perspective of a bystander.

> My uncle Weizheng is a man of outstanding talents in our lineage. He is filial, friendly, and particularly excels in business matters. His father, Suwei, . . . had six sons who grew to adulthood. [Weizheng] was the eldest. The next was Beixuan, then Jinzhai, then Lizhen, then

Tianyi. Each of them exerted himself in agriculture. Only the sixth son, Changran, studied for the examinations, but he was not lucky. Initially, Suwei had little inherited property and his family had no surplus. Though he supervised all his sons strictly and carefully, still they were barely able to survive. While young [Weizheng] studied medicine for the eyes; when he grew up he worked as a doctor. He gave the payments he received to his father, keeping not even the least bit for himself. The family relied on this to avoid bankruptcy.... When Suwei got old, his health and spirit were both weak, and the family members had grown very numerous. The family income was barely sufficient to meet their expenses. Because of this [Weizheng] took it on himself to support [the family]. He was skilled at management and was able to motivate all his brothers to work diligently and economize together with him. The whole family got along. Perceptive people early on predicted that his family would surely flourish. In this way, over the course of several dozen years, although the funerals of his two parents, his wife and brothers, and the marriages of brothers and his nephews followed one after the other, the total expenses amounting to not less than several hundred taels, he never had to borrow money from others, and was even able to add to the property [by purchasing] bottom soil and topsoil rights, hill land, and unirrigated land worth in all several thousand or more taels.... If it had not been for his warm and filial character, and his managerial ability, how could he have been able to motivate his brothers to exert their efforts together, so that when they were old it was just like when they began, and achieve this?[38]

The key to the success of the six Gu brothers was that they "exerted themselves together from the start until they grew old," in other words, they consistently maintained the lifestyle of a large family. Although the formation and development of this large family depended on the "warm and filial" character and economic acumen of the family head, the document also points out that this sort of large family could respond relatively effectively to the socioeconomic environment of the time. It offered economic opportunities that no small family could match.

Large families of Qing Fujian could usually be sustained for no more than three or four generations. The individuals critical to determining the timing of division were the married brothers and cousins of the second generation. As the size of the family expanded, the consanguinal relationships between these members gradually grew more distant; different kinds of contradictions grew more serious, and the division of the household became unavoidable. Once the household was divided, the size of the constituent families was reduced, and the original economic structure based on cooperation and division of labor was bound to suffer to some degree. It therefore had to be supplemented by other forms of social organization, such as lineage organizations. The transformation from large family to lineage organization was thus a very natural developmental trend. In a sense, the emergence and development of lineage organization was the inevitable result of the disintegration of the large family.

The Development Cycle of the Family

Family structure can change through the medium of division of the household estate in one of two different directions—that is, small families may expand into large ones, and large families may divide into small ones. But since the maximum potential limits on development differ from family to family, the resulting domestic cycle also differs. Even families with similar potential development maxima might still follow different cycles if the circumstances of household division differ. The possible development cycles of each of the different kinds of family are reflected graphically in Figure 2.1

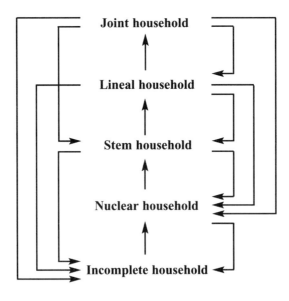

Figure 2.1. Potential Development Cycles of Different Household Structures

In the chart, the inner lines reflect the process of development from smaller to larger family, and the outer lines the process of disintegration from larger to smaller. At each stage in the cycle, there is more than one possibility for further development, which implies that there are numerous possible development cycles. But in practice, because of the restrictions of the customs of the inheritance system, some transformations were extremely unlikely, so the relative probability of occurrence of the different cycles differs. Therefore we must look specifically at the manner of household division in each kind of family in order to understand the predominant patterns of transformations and the predominant domestic development cycle.

Under normal circumstances, a nuclear family could continue to develop until it became a stem family. But in certain exceptional circumstances a nuclear family could also disintegrate. The early Ming cases of the Yuan of Chong'an County and the Zhou of Jianyang, discussed above, provide examples of this. When a nuclear family divided its estate, the result was usually that the sons of the second generation formed a number of incomplete families. Thus this development cycle was a fluctuation between two different types of small families, nuclear and incomplete. In some cases, a nuclear family, consisting of the parents, that is, of the first generation, might survive the division. But this reduced nuclear family would disappear when they died. It had no potential for further development, and so did not affect the character of this development cycle.

A stem family could continue to expand into a lineal family, or it could disintegrate directly into a number of small families. When a stem family disintegrated, the result was usually one nuclear family and a number of incomplete families headed by members of the second generation. Thus, in the case of the Chen family of Fuzhou discussed above, after household division there were three families made up of the sons of the second generation, of which one was a nuclear family and two were incomplete families. This demonstrates that if the maximum size to which a given family could develop was the stem family, then the development cycle consisted of a fluctuation between large family and small family phases. In mainland Fujian in the Ming and Qing, division of a stem family was rare. This may have been because such a division would have led to the formation of several incomplete families, which would have been disadvantageous for the members of the second generation, and so was not sanctioned by custom. Naturally, if division took place while both parents were still alive and only one son was married, then household division would lead not to the appearance of an incomplete family, but rather to two nuclear families, one being the family of the parents and the unmarried sons, and the other the family of the married son. However, such a straightforward division between parents and a single son would have been a clear violation of traditional Chinese morality, and hence did not generally occur.

The possible transformations of a lineal family were more complicated. It might continue to develop into a joint family, or it might divide into a number of stem families, nuclear families, or incomplete families. If the parents in a lineal family lived to an old age and all of the sons were already married, the parents themselves might initiate the division, dividing the family into a number of stem families and nuclear families. If the parents died young, and their sons were not all married, the family might continue to develop into a joint family, or it might divide into a number of nuclear and incomplete families. The experiences of Lin Zexu's immediate ancestors illustrate these various possibilities.

In 1758, Lin Zexu's great-grandmother divided the family for her sons. "The fields and houses inherited from the ancestors were divided into five shares, and distributed evenly among the five sons." Lin Zexu's grandfather was the fourth son, and the marriage of his own eldest son was arranged not long after this division, which suggests that each of the five brothers were all already married prior to the division, and some of them may already have formed their own stem families. The result of this division was thus the disintegration of the lineal family into a number of nuclear and stem families.

Prior to the death of Lin Zexu's grandfather, two of his four sons were married and the other two were still single. This was therefore a type of partial lineal family. After his death, as we have seen, because of the complete bankruptcy of the family, the sons were unable to maintain the lifestyle of a large family and divided into two nuclear and two incomplete families. We can speculate that, had economic circumstances permitted, the family might have continued to develop into a joint family and only divided the estate once all four brothers had married.

After the funeral of his own father, Lin Zexu's father made his living as a teacher. "He worked hard and saved money for two years. He took a wife née Chen, and had two sons. The elder was Zexu; the younger Peilin." By 1826, Zexu and his brother had both married, but they still lived and owned their property in common with their father. The family was thus a lineal family. In the eleventh month of that year, Zexu's furlough from office came to an end. "He did not dare to remain at home for even one more day." Because his father was elderly, it was thought best to divide the family estate immediately. At the time, Zexu's eldest son was not yet married, so after the division his family could only have been a nuclear one.[39]

These three episodes of household division cover two complete development cycles, averaging thirty-five years' duration. The basic family development cycle involved fluctuation between small and large family phases. But because Lin Zexu's grandfather and father were both younger sons and the time between each household division relatively short, the family structure of their own family after division must have been comparatively simple. So these cases do not fully express all the potential development cycles of a lineal family. In my opinion, under conditions of early marriage and early childbirth, and hence a generational period of about twenty years, where the initiator of household division was over sixty, it was quite possible that the eldest of his grandsons might already be married at the time of division. This would mean that within the lineal family there might already be one or more large families oriented around the second generation. When a lineal family of this kind divided its estate, if it was the second-generation sons who initiated the division, then even after division several large families persisted, and the cyclical fluctuation between large and small families no longer obtained. Naturally, if it was the grandsons of the third generation who divided the estate, then division resulted in a number of small families. A document of division dated 1532 provides an example:

> I, née Yanling [i.e., Wu] was married to Yuan Ru'nan, taboo name You, style Jiqing. We had four sons. The eldest, County Student Tingqin, married a woman née Zhu but died early without posterity. The second son, County Student Luan, married a woman née Xu, and also died early without posterity. The third, Tribute Student by Imperial Grace Qiao, married a woman née Xu and then a woman née Shen, and has five sons. The fourth, Military Provincial Graduate Feng, married a woman née Liu. Alas, Third Son died in 1532. So I called on the affines and agnates to discuss matters. It was decided to divide the estate inherited from the ancestors into four equal shares, which were given the names Wen, Xing, Zhong, and Xin branches. Because the senior Wen branch had no posterity, the eldest son of Qiao, named

Guangtao, was designated the heir. The Xing branch of the second
son also had no posterity, but Guangbo has been raised as Luan's
adopted son. When third son Qiao was dying, in the main hall I
announced: "Qiao's second son, Zhonghan, should be designated as
heir to Luan. But since Guangbo was raised by Luan as adopted son,
the family's property should be divided into two equal shares, to be
given the names Ling and Guan branches." This arrangement of the
branches was approved by the affines and agnates. The estate of the
Xing branch has been divided as planned in this way, in order not to
betray the ancestor's sentiments toward adopted kin.[40]

This document actually records the simultaneous division of the estates
of two different generations, the whole of the second generation of
the original family, and some of the members of the third. According
to the genealogy, Yuan Jiqing, the first-generation head of this large
family, was born in 1734, seventy-two years prior to this division.
When Jiqing and his brother divided their estate in 1757, their father
had written "you two [brothers] are both married and have already
had [my] grandsons." Fifty years later, when Jiqing's widow supervised the subsequent division of his estate, their eldest grandson must
himself have been an adult with children of his own. After division of
the second generation into branches, at least the second and third of
these branches may also have formed stem or lineal families. However, because the eldest and second sons of the third branch were designated as heirs to other branches, and the adopted son and the designated heir of the second branch seem not to have lived together and
owned their property in common, the third generation also underwent
household division at the same time. Obviously, had it not been for
the particular circumstances that led to the division of the estate of
members of the third generation, the development cycle of this lineage
family might not have followed this pattern of fluctuation between
large and small family phases, but rather continued to develop as a
large family. Unfortunately, in the surviving documents of household
division of this type, the age and marital status of the members of the
third generation is generally not discussed, so it is impossible to know
if this possibility was ever realized.

Household division would cause a joint family to disintegrate either
into a large family or families, or into a small family or families. The
chief factors determining which possibility was realized were the
family structure prior to division and the circumstances of the division
itself. In the Wanli period of the Ming, Chen Damao of Yongchun
County wrote biographies for his father and himself in which he de-

scribed in detail the changes in their family over two generations. The document is of great value in explaining the internal structure and development cycle of the joint family.

[My father, the other uncles, and] Uncle Guangzu cooperated together in managing the family. Whenever they accumulated any savings, they successively purchased land, which in total came to earn 222 piculs rent. From this [property], they agreed to set aside 5 piculs to serve as the estate to pay for the spring and autumn sacrifice. . . . [Then Father and the other uncles] first divided [the family estate] with Uncle Guangzu. Uncle [Guangzu] lived at Niudi. Father, Second Uncle, and Third Uncle moved to Guanludou. The [three] brothers continued to eat together.[41] They were sincere in their mutual feelings, and no grudges divided them. They followed rules. There were fixed regulations for the expenses of weddings and funerals. When a son or grandson chose a wife and married, the amount was fixed at fifteen taels. In 1579, Second Uncle died. His widow was six months pregnant, and gave birth to cousin Weijin in the second month of 1580. Father and Third Uncle raised him with the same heart. In 1592, Third Uncle and Father discussed and decided to divide [the family estate]. The land acquired since the division of the estate with Guangzu earned a total rent of 346 piculs. A portion earning 63 piculs rent was used to redeem a loan of 34.5 taels that had been contracted from Chen Jinniang to finance the purchase of land; a portion earning 38 piculs had been privately purchased by uncle Ju; a portion earning 37 piculs rent had been privately purchased by elder brother Zu, and a portion earning 59.1 piculs had been privately purchased by Father. They further set aside a portion earning 10 piculs to supplement the shortfall in brother Zu's marriage expenses, 15 piculs' worth for [the marriage expenses] of Weijin, and 13 piculs' worth for Guangsun, to which was added two taels. There remained land earning 95 piculs rent, which was evenly divided into three shares on the basis of the rent the land earned, without reference to the cultivated area. Each obtained land earning 31 piculs rent. . . .

I am thirty-three years of age. My father is elderly and wishes to avoid trouble. Eldest Brother was conscripted and died in battle. . . . Second Elder Brother and I worked together to manage [the family]. We calculated carefully, and family members did not have to fear hunger or cold. We paid our taxes early, thus avoiding having the government runners coming to press us for the tax. In all, eighteen weddings were arranged for the boys and girls in the family, without any partiality in favor of those who came earlier or later. The funeral arrangements for both Father and Mother have been made, strengthening our filial piety. In order to recover our old property, my brother and I each contributed over 300 taels of our own money to redeem property that had previously been mortgaged. . . . The family had more than thirty members in all, living together and eating meals in common. There were fixed regulations for the expenses of weddings and funerals. Young and old all got along happily together, harmoniously and without mutual suspicion. . . . Eldest Brother in managing the family did not have any capital of his own, so he did not generate any private savings. Second Elder Brother and I had private capital, which we used to generate income, accumulating fully one hundred taels, but we used this money to redeem the mortgages and to reclaim land, and there was no squabbling over this. Now we take all the current property and divide it into three shares. Eldest Brother's son Zhu obtains one share; [Second Brother's sons] Xi and Kai together get one share; [my sons] Zhen, Xuan, and Lu together get one share. This document of household division has been prepared. [The property] of each family is not muddled together. This will enable the descendants to remain at peace over the long term, [demonstrating] etiquette and yielding [where appropriate]. This is what is most important.[42]

Chen Damao's father and three uncles originally formed a joint family. After the first division of the estate, the eldest uncle formed his own family, while the three other brothers continued to live in common, making up a new joint family. Prior to the second division, one of the nephews, that is, a member of the third generation, had already married, and his branch had thus already developed into a stem family. In the second division, the three remaining uncles divided their estate, resulting in the formation of one stem family and two nuclear families. Chen Damao's father was the youngest of the uncles; after division of the estate he continued to live together with and own his property in common with his sons. His own family thus developed from nuclear family into stem family and then into lineal family. After his death, his sons continued to live together and own property in common, once again forming a joint family. At the time of the second division, which was conducted by Damao himself, the third-generation members of the joint family had all already married, so at least two of the branches themselves consisted of large families oriented around the second generation. The parties to this division of the estate were the members of the second generation. If the members of the third generation of the different branches did not immediately further divide their estates, then each of them would have been able to maintain the lifestyle of a large family, forming a stem family (in the case of the senior branch) or a lineal family (in the case of the second and third branches). Thus the development cycle of a joint family did not normally involve a fluctuation between large and small family phases, but rather the continuous development as a large family.

In a joint family, division of the estate most often occurred when the members of the second generation were aged and most members of the third generation were already married. In this situation, if the parties to the division were the members of the second generation, the large family did not completely disintegrate. But under certain exceptional circumstances, the parties to the division might be members of the third generation, which meant the complete disintegration of the large family into small families. For example, the document of household division of a woman née Lü, married into the Huang surname in Minxian, dated 1906, reads:

> My husband was one of three brothers. . . . They either studied for the examinations or engaged in trade, each according to his own abilities. Thus younger brother Shuzhao engaged in commerce, but he died early. Younger brother Shuyan had a will to study, so he happily did so. I had four sons. . . . Because younger brother Shuzhao died without any descendants, our fourth son, Kun, was made his heir, to preserve his house. . . . My late husband left a legacy solemnly commanding his sons to maintain their enterprise [together] in order to expand their property. The sons received this legacy and respected it well. So for many years they were very successful in business. . . . Now, all the property and businesses, aside from some to be set aside as a sacrificial estate and some to be set aside as a retirement estate *(yangshan)*, will be divided into five even shares. My husband's younger brother Shuyan will obtain one share, and our son Kun, who has been adopted out [to serve as heir to Shuzhao] will also obtain one share.[43]

In this case, the joint family that had existed prior to the division was in fact centered on the second-generation lineal family headed by Lü's husband, with the other second-generation families of his brothers affiliated to it. After division, the status of these other families was downgraded, because each received a share equal to that of the individual third-generation members of the lineal family. This kind of household division, in which the parties to division were the third-generation members, occurred only relatively rarely, perhaps because it did not accord with customary practice. In an era when the large family was idealized, organizing a new family based on the second generation of the previously existing joint family was considered preferable and more practicable. We can therefore deduce that a joint family would usually develop according to a cycle whereby the families of the second generation were the parties to division, such that household division led to the organization mainly of stem and lineage families. This is the most common pattern found in surviving household division documents and genealogies from Ming and Qing Fujian.[44]

* * *

Our study of household division in Ming and Qing Fujian has shown that, for most families, the maximum potential extension of the development cycle was not a stem family but a lineal or joint family. We have also discovered that the lineal or joint family did not inevitably disintegrate into a number of small families but could potentially continue to develop further as a large family. On the basis of this analysis, we can conclude that, under conditions where the family estate was divided in each generation, the basic pattern and long-term development cycle of family structure in Ming and Qing Fujian was reflected in a dynamic equilibrium between large family and small family phases. Leaving aside exceptional transformations in family structure, we can say further that, within this cycle of family development, large families may have had greater potential to develop further than small families, so in a sense the large family occupied the dominant position. However, although people made every effort to maintain the lifestyle of a large family, with the passage of generations such families found it increasingly difficult to avoid disintegration. This cycle of family disintegration encouraged efforts to find more sustainable and stable bases for cooperation. The result was that inheritance lineages gradually replaced large families of many generations living together.

The Special Character of Family Structure in Qing-era Taiwan

Large-scale settlement of Taiwan began with Zheng Chenggong's recovery of the island. After Taiwan was reunited with China under the Kangxi emperor, a prefectural government under the authority of Fujian Province was established there. It was only in 1885 that Taiwan was established as a separate province. Therefore, the family lineage organization and social transformation of Taiwan during the Qing also falls within the scope of this work.

The historical development of Taiwan in the Qing was a process whereby an immigrant society was transformed into a settled society. Chen Kongli has characterized Qing Taiwan society as follows:

> In terms of population structure, aside from the small number of indigenous inhabitants, the majority of residents were people who had migrated in succession from the mainland. Population increase was

relatively rapid; men were more numerous than women. In terms of social structure, the migrants basically organized themselves according to their different native places, forming social groups based on ties of locality. A few powerful men became major landlords and heads of wealthy families; the other migrants became tenants and artisans. Class and occupational structure were thus relatively simple. In terms of economic structure, because this was a period of early development, the basis for the subsistence economy was weak while the commercial economy was relatively advanced. In terms of political structure, the power of the state was weak, and it was unable to govern effectively. The large villages depended mainly on local elites to implement administration. As for social contradictions, those between the state and the people, and between people from different native places, were the most striking, and to a certain extent these obscured class contradictions. Add to this swarms of vagrants, bandits running wild, and frequent incidents of turmoil, and society was most unstable. The whole of society was still in the process of becoming organized and integrated.

Therefore, though the immigrant society of Qing Taiwan "had many of the characteristics of mainland (especially Fujian and Guangdong) society, it also had many local characteristics that had developed in this new environment. It was neither a simple transplantation of traditional Chinese society nor a completely different society from that of the mainland."[45] This turbulent and unstable social environment affected family structure in Qing Taiwan, differentiating it from the development cycle of the traditional family and giving it characteristics distinct from those of the mainland.

The *Reference Materials Appended to the Common Law of Taiwan,* compiled early in the period of Japanese occupation, contains almost a hundred historical documents relating to household division and the inheritance system, which illustrate family structure and the household development cycle in Qing Taiwan.[46] On the basis of the sixty documents of household division, it appears that most families had developed into lineal or joint families prior to division. There are only a few cases of stem families dividing. The maximum limits of expansion of these sixty families, arranged according to historical period, is illustrated in table 2.1

The table shows that, at the time of household division, only 6 percent of the sixty families were stem families; 55 percent were lineal families, and 38 percent were joint families. This demonstrates that, in Qing Taiwan, the maximum potential size of the family structure was usually the lineal or joint family, and the basic pattern was more or less the same as in mainland Fujian. However, these documents of

Table 2.1. Maximum Expansion of Sixty Households in Qing Taiwan

Period	Stem family	Lineal family	Joint family
Qianlong	0	5	0
Jiaqing	0	4	3
Daoguang	0	6	5
Xianfeng	1	2	2
Tongzhi	0	5	1
Guangxu	3	11	12
Totals	4	33	23

Source: *Taiwan shihō furoku sankōsho.*

household division also reveal three exceptional practices associated with the household division and inheritance systems, which reflect certain special characteristics of family structure in Qing-era Taiwan.

First, families without heirs were relatively common. *Reference Materials Appended to the Common Law of Taiwan* includes a number of documents connected to property of a family with no heir. These are generally called deeds of Entrustment *(tuofu)* or of Entrustment to an Orphan [Heir] *(tuogu).*[47] Such deeds can basically be divided into two types. In the first, a proprietor who is near death entrusts his family estate to a lineage member or close relative or neighbor, in order to provide for him to designate an heir or conduct sacrifice in the future. In the second, the proprietor has died without an heir or a will, so lineage members or other relatives together draw up a contract to take over ownership of the relevant property and responsibility for the relevant duties.[48] Obviously, in any of these circumstances, the heirless man's family would not develop into an ordinary large family. Because of the unbalanced sex ratios of Qing Taiwan, poor men generally found it impossible to marry, and so this sort of family was probably most common. Inadequate resources would have been a particular problem for the first few generations of migrants who had only recently arrived in Taiwan and established an estate, as is suggested in the two following documents:

Entrustment of an Orphan Heir, 1832
The maker of this document for the entrustment of an orphan heir is descent-line elder brother Chen Zhuang. . . . My father and I came to Taiwan to make a living. We were hardworking and frugal, and established [an estate] and a succession which ought certainly to be trans-

mitted. Who could have expected that the lot granted by Heaven should have such limits, that our bloodline should be cut off here? Since I am already seventy years old, what do I have to rely on? It must be that Heaven wishes to see me destroyed. . . . Now I am troubled by serious illness, like the sun setting behind the western mountains. I gasp for breath, and there is nothing to be done. Now I publicly entrust my estate to my orphan heir, descent-line younger brother Chen Qitian, to manage as his own. He is to take care of the incense burner on behalf of my father and me on the taboo and sacrificial days in spring and autumn, and maintain the sacrifices in perpetuity. . . . I sincerely fear that in the future this property might be sold or ruined, and the incense not burned at the appropriate time, so I have assembled various people, all of whom have gathered here. The record of the estate is on this day transformed by burning [i.e., communicated to Heaven], in order that its ruin might be prevented.[49]

Contract, 1847

The makers of this contract are maternal grandson Kexi and lineage nephews Biaoyin, Deyue, Youdao, Fuwang, Fuzhu, and others. . . . Our lineage uncles, brothers Pairou and Paiyan, since moving to Taiwan have been hardworking and frugal, and have personally acquired and opened up lands, dwellings, and mountain lands. All are recorded in the pioneering contract *(kendan heyue)*, spelled out explicitly as clear evidence. Now both brothers have unfortunately died, and they have neither married nor adopted descendants. The nephews reflect that they are our close relatives from a common origin who have left no posterity, and we cannot bear that there is no one to rely on [to ensure the maintenance of] their sacrifices. Therefore we have gathered the affines and agnates to come to a collective decision. Lots are to be drawn for [the right to rent] the three plots of property. The total annual surface rent comes to 13.5 piculs of rice. Each year, 8.5 piculs of the surface rent is to be set aside to meet the expenses of the sacrifices, which will be conducted by us seven men in rotation. Each year, after the mountain tax and the expenses of sacrifice have been paid, the surplus rental rice is to be accumulated and lent out to earn interest, in order to meet the expenses of establishing an heir and arranging a marriage for him.[50]

Both these families of early migrants were incomplete families. Had their marital situation been normal, their families might well have been able to develop into large families, and they would not have faced the problem of being heirless. But for these early first- or second-generation migrants, establishing property may have been an even more pressing concern than establishing a family, which meant that the tragedy of dying without posterity was common. Both these families left behind some property, so at least in terms of establishing an estate they had been relatively successful. Migrants who had not even been able to establish an estate could hardly even consider establishing a family.

Every society has people who die without posterity, but the consequences for family structure can vary considerably. In mainland Fujian in the Ming and Qing, men could adopt from outside the lineage or designate another lineage member as heir, which made it possible for a weak small family to develop into a powerful large family. In Qing Taiwan, there were also adopted heirs and designated heirs, but so many heirless families appear in the documents that such heirs were probably relatively rare. I believe that, in the early immigrant society of Taiwan, it was not easy to adopt heirs from outside or to designate heirs from within the lineage. The latter was particularly difficult, for normally only someone of the appropriate generation within the family could be designated heir. This was something the migrant far from his home village might dream of but probably could not accomplish. In fact, it was precisely because men without heirs had no hope of designating an heir while still alive that their property might be transferred to lineage members or neighbors, who could be called on to conduct sacrifice or install an heir on their behalf after they died. This practice of entrustment in order to arrange for inheritance of property and the maintenance of sacrifice was a Taiwanese version of the traditional mainland practice of designating an heir. But the family structure of the man who lacked an heir would be completely different in the two arrangements. Obviously, entrustment only ensured that the sacrifices to the heirless man would be maintained; it did not enable his family to continue to develop normally. As for a family that lacked both heir and property, even the maintenance of their sacrifices could not be entrusted, so after his death the proprietor could only become a hungry ghost. In the Qing, charitable facilities such as graveyards and altars for hungry ghosts were established throughout Taiwan specifically to deal with the burial of and sacrifices for these men who died without heirs, which suggests that such heirless families must have been numerous.

*   *   *

Second, the development of the large family was unstable. We have seen that, in mainland Fujian in the Ming and Qing, lineal families usually divided their estate only once the second generation had already married, and joint families only once the third generation had married. In the small number of families for which this was not the case, there were usually exceptional circumstances. However, in Qing Taiwan, the estate was often divided before the second-generation members had married. This meant that the development of the large family in Qing Taiwan was less stable, or less likely to succeed, than on the mainland. For example, when four brothers of the Xiao surname divided their family in 1770, only two were married. A family in Taizhong divided its estate in 1799, when only five of seven members of the second generation had married. Another family in Jiayi divided its estate in 1838, when only four of the six members of the second generation were married. The Wang family divided its estate in 1894, when only one of the three brothers was married.[51] There are many other similar cases. In these circumstances, the development cycle of the large family was not exactly the same as on the mainland, as the following three documents of household division reveal.

Document of Household Division, 1838

The maker of this deed is stepmother Zheng. My late husband first married a woman née Cai. Between us we had six sons. . . . Because our family had bad luck, Eldest Son unfortunately died young. Fourth Son was adopted out to serve as heir to my husband's elder brother. Then wife Cai and my husband died in quick succession. . . . Now, fortunately, Second and Third Sons have both married. Although Fourth Son has been adopted out, we have also explicitly arranged his marriage. . . . I have invited the agnates of the branch and the lineage head, and we have collectively decided as follows. First, three plots of varying sizes located at Dongshiding Jijigang are given to the adopted son to inherit as his own property, in order to support the sacrifice to husband's elder brother. Also, one ward at Zhuxiaopo Daqiyuan is set aside to serve as my retirement estate. The remainder is divided into five even shares, to be chosen by lot, for each man to manage separately. Fourth Son has no claim on these. The estate left behind by husband's elder brother belongs to Fourth Son. Eldest, Second, Third, Fifth, and Sixth Sons have no claim on it. Fifth Son, Sixth Son, and Eldest Grandson have not yet been married. To make preparations in advance for their wedding, the land at Zhongzhenyuan will be set aside. Fifty large silver dollars *(dayuan)* should be spent on each wedding. . . .[52]

Contract of Household Division, 1838

The makers of this deed of household division are eldest [brother] Zu, second [brother] Qin, and third [brother] Zhangtong etc. . . . We have decided we wish to live and eat separately. . . . The plot of dry land above Wangtianshejiao is to serve as the corporate estate for the sacrifices to the ancestors, to be managed in rotation by the three branches, one after the other, to cultivate and harvest, and used to meet the expenses of the sacrifice and to pay the tax. It is also decided that since Third Brother is not yet married, from the second month of this year (1838) until the second month of 1840, he will manage this corporate estate, cultivating and collecting the harvest for two years, in order to meet the expenses of his marriage and pay the tax.[53]

Document of Household Division, 1853

The maker of this document of household division is father Sancai. ... My grandfather and father first established an estate and transmitted a plan to posterity. Serving as heir, I inherited these. Now I am also old. So I have called on the elders of the branch to divide the estate inherited from my grandfather and father, which is worth about 400 large silver dollars. The complication is that my mother is still living, and I fear that she will have no capital to support her living expenses. Also I have five young sons who are still children and haven't yet grown up. Only my eldest son Tianze has grown up and married, and he desires to live separately in his own family. So I have invited the relatives of this branch to discuss this, and we have agreed that, from the legally purchased land at Shuibintou, the rights to a portion worth forty large silver dollars is to serve as my mother's retirement estate (shanlao). As for the five sons who have not yet grown to maturity or married, land worth 300 large silver dollars is to be divided into five equal shares, with each share being worth sixty large silver dollars, to meet the expenses of taking a wife. Although the estate inherited from grandfather and father should be divided among the descendants at the appropriate time, on reflection it would not do to make no arrangements for myself. So the remaining sixty large silver dollars' worth of purchased land will be retained as a retirement estate for me and my wife. ... Once all of this has been arranged, there is no remaining money left to give to eldest son Tianze. So I have divided the furniture and family utensils and the remaining seed from spring into six equal shares.[54]

These three examples demonstrate that, if the members of the second generation were not all already married when household division took place, then some of the families formed after the division would be incomplete families. Moreover, the speed at which large families disintegrated made it unlikely that any of the families of the second generation were large families. In other words, division meant the complete disintegration of the original family into some number of small families. Thus, where the development of the large family was unstable, the trend was toward declining size and complexity of family structure.

This sort of document of household division always includes provisions for the wedding expenses of those parties to the division who are not yet married. This appears to be an aspect of household division that became accepted through common practice, which shows that traditional household division practices had undergone a fundamental change. According to customary law in mainland Fujian, household division could only be initiated once the second-generation members were all married, and this was precisely the basis on which large families could develop in the long term. Providing for the marriage expenses of individuals unmarried at the time of division implied that the large family could actually arrange for the fulfillment of its responsibilities even before all the members were married, which greatly accelerated the disintegration process. This suggests that the unstable development of the large family in Qing Taiwan was not just a matter of chance, but rather reflected inexorable development trends.

*   *   *

Third, a single large family might have multiple components. The multiplex families of Qing-era Taiwan can be divided into two basic types: multiplex families resulting from the process of immigration; and multiplex families resulting from multiple inheritance, that is, of a single individual serving as heir to more than one person. The former type is described in the following two documents:

Document of Household Division, 1793

The maker of this deed, née Guo, married into the Han surname. After I married Duzhai, I observed that his manner in life was filial, cordial, and honest. He managed his affairs in accord with the will of the ancestors. Thus I knew that his descendants would be flourishing. He had six sons. Eldest son Gaoze, second son Gaoxiang, and third son Gaorui were all born of his previous wife née Fang. Fourth son Gaozhu was born of concubine Hua. Fifth son Gaofeng and sixth son Gaolin were born to me. My husband died nine years ago, in 1785. ... So I had [Gao]ze and the others invite the lineage head, third branch uncle Xiwen, to discuss things together. It is decided that the land, shops, and dwellings in Taiwan and Zhangzhou belonging to the Prosperous Record enterprise *(Hengjisuo)*, totaling in all 64,280.952 taels, should be disbursed as follows: 7,837.488 is to be retained as the corporate property of the Prosperous Record enterprise. 3,209.09 is to be used to repay debts and to pay for the installation of the ancestral tablets in the lesser-descent-line ancestral hall. 1,639.2 will serve as my retirement estate; 411 will serve as Concubine Hua's retirement estate. After our deaths, once the funeral expenses have been met, the surplus [from these two items] will serve as our sacrificial estate. 1,840 taels is to pay for the marriage expenses of Gaolin and the two younger sisters; 395.2 for Gaorui to find a new wife. 3,484.6-

worth [of land] is to be given to Eldest Grandson to earn the rent. 3,415.4-worth is to serve as an educational estate, to encourage the descendants over the generations to become educated and enter the County School. Those who do will enjoy the rental income and manage the land. . . . The remaining 42,019.24 is divided into six even shares. . . . Fourth [Son], whose branch is named Yu, together with his birth mother, concubine Hua, are in Taiwan. The numerous should not accommodate the few; I have chosen the share which they shall be given. Beyond this division, any surplus property ownership of which was not declared, or debts that have been owed us for many years are to be incorporated into the corporate property.[55]

Document of Household Redivision *(zaifen jiushu)*, 1884

The makers of this document of redivision are the wives of Guo Weishu, née Cai and Zhao, his sons Fuduo and Qicai, his grandson Gantang, second branch nephews Fuqi and Futing, and third branch nephew Guangxi etc. . . . Our late husband Weishu crossed the sea to Taiwan at a young age, made his living in trade, and established an estate. Reflecting that relatives ought to treat one another with intimacy, and unable to bear being selfish, in 1877 he returned to the mainland and drew up a contract of household division in four copies. He divided the dwellings and property that he had acquired on previous trips back to the mainland into four shares, and distributed these to second branch younger brother Weijian, third branch nephew Chengjia, fourth branch nephew Guangxi, and his own eldest son on the mainland, Fuduo, with each one getting one share. In addition, he established corporate property on the mainland from which the four were to collect the rent in rotation. From the shares in the Pivot of Abundant Profit *(Longyishu)* enterprise at Bicheng, he took 1,000 silver dollars' worth and recorded that this amount belonged to Weichan. . . . As for the property in Bi[cheng], Weishu returned [to Taiwan] in 1879 and drew up a document of household division with five copies, which divided the property into five equal shares, one each of which was distributed to eldest son Fufeng, second son Anran, third son Zizai, third branch nephew Chengjia, and fourth branch nephew Guangxi. Each man also received 1,500 silver dollars. Because Anran and Zizai were still young and at school, they were each given an additional 500 silver dollars. All the funds were [in the form of] shares in the Pivot of Abundant Profit enterprise. In addition, from the corporate property he established, worth 7,500 silver dollars, each person was given a share worth 500 silver dollars. Weishu personally retained control over the 5,700 silver dollars in the corporate account of the enterprise. . . . It could not have been expected that last year he should die. Second branch nephews Fuqi and Futing raised the issue that they had not received shares in the property at Bi[cheng], nor did they receive a greater share [in the property on the mainland]. We [the two wives] respect our late husband's cordial intentions; we cannot bear that he should be seen as partial. So we have gathered the sons and nephews, and agreed openly with the relatives that the shortfall of the second branch should be made up for with shares in the Pivot of Abundant Profit enterprise. The deeds and documents to the corporate land have been inspected by the sons and nephews, and this document of redivision has been drawn up in six copies. Each party is to hold one copy, to serve as the final proof. By this single effort we may produce lasting peace, on the one hand accomplishing our late husband's refined cordiality, on the other preventing conflicts in the future.[56]

These two cases illustrate that wealthy migrants to Taiwan in the Qing might have property both on the mainland and in Taiwan, which meant they had a dispersed multiplex family. The basic characteristic of such a family was that the family members owned an estate in common but lived separately. As a result, the family was a unified body from the point of view of property relations, but comprised a number of mutually independent units from the point of view of living arrangements. In the first case, even before household division, wife Guo on the mainland and concubine Hua on Taiwan each handled her own affairs separately. The situation in the second case was even more complicated; it might be described as a multilevel multiplex family. Before the division, Guo Weishu and his brothers on the mainland lived separately but held their estate in common, and thus comprised a joint family with two components. Guo Weishu's mainland wife and his eldest son lived separately from his Taiwanese wife and the younger sons, but they also held their estate in common, and thus comprised a lineal family with two components. This complicated multiplex family underwent three divisions of its estate in the course of two generations before finally disintegrating. In this kind of multiplex family whose members owned property in common but lived separately, even though the property was owned by the large family, the main unit of social life was generally a small family. Thus, in practice, concubine Hua and her son in the first example, or wife Cai and her sons in the second, could not easily develop a large family and, realistically, could potentially develop only into a stem family. Moreover, without property relations tying the members together, this kind of multiplex family would tend to disintegrate rapidly, and was therefore not likely to develop over the long term with any stability. In the second case, when Guo Weishu divided his estate for the second time in 1879, his second and third son "were still young and at school." I believe that a multiplex family that had developed during the process of immigration remained consistently in a state of transition between large and small family phases, and can be said to display simultaneously characteristics of both.

*   *   *

The multiplex family created by multiple inheritance was not peculiar
to Qing Taiwan. But because heirless families in Qing Taiwan were so
common, and designating an heir relatively difficult, multiple inheritance may have been relatively common. Multiplex families that developed in this way were usually also characterized by residential separation but common ownership of an estate, since those sons who had
been designated someone else's heir shared ownership in the estate of
their birth parents with those sons who had not. Documents of household division from Qing Taiwan show that it was common for sons
who had also been designated someone else's heir to participate in the
allocation of the birth parents' estate as well. For example, a deed of
the Division of the Estate of the Li surname, from 1876, reads:

> Of the paddy and dry land and dwellings that have been established,
> aside from [a portion] which is set aside as our retirement estate, and
> property given to adopted heirs Yupan and Yutai, the remainder is to
> be divided evenly among Yubi, Yuqing, Yuchen, and Yubing. The dwell-
> ings and furniture and utensils are divided evenly into six shares.[57]

An 1895 document of household division reads:

> My husband . . . had two sons, Bingyu and Bingjun. . . . Bingjun was
> adopted out to serve as heir to his father's younger brother Wuzhong,
> to inherit the estate of the fifth branch together with Bingyou of the
> sixth branch. They have already drawn up a division document, for
> which there is reliable evidence. Considering that Bingyu and Bingjun
> share the same spirit and are branches of the same tree, that is, they
> are the closest of relatives [i.e., full brothers], rather than each inherit-
> ing separately, would it not be better to come to a compromise to-
> gether, and thus to esteem the closeness of hands to feet? . . . There-
> fore I have called on the affines and agnates of the branch and lineage
> to come to our house to serve as witnesses. From the estate that was
> inherited through household division by my husband, which earns a
> rent of sixty piculs, ten piculs' worth is set aside to serve as my retire-
> ment estate, and five piculs are to be given to Bingjun, who has already
> left, which leaves forty-five-worth to go to Bingyu.[58]

In general, taking responsibility for someone's sacrifice was a necessary
condition of inheriting his property. A man designated as someone
else's heir had to take responsibility for sacrifice to his own birth
parents in order to inherit from them. For example, the previously
cited document of household division of the Li family clearly requires
that after the death of the widowed mother the income from her re-

tirement estate should be jointly inherited by the son who had been designated his relative's heir and the son who had not been, "to conduct sacrifice in rotation to their father and mother." This sort of multiplex family, with separate residences but joint property, was clearly a product of the practice of joint sacrifice. However, even under joint sacrifice, if the son designated somenone else's heir continued to live with and own property in common with other sons, then this sort of multiplex family did not really develop. For example, the 1893 document of household division of the Liu surname prescribes:

> [The makers of this deed are Shen]yue and his two brothers. . . . At a young age Shenyue was designated as the heir of his uncle Boyuan, all of whose property was divided between him and his cousin Tengjiao. But [his share of the] property remained under the control of his father Qinqi, and he continued to eat together with this family for a long time. No distinction was made between [the different brothers]. Now they have decided to live separately, so it is necessary to allocate the interest [on the capital Shenyue inherited from Boyuan]. Together we have called on the lineage head and branch relatives to decide things. The property that [Shen]yue originally inherited and the property left behind by birth father Qinqi will be combined and divided evenly.

Here, because the son who was designated as another's heir never lived separately from or divided the estate with his siblings, a real multiplex family never developed.

It should be noted that the decision as to whether or not the son designated as an heir would continue to jointly worship his birth parents was rarely taken in advance, but rather was usually made only during the process of division of the estate of the birth parents. Thus, this sort of multiplex family was often latent, only becoming actual at the time of household division. As a document of household division dated 1868 explains:

> We reflect that our parents gave birth to us four brothers. . . . But second brother Ying was designated the grandson of ancestor Ding, so one of the four branches [of our family] lacked posterity. At the time, Ying had three sons. . . . When he was dying, he reflected that trees have their roots, and streams their source. He had his second son, Hou, return to [serve as posterity of] the second branch [of his original family]. . . . For this reason we have invited the heads of the lineage to decide things. The rent from two plots of land, one redeemed and the other newly acquired, is to serve forever as the sacrificial estate, to rotate through the four branches to pay the costs of the sacrifice. The remaining fields, dwellings, and family implements will be assessed in value and divided evenly into four shares.[59]

This document suggests that, in a situation where joint worship was common, the son designated as heir to another could at any time request that he be permitted to jointly sacrifice to the descent line of his birth parents, which also gave him the right to inherit a share of their property, and thus transformed the latent multiplex family into an actual one. Naturally, if the designated son relinquished his demand to jointly worship his birth parents' descent-line, then this multiplex family no longer existed. But this was only determined at the time of household division. In other words, prior to the division of the estate, there existed the potential for joint worship, and hence a latent multiplex family. I believe that this sort of multiplex family growing out of joint worship was fundamentally no different from the multiplex family created by immigration, since both could simultaneously display characteristics of large and small families. But in terms of the development cycle, the two clearly were different. Whereas the multiplex family created by immigration remained consistently in a state of transition between large and small family phases, the multiplex family created by joint worship reflected the temporary return of a small family into a large one. In a sense, neither of these two kinds of multiplex families was really a stable large family, but rather a large family in the process of disintegration. Therefore, neither the multiplex family created by immigration nor the multiplex family created by joint worship can be considered identical to the traditional large family.

*   *   *

In sum, the heirless families, unstable large families, and multiplex large families of Qing-era Taiwan all represent to different degrees variations on the ordinary development cycle of the traditional family, and collectively represent a trend toward declining size and complexity of family structure. But leaving aside such exceptional forms, there were also large families in Qing Taiwan which developed with some stability—namely, lineal and joint families in which the second-generation members were all married prior to household division. The development cycles of such families were essentially similar to those on mainland Fujian. In order to clarify the basic pattern and special characteristics of family structure in Qing Taiwan, I have reclassified the families described in the documents according to this typology. The results are shown in Table 2.2. The table shows the maximum limits of expansion of seventy families. 47 percent grew into stable large families; 21 percent into unstable large families; 17 percent into multiplex

Table 2.2. Household Structure in Qing Taiwan

	Stable Large Family	Unstable Large Family	Multiplex Family	Heirless Family
Qianlong	3	1	1	0
Jiaqing	6	1	0	1
Daoguang	7	2	2	6
Xianfeng	4	1	0	0
Tongzhi	5	0	1	0
Guangxu	8	10	8	3
Totals	33	15	12	10
(%)	47	21	17	14

Source: *Taiwan shihō furoku sankōsho.*

families; and 14 percent into heirless families. Thus, in Qing Taiwan approximately half of all families did not develop into stable large families, which explains the general trend toward declining size and complexity of family structure.

Most scholars believe that instability and diminishing family size are common characteristics of migrant families. But it should also be pointed out that, by the middle of the nineteenth century at the latest, Taiwan had already gradually become a settled society. Nevertheless, large families were still not appearing in any numbers. Of the twenty-eight Taiwanese families in the Guangxu period in Table 2.2, only eight, or less than one-third, were stable large families. This demonstrates that the development cycle of Qing Taiwan families was not determined solely by the immigrant environment but also by other important historical factors. Because the commercial economy of Qing Taiwan was relatively highly developed, the cooperative division of labor within the family was weakened, and the economic advantages of the large family may have no longer held. The trend toward diminishing family size in Qing Taiwan was thus part of the process of the modernization of the traditional family.

Finally, it should be noted that the historical characteristics of family structure in Qing Taiwan had important implications for the development of lineages. On the one hand, widespread incomplete families meant that few inheritance lineages formed through household division, so the majority of lineage organizations in the early immigrant period were contractual lineages. On the other hand, because the development of large families was unstable, the appearance and development of the inheritance lineage was accelerated, so once immigrants had settled, the inheritance lineage quickly became the predominant lineage form. Moreover, the widespread practice of joint worship greatly complicated the inheritance relations of family lineage members, which frequently led to different kinds of lineage organizations developing in a mutually interconnected way. Thus family structure and development cycles are essential to understanding lineage organizations in Qing Taiwan, a subject that will be resumed in Chapter 4.

3
A Basic Typology of Lineage Organization

The Taiwanese scholar Tang Meijun suggests that the Chinese lineage is an unusual form of kinship organization in that it simultaneously embodies three principles of social organization: consanguinal ties, territorial ties, and ties of common interest.[1] This interpretation helpfully draws attention to the multifaceted nature of lineage organization. But if the analysis goes no further than this, we run the risk of conflating rather different types of lineage organization, making it impossible to explain the historical characteristics of lineage organization and its developmental trends. I believe that no actual lineage organization could possibly have fully embodied all three of these organizational principles at any given time; rather, the tendency was always for one principle among the three to dominate. Lineage organization can therefore be divided into three basic types: the inheritance lineage, a lineage based on consanguinal ties; the control-subordination lineage, based on territorial ties; and the contractual lineage, based on ties of common interest. This chapter analyzes the structure, functions, and operative mechanisms of these three types of lineage organization.

The Inheritance Lineage

The defining characteristic of an inheritance lineage is that the rights and responsibilities of each member of the lineage are determined by inheritance relations. Inheritance relations are largely determined by relations of consanguinity, so the inheritance lineage is a form of lineage organization based on consanguinal relations.

The formation of an inheritance lineage is primarily linked to collective inheritance of wealth and social position, and is thus the result of incomplete division of the household estate. It is generally held that the chief characteristic of the traditional Chinese system of property inheritance is partible inheritance, that is, the estate of the father is completely divided among the sons. But in fact, in order to lessen the shock that division of the household estate caused for the traditional family, it was common practice for people to employ such practices as dividing the estate without dividing sacrificial rights and responsibilities, dividing the estate without changing the household registration, and dividing the household without dividing the property. Each of these methods involved some kind of collective inheritance, of either the sacrificial responsibilities of the descent-line, household registration, or property, which meant that, after the division, lineage members continued to maintain cooperative relations. This is what transformed a family into a lineage. The document of household division of the Ouyang family of Taining County, dated 1809, records:

Ritual has five constant principles, of which none is more important than sacrifice. . . . Our family is assembled here as a lineage. The descendants hope to flourish. It is particularly important that arrangements for sacrificial matters be made in advance. For this reason, we have reverently set aside sacrificial fields earning 52.2 piculs rent to meet the expenses of the spring and autumn sacrifice and grave cleaning for grandfather Maohui, and venerable grandmother Gong. The sacrificial items and the regulations for the rituals are all recorded in detail in [another] volume. The members of the first, second, and third branches are to take charge of the performance of the ritual and the collection of the rent in rotation forever. They must not try to bring forward their position in the order, or worry that their position is too far back. Nor are they permitted to collect the rent for themselves or to sell the land off illicitly. If this kind of bad conduct takes place, the registers should be consulted in public discussion. If [the violator] still does not respect [the decision], the matter must definitely be referred to the authorities to impose punishment. If the members of the lineage become numerous and the funds insufficient, only the sacrificial items need remain fixed; the size of the feast and the amount of meat to be divided can be changed to meet the needs of circumstance. It is only to be hoped that in every generation the descendants will prepare the objects and perform the ritual with the utmost love and respect. In [the world of] darkness this will agree with the spirits and in that of light this will encourage warm feelings within the lineage.

Our reigning dynasty following historical precedent has established the *baojia* system, so that the population registers can be investigated and tax responsibilities checked. Each *bao* has a head, who is put forward by the community. Within each *jia* are households who are subordinate to the *li* head. The *li* heads are referred to by the names of the first ancestors of each surname to be entered in the registration. Their descendants take on the responsibilities [of the *li* head] in rotation. This is also referred to as the annual management rotation, and involves being specifically in charge of pressing for tax payment for one year. Within the *li*, when the secretary (*celi*) draws up the tax list and the tax collector (*tucha*) comes to press for tax and receive the customary gifts, [the *li* head] handles the negotiations, oversees matters, and makes decisions accordingly. As for the decennial rotation of responsibility for the conduct of sacrifices at the village altar,[2] the expenses are not fixed, but [the provisions for] the feast and the distribution of meat must be sufficient.

Our family was registered in the seventh *jia* of the second ward of the county town. We serve as *li* head together with the Ye surname. Later the Liao surname was also entered into the registration. We are [collectively] responsible for [the sacrifice] once every ten years. [When it is our turn,] the Ye take responsibility for the sacrifice in the middle of the seventh month; we Ou[yang] take responsibility for the sacrifice at the beginning of the tenth month; the Liao take responsibility for the sacrifice at the Clear and Bright (*Qingming*) Festival in the third month of the following year. To the right of the altar in the *li* are some shops on which rent is earned. The rent is divided among those whose turn it is in the rotation to conduct the sacrifice, and the households of the *jia* also contribute, but in fact the amounts are insufficient. For this reason I have established fields earning two piculs' husked rice rent to serve in perpetuity as the fields [to meet the cost of our, the] Ouyang surname's [responsibilities] in the annual tax management rotation. From the rent collected each year, after the customary gifts for the secretary and the tax collector and the tax on the land have been paid, there should remain more than thirty piculs, which is to be saved until it is our turn in the decennial rotation. The full amount should then go to provide the sacrificial items; detailed regulations for this follow. This land is to be managed in the same way as the rest of the corporate property is administered. I only hope that in the future the descendants will not expropriate this property or divide it up, but each time the sacrifice is held they will carry it out wholeheartedly. It may be that since the spirits scrutinize us, the people of the *jia* will stress trust and build harmony. This would indeed be fortunate.

Educational fields are established in order to educate the talented, to let them study without distraction and devote their will to scholarship, in order that they will be worthy of being chosen to serve the court. . . . When our grandfather had just arrived in Taining, he was not even able to earn a living, so how could he think of devoting energy to study? Because I have exerted my full spirit and energy, without regretting the hardships, I was able to purchase fields and a house, and become a native of Shanyi, able to pay taxes and participate in the examinations. This has been done out of the desire to bring glory to the ancestors and enrich the descendants. I myself consider that our fixed property is now sufficient to meet our needs, but I am concerned that luxury leads to dissipation. So in the free time I have had to manage household affairs, I have given both encouragement and warning to you brothers and nephews, anxiously hoping that you will soon succeed. Now we have obtained the protection of Heaven, and you have not disappointed my hopes, since in succession [several of] you have become County School Students. Now I am still concerned that you will be short of money to conduct your studies, which will make it difficult to succeed in the examinations. So I have specially established educational fields earning a rent of fifty piculs, the income to be collected by and distributed to the County School Students. In the future, anyone who succeeds in literary or military study and passes the examinations to enter the literary or military county schools, or who is named in the provincial or national examinations, shall get the whole rent to himself in the year of his success. He is to select an auspicious day to report this to the ancestors, inviting the elderly and respected from within the lineage to celebrate together. . . . Brothers and nephews who pass the examination in the same year will each receive the full amount for one year according to their generational order. Once each of them has had a turn, the income will revert to being sharing evenly by all the eligible who are living. Those who are appointed to hold office and earn a salary, or whose appointment has been announced, regardless of whether this was by purchase, are not eligible to receive the income. In this way, the descendants will have something to rely on, and talent can be cultivated, and prepared for selection by the state. In this way we can continue to be a literary and refined family, and the descendants for generations will surpass one another in their exertions.[3]

The Ouyang were originally registered in Nan'an County in Quanzhou Prefecture and had moved to Taining in Shaowu in the early Qianlong period. The document above describes the first division of the estate after their move. In the division, portions of the estate were set aside as "sacrificial fields," "fields [to meet the cost of our, the] Ouyang surname's [responsibilities] in the annual tax management rotation," and "educational fields," to be collectively inherited by the descendants to enable them to meet the expenses of collective sacrifices and *lijia* responsibilities and to encourage academic success. As a result, even after the division of the household, its former members continued to maintain extremely close cooperative relations. This in turn meant the formation of an inheritance lineage.

Membership in an inheritance lineage was determined on the basis of personal relationships of inheritance. In general, only the direct descendants of an ancestor whose estate was inherited could become members of his inheritance lineage. This is demonstrated by the

"Record of the Sacrificial Land of the Gen Branch" of the He surname of Lujiang, Jianyang County:

> In our lineage, the right to receive a share of sacrificial meat from the sacrificial property left behind by Puxuan has rotated for a long time among all the descendants of the Gen branch, without any dispute. The Zhen and Kan branches do not have any claim. The lines of inheritance are clear (*ming dipai*). As for the sacrificial estate established personally by Wenmao, and the duty to worship the ancestor and sweep the grave, it is only the descendants of Wenmao who prepare the wine in rotation and attend the feast. The descendants of Wenzheng do not have any claim. This is determined based on the origins [of the sacrificial property] (*su youlai*).[4]

The term "lines of inheritance" refers to those descendants who inherit a share in the estate endowed by an ancestor; the term "origins of the sacrificial property" refers to the ancestor who has endowed an estate that is inherited collectively by his descendants. The emphasis is slightly different, but both make the same point. The rights associated with sacrificial property were collectively inherited only by the direct descendants of the ancestor who had established that estate. Anyone who was not his lineal descendant had no claim on it.

Inheritance lineages therefore necessarily placed great emphasis on the inheritance relationships of their members, which led to such practices as reporting new male members of the lineage (*baoding*) and re-compiling the descent-line records (*qingxi*). According to the genealogy of the Yuan of Chong'an:

> It is decided that on the first day of every New Year the new male members of the lineage born in the preceding year must be reported and verified. If they turn out to be adoptions of people who are not consanguinal kin, they may not be entered into the membership register. Every five years when it comes time to recompile the descent-line registers, if there are [descent-lines] for which there is no living male or [individuals] who lack heirs, the whole lineage should collectively choose and designate an heir in a timely manner. If anyone ought to accept an heir but refuses to, the lineage head (*zuzhang*) should not let him get away with it.[5]

The purpose of reporting new male members of the lineage and recompiling the descent-line records was to confirm the inheritance relationships of the lineage members, in order to prevent potential conflicts over rights of inheritance from arising.

Lineage regulations from Ming and Qing Fujian often strictly restricted the selections of heirs, forbidding those "whose origins are not the same" who might "muddle the descent-line." For example:

Designating an heir (*jisi*) is done in order to make up for shortcomings owing to natural circumstances and to extend the sympathy and love of the ancestors. So the heir should be chosen from male relatives according to the closest mourning grade. If there is no one within the mourning grades, then another lineage member may serve. The designation is to be made collectively; there should be no dispute. . . . Adopting someone of another surname would cause what is known as muddling the descent-line and should be rejected on principle.[6]

According to this, any member of a household who did not have a consanguinal relationship with the relevant ancestor was excluded from the inheritance lineage. In 1757, Yuan Shaowu, whose adoption of Tiansun was discussed in the preceding chapter, divided his estate between his adopted son and his birth son, Jiqing. The document of division stresses:

Now Tiansun has grown up. He is adopted, and in principle should not be given a share in the household estate equal to that of a direct descendant, nor should he worship the ancestors in rotation with them. . . . For example, for the sacrificial property of my ancestor Gengwu, which is held corporately by the Zhi, Ren, and Yong branches, and the sacrificial property of my father Xingsan, which is held corporately by the Yuan, Heng, Li, and Zhen branches, my birth son is to conduct the sacrifice and clean the graves, to be the host [at the feast], and to collect the rent [from these properties when it is his turn in the rotation]. Tiansun does not have a claim on the worship or cleaning of these graves [nor on the property that supports these activities]. As for the property which I have set aside as my own retirement estate (*shan*), my intention was for my birth son and my adopted son to manage this as sacrificial land in rotation. But according to the laws and the advice of the elders, an adopted son may only participate in the feast, and there has never been the precedent of his conducting the sacrifice in rotation with the birth son. . . . [So] I additionally set aside property earning six baskets (*luo*) rent to give to [Tiansun] and his son, to conduct sacrifice and grave cleaning themselves in the future.[7] My retirement and sacrificial property is given entirely to [birth son] Jiqing to pay for the sacrifice, collect the rent, and pay the tax. The adopted son should not overreach [propriety] by questioning this.[8]

In 1806, Yuan Jiqing's widow divided the household estate on behalf of her adopted grandson, Guangpo, and the designated heir, Zhonghan, and stated clearly:

The sacrificial property left behind by Shaowu and grandmother is managed in rotation by the Wen, Xing, Zhong, and Xin branches. [Adopted son] Guangpo does not participate in the rotation. But in the rotation of the sacrificial property of my husband Jiqing and myself, when it is the turn of the Xing branch, [the designated heir] Zhonghan receives a share of 590 baskets, and Guangpo a share of 210 baskets. The tax is to be paid in this same proportion, so that neither of them is taken advantage of.[9]

This shows that an inheritance lineage in the strictest sense could exist only among lineage members whose consanguinal relationship was clear and straightforward and who all shared a common ancestor. In other words, direct consanguinal relationships between all the lineage members was the prerequisite for and fundamental basis of an inheritance lineage.

*   *   *

After an inheritance lineage had formed, the rights and responsibilities associated with it had to be reallocated with each passing generation,

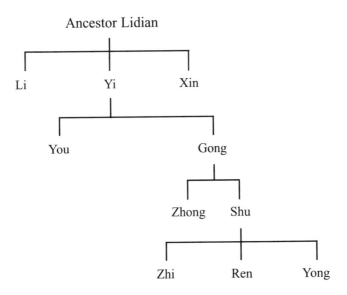

Figure 3.1. Organizational Structure of the Su of Pucheng

and the scale of the inheritance lineage could expand accordingly. An inheritance lineage that was able to continue to develop through the ongoing fragmentation of the associated rights and responsibilities was generally characterized by internal divisions into branches (*fang*), or segments. Moreover, any member of an inheritance lineage could potentially leave a further collective inheritance for subsequent generations, thereby creating a new inheritance lineage within the original one. An inheritance lineage would therefore tend to develop into a multibranched, multilayered pyramid-shaped structure. The rights and responsibilities of each individual member of the lineage were determined by his position in the branches and in the generational order. In other words, members of an inheritance lineage who belonged to different branches and different generations occupied different positions in the lineage. This is clearly illustrated by a 1930 "Document of division" of a family of the Su surname from Pucheng. The estate was divided among three sons, whose households were given the names Zhi, Ren, and Yong branches.

1. The ancestors have left behind sacrificial property at Wudun in the name of Lidian. The annual rental income is 300 piculs. Since previous generations, the conduct of the sacrifice has rotated between the Li, Yi, and Xin branches. My ancestor belonged to the Yi branch, which is further divided into the You and Gong sub-branches, each of which earns the income from the property once every six years. Now our Gong branch has further divided into the Zhong and Shu sub-branches. Our Shu branch earns the income from the property once every twelve years. In the future, when it is our year to earn the income, you [the members of the] Zhi, Ren, and Yong branches will collect it in rotation one after the other. The details of the rent, the property, and the tenant are all recorded clearly in the genealogy, so they are not recorded here.

2. The ancestors have left behind sacrificial property at Xianyang in the name of Chengpei. The annual rental income is 200 piculs. . . . Since previous generations, the conduct of the sacrifice has rotated between the You and Gong branches. [The Gong branch is divided into the Zhong and Shu sub-branches.] . . . In the future, when it is the turn of the Shu branch to earn the income, you [the members of the] Zhi, Ren, and Yong branches should collect the rent and manage the property in rotation one after the other.

3. The sacrificial property at Qingyun in the name of Chuikun earns a current annual rent of 100 piculs. The sacrificial property of Yingyu at Wudun, which was the retirement estate of Madam Su née Ji, earns a rent of 300 piculs. The estate for the accompanying sacrifice (*fusi*) to Luanchun at Wudun earns a rent of over 20 piculs. Since

previous generations, the conduct of this sacrifice has rotated between
the Zhong and Shu branches. In the future, when it is the turn of the
Shu branch to earn the income, you [the members of the] Zhi, Ren, and
Yong branches should collect the rent in rotation in order.
    4. The educational estate endowed by Tingzang at Xianyang earns
a rent of 50 piculs. It is already recorded clearly in the original document [of household division] that those descendants of the Zhong and
Shu branch who become County School Students collect the income. . . .
    5. The different sacrificial properties and education rental [proper-
ties] left behind by the ancestors, as well as my retirement estate, earning over 200 piculs dry unhusked rice rent, is presently collected and
managed by me. When your mother and I are dead, you [the members
of the] Zhi, Ren, and Yong branches will earn the rent and manage
the property in rotation.[10]

The Zhi, Ren, and Yong branches, which were established by fifth-
generation members of the Su, had different rights to the lineage property endowed by each preceding generation. Each of the three branches
had a one-third share of the lineage property established in their
father's generation, a one-sixth share of that of their grandfather, a
one-twelfth share of that of their great-grandfather, and a one-thirty-
sixth share of that of their great-great-grandfather. This was the case
because, at each different level of the inheritance lineage, shares in the
rights to lineage property were determined on the basis of the number
of branches and generational order.
    The formation and development of the inheritance lineage were
conditioned and restricted by inheritance relationships, and inheritance relations were in turn based on relations of consanguinity. So
the ideal inheritance lineage required complete, accurate, and reliable
genealogical records. But this is not to suggest that the existence of
complete, accurate, and reliable genealogical records necessarily implied the existence of an inheritance lineage. By an inheritance lineage
I mean more than simply a vaguely defined descent group, but rather
a highly regulated lineage organization with practical functions. Many
lineage genealogies of Ming and Qing Fujian contain relatively complete descent-lines but no suggestion of regulated cooperative relationships between the lineage members. This kind of descent group, with
a genealogical connection but no practical function, should not be
considered an inheritance lineage. Thus the "General Rules" in the
genealogy of the You surname of Fulong in Jianyang prescribe:

    In cases [where a member] had moved away and settled elsewhere,
    and [his descendants] multiplied into a large branch, the old geneal-

ogy has been consulted for confirmation. If there turned out to be a record of someone in a particular generation migrating to settle in a particular place, and the descent-line records are in accord, then they have been entered [into the new genealogy]. Otherwise, we have not dared to include them, out of concern for confusing the descent-line.

All cases of a member of the lineage having married uxorilocally or moved away must be recorded in detail, so that in the future should he [or his descendants] wish to return to the descent-line and be entered in the genealogy, their origins can be sought.

Although the descent-lines have branched, the ancestral tombs were originally collectively owned. In the past, because the genealogy was not clarified, the distant branches ceased to participate in the rituals, and only the descendants living nearby sacrificed there. With the passage of many years, some descendants in distant places cunningly contested the benefits from the mountain [lands around the tombs]. The descendants living nearby [responded that] the distant relatives had for years not participated in the collective rituals, thus seriously losing sight of the virtue of [putting value] on their common origin. Now the genealogy records all of the hill sites. The ancestral tombs are considered to belong collectively to all those who share the common ancestor, but, as in the past, the hills [around the tombs] are under the control of the descendants living nearby. Descendants living at a distance are not to use the pretext that they share a common ancestor to vie for the benefits from the hill lands and thereby incite quarrels.

Obviously, among the residentially dispersed members of the You, even though the genealogical record was clear and reliable, because the more distant branches had lost their inheritance rights to the lineage property, they had no real cooperative relations with the "descendants living nearby." So these You, despite having jointly compiled a genealogy, could form only an idealized inheritance group and could not possibly have formed a functional inheritance lineage.

* * *

In an inheritance lineage, the rights to manage and collect income from collectively inherited property generally rotated, usually annually, through the branches, or segments, descended from the ancestor who had endowed the property. For example, the rule of the Yang lineage of Jinzhang in Pucheng was that:

Each branch has established its own sacrificial property. The right to collect the rent and conduct the sacrifice rotates within the sub-branches of that branch according to seniority. . . . If there is bullying or the order becomes muddled, the lineage head should resolve things. The whole lineage should recover the rents that have been already collected and give them to the person who is supposed to have received them, and also agree on what sacrificial objects should be paid for [by the offender] as punishment.[11]

Jianyang County Magistrate Chen Shengshao's *Wensu Lu* (Record of enquiry into customs) provides another example:

> The gentry and common people of Jianyang all have rotating rental income for sacrifice. Major descent-line branches have their turn [to collect the rent] every five or six years; minor descent-line branches have their turn [to collect the rent] every fifty or sixty years. Whoever's turn it is in the rotation is responsible for paying the tax, repairs to the ancestral hall, the supply of sacrificial items to be sacrificed to the ancestors in spring and autumn, and the distribution of the sacrificial meat. If there is any left over, it belongs to the rota holder.[12]

Anyone who held a position in the rotation of lineage property had the right to collect certain benefits from it, and also had to take on certain responsibilities. These rights and responsibilities were closely connected. Moreover, because each branch had its own turn in the rotation, the rights and responsibilities associated with the lineage were distributed evenly across the branches.

In 1850, the three branches, known as Tian, Xing, and Jian, of a household belonging to a Xie lineage in Shunchang divided their household estate. The father, Xiabiao, drew up "Regulations for the Sacrificial Property Consisting of Fields and Houses and for the Conduct of Sacrifices," which describe in some detail how the rotation system was set up:

> 1. The fields and houses newly established as the sacrificial estate for me and my wives are to rotate among the Tian, Xing, and Jian branches in order according to seniority, each branch collecting the rent and conducting the sacrifice in turn. [The branches] should not jump their turn. Only after I and my second wife née Ou are both dead is this rotation to begin. My first wife née Zhang died long ago. . . . In the future, whichever of the Tian, Xing, and Jian branches whose turn it is to collect the rent should, on the occasion of the spring and autumn sacrifices, prepare the three sacrificial animals, sacrificial grains, fruits, vegetables, paper money, candles, and other sacrificial objects, and offer them at the graves of myself, Madam Zhang, and Madam Ou. They should do so wholeheartedly, and not merely as a gesture. Violators are to be fined 50 baskets of unhusked rice, which is to be saved to meet common expenses.
>
> 2. Whichever of the Tian, Xing, and Jian branches whose turn it is to conduct the sacrifices at the graves of myself, Madam Zhang, and Madam Ou should prepare the rice to be given to each male member

(ding) of the lineage in advance of the spring sacrifice. Each male member of the lineage is to receive one catty *(jin)* of sweet rice. In advance of the autumn sacrifice, they should prepare the cakes to be given to each male member of the lineage. Each male member of the lineage is to receive one catty of rice cakes. Any [household] that has new male members must pay the reporting fee of one hundred cash to the rota holder in order to record their name, to ensure that in future they receive the rice and cakes distributed to the lineage males. Anyone who becomes a civil or military County Student is to receive an additional catty of rice and cakes in spring and autumn. Anyone who passes the provincial or metropolitan civil or military examinations is to receive a further additional catty each in spring and autumn. Those who attain the age of sixty are to be given an additional catty each in spring and autumn. For each additional ten years of age, they are to receive a further additional catty each. On the day of the sacrifice, prepare a feast and invite male and female descendants of the three branches to partake of the foods that have been sacrificed. Young and old share equally. The dishes and drinks should not be excessive, or else the costs will become prohibitive and it will be difficult to continue. Those who wish not to attend may do as they please; there is no need to prepare dishes and drinks to send to them.

3. The schedule for the spring and autumn sacrifice at the graves is: In spring, the sacrifice should be within five days on either side of the Clear and Bright Festival. In autumn, the sacrifice should be held within five days on either side of the beginning of the White Dew.[13] Anyone who worships prior to these periods or who has failed to worship by the time they end is to be fined 10 baskets of rice, which is to be saved to meet common expenses.

4. Prior to the spring and autumn sacrifice, the rota holder should go to the tomb and clear the weeds in order to tidy it up. Violators are to be fined 20 baskets of rice, which is to be saved to meet common expenses.

5. An additional registration volume has now been set up [to administer] the rotation of rent collection and the conducting of sacrifice. It is to be held in rotation by the rota holder. The previous rota holder must pass on this volume to the new rota holder by the fifth day of the first month of the year, to hold onto and follow in conducting [the sacrifice]. Anyone who allows it to fall apart, conceals it, or alters these terms is to be fined 30 baskets of rice, which is to be saved to meet common expenses.

6. On the day of the worship at the graves in spring and autumn, the descendants in the Tian, Xing, and Jian branches must all go to the grave to conduct the ritual, the more the better. It is not permitted to be absent out of laziness or lack of respect.

7. I have not established any educational lands. If any descendants of the three branches are able to become County School Students in the future, they will be entitled to receive the rent from fields and dwell-

ings belonging to the sacrificial estate of myself and my wives for one year. This expresses our intention to promote talent. The manner by which they take responsibility is to be the same as the regulations for the rotation of the sacrifice. Military Students and those who purchase titles may not ask to receive [this income].

8. The land tax, service levy tax, autumn rice taxes and the rent due [to the bottom-soil landlord] on the sacrificial property is to be paid in full each year by the rota holder for that year. The rota holder should pay as early as possible, so the accounts can be kept clear. There must be no shortfall. If anyone violates this, the Tian, Xing, and Jian branches are permitted to suspend their collection of the income from rents on fields and houses in that year and use this to pay on their behalf.

9. In all cases of sacrificial fields being ruined by flooding, houses burning down, roofs starting to leak, or [sellers of property] demanding further payment or obstructing our acquisition of permanent ownership rights, rice that has been collected from violators [of these rules] should be used to meet expenses. If there are no funds from punishment available, the members of the three branches should together raise funds, divide up the construction work, or provide the materials.

10. In the past, when my younger brother and I divided our estate into the Yue and Xing branches, I obtained two rice-drying grounds at the place known as Lixiang Houmenshan, on which 20 rice-drying sheets can be laid out. Later I purchased one rice-drying ground from the Lu surname at the place known as Xiahoumen, on which 8 sheets can be laid. The drying grounds in these two places can be used to lay out sheets and dry rice by whichever of the Tian, Xing, or Jian branches holds the sacrificial rota for that year. Each year, the [rights to] dry the rice should be allocated according to the rota. This should not be contested.

11. The fields and dwellings of the sacrificial property may never be split up or sold off by the descendants. Violators are to be reported by righteous descendants to the state officials to investigate and punish according to the law.[14]

This text shows how explicitly the rights and responsibilities of lineage members were defined in a system of rotation through branches. If each member of the lineage acted conscientiously in accordance with such regulations, then the system could function fairly and rationally. In principle, an inheritance lineage could persist and develop only on the basis of fair cooperation. But in practice some participants would inevitably fail to fulfill their responsibilities, violating the principle of fairness. Therefore it was necessary to have recourse to external sanction to ensure the stable development of the inheritance lineage. For example:

With respect to the sacrificial property of Hongji, Zongchen, and Shaowu, in the past there have been cases of the person whose turn it was in the rotation failing to conduct the sacrifice or pay the tax. This sort of thing is not only an offense to the ancestors but may also get the whole lineage into trouble. Now the lineage and branch heads have gathered, discussed, and agreed that if anyone dares to fail to pay the tax when it is his turn in the rota to collect the income of the sacrificial land, the full amount of the rent when their turn in the rota comes again in the future is to go to the ancestral hall, to expand the corporate funds available to support the educational and examination expenses of candidates for civil and military [examinations]. They are never again to have a turn in the rotation.[15]

When Xie Xiabiao drew up regulations and a "sacrificial register" (*jibu*) for his descendants, he stressed that:

I have considered that, as my descendants develop, there will be some who are truthful and others who are treacherous. There may be evil schemers who conceal the register of the household division and will not reveal it, so that it becomes impossible to check up on the land and houses and regulations registered therein. Those whose turn it is to collect the rents and conduct the sacrifice will then have nothing to guide them. So I have additionally set up this [sacrificial] register, to be held in rotation, and determined when the register is to be handed over, and fixed a punishment in rice to deter [potential violators]. This is all done out of my desire that you [the descendants] cherish being frank and straightforward, and reveal your true feelings to one another, and to prevent secret schemes and bullying among the kin.[16]

Genealogies of Fujian lineages from the Ming and Qing periods contain many such references to regulations, registers, and sanctions, reflecting the growing regulation of inheritance lineages.

To lineage members, inheritance rights to lineage property established over the generations were not simply a right to income but also a relatively stable form of ownership or possession. Even lineage members who had moved away generally retained corporate inheritance rights over lineage property in their old home. In 1876, Cai Shangfeng of Jianyang County was harshly punished for encroaching on the rights of ownership of lineage property of a lineage member who had migrated to Tieshan County in Jiangxi. According to the *Genealogy of the Cai of Lufeng*:

Cai Shangfeng has dared to privately sell off one burial place at the grave of our founding ancestor, Tianzhao, at Dapingzhai, Nantai, Jianyang County, Fujian, to a man named Wang to hold a burial. . . . This was only discovered this year at the Clear and Bright festival when we went to sacrifice and sweep the graves. Everyone has discussed and agreed that all the property and the rights to sacrificial fields, grave lands, and tea mountains that belong to Shangfeng's household are to be confiscated and transferred to the management of the sacrificial estate of Kesheng, to be sold off to meet the expenses of sacrifice and cleaning of the grave. The sons and nephews of Shangfeng's family are not to make complaints or cause problems in this regard in the future.[17]

In 1790, members of the Wang lineage of Jianning drew up an agreement specifying in detail the lineage property rights of members of the lineage who had emigrated to Guangchang County, Jiangxi.

The makers of this contract are the descendants of the branches of Chenghai and Chengqing. We agree that the two plots of sacrificial land established in the name of Yunxi and belonging to his descendants . . . which together earn an annual rent of eight piculs which is to be used in perpetuity to pay for sacrifices to Yunxi, have been managed for many years without any problem. The descendants of Chengyuan moved to distant Jiangxi, and it became impossible for them to cultivate the land, so they entrusted it to the descendants of Chenghai and Chengqing to manage on their behalf. These two branches originally agreed that when they conducted sacrifices at the grave of Yunxi on the day after the Clear and Bright Festival they would also offer accompanying sacrifice to Chengyuan, and they would never be remiss or delay. Recently, this sacrifice has been delayed or shirked, wronging those who come from distant places to sacrifice, making it impossible for them to return home on schedule. Also the sacrificial land has been mortgaged away, and the boundaries of the land have become confused, damaging this estate. Those who come from distant places to sacrifice curse them angrily. Such kinds of problems are numerous, and it is difficult to express the true feelings of respect for the sacrifice. Now the descendants of the branches of Chenghai and Cheng-qing have discussed together and agreed to call on the relatives to label the two plots of sacrificial land with the names Tian and Di, and to divide them into three equal shares. The share belonging to Cheng-yuan's branch is to be entrusted to the other two branches to manage, each branch managing half. Thus the three shares have now been organized into two shares. Each year, should there be any people from outside the Chenghai branch who come to participate in the sacrifice and sweeping of the graves [i.e., if someone from outside the branch makes a claim on the income from the estate], the Chenghai branch should handle this. If there are any people from outside the Chengqing branch who come to participate in the sacrifice and sweeping of the graves, the Chengqing branch should handle this. The two [issues] should not be muddled together. Today the matter has been settled through the adjudication of the kin. The sacrifice is to be conducted the day after the Clear and Bright Festival, and should not be

delayed. . . . If the descendants of Chengyuan's branch return to the
descent-line in the future, the other two branches shall each split off one
share, and return it to them so they can conduct the sacrifice.[18]

This agreement illustrates that, even after they had entrusted the relevant inheritance rights to lineage members in Jianyang, lineage members who had migrated to Jiangxi still retained rights of ownership and
rights to earn income from the lineage property. Even after the sacrificial lands were divided up in 1790, these emigrant lineage members
continued to enjoy the right to a share of income, and could use "returning to the descent-line" (*guizong*) as the justification for recovering
their ownership rights.

Sometimes out–migrants had to yield their inheritance rights to
other lineage members because they were no longer able to fulfill the
relevant obligations in the native place. This led in turn to the disintegration of the inheritance lineage. In his "Self-Compiled Preface on
Moving to Chongzheng," dated 1374, Ye Yigao of Jianyang wrote:

> When the prominent generals of the dynasty fought their way down
> from Shaowu to Jianning, I fled from the fighting with my family to
> Chongzheng. When we arrived in Shezhou we lived with the family of
> my concubine's father Li Wujie. . . . After the fighting was over, we
> returned to our old home, and I told my elder brothers that I had found
> a good place to live and decided to settle there. Coming back and
> forth to participate in the spring and autumn sacrifice at the lineage
> school (*shuyuan*) would be quite troublesome, so I entrusted the fields
> and hills left behind by the ancestors to my brothers, to collect the
> rent in order to conduct the sacrifices in the shrine, thereby fulfilling
> my sentiments of requiting my origins while also limiting this ongoing
> burden.[19]

In 1575, members of the Chen lineage of Longxi drew up the following contract:

> Great-grandfather Shiliu had two sons. The eldest, Chen Gongsan,
> also had three sons, who moved to Ganhua, Juren, and Longxi, regis-
> tering as three households. Shiliu's second son remained in Guqi. . . .
> Because the ancestral hall and the ancestral graves are distant, and it is
> difficult to prepare the sacrificial items, the sacrificial animals and
> wines each year, Youshan and others of the three households have
> today agreed to entrust the mountain lands established by the found-
> ing ancestor to the Second Branch, known as the Renfeng branch. [The
> members of the Renfeng branch] are to use the rent collected each
> year to meet the expenses of sacrifice at the hall and graves. If descen-
> dants of the Senior Branch should once again prepare the sacrificial
> animals for sacrifice at the hall and graves themselves, then the income

from the hills should again be divided evenly among the two branches, and the descendants of the Renfeng branch may not seize it for themselves.[20]

In this case, because the members of the lineage who had moved away abandoned their inheritance rights to the lineage property and no longer retained any kind of cooperative relations with the lineage members who remained behind, the original inheritance lineage disintegrated.

*   *   *

Even in residentially concentrated lineages, inheritance rights might be transformed for a variety of reasons, and this could also lead to the division or disintegration of the inheritance lineage. I will illustrate this with several examples. The genealogical records of the Xie lineage of Shunchang provide one case:

> In 1831, elder cousin Longyang of the Ren branch became involved in a lawsuit with Zhou Lianhui, a salt merchant from Jinjiang. At the time, a body of merchants rose up and used their wealth and power to bully Longyang, who was not powerful enough to resist. I helped him with one thousand taels of silver, but this was not enough. I again helped him with 180 taels, and this was still not enough. Longyang had no choice but to divide up the corporate land belonging to the ancestral hall of grandfather Yaoting and land purchased with the interest earned on the educational lands, earning a total annual rent of 700 baskets, so that he could sell [his share] to raise money.[21] In the circumstances, I could not prevent him. I allowed him to assess the land and divide it into two even shares, one each for the Ren and Yi branches. A contract of agreement and a declaration were drawn up, which each of us took [one copy of] to serve as evidence. The share of the Ren branch was sold. Our Yi branch's consisted of fifteen plots of land, earning a rent of 340 large baskets. . . . Therefore I got together with my two brothers, and we agreed that the estate would not be divided or sold, but rather that the right to collect the rent would rotate between our three branches, the Ri, Yue, and Xing branches, in order. . . . In the future, if the Ren branch is able to redeem the land that has been sold off and return it to the ancestral hall, our Yi branch will immediately cease [the rotation] of this newly acquired sacrificial land and return it to the management of the ancestral hall, to express our celebration at this new unity.[22]

Another example comes from the "Record of Luo's Educational Fields" in the genealogy of the Zhan surname of Pucheng County:

> This sacrificial property earns a fixed rent of 5,805 catties. In 1887, Dadi, Wudi, and other descendants of the Kunyuan branch collec-

tively sold a portion of this total earning 2,950 catties to the Ji surname. In the future, the descendants of the Kunyuan, regardless of
whether or not they are County School Students, may not interfere
[with the remainder of the estate].[23]

The "Overview of the Sea [Rights] Dispute" in the genealogy of the
Zhu surname of Xianyou records:

> Our founding ancestor, Yizhai, left behind one plot of coastal marsh
> in front of our dwelling. It was held for 300 years. In 1475, [Zhu]
> Bangji and Cai Yuanzhao got into a lawsuit over the eastern
> boundary. The prefectural authorities investigated on the spot, judged
> in our favor, and gave us a document to serve as proof. Our branch
> and the Shicheng branch each managed half the beach. In 1548, Cai
> Dao once again fought over the western boundary. This time the
> Shicheng [branch] brought suit, at a cost of several taels, which was
> borne entirely by the Shicheng branch. The result was that the Shi-
> cheng commended (*xian*) fifteen plots of coastal land to the family of
> Supervising Secretary Zhang of Putian, renting it back from him each
> year to cultivate shellfish. But the tax obligation [remained under] our
> household registration, which was an impossible burden. The whole
> lineage gathered and reflected that our ancestors had held this beach
> for a long time. How could we simply abandon it? Weifeng and others
> of the senior branch held up the document given to Bangji, but would
> not spend a single [copper] cash. It was only Shijie, Shi'ang, You-
> zhong, Ziyi, and others of the second branch who got the money
> together, by collecting funds from the holders of the plots of the shell-
> fish banks inherited by members of the branch, according to the
> number of plots. They reported this to the officials and were permitted
> to redeem the contract of commutation to the Supervising Secretary at
> the current price of the land, which was .82 taels per plot for a total of
> fifteen taels. Now the eastern and western borders have been regu-
> lated for a long time with no problems. The half of the beach that
> used to belong to the Shicheng branch is now held by the branches of
> Shijie and others, who manage it on the basis of the present contracts,
> so the original proclamation by the prefecture and the private agree-
> ments need no longer be recorded.[24]

In each of these three examples, the division and sale of lineage property led to the division or disintegration of an inheritance lineage. But
there are differences in the specific outcomes of the different cases. In
the first and second cases, certain members of the lineage sold off their
shares of the lineage property, whereupon the inheritance lineage disintegrated. But other members of the lineage continued to practice collective inheritance of their share of the lineage property, so they were
able to form a new inheritance lineage. In the third case, the division of

the rights to the management of the shoreline in 1475 meant the formation of two new inheritance lineages. The transfer and sale of the shoreline rights after 1548 led to a further subdivision of the property rights of the Shicheng branch and the appearance of a new lineage organization comprising "the branches of Shijie and others." These examples demonstrate that division of lineage property would lead to changes in the scope of cooperative relations between lineage members, with the original inheritance lineage disintegrating into some number of smaller inheritance lineages. But when lineage property was sold off, there remained no basis for cooperative relations, and the inheritance lineage disintegrated completely.

*   *   *

Because only the relatively wealthy stratum in society would have been able to leave lineage fields or other kinds of property to their descendants, inheritance lineages that owned income-earning property must have been few in number. In fact, the vast majority of inheritance lineages in Fujian history were based, not on income-earning property, but rather on the inheritance of *lijia* household registration and the responsibility to maintain the sacrifice to the descent line. The genealogy of the Huang surname of Shaowu provides an example of the first type:

> Within the tenth *jia* of the *li* service levy system there is a registration under the name Huang Tianci, which is collectively held by the lineage. In the Ming, the service levy responsibilities of the *li* head were extremely onerous. Later, Gongbao's registration was transferred to the eighth *jia*. The descendants of Shouyi were few in number, and we gradually became unable to handle the levy. In 1659, Tinghui and his brothers were transferred back to our household [registration] to help fulfill the service levy. . . . In the Yongzheng period (1723–1735), Zhou Liang of the most junior sub-branch of the Shouyi branch was transferred out of this registration. In 1750, his brother Xingliang was transferred back to this registration.[25]

Under these circumstances, even though the lineage members owned no collective property whatsoever, collective inheritance of household registration and service levy responsibilities implied the formation of an inheritance lineage. In this kind of inheritance lineage the responsibilities associated with the household registration system were commonly also allocated by means of rotation through the branches or segments. Thus, "our original ancestor left [a registration] in the registers of the tenth *jia* of the first ward of sector 4, responsibility for which originally rotated through the three main branches, the Dechu branch descended from Shouyi, the Degui branch descended from Shou'er, and the Degao branch descended from Shousan. . . . Now the descendants who have divided off from Shouyi . . . also take a turn in the rotation of responsibility."[26] As Chapter 5 will demonstrate, collective inheritance of household registration was common practice in Ming and Qing Fujian, so this sort of inheritance lineage must also have been common.

Similarly, there were some inheritance lineages which, though without lineage property, still collectively inherited the responsibilities connected with ancestral sacrifice, and hence also formed inheritance lineages the main purpose of which was collective ancestral sacrifice. Chen Shengshao's *Wensu Lu* describes an encounter Chen had while serving as magistrate of Zhao'an during the Daoguang period (1821–1850):

> I happened to go out on official business, and ran into a continuous line of men and women bearing wine and meat hurrying on the side of the road. I enquired of them, and they replied: "We have no sacrificial estate, so each [family] has prepared several vessels of dishes, and we are gathering with the uncles to sacrifice together. When the sacrifice is over we remove the sacrificial foods and leave."[27]

This kind of inheritance lineage, linked to sacrificial activities, was usually based on collective inheritance of some kind of site or facility dedicated to ancestral sacrifice, such as an ancestral dwelling, a grave, or an ancestral hall. In such cases, too, the cooperative relations were usually characterized by the allocation of responsibilities through rotation through branches. For example, the "Regulations of the Shimei Wu" of Fuzhou specify:

> 1. The lineage together carves spirit tablets of the generations of ancestors, which are entered into the ancestral hall, in order to venerate their virtue and repay their merit. . . . The descendants of each branch, in addition to erecting small tablets in their chamber (*qin*) [i.e., within their own residence] to which they offer sacrifice themselves, also set up a small placard together, on which are carved the names of the generations of ancestors of that branch, and the placard is entrusted to the ancestral hall to enjoy the general sacrifice (*xiaji*). Ancestors more than five generations distant are considered distant ancestors, and [their tablets] are arrayed in the east and west side chambers of the hall and receive sacrifice at the major sacrifice at the festival of Middle Origin.
> 2. The ancestral hall is the dwelling place of the spirits of the

generations of ancestors. . . . At the Lantern Festival, the caretakers of the hall should prepare lanterns and candles. The branches in rotation select eight men to prepare the sacrificial items, suspend the lamps, and conduct the ritual of celebrating [the ancestors] and enjoying [the lanterns]. In the autumn, during the seventh month, at the festival of Middle Origin, the caretakers of the hall should prepare incense, candles, and paper money, and collect funds from each branch. . . . When the whole lineage is assembled the ritual of offering food is conducted. It is permitted to offer major sacrifice to the tablets of the distant ancestors in the east and west side chambers. In the ninth month, the caretakers of the hall prepare incense, candles, and paper money, and collect funds from each branch. . . . When the whole lineage is assembled the general sacrifice is conducted.

3. The correct times for sacrifice and sweeping of the graves are in spring at the Clear and Bright festival, and in autumn at the Chong-yang festival. Sacrificing at the graves at the New Year is not in accordance with the canons on sacrifice. Those who have sacrificial property naturally must not fail to sacrifice. Those who have no sacrificial estate should not fail to sacrifice on account of poverty. . . . At the [grave] of the founding ancestor, the whole lineage conducts the general sacrifice in spring and autumn. Each branch sends one male member, and expenses are collected according to branch. At the feast eight dishes are permitted. The branches of the descendants conduct particular sacrifice (*teji*) at the graves of their own ancestors in spring and autumn. The branches of direct descendants rotate responsibility for this. It is not permitted to neglect these rituals.[28]

The ancestral sacrificial activities of the Wu lineage members can be divided into two categories, general sacrifice (*xiaji*), involving the whole lineage, and particular sacrifice (*teji*), conducted by individual segments. Both categories involved collective sacrificial activities, so the expenses associated with them had to be allocated collectively among the descendants, either by branches collecting funds in rotation or by branches taking responsibility in rotation. Thus the need to conduct collective sacrifice to multiple generations of ancestors led to the formation of a multilevel inheritance lineage in which degrees of kinship relations were distinguished and different levels of obligation clearly separated.

In a sense, sites for ancestral sacrifice such as ancestral dwellings, ancestral graves, and ancestral halls, were really just a particular form of lineage property. For lineage members, participation in ancestral sacrifice was not only a responsibility but also a right. This is demonstrated by the Guangxu period "Ancestral Grave Hill Agreement" of the Liujiang He lineage of Jianyang:

The makers of this agreement, in which [the details of] the ancestral
grave hill are clearly recorded to prevent conflict, are the descendants
of He Mozhai.... The grave of the sixth-generation ancestor of our
lineage, Mozhai, and his wife née Chen, is located at [place-name].
... There is a stone inscription erected there. The descendants of the
branches descended from him, the first, second, and third branches,
[whose founders] are named in the genealogy as Zongcheng, Zongyi,
and Zongqu, should all climb the hill to sacrifice and sweep the grave,
and manage the property in perpetuity. The descendants of Wenzheng
may not participate. The grave of the seventh-generation ancestor,
Zongcheng of the first branch, whose taboo name was Di, whose style
was Shun and whose literary name was Zhurun, is located at [place-
name].... There is a stone inscription erected there. The grave of
the tenth-generation ancestor, Yuanhong, and his wife née Chen, is
located at [place-name].... There is a stone inscription erected there.
The descendants of the first branch may ascend to these graves to
worship and sweep. The descendants of the second branch descended
from Zongyi and the third branch descended from Zongqu may not
ascend the hill and conduct further burials there. The grave of Yuanyou of the thirteenth generation, together with his wife née Zhang, is
located at [place-name].... There is a stone inscription erected there.
The grave of the fifteenth-generation ancestor, Xiasun, and his wife
née Xiao is located at [place-name].... In autumn 1890, a stone inscription was newly erected there. Only the descendants of Yuanyou
may ascend to the grave to worship and sweep the grave. The descendants of the other sub-branches of the first branch descended from
Zongcheng may not ascend the hill and conduct further burials there.
In sum, this chart records the hills, the graves, and the descendants of
the branches of each ancestor who manage the property. Other
branches should not make trouble. If all the members of the lineage
can each observe the regulations, then all will be well. If powerful
bullies try to take over [the grave lands] or there are illicit burials on a
pretext, the lineage members of each branch must order them to dig
out [the bodies] and move them elsewhere, recover the land, and discuss more serious punishment. Otherwise appeal may be made to the
authorities. Partiality must not interfere.[29]

In this case, the various sacrificial activities depended on the collective
inheritance of the graves of different generations of ancestors by the
lineage members. In the Ming and Qing period, which saw growing
privatization of ownership of uncultivated hills and forests, people
attached great importance to the maintenance of ancestral graves, and
sacrificial activities centered on ancestral graves became more common
and more impressive. The *Joint Compilation of the Genealogy of the
Liang Surname* of Pucheng records:

> It is the responsibility of the descendants of each branch to carve and erect stone inscriptions for the ancestral graves of each branch, and to personally repair the graves. It is not permitted to neglect the sacrifice and sweeping or to rely on outsiders to conduct the sacrifice and sweeping, which would lead to the grave no longer being recognized, and eventually just disappearing. The trees provide protection and shade. Anyone who would secretly cut them down is to be considered unfilial, and the whole lineage should punish him.[30]

According to another genealogy, "One who esteems sacrifice, regardless of whether his ancestors are buried at a distance of one hundred *li*, or several dozen *li*, or only a few *li*, in each case erects a small structure nearby, known as a tomb shrine."[31] This kind of grave sacrifice generally had to be conducted generation after generation, and so came to be the most systematized of sacrificial practices within a lineage. Broadly speaking, the practice of sacrificing to certain ancestors for generation after generation had already emerged in Fujian in the Song. By the Ming and Qing, this type of sacrificial activity included household sacrifice, grave sacrifice, and ancestral hall sacrifice (see Chapter 5).

The expansion of ancestral sacrifice was of course not unconnected to the development of lineage property, but it did not depend on it. The Pucheng genealogy records:

> The system of the ancient kings was that those who had property [used the income from it] to sacrifice to their ancestors. Those who had no property offered grains and fruit. . . . But what is appropriate differs between antiquity and the present day, and customs differ between localities. If it is necessary to wait until there is land before one sacrifices, then how many people are there who would be able to express their sincerity in recalling their origins?[32]

In other words, if the ancient principle that only people with property could sacrifice to their ancestors had been strictly adhered to, then ancestral sacrificial activities would never have become common. Since such activities did become common, our understanding of inheritance lineages should therefore not be restricted to the small number of wealthy lineages with extensive lineage property.

Lastly, it should be pointed out that an inheritance lineage often performed multiple functions simultaneously, and so the form it took could also be complex and everchanging. Therefore, the inheritance lineage could be defined and analyzed from a number of different perspectives. In the preceding discussion, I analyzed the basic functions and development mechanism of the inheritance lineage in terms of the chief objects of collective inheritance—namely sacrificial responsibility, household registration, and lineage property. But in practice, an inheritance lineage's functions could also extend into irrigation, transportation, trade, manufacturing, education, religious and charitable matters, as well as other areas too numerous to list. The potential development path of an inheritance lineage could also be quite complex, and a few specific cases cannot encompass all the possibilities. For example, the "Record of Hekou Market" in the *Ninth Compilation of the Genealogy of the Zhang Surname of Qinghe* from Shunchang records:

> Jiuxiu had four sons. . . . Only Silang worked as a farmer, and he alone maintained the original land at Shibi. He was the fourth-generation ancestor. In 1175, he purchased one plot of hill wasteland, known as Hekou, from Zhang Tinglang, for 9 strings of cash. During the Wanli period, a market was opened. The rule used to be that the rent from the dwelling, shops, and the open plots at Upper Plot and Lower Lane were evenly divided by the three branches. There was also handed down a plot of open land on which was built a shed, which was managed in rotation and the rental income used to pay for the expenses of spring and autumn sacrifice to Silang. There was also handed down a grave plot. In 1833, the whole lineage, led by Chengwu, Ronglun, Huashen, and others, began to construct the Hall of Fragrance of Virtue *(Dexin Tang)* ancestral hall. The three branches had previously decided to give Yishan the land at Yuping Gangtou to be his own property. A boundary stone was erected to serve as proof. . . . The ox plot; the manure basket plot; the theatrical stage built above the rice plot; the tea pavilion built by Guishao; the press for making oil; the site of the Wutong temple; and the land beside the crescent of the road to the bridge at Xiwang Monastery, were all established by Silang with his own funds. Every inch of the land all around the market is property that was purchased by Silang and his wife. I am not recording falsehoods. I have consulted the original genealogies of several generations. So all is recorded clearly to serve as a record for the generations.[33]

The different kinds of lineage property mentioned in the document were connected with commerce, sacrifice, and other public matters such as cultural and religious affairs, irrigation, and communications. The Zhang lineage organization that formed on the basis of this lineage property was certainly involved in these multiple functions, but not in a static and unchanging way. Nor were these different functions consistently performed by a single lineage organization. Basically, from the Southern Song to the mid-Ming, the plot of land known as Hekou was collectively inherited by the descendants of Silang, but during that period Hekou was simply hill wasteland. When a market was first constructed in the Wanli period, the various commercial facilities were divided among the three branches. In other words, they belonged to three separate inheritance lineages. At the same time, sacrificial property and sacrificial activities continued to be "managed in rotation," so the inheritance lineage centered on Silang must have persisted. In 1833, under the leadership of a few lineage members, the lineage constructed the ancestral hall. As we shall see in the next section, this suggests that the inheritance lineage centered on Silang was transformed into a control-subordination lineage. The stage, tea pavilion, oil press, temple land, and other lineage property was collectively owned by this lineage centered on Silang, which was initially an inheritance lineage and later a control-subordination lineage. The expression "established by Silang with his own funds" refers to property purchased not by Silang himself but rather by the lineage organization made up of his descendants. This example shows that an inheritance lineage might change as a result of the division of or transformations in its functions, but changes to the lineage might also be reflected in such divisions or transformations. Usually when we consider an inheritance lineage to have undergone fission or disintegration it is on the basis of changes to its chief function. But from the perspective of its other functions this same inheritance lineage might persist and develop further, or it might transform into some other kind of lineage organization.

*   *   *

In general, the chief function of inheritance lineages was to ensure the smooth transmission of the descent-line, so such lineages were especially concerned with the collective inheritance of property and social position. In Ming and Qing Fujian the most common form and fundamental connotation of the inheritance lineage was an organization that served to promote long-term close cooperative relations among lineage members on the basis of the collective inheritance of descent-line, household registration, and lineage property. Other larger-scale public functions, such as irrigation, transportation, education, and social welfare, were mostly performed by control-subordination lineages or contractual lineages. Therefore, when inheritance lineages were transformed into other kinds of lineage organizations, it was usually these functions which were the first to be yielded to the new organization.

Control-Subordination Lineages

The defining characteristic of a control-subordination lineage is that the rights and responsibilities of each lineage member are determined by his relative social position, in other words, by relations of control and subordination between the members. Because such relations of control and subordination usually arise in residentially concentrated lineages, the control-subordination lineage can also be understood as a form of lineage organization based on ties of common locality. In the previous section, I showed that in an inheritance lineage, changes in the inheritance relations of lineage members invariably led to the division or disintegration of the inheritance lineage. Even without obvious changes in these relations, changes in the way lineage members' responsibilities were managed could also cause changes in the nature of the lineage—namely, the transformation of an inheritance lineage into a control-subordination lineage.

*   *   *

The Wang surname of Beixiang in Pucheng had two sacrificial properties, endowed in the name of Shouyi and grandmother Zhou, which together earned rent of over 350 piculs. The rent was originally collected by the seven main branches in rotation, and the branch whose turn it was to collect the income took on "the sacrifice and sweeping of the graves at the Clear and Bright Festival, and the tax payment" as well as other responsibilities. In the Guangxu period, a portion of the rent totaling 150 piculs was set aside for the purpose of supplying "incense and lamps" at the festival of the Winter Solstice; "the costs of the sacrifice at the Clear and Bright Festival," and educational expenses. This portion of the estate was put under the management of the Wang ancestral hall, the Shrine of Modesty and Filiality (*Qianxiao Ci*). The remainder of the sacrificial estate was distributed evenly among the branches of descendants: "The descendants of the seven branches, who had originally rotated the right to collect the rent, were organized into shares. The shares drew lots on the basis of which were specified the tenants from which each branch would collect the rent. It is not permitted to transgress and seize [what does not belong to one's own branch], thereby causing conflict and confusion."[34]

On the surface, this seems to be merely a change in the method by which lineage property was managed, with no effect on the inheritance rights of lineage members. But closer analysis shows that when a few lineage members obtain the right to allocate lineage property and the responsibilities associated with it, then the remainder of the lineage members are forced into a subordinate or dependent position. The "Agreement by the Descendants of the Seven Branches on the Transfer of the Sacrificial Properties to the Ancestral Shrine" of the Wang of Beixiang, dated 1903, records:

> 1. In 1891, this ancestral hall decided to place a portion of the land of grandmother Zhou's sacrificial estate[35] earning 51.5 piculs rent under the management of the ancestral hall, to meet the expenses of incense and lamps for the Winter Solstice and of repairs. Furthermore, this year, the descendants of the seven branches have talked things over again and decided to place a portion of the land from Shouyi's sacrificial estate earning 85.1 piculs rent under the management of the ancestral hall, to pay the tax and the expenses of the sacrifice at the Clear and Bright Festival each year. These two rents that are to be collected by the hall have been transferred from the sacrificial property of Shouyi and grandmother Zhou. Not the least amount comes from other branches. Therefore, the income from and the expenses paid out of this rental property each year must be managed by people chosen by the members of the seven branches descended from Shouyi. The descendants of other branches are not permitted to interfere in the management, but they are entitled to a share of the cakes and meat distributed to adult male lineage members at the Winter Solstice, in accord with the regulations. Descendants of later generations are forbidden to contest these management rights on a pretext. This is to serve as proof.
>
> 2. A portion of the lands from the sacrificial estate [of Shouyi] earning 21.6 piculs rent, has been set aside as educational lands in order to encourage the descendants of the seven branches to study. The rights to this land are to be enjoyed only by those members of the seven branches who have a will to improve themselves.[36]

Management by "people chosen by the members of the seven branches descended from Shouyi" means unified management by a small number of directors chosen from the seven branches. This is fundamentally different than management by rotation through branches:

> Once [these portions of the estate] are placed [under the management of the ancestral hall], the full rental income and the expenses for sacrifice and cleaning of the graves are to be managed by the directors of the ancestral hall in perpetuity. The descendants of the seven branches are not permitted to cause any trouble over this.[37]

In other words, the members of the lineage who were not directors had now lost their rights of control and management over the relevant

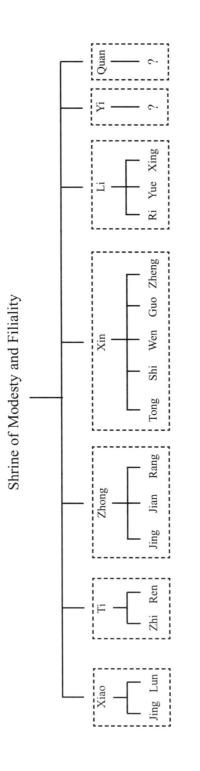

Figure 3.2. Inheritance and Control-Subordination Lineage Organizations of the Wang of Beixiang

lineage property. They retained only the right to receive a specified amount of the cakes and meat distributed to adult male lineage members, a right that differed little from that of the "descendants of other branches," that is, branches not descended from Shouyi. At the same time as this lineage property was placed under the control of the hall, the remaining lineage property was divided among the branches. The portion received by each branch earned about thirty piculs of annual rent. Now that this sacrificial income was administered by the branches separately, it could no longer be used for the collective affairs of the seven branches, but only for the individual affairs of each branch. This property was now collectively inherited by the members of each branch. Therefore, seven inheritance lineages, each consisting of a single branch, also formed under the umbrella of the Shrine of Modesty and Filiality. The various lineage organizations of the descendants of the seven branches descended from Shouyi after the transfer of part of the sacrificial income and division of the rest are represented graphically in Figure 3.2

In the figure, the solid lines represent the limits of the control-subordination lineage, and the broken lines the limits of the inheritance lineages. The inheritance relations of the Yi and Quan branch are unclear, and it may be that they had not yet formed proper inheritance lineages. The control-subordination lineage centered around the Shrine of Modesty and Filiality also included other branches besides the seven branches descended from Shouyi, but these are not indicated here. The figure shows that, after the transfer and division of the sacrificial income, what had originally been an inheritance lineage oriented around the sacrificial estates of Shouyi and grandmother Zhou was transformed into a control-subordination lineage oriented around the Shrine of Modesty and Filiality, which included within it seven inheritance lineages at a lower level. What caused this transformation? The Wang's "Agreement" provides a brief explanation:

> I have noticed that whenever rich landlords and tax-paying households divide their fields and property, they must set aside sacrificial rent-earning property for the Clear and Bright Festival, to allay the long-term concerns of the descendants. When the households are all flourishing and the descendants are all wealthy, the rent is collected and responsibility is taken for the sacrifice in rotation according to regulations, and everyone benefits greatly. But when wealth declines, some branches flourish and others are bankrupted. The idle and lazy descendants may mortgage their rights to collect the rent to other people years in advance of their turn, and when their turn comes, their

household hasn't the least income. They are still as poor as before, and they even evade or default on the tax they are responsible for paying that year. The sacrifice and cleaning of the graves in the hills is abandoned. It even comes to the point where the government tax collectors press for the tax and make arrests. Disputes break out within the household. The ancestors establish rent-earning sacrificial property for the benefit of the descendants, but, perversely, the descendants make trouble or bring shame to the ancestors because of the rent-earning sacrificial property. Having said this much indeed makes one sigh. I believe that when thinking about potential troubles, one ought to try to prevent them in advance, and when problems have already arisen, one ought to seek good ways to resolve them. Just as different trees grow to varying heights, among many people how can one not worry about some prospering and others declining?[38]

This suggests that economic differentiation among lineage members was the basic cause of the transformation of an inheritance lineage into a control-subordination lineage. Generally speaking, after the formation of an inheritance lineage and subsequent segmentation over several generations, such economic differentiation was usually inevitable. To make ends meet, impoverished members of the lineage were forced to sell off or mortgage their rights to earn income from lineage property in rotation, such that when their turn came they found themselves unable to pay the taxes due or fulfill corporate responsibilities. This gave rise to various kinds of irreconcilable problems within the inheritance lineage. Once the economic differentiation of lineage members had reached a certain point, it became difficult to sustain the rotation of responsibilities through the branches. Under such circumstances there were two possible options. The first was to divide the lineage property and its related responsibilities, which would mean the disintegration of the inheritance lineage. The second was to implement unified management of the lineage property and its related responsibilities, which would mean the transformation of the inheritance lineage into a control-subordination lineage. In theory, division according to branches was fair and rational, so it was more easily accepted by the majority of lineage members. But in a residentially concentrated lineage, there were inevitably some enduring common concerns that could not easily be divided. Such concerns were not likely to diminish as wealth became polarized, but could only increase. As a result, even if the lineage property was divided among the branches, it was generally also necessary to set aside some lineage property to be managed collectively, in order to meet these collective concerns. Thus the transformation from inheritance lineage to control-subordination lineage was a logical development. The Wang of Beixiang's "Agreement" on the transfer and division of their sacrificial estate declares: "There is no excellent method of honest intentions which surpasses this one." This is not necessarily simple flattery on the part of the person who wrote this text, but rather may reflect the prevailing social psychology of the time.

Chen Shengshao, while serving as an official in Shaowu prefecture in the Daoguang period, tried to compel unified management of sacrificial property in order to reduce tax resistance and the need to press for tax. He wrote:

> When ancestors divide their household estate, they set aside a certain number of *mu* as sacrificial property, in order to meet the expenses of the spring and autumn sacrifices and the greeting of the ancestors at the New Year. The feasts where the whole lineage gathers and the semiannual tax responsibilities are paid for out of this. It is managed in rotation, and is known as sacrificial rental property (*jiaozu*). But descendants who fall into decline before it is their turn in the rotation may sell off the rights to collect the rents to others, or may be heavily indebted. When their turn in the rota comes, and they must make the expenditures and pay the semiannual taxes, there is simply no way they can even hope to do so. When the tax collectors arrive, they assess responsibility for the tax on any available pretext. Over the years, the accumulated shortfall may be considerable. [Establishing] sacrificial property is an excellent practice. But after a long time has passed, the problems of tax resistance and tax pressure arise. I proclaim that from within the lineage one man who is fair and upright should be chosen to take special responsibility for the tax. He must put the public good first, and private benefit last. Thus they will know the humaneness of venerating the ancestors and respecting the descent line, and will also know the dutifulness of venerating the ruler and obeying their superiors.[39]

Chen believed that in order to ensure the timely payment of land tax on sacrificial land, the pressure of the state administration was necessary to encourage the transformation of inheritance lineages into control-subordination lineages. But in fact the emergence and development of a control-subordination lineage was the inevitable product of contradictions internal to the lineage, not of government pressure.

To prevent such anticipated problems from arising, some landlord families arranged for unified management of certain collective concerns when the household estate was first divided. This meant that the descendants formed a control-subordination lineage and an inheritance lineage simultaneously. For example, when the Ren and Yi branches of the fifteenth generation of the Xie surname of Shangyang in Shunchang County divided their estate, they established sacrificial property (*jichan*) that rotated through the branches, and also corporate property (*gongchan*), which was managed by a specific person "in order to meet the expenses of repairing the ancestral hall and corporate matters."[40] When Xie Xiabiao of the next generation divided his estate among his three sons, aside from "sacrificial property to be collected in rotation," and "educational fields," he also established corporate property under unified management, "to be used in the future for the expenses if the two sacrificial properties collapse or fall into disrepair." He also declared that:

> The manager of the corporate property is permitted to take twenty thousand cash each year from the corporate account to serve as salary for his labor and to meet office expenses. . . . The manager is also to look after the expenses and affairs of the construction of the boat for the planned charitable ferry crossing. He must not evade this responsibility.[41]

In this situation, those who managed the corporate property also gained control over the collective matters of the lineage, which implied the formation of a control-subordination lineage.

A control-subordination lineage could also form when a lineage organization that was disintegrating or had already disintegrated was reorganized and reunified through donations of funds to the lineage by a small number of lineage leaders for the repair of ancestral graves, construction of an ancestral hall, compilation of a genealogy, or establishment of lineage property. In the reorganization process, a group of powerful or respected members would invariably emerge within the lineage, giving the reorganized lineage organization the character of a control-subordination lineage. Generally speaking, any lineage organization that had a relatively long history might potentially be reorganized, and hence take on the character of a control-subordination lineage, any number of times. The many forms that a reorganized control-subordination lineage might take are discussed in more detail in Chapter 4.

*   *   *

After the formation of a control-subordination lineage, its members were divided into two separate interest groups: the dominant and the subordinate. The two groups can be distinguished by their different rights and responsibilities. The dominant group within a control-subordination lineage comprised the lineage and branch heads and the local gentry, as well as professional managers such as hall managers and directors, and possibly other lineage members who enjoyed certain special rights. For example, the regulations of the branch hall of the Jintang Wang surname of Fuzhou state:

> Each year for the sacrifices in spring, Clear and Bright, Middle Origin, Chongyang, and Winter Solstice, one adult male from each household may attend the feast. The lineage and branch heads, the managers and assistant managers, the gentry of the hall, and, if they are old enough to use chopsticks, the descent-line heir (*zongzi*) and descent-line grandson (*zongsun*) are also specially invited to the feast. At the sacrifice of the Winter Solstice they are not required to pay the fee for adult males.
>
> The descendants within the lineage who contract to cultivate the corporate property owned by the hall must pay the rent in processed and clean rice. There must not be delays or shortfalls in rent payment. In the event that there are such problems, the lineage and branch heads and the managers and assistant managers may decide to cancel the tenancy rights and look for other tenants. [The defaulters] are not permitted to enter the hall and participate in the sacrifice. Only once the money owed has been paid in full are they allowed to enter the hall again.
>
> Collection and disbursement of the rental rice of the ancestral hall is to be discussed by the lineage and branch heads and the managers and assistant managers three days in advance. Whether the rent is to be collected in full or in part, whether the rent is to be sold, and the price that is decided, should be written on a notice to inform the lineage members. No one person may monopolize [the decision]. Only after the lineage and branch heads, the gentry of the hall, and the managers and assistant managers have decided things clearly is it permitted to sell the rice. Nor is it permitted for the rice to be privately lent or sold. If the rent is stored with the manager, it should be sealed under the mark of the lineage and branch heads. This is also the case if it is stored with the assistant manager. . . .
>
> All the contracts, deeds, accounts, cash, and rent of the hall should be distributed evenly among the managers and assistant managers. Each year at the festival of Middle Origin all [the managers] should assemble in the hall and audit the account books. At the Winter Solstice, they should update the accounts clearly, disclosing them in the hall and rotating the recording. When all of the account books have been submitted, the manager and assistant managers next draw up clearly the list of the names of those whose turn in the rotation it is to take charge of the spring, summer, and winter sacrifice [in the hall] and the Clear and Bright and Chongyang sacrifice [at the graves] and post the lists in the hall to inform the lineage members. If there is no man-

ager or assistant manager, the lineage and branch heads are to divide the documents and funds evenly. . . . Anyone who does not respect the common decisions is to be reported to the authorities for investigation.

If our ancestral hall, the temples to the Civil and Martial Sages, the various ancestral graves, or the contents of the hall are damaged, the manager and assistant managers are required to discuss making repairs immediately. This is not to be put off.[42]

In this lineage, the lineage and branch heads, gentry members, the manager and assistant manager, and the descent-line heir and descent-line grandson all enjoyed special hierarchical rights and together comprised the dominant group of the lineage. In the actual functioning of a control-subordination lineage, the special rights and functions of individuals in the dominant group could be quite different, and these need to be analyzed in concrete terms. The lineage and branch heads were respected figures in the lineage. These positions were usually filled by the oldest individuals in the senior surviving generation. Thus, "the selection of the lineage head and branch heads must be on the basis of who is the most respected in terms of generational position, age, and reputation."[43] The special rights of the lineage and branch heads were the right to make decisions about lineage affairs and the power to provide moral leadership and impose punishment on lineage members. The lineage regulations of the Shi surname of Xunhai in Jinjiang County explain:

Lineage and branch heads have been established from the lineage [membership]. They should handle all those matters which can be investigated clearly and resolved in accordance with the actual circumstances. They should assemble those who have official titles in the main hall, with fair hearts investigate who is right and who is wrong, beat those who have committed major faults, and fine those who have committed lesser faults. Before the [spirit tablets] of the ancestors resentments should fall away and good relations be renewed. If there are powerful and fierce people who do not obey, or people who act violently or who bring lawsuits, the whole lineage together should denounce them, in order to correct the violent and perverse.

With regard to marriages and funerals . . . the lineage and branch heads should investigate whether there are really people who put them off because of lack of funds, provide the appropriate assistance from the corporate accounts of the lineage, and ensure that they are held in a timely fashion. If money is wasted and the ceremony not held immediately, the person responsible should be beaten and the lineage head pay restitution. This is in order to relieve collective [economic] hardship.

Scholars, farmers, artisans, and merchants should all be hardworking and frugal. . . . If there are unworthy descendants who give up their occupations and join up with criminal elements, open gambling dens, or engage in usury, with the result that other members of the lineage are lured into bankruptcy and shame, this is indeed hateful. In the future, if the lineage and branch heads know for a fact that people have lent money for gambling, [these people] should not be permitted to recover the money, and the lineage members are to be ordered to the main ancestral hall to punish and correct them, allowing them to turn away from their errors and become new men. Those who do not change are to be sent to the authorities to be investigated and dealt with. This is in order to get rid of weeds.

The women's chambers most require strict control. It is not right that men and women should pass things from one to the other. . . . If unfortunately there should be rumors of illicit intercourse between the sexes which are investigated and confirmed, the branch head should assemble the lineage. The male should be punished severely, and his name expunged from the genealogy. Whether or not the woman has a son, she must be sent back to her natal family. This is in order to preserve customs and morality.

When a household estate is divided, the lineage and branch heads must conduct the division, ensuring that the shares are fair. Fathers and mothers must not be partial; brothers must not be selfish. Violators must pay a fine to the hall. This is in order to prevent conflicts.

When descendants see their venerable elders, they must be respectful and proceed with their hands clasped. They may not arrogantly or disrespectfully use the terms "You" and "Me." If they offend and are cursed, regardless of whether this is right or not, they should bow their heads and accept it. If in fact they are in the right, they should still maintain dignity, explaining the situation to their venerable elders. They are not to lose their temper and argue. . . . This is in order to stress respect and love.[44]

These are only some of the rights of lineage and branch heads; it is by no means an exhaustive list. Because lineage and branch heads were the naturally respected elders of the lineage, they frequently enjoyed rights without having to take on responsibilities, so their special position was particularly stable.

Aside from the lineage and branch heads, other aged and respected figures in the lineage also enjoyed certain special rights. Thus:

Of the five types of good fortune, longevity is the most important. One does not attain it by sheer luck. All those who have reached the age of sixty are given one catty of "longevity meat" [distributed at the sacrifice]; those who are seventy, two catties; those who are eighty, three catties; those who are ninety, five catties; those who are one hundred, ten catties. This is in order to respect the aged and venerate the elderly.[45]

The positions of descent-line heir and descent-line grandson were usually filled by the senior descendant of the senior branch, whose generational position would normally be junior to that of other lineage members. In Ming and Qing Fujian, the installation of descent-line heir was not very common. His chief function was limited to presiding over ancestral sacrifice, which was a special right of little substance (see Chapter 5, part 1).

The gentry, ordinarily those members of the lineage who had passed the examinations or earned a civil or military official title, were the honored members of a control-subordination lineage. The special rights they enjoyed consisted mainly of rights to participate in discussions of lineage affairs, control over lineage property like "educational fields," and the privilege of having their tablets installed in the ancestral hall after they died. The involvement of gentry members of the lineage was usually required in planning and decision making about the most important affairs of the control-subordination lineage. Especially in matters involving the state or relations with other lineages, it was often only the gentry who could deal with the situation. Some lineages even required that sacrificial activities be presided over by gentry members who had obtained their position through examination. Thus, "the officiant of the sacrifice should in the first instance be [the lineage member who is] an examination graduate; next, a Graduate by Inheritance, Graduate for Preeminence, Tribute Student, or Tribute Student second class; next, the Tribute Student by Purchase first, second, or third class whose position in the generational order is most senior. Those who begin their careers through purchase of a degree and those whose position in the generational order is venerable but who have not yet obtained official title are not to vie for this role. The sacrificial assistant is also to be chosen from the descendants in this way."[46] More important, the formal regulations of a lineage were undoubtedly determined by the gentry stratum, and largely reflected and served their values and special interests as a class. Thus the gentry were the main rule makers and planners of the control-subordination lineage; they were its real leaders.

Because degree-holders were considered the hope and model for the whole lineage, lineages often had funds dedicated to preparing candidates for the examinations. For example:

> Our lineage has established special rules for the educational fields. If a single man enters the County School, he earns the full [income] himself. If two men do, they share it. If there are three, four, five, or six

men, then they share it equally, and as soon as anyone else enters the County School he also joins the group [of men who receive a share]. If there is a new Provincial Graduate, distribution is suspended for a year, and he receives all the funds in order to supplement his examination expenses. If all those who have previously [become eligible for a share] have died but no replacements have yet appeared to take their place, the income should be saved corporately and used to hire a famous teacher to encourage later students. Once these later students have accomplished themselves, the funds should again be distributed to meet their educational expenses.[47]

Some lineages did not establish a specific educational estate but included provisions for educational expenses in the general expenditures of the ancestral hall. For example:

> Descendants of the branches of our lineage hall who enter the County School or become Stipendiary Students are to be given four thousand cash from the collective account of the branch. Students by Inheritance, Preeminence, Excellence, or Tribute should be given eight thousand. Provincial Graduates receive the full income of the sacrificial estate of the ancestral hall for one year. This is doubled for Metropolitan Graduates. Those who receive a post or a title by purchase are not covered by these regulations.[48]

In addition, the esteemed degree-holding members of a control-subordination lineage could have their tablets entered in the hall in accordance with regulations to receive sacrifice and could extend this honor to their paternal ancestors. The "Regulations for the entry of tablets into the hall" of the *Hall Record of the Sanshan Ye* of Fuzhou prescribe:

> 1. One who begins his career through the examinations and becomes eligible for an official post or, though not eligible for a post, is placed in the lists of Provincial Graduates or Students by Tribute Second Class, Preeminence, or Excellence may have his tablet and that of his father entered [into the hall to receive] sacrifice. One who actually serves as an official of Rank Two or Three (*pin*), but not one who has held this as an honorary title or rank, may also enter the tablet of his grandfather. One who serves as an official of Rank One may also enter the tablet of his great grandfather. This follows the example of the dynastic enfeoffment privileges for one, two, and three generations.
> 2. One who begins his career not through the examinations but rather through military merit or by purchase, if appointed in the provinces to an office at the circuit, prefecture, department, or county, whether or not he has actually assumed his post, or if appointed at the capital to the position of Secretary, Vice-Director, or Director within the Six Boards may have his own tablet as well as that of his father

entered [into the hall to receive] sacrifice. One who actually serves as
an official of Rank Two or Three, but not one who has held this as an
honorary title or rank, may also enter the tablet of his grandfather.
One who serves as an official of Rank One may also enter the tablet
of his great grandfather, according to the example of those who begin
their careers through the examinations. These regulations do not apply
to those who hold miscellaneous offices in the capital or in the provinces, even if they are already appointed.

3. Annual Tribute Students, Tribute Students by Grace, and Tribute
Students by Purchase first, second, or third class, who have either
been appointed or actually held the position of Assistant Instructor in
the Confucian school on the basis of military merit or purchase, may
have their tablet, as well as the tablet of their father, entered [into the
hall to receive] sacrifice.

4. The rules for one who begins his career as a Military Metropolitan
Graduate are the same as for the civil branch. Those who hold military appointments or serve in the army are especially important. Aside
from those who have been given honorary rank and title or those who
have been appointed to an office but have not actually served, one
who attains the position of Brigade Commander or higher may have
his tablet as well as that of his father entered [into the hall to receive]
sacrifice; one who attains the position of Regional Commander may
also have that of his grandfather entered; one who attains the position
of Provincial Military Commander may also have that of his great-
grandfather entered.

5. Annual Tribute Students, Tribute Students by Grace, and Tribute
Students by Purchase first, second, or third class, who are aged seventy or above, regardless of whether or not they have already requested
recognition, may all have their tablets entered to receive sacrifice.
Their age should be written clearly in vertical lines on their tablets.[49]

These regulations fully illustrate the hierarchy of special rights enjoyed
by degree-holders. In a control-subordination lineage, the installation
of one's tablet in the ancestral hall to enjoy collective sacrifice by the
whole lineage was the ultimate ritual consideration and special right.
This right was strictly controlled in every lineage. The Ye lineage's
"Regulations on the Entry of Tablets" explain this in general terms:

Our hall was established by Gongzhan. The seven branches originate
in the generation [the names of all the members of which include the
character] Shen. The twenty-five branches originate in the generation
[the names of all the members of which include the character] Chang.
For all [these ancestors], tablets are installed without discussion. Since
the Chang generation, the sons of the surname have become numerous.
If tablets were installed for all of them indiscriminately, not only would
it be difficult to accommodate them all on the niche, but the important
rituals could be said to be almost defiled. In accord with reason and

circumstance, the introduction of distinctions is unavoidable. In the ancestral halls of the Lin of Houguan and the Chen of Luojiang, the criteria for the making and installing of tablets of lineage members in the hall are official position, rank, and examination success. Thus restrictions are clarified and encouragement expressed. Those selected on the basis of merit must have received state rewards for exceptional filiality, loyalty, or virtue. Where solid evidence is known, official position or examination success is irrelevant; they may receive sacrifice. This is in order to esteem proper conduct and guard against false claims. Selection may be determined on the basis of a combination of age and merit. We have repeatedly consulted existing regulations, and all of them do it in this way.[50]

The thrust of these regulations is that, aside from the collective ancestors of the whole lineage and the degree-holders, the only members of the lineage who could have their tablets entered in the hall to receive sacrifice were those who were granted state rewards or titles for merit, those who attained a great age, and those who made important contributions to the lineage itself. In the Ye lineage, the criteria for "selection on the basis of age" were "the attainment of one hundred years of age and meeting the qualifications for requesting the construction of a memorial arch [from the state]." For "selection on the basis of merit," the criterion was "establishment of sacrificial property or sacrificial fields in the amount of one thousand taels or more." Other lineage members were generally permitted only "to enter tablets for accompanying sacrifice (fusi)," for which the criterion was "contribution of ten thousand cash to the corporate account."[51] Thus the special position enjoyed by the gentry in a control-subordination lineage was something that other lineage members found difficult to match.

Professional management positions such as managers and directors could only be filled by wealthy or "virtuous" members of the lineage. Thus:

> For the general manager of the hall, a man who is upright and proper should be selected. The lineage and branch heads and the gentry members of the hall should collectively choose him at the appropriate time. Only one who is filial, charitable, and prosperous is suitable to hold this office. One who is filial won't be able to bear stealing from the hall's money. One who is charitable will not dare to waste the hall's money. One who is prosperous will not embezzle the hall's money for himself. One who has been selected may not evade the responsibility.[52]

The chief obligations of management personnel were to administer lineage property and to ensure that collective responsibilities were fulfilled. There was frequently a division of labor within the group of managers:

> Each year, one General Manager and one Assistant Manager are appointed through rotation, one of them to collect and issue the accounts, one to be in charge of managing affairs. From the lineage, a dozen or more honest and careful men are selected and arranged in a rotation in order. Those who have not been selected in this way must not participate in the rotation.[53]

Because professional management personnel held the right to administer the financial affairs of a control-subordination lineage, their selection was considered very important. Some lineages required that managers of lineage property have guarantors, with the guarantor and the administrators sharing economic responsibility:

> One man is collectively selected to manage the corporate accounts. Several members of the Ren and Yi branches with considerable property are in charge of the selection. It is not permitted for the poor to interfere or people with their own ideas to obstruct things. Once the selection has been decided, those in charge of the selection write a pledge of guarantee, signing it themselves, as proof. If the person selected is not honest, and later [corporate property] is embezzled and disappears, the descendants are permitted to demand restitution from those who were in charge of the selection. Only when the person selected as manager has passed on the job to the next person, and it has been verified that there has been no embezzlement or losses, is the pledge of guarantee by those in charge of the selection returned to them and rendered void.[54]

Despite the criteria that managers should be prosperous or "good and capable" and the various additional restrictions imposed on their administration, lineage administrators nonetheless frequently did view lineage property as a source of profit and tried to embezzle it through every type of force or fraud. For example, the genealogy of the Zhou surname of Pucheng records:

> Alas, in 1867, when the repairs to the ancestral hall were completed, the members of the lineage decided that Sanle and Sanwei were wealthy and reliable, and selected them to manage the rental income of the hall, to save it up to pay for the compilation of the genealogy. This year we are compiling the family registers, and not only have they not handed over [the list of] donations, but they have also swallowed up several dozen years of the hall's rental income, starving the ancestors to fatten themselves.[55]

This type of misdeed could be considered an example of embezzlement by force. The administrator of the public accounts of the hall of the Xie of Shangyang in Shunchang County enriched himself through fraud. The "Contractual agreement of the Shangyang ancestral hall" records:

> On the sixth day of the second month of this year (1865), the descendants of the Ren and Yi branches, descended from ancestor Yaoting, agreed as follows: "In the past, the originally established regulations required that by the fourth day of each New Year, the person in charge of the corporate accounts should gather the Ren and Yi branches and calculate whether or not there is a surplus in the corporate accounts based on the income and expenditures. This is to be recorded in the account books, which everyone is to sign, in order to prevent embezzlement. Investigation has revealed that the public calculation has not been done since 1837. According to the records in the previous account books, the annual surplus of income over expenses from the corporate property of the hall should be several hundred thousand. Now more than twenty years have passed without any assessment. It is urgent that we assemble in the hall, openly audit the accounts, and recover the money."
>
> Shouchen, the man in charge of the corporate accounts, was interrogated about this. He answered: "In 1858 the Long-haired [Taiping] rebels occupied Shangyang, killing, burning, and pillaging. The account books and deeds were all lost. . . ." Investigation revealed that, after the retreat of the bandits, Shouchen had searched for and found a box of documents concerning inherited property. Why did he conceal this and not first tell us all about it? Only when everyone was voicing their opinions, pointing at him and criticizing how he had obtained this box, did he admit it and hand it over. His fault in confusing and obscuring the matter was evident. . . . Now all the relatives have agreed that Shouchen's punishment shall be that he must determine and donate to the hall an appropriate amount of his own fields. This will give a clear warning. Shouchen was positively willing to make this donation, for he recognized his mistake and wanted to improve. This is indeed something to be pleased about. The records prior to 1858 were lost at the hands of the Long-haired rebels, and there is nothing from which to recover their contents, so it is best that they be canceled, and not be discussed any further. But naturally the property of the hall should not just be lost forever. The Ren and Yi branches are commanded to collectively investigate and recover it, and return it to the hall to be managed. If it turns out that property has been embezzled by Shouchen, and there is clear evidence for this, then he ought to make restitution of double the amount he has embezzled. If this is not the case, then there is no need to discuss it further. . . . Since Shouchen has handled the corporate accounts for many years and is very familiar with them, he is ordered to continue to manage them honestly and carefully. There is no need to discuss replacing him as manager.[56]

The manager of this lineage's corporate property treated it as his own private property. Moreover, even after his misconduct was brought to light, because of his experience and familiarity with the accounts, he was permitted to keep his position. This shows that the special rights of management personnel in a control-subordination lineage could be extremely stable.

The "wealthy" or "virtuous" in a control-subordination lineage often had other ways of obtaining certain special rights besides serving as professional managers. In most control-subordination lineages, most lineage property came from donations. Members who donated to the lineage property usually received certain corresponding special privileges in return. In 1796, forty-two "donation heads" (*juanshou*) belonging to the Yu surname of Shulin, Jianyang County, contributed to the purchase of sacrificial fields "because the fields left behind by the ancestors included insufficient sacrificial property." A declaration was made that:

> Unfortunately, among the descendants of this hall, only these forty-two households were really willing to donate. So each donated the sum of five taels in silver dollars to the hall for the rota holder to purchase tax-bearing lands to expand the sacrificial estate. Each year on the day of the autumn sacrifice, these donation heads must be invited to assist in the sacrifice and partake of the feast. Generations to follow may enjoy the bounty of the ancestors, in order to commemorate their humble contributions.[57]

In 1837, the Yu surname found it "difficult to meet the different expenses and various accounts." Twenty-four "donation heads" again came forward, each of whom "contributed ten silver dollars for the purchase of fields to assist in the repair of the ancestral hall, with the excess to be used to expand the property of the sacrificial estate." Once again, the donors were remunerated with the right to be "invited to assist in the sacrifice and partake of the feast. Generations to follow may enjoy the bounty of the ancestors."[58]

In a control-subordination lineage, the most effective way to collect money was to expand the criteria by which tablets could be installed in the ancestral hall and to demand "spirit tablet fees" (*shenzhu qian*) from those who wished to install tablets. Lineage members who had installed tablets in the hall were usually allowed to receive shares of sacrificial meat or to participate in feasts. For example, in one lineage, "the tablets that have been entered into the hall to receive sacrifice in the past number 293 in all. On the day of the autumn sacrifice, each is entitled to receive half a catty of the sacrificial meat."[59] Some lineages used the term "payment to obtain [a share of the] sacrificial

meats" (*nazuo*) to collect funds from within the lineage. The genealogy of the Ping surname of Houju in Jianyang records:

> In 1690, the tenth-generation descendants Guoren, Guoyong, and
> others took charge of the affairs of the hall. They generously consid-
> ered the repair of the hall to be their personal responsibility.... But
> the harvest that year was poor, and the funds were not sufficient. So
> they assembled the lineage to discuss things, and immediately began
> the practice of [requiring] payment to obtain sacrificial meat. At the
> time the gentlemen who happily donated money included two in the
> Le branch, twelve in the Yu branch, and four in the Shu branch. De-
> pending on how much they donated, they obtained one or two piculs
> of sacrificial meats (*zuo*).[60]

In these circumstances, a donation to the ancestral hall was really a
type of investment. Since the privilege of obtaining a share of the sacrificial goods could be transmitted through inheritance, one's descendants would also enjoy specific rights of control over lineage property.

Early in the formation of a control-subordination lineage, ordinary
lineage members might also enjoy rights such as a share in the distribution of sacrificial meat and participation in feasts. However, this
right was invariably restricted as the size of the lineage membership
grew. A document from the Xu surname of Donghai in Pucheng
records that, as "the income of the hall is not great, it would indeed
be difficult to distribute sacrificial meat to all. Rightly, only those who
hold management positions should receive a share."[61] Another account
from Ouning County records, "only the administrators should personally attend the sacrifice, clear up the accounts, and partake in the feast.
It is not necessary to distribute sacrificial meat to all of the members."[62] Most lineages also had regulations that anyone who violated
the rules of the lineage was forbidden from participating in the distribution of sacrificial meat or in the feast.[63]

From a purely economic perspective, the chief benefit of the control-
subordination lineage for ordinary lineage members was charitable
relief, which is one of the chief reasons why lineage organization was
praised in the past. But, in practice, the charitable aid offered by a
control-subordination lineage to lineage members tended to be mini-
mal and should not be exaggerated. The lineage regulations of the Fu
surname of Jianyang County, for example, prescribe:

> 1. Members of this lineage who are sick but are unable to
> seek medical attention should be assisted accordingly to obtain
> medicine.

2. Members of this lineage who are weak and alone, the widows, widowers, and orphans, should be given three cash per year.

3. All those in the lineage who have funerals to conduct should be given one cash. Those who are poor and do not have a coffin should be given the full expenses of the coffin for burial. If the wives and brothers are poor and will find it difficult to conduct [the funeral], they should be assisted with five cash or more.[64]

This sort of charity, consisting of only a few cash in each case, was of merely symbolic importance. In general, the income from lineage property belonging to a control-subordination lineage was mainly used not for charitable relief but for sacrificial activities, promotion of education, and other collective matters. This is why sacrificial fields, educational fields, and fields dedicated to tax and corvee payment were the most common forms of lineage property in Ming and Qing Fujian, and property dedicated to charitable relief for lineage members was extremely rare.[65]

*   *   *

The main function of a control-subordination lineage was to maintain the traditional social order and effective control over the basic level of society. In a residentially concentrated lineage, control of lineage members was an essential condition for more general social control. Every lineage had lineage rules, known as Regulations, Prohibitions, Admonitions, Pacts, Ancestral Hall Rules, or Genealogy Conditions, which imposed restrictions of many different sorts on the behavior of lineage members. Lineage rules touched on marriage, inheritance, occupation, funerals, lineage ideology and structure, management of lineage property, sacrificial practices, interpersonal relations, respect for the state, upholding of the law, and other areas. Such rules were often strictly enforced. For example, in the lineage regulations of the Zu surname of Tunshan in Ouning County, each of the eighteen rules includes a sanction to enforce compliance and punish violators. Punishments include fines, cutting off the receipt of sacrificial meat, and handing over the offender to the state authorities for investigation. The most serious was "exile from the lineage," or "wiping out the name in the genealogy." The Zu have been a residentially concentrated lineage since the Song–Yuan period, and in the Ming and Qing formed a closely organized system oriented around their ancestral hall, so their lineage regulations may have been particularly effective (see Chapter 4, part 1).[66] In addition to such regulations, the dominant group in a control-subordination lineage could make use of economic measures or moral education to strengthen the self-identity and the cohesion of the lineage, and thereby better maintain control over the membership.

The dominant group in a control-subordination lineage was invariably involved actively in various aspects of local affairs as part of its efforts to establish control over local society. Much of the estate of such a lineage was generally held in the form of immobile property, the income from which was dedicated to collective purposes. For example, the Regulations for the Conduct of Sacrifice of the Fu and Shou branches of the Xie surname of Shangyang in Shunchang records:

> 1. Gui Hill in Wurongbao, which was purchased by individual generations of ancestors, and which is linked to a plot of foundation land [i.e., land suitable for construction] extending as far as the bank of the stream, was previously donated to the locality for the Temple to the Eight Sages (baxian miao). On account of [the donation of this] temple land, at the sacrifice conducted annually in the middle month of spring and autumn, the officiant of sacrifice is to provide three catties of pork and a half-catty of goat from the bounty of the spirits. There is also a plot of land that has been donated for the Temple of Favorable Relief (shunji miao). Now the Palace of Longevity (wan-shou gong) has already been built, interior and exterior, left and right, front and back, for each of the gods to receive sacrifice. When [the people of] the locality collectively receive the bounty of the god, it is up to the lineage head to decide how the specific quantity of rice and cakes is to be collected and disbursed.
>
> 2. The rent from the plot of land donated by individual ancestors to the temple of Favorable Relief for incense and candles to worship the gods is to be collected by the temple keeper directly from the tenants, and he is also to pay the taxes himself. But the vegetarian cakes offered to the gods using the income from this land are to be collected by the lineage head for his own use. The lineage members may not struggle to obtain these or the above-mentioned rice cakes from the bounty of the god.
>
> 3. The individual ancestors have donated land to pay for the ferry-man's salary, his house, and sacrificial property. If this is not inspected for a long time, there is a danger that it may be seized by others, or the ferryman may sell it off illicitly, or unfilial descendants may claim it as their own property and band together to divide it up or sell it off illicitly. If this is kept secret and not made known, there will be no way to investigate the problems. So precautions must be made in advance. . . . [This property] will be managed by the fair and upright lineage head, who will regularly inspect it. Thus someone will take personal responsibility. The lineage head must also responsibly investigate and resolve [problems]. If it is lineage members who have seized or sold off the land, then the situation should be resolved on the basis of the family

regulations. If outsiders have seized it or the ferryman has sold it off illicitly, the lineage head is permitted to call on the members of each branch and turn to the community to discuss this in accord with reason. If [the offenders] resist and the land is not returned, this should be reported to the authorities to recover. No one may shirk and not come forward. Violators will be fined.

4. The stone guardrail and staircase of twenty steps in front of the temple of Favorable Relief were donated and constructed by second-generation ancestor Decheng. Several hundred years have passed and no one has taken on the job of repairs. In the future if there should be any damage, it is hoped that virtuous descendants will inherit [the ancestor's] ideals. If anyone takes it upon himself to donate funds for repair, the vegetarian cakes from the bounty of the god of this temple should be given to him. If no one is able to pay for repairs, the lineage head should solicit funds, or retain the income from the sacrificial property, in order to pay the costs. This would also be a way to bring glory to the ancestors. Unfilial descendants who interfere should be given a warning by the lineage head.[67]

These collective facilities, funded by donations from and constructed by ancestors of the Xie surname, were a special kind of transformed lineage property and inevitably fell under the control of the lineage organization to some degree. In Ming and Qing Fujian, many kinds of collective local matters were undertaken by multiple lineage organizations cooperating together, or were controlled and monopolized by a small number of powerful lineages. This was the basis on which control-subordination lineages developed control over local society.

*   *   *

Under normal circumstances, a control-subordination lineage required that its members restrain their personal interests in favor of collective interests and maintain friendly relations with other people in the locality. But when contradictions broke out between lineages, the lineage demanded unity in the face of the opposition. Thus:

In matters concerning the whole lineage, surplus corporate funds that have accumulated over the years are to be used in common for the common good. If there is not enough, then money should be solicited from the . . . adult males of the lineage to meet the common need. If there are lineage members who are being bullied by outsiders, everyone should exert themselves on their behalf. If anyone in the lineage feels differently, the whole lineage should cast him out.[68]

These behavioral restrictions, intended to prevent maltreatment at the hands of outsiders, served not only to strengthen the cohesiveness of lineage members but also to maintain control over local society. Inter-lineage feuding in Ming and Qing Fujian was usually directly or indirectly related to struggles over control of local society. Biographies in the genealogy of the Xue surname of Fengxi in Xianyou County provide several examples:

> Zigan acted heroically whenever he saw the opportunity to do right. He and Zhu Fengqi, Fengzhou, and Jianshi and Zhao Xianwen and his brother, all of Dongsha, formed into a society. They detected that the Zhu family had over one hundred *mu* of mountain land on which they paid no tax. Within our lineage there was a household registration under the name Zhu Guangzai that was registered as having several dozen *mu* of mountain land, on which a [tax] burden had been due for many years. It was ordered that the tax obligations be transferred. At that time, the two brothers Zhao served as mediators, trying to persuade the Zhu. The Zhu agreed, so our lineage was relieved of this tax obligation. [Zigan] also donated money to construct irrigation works at Houyang, which irrigated over one thousand *mu* of fields. The people obtained the bounty, and our lineage was also able to earn the benefit of holding the position of dike head. This is only a general picture, but it is enough to show that he need not be embarrassed about his conduct in life.

> When Fuwu was in the prime of life, wealthy monks of Quan'an-zhuang noticed that the irrigation works at Houyang could be used to irrigate their reclaimed land at Beizhuang. They tried to arrange this but didn't succeed. So they hired a stoneworker to get some stone ready, and in one night constructed an irrigation channel to divert the water to their land. Fuwu stood up himself and gathered a group of people to destroy the channel. The monks relied on their wealth to bring a suit at the two Provincial Offices [i.e., the Provincial Administration Commission and the Provincial Surveillance Commission]. The judgment [went against] the monks, who were ordered to disperse. Only one monk and one novice were allowed to remain to look after the monastery. . . . The water from Houyang serves seven *jia* and irrigates over 2,000 *mu*, all of which depend on this dike. If it were diverted away, then all this land would immediately turn to stone. Moreover, the position of dike head is held by our lineage. Recently the reclaimed land became the property of Chen Sanfu of Quanzhou. He also went through a mediator to offer us fifty taels, on the pretext that he wished for a share of the excess water. This is a most important matter. If in the future there should be any who greedily think of profit and don't consider the consequences, they wrong the ancestors. Take care! Be warned!

> When Shuyun was young he had a gallant spirit. In 1760, a local tyrant named Chen Rang from Nanzhuang village in this county relied

on his strength to transgress limits. He took over the scales at Tumen Harbor, looking down on our lineage, controlling the visiting merchants, ganging up with the troops and *yamen* runners, and doing evil without restriction.... This was difficult for us to accept. [Shuyun] learned that Rang patronized a prostitute with whom he stayed at a brothel at Nanling. He assembled and led a group of over thirty younger relatives, who secretly took up weapons, broke down the door, charged in and seized him, and then beat him severely, holding him by the neck and gouging out his eyes, carving up his anus, and covering his body with wounds. Rang was a strong and vigorous man, and after [his allies] carried him to the county *yamen* to show his wounds it took three days for him to die.... The county magistrate had frequently heard of Rang's evil deeds, so he took a soft line on punishing the offenders. ... Surely the ancestors provided secret assistance here.

Zizhen had great foresight and quite a gallant spirit. In the first month of the year, Jiaxiang, Luguan, Guiniang, Xiongsun, and others were chatting at the pavilion at Qingze, when the son of Huang Fu from Liuzhai happened to pass by carrying peanuts to [the market] at Feng-[ting]. They cursed him and chased him, so he dropped his peanuts and fled, and reported them to the county *yamen* as highwaymen. At that time, in the matter of the Zhang family land, it was [the Huang] who had [bought this land from us and then] resold it [to the Zhang]. Because of an ongoing lawsuit we were not permitted to redeem the land. So the [new] suit claimed that accumulated resentment was behind the matter. [Zizhen] was afraid that we would lose face, so he thought it best to use his own money to fight the suit.... Those who started this fiasco were naturally to blame. But the situation grew out of control, and the Huang happened to be our old enemies, so the only thing to do was to temporarily accumulate the income from the sacrificial property [to pay the suit]. In the future, those who deliberately cause misfortune may not use this example as an excuse.

In 1790, Erzong of the fifth branch and Shuqin of the senior branch got in a fight over some rent with a local bully named Zhuang Gong, who lived in Feng[ting] market. Gong went first to the judicial office at Fengting to make a report and be examined. Arrogant because of his wealth, he made the details widely known. Later he exaggerated the matter and brought the suit to higher and higher levels, falsely involving Shichou and his son from our lineage, planning to make our lineage lose face.... Observers all exclaimed: "Zhuang [Gong] has such influence, and the Xue are hiding in fear and don't dare fight his suit. It must be that they are guilty," and so on. The experienced members of our lineage heard these hateful things. They took on the outrage collectively and recognized what was right to do. They said, "Even though this affair started because Erzong and Shuqin got in a fight over water rights with Zhuang Gong, now the case has exploded to this level. If we now lose our footing, the stink will endure for a thousand years. This is a matter of our face, so it is agreed that we should bring a lawsuit against Gong, on the grounds that he owes us rent." . . . On the day of the interrogation, we relied on Shuxiu and Shichang and others to follow the case and make arrangements. Magistrate Wu decided that the circumstances were as we reported. Zhuang Gong and his son held their heads and wept, requesting that there be an investigation and resolution on the basis of their claim that we had taken knives and rushed to their home, coming in numbers and beating them severely, setting fire to their sheds, preventing them from cultivating the land and obstructing the payment of tax, and other evil deeds. The magistrate didn't listen and sent them under escort to get the rent that was owed. They had to express their willingness to end the suit. The members of our lineage danced home happily. Zhuang Gong lost face and was embarrassed. . . . The members of our lineage were overjoyed.[69]

These examples involve taxation, irrigation, marketing, and property, but in every case the key factor that united lineage members was the lineage's prestige or face (*timian*). In the interests of face, calculations of profit and loss and distinctions of fact from falsehood all became irrelevant. Face was a symbol of lineage power, a reflection of the lineage's control over local society. So anyone who came forward in inter-lineage feuding and vied for the face of the lineage was seen as a righteous man who ought to enjoy the respect of the lineage members. One genealogy records: "those who are able to respond to big disasters, prevent great shame, and protect all the sons of the surname are those on whom the whole lineage relies. They should be worshiped [in the ancestral hall], in order to demonstrate their merit."[70] Much territorial lineage feuding in Ming and Qing Fujian appears on the surface to be wholly irrational, involving conflicts over trivialities. But in fact these conflicts had deep historical roots and were determined by the social structure of the time.

*   *   *

Because the chief organizational purpose of a control-subordination lineage was control over local society, ties of common locality were the essential link between the lineage members. Ties of consanguinity had only symbolic importance; adopted sons and their descendants, who were excluded from inheritance lineages, could usually be accepted into control-subordination lineages. The genealogy regulations of the You surname of Liutian in Nan'an County proclaim that adopted sons contribute to "the flourishing of the lineage branches, and the splendor of our gates," so they may one and all be recorded in the genealogy "in accordance with custom." "Under their name is to be written that they are adopted sons. They are not permitted to lead the sacrifice for the main descent-line, since distinctions should naturally still be made."[71]

In some control-subordination lineages, descendants of adopted sons tried to shed their subordinate status or even assume a dominant position. For example, in the Wanli period, Luo Qianyu of Hui'an County declared himself a descendant of the descent-line heir of the main branch of his lineage. The other members of the Luo lineage gathered together and attacked him, denouncing him as the "descendent of adopted son Huang Laobao" and widely distributing "indignant poems" and "explanatory documents" to straighten out the situation.[72] In the Kangxi period, the Xue surname of Fengxi in Xianyou had an adopted son named Foqi. At the time of the sacrifice, "because he was the eldest, he firmly desired to hold the superior position. The group scolded and prevented him." In the Qianlong period, another adopted son, Shenqi, "unreasonably desired on the basis of his seniority to be the leader of the sacrifice. This was reported to the officials and it was several years before this was dealt with and things went back to the way they should be."[73] In the late Qing and early Republican period, the Guo surname of Quanzhou recorded a certain Xingui as an adopted son in the genealogy. As a result, "seventy-nine men opposed the compilation of the genealogy," and this led to a protracted lawsuit.[74]

Even where there were serious contradictions between adopted sons and natural sons, the ties of common locality among them made it possible for them to form a common control-subordination lineage. On the other hand, lineage members whose consanguinal ties were clear and direct but who had moved away found it difficult to be accepted into a control-subordination lineage. The genealogy of the Shi surname of Xunhai in Jinjiang records:

> Within the descent-line are some people who share the same Shi surname. Their family is very learned. They live at Linghou village in Hui'an. The draft of the old genealogy records that they went to Xunpo five generations ago, so their descent-line was still temporarily included [in the previous edition], the idea being that true [kin] should be recognized and direct descendants [of common ancestors] included. When [I] compiled the genealogy, I omitted this branch for the first

time, because they already consider themselves descendants of another descent-line. . . .

Note: when their branch was still small, my great grandfather Shuode went to where they lived, desiring to recognize them [as kin]. But because they were afraid of getting tied up with our tax obligations, they refused.[75]

These residentially dispersed lineage members, though included in the same genealogy, should not be considered as comprising a single control-subordination lineage. Each residentially concentrated group of kin had its own organizational goals and did not belong to the same system of social control. In Ming and Qing Fujian many residentially dispersed lineage organizations had collective lineage property, lineage graves, and ancestral halls as well as genealogies, yet were not control-subordination lineages but contractual ones. In fact, simply moving away could be enough for lineage members to escape the control of a control-subordination lineage. The genealogy of the Zhan of Pucheng County records:

Zhan Xianchang, of the Su branch, known in childhood as Meizhi, now lives in the Yanping prefectural city, where he has opened the Yufengsheng rice shop. His father moved from Pucheng to Nanping city in Yanping in the Xianfeng period (1851–1861). His household was extremely wealthy. In accordance with the current regulations of the office in charge of compiling the genealogy, . . . Xianchang ought to contribute 72 silver coins of 100 *yuan*, a total of 72 taels of silver. . . . On October 27, 1904, [lineage] officers Xianquan and Shihuan were sent to Yanping [to collect]. They spent over 30 *yuan* on the return trip. Xianchang not only refused to pay their expenses, he also wouldn't pay the fee due from adult male members of the lineage. He spoke most impolitely, and in the end they came back empty-handed. There was nothing else to be done, so on August 12, 1905, the ancestral hall brought suit, asking the county magistrate to transmit a document to Yanping to press him for the contribution. He still refused to pay. Such a person, who has not got his ancestors in his heart, is a case of what is called rich but immoral. It would not be going too far to cut off his new branch from the genealogy. For the moment we simply reflect that he is a relative who comes from the same origin. Xianchang is just a small-town philistine. It's not worth haggling with his sort.[76]

This demonstrates that only in the context of a residentially concentrated lineage could effective control be exercised over lineage members, and hence only in this context was it possible for a control-subordination lineage to develop.

*   *   *

The formation and development of control-subordination lineages reflect the localization and politicization of lineage organization. In the Ming and Qing, intensifying social contradictions and weakening state power led people to concentrate residentially for self-protection, which strengthened the relations of control and subordination among lineage members and encouraged the rapid development of control-subordination lineages. However, as control-subordination lineages were established on the basis of class opposition and class oppression, they invariably contained irreconcilable internal contradictions and depended on the support of the powerful and privileged groups within the lineage for their existence and development. This is why, although residentially concentrated lineages were common throughout Fujian, truly powerful control-subordination lineages were quite rare. In some cases residentially concentrated lineages formed control-subordination lineages but lacked sufficient wealth and authority to exert effective control over local society. Certain of their functions might therefore be taken over by contractual lineages. The political functions of the control-subordination lineage should therefore not be overestimated.

Contractual Lineages

The defining characteristic of the contractual lineage is that each lineage member's rights and responsibilities are determined by contractual relations. Because the contractual relations between lineage members were typically established on the basis of equitable mutual benefit, the contractual lineage is a form of lineage organization based on relations of common interest.

The formation of contractual lineages was generally associated with collective investment in collective undertakings by lineage members. The basic unit of investment usually took the form of a share (*gufen*), so in terms of administration and allocation of income, the character of a contractual lineage resembled that of a corporate organization like a limited partnership. The "Record of the Collection of Funds for the Purchase of Sacrificial Property for the Clear and Bright Festival," from the genealogy of the Zhan surname of Pucheng, records:

> In 1865, the hall was completed and the sacrifice prepared. . . . But there remained a shortfall for the sacrifice at the Clear and Bright Fes-

tival. Xianfeng regretted this, so he called on eight descendants of the lineage to donate five silver dollars each to purchase a garden, earning an annual rent of 8,000 cash. The name Tracing the Distant (*zhuiyuan*) was chosen as the name of the society (*tang*). In 1872, he again called on eight men of like mind to donate seven silver dollars each for the purchase of a shop earning an annual rent of 12,000 cash, and similarly chose the name Shared Ambition (*hezhi*) for the society. In 1887 and 1902, he further added two more societies, one called Sincerity to the Origins (*dunben*) and the other Forever Respectful (*yongjing*). Each society had eight members, who contributed five foreign silver dollars each. But no property was purchased. . . . Each society earned eight foreign silver dollars in interest annually, which was used to help meet the expenses of sacrifice. Each year at the time of the Clear and Bright Festival, all those who belonged to one of the societies went respectfully to the hall to assist in the sacrifice. For each share, one man and one woman were allowed to attend the feast, and the leftovers were divided completely.[77]

The various societies that conducted sacrifice at the Clear and Bright Festival were all nominally subordinate to the Dongmentang Hall of the Virtuous (*xianci*), but actually they always maintained an independent character. Only those who had purchased shares in the societies and their descendants were entitled to participate in the activities associated with them and to have a share in their income. They were strictly exclusive. These societies were thus a form of contractual lineage organization based on common interest and organized on the principle of share ownership.

In a contractual lineage, the interest of lineage members in lineage property could be transmitted through inheritance, alienated, or sold. For example, the *Genealogy of the Yingchuan Chen Surname of Jianyang* records:

In the ninth month of 1591, descendants of the third branch Wengao, Wenkui, and [Wenyue's son] Dezhong together purchased fields, including bottom soil rights, on which late harvesting rice was cultivated and [earning rent] of 3 official piculs, from Chen Zhangsheng of Yejiaqu in sector 5 of Shaowu County. . . . The seller continued to work the land, and each year paid 6 piculs of unhusked rice in rent. In the Yongzheng period, Wenyue's descendant Shifu sold off his share of this income worth 2 baskets. Wenkui's son Juesheng sold his share worth 2 baskets to Wenshun's descendants Shiyi and Shijun. In the Qianlong period, Shiyi's son Guangheng sold the final rights to his share worth 2 baskets to Shijun. [The income from this] share was collected together with that of the branch [descended from] Wengao.[78]

124 Zheng Zhenman

This lineage property had originally been purchased with funds collected from the Chen lineage members to serve as the sacrificial estate of ancestors Ying and Gui. The income was then used to pay for collective sacrificial activities by the investors. During the Yongzheng and Qianlong periods, share ownership rights were transferred through purchase and sale to different members of the lineage, but this did not lead to the disintegration of this contractual lineage.

In its early stages, a contractual lineage usually comprised only a small number of relatively wealthy families. But because the relevant shares were inherited by the descendants of the original shareholders, the individual participants gradually transformed from households into inheritance lineages, or even into control-subordination lineages. Under certain conditions, inheritance or control-subordination lineages themselves might invest together from the start, forming a contractual lineage based on share ownership in which the shareholders comprised different lineages. This contract of the Zou lineage of Longzu Township, Changting County, dated 1779, provides an example:

> The makers of this contract, the descendants of [Ye]sheng, and the descendants of his nephew twice removed, Lichong, whose names are Yuzu, Hongsheng, Xiongyun, Zhongyan, Xiongyan, Yiyan, Shengqian, Weiyao, and others, hereby found the Gongping market at the river mouth of this township. Young and old are both delighted; everyone exerts himself enthusiastically and with one heart. Each has willingly donated his own tax-bearing land to serve as the site of the market, and together they have constructed shops and a small warehouse, the expenses of which have been allocated among eight equal shares. The branch descended from Yesheng has paid for its share of the expenses for the market out of the public accounts of their ancestral hall. [The branches descended from] Lichong, Xiong, Ximeng, and Yongsheng together own half the shares, and the [Ye]sheng [branch] the other half. In the future, the rental income from the Gongping market is to be divided into eight shares. The [Ye]sheng branch will receive four shares' worth; the branches descended from Li[chong] will also receive four, such that each year the two branches will each receive half the income. As for the collection of rents each year, it has been agreed that the [Ye]sheng branch shall choose four men to serve as managers, and the Lichong [and the other three] branches shall also choose four. When it is the time to collect the rents, these eight men are to be informed and assemble together to collect and evenly divide the rent. This agreement is not to be violated, nor may one or two men take this over themselves. Because we are afraid that what is said orally can not be used as proof, we have drawn up this contract together, and given a copy to each party, to serve forever as evidence.[79]

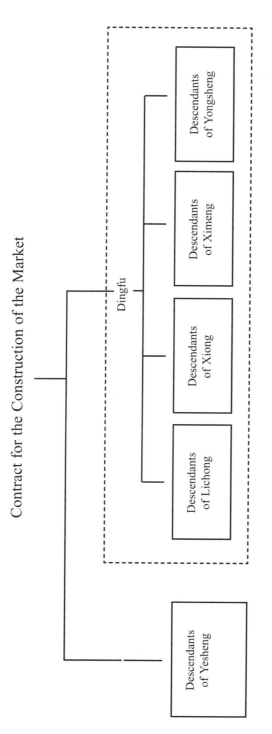

Figure 3.3. Organizational Structure of the Zou of Longzu

The Zou had settled in Longzu in the Southern Song, and by the early Ming had divided into the Yesheng and Dingfu branches.[80] Yesheng was the senior branch. Lichong was Dingfu's fourth-generation descendant, and Xiong and Ximeng were Lichong's son and grandson respectively. The generational position of Yongsheng is unclear, but he too was a direct descendant of Lichong. The Yesheng branch had built a private ancestral hall in 1756, while the descendants of the Dingfu branch did not build their own hall until 1794.[81] Thus, when the market was established in 1779, the Yesheng branch was already a control-subordination lineage, while the descendants of Lichong, Xiong, Ximeng, and Yongsheng comprised four mutually independent inheritance lineages. These different lineage organizations, each oriented around an ancestor of a different generation and each with its own distinct character, were the shareholders who invested in the establishment of the market. Through this contract the five lineages, one control-subordination and the other four inheritance, together formed a contractual lineage. The organization of their corporate estates is expressed graphically in Figure 3.3. Note that this is not a descent-line chart, but an organizational one. For example, since Xiong was Lichong's son, the shareholders of the Xiong branch were also shareholders in the Lichong branch.

The broken lines of the chart show that there was as yet no lineage organization centered on Dingfu, so his descendants participated as four independent inheritance lineages in the establishment of the market, forming a contractual lineage along with the descendents of Yesheng. Later, the Dingfu branches added new shares by making additional investments, which led to changes in the structure of the contractual lineage. According to the records:

> In the spring of 1792, the lineage decided to build a temple to the Empress of Heaven (*Tianhou*) [i.e., Mazu] in Gongping market. We the descendants of the four gentlemen of [the Lichong branch] invited the descendants of Liheng to participate in the market, and they happily agreed. Therefore the amount originally paid by the four branches to establish the market was divided by five, and the difference repaid [by the Liheng branch] to the original four. Naturally, this was all done openly. In the future, rental income from the marketplace of Gongping market is to be paid half to the descendants of [Ye]sheng, and half to the branches of Lichong, Liheng, Xiong, Ximeng, and Yongsheng in the Shugong branch together. All of the contracts signed in regard to this matter have been recorded in large books, which have been distributed to each branch to serve as evidence.[82]

Now the contractual lineage associated with the Gongping market comprised six participants, one control-subordination lineage and five inheritance lineages. The relations of interest and responsibility between these six participants were determined by the shares held by each, as specified in the contract.

Within the larger Zou lineage there were other contractual lineages, most of which had been formed through collective investment by a small number of lineage members. For example, a contractual lineage called the Soaring Dragon Society (*longxiang hui*) within the Mazu temple, was set up specifically "for the annual celebration of the birthday of the Sagely Mother in Heaven in the third month." This society had "forty-eight men in all, who are divided into four groups (*hui*); at this time each member contributes two silver dollars." This society adopted a system of administration by annual rotation and had a very tight organizational structure. According to their records:

> It was collectively agreed that the money should first be held in rotation by the first group, then the second, then the third, and then the fourth, [and loaned out] to earn interest. When the rotation is complete, it starts again at the beginning. By 1812, the capital had grown to 506 silver dollars. In the future, any member of a group who wishes to retire from it is only entitled to recover his original 2 silver dollars.[83]

After 1812 the society spent 495 silver dollars to purchase three plots of land and continued to administer the cultivation of the land by rotation through the four groups.

> If nobody in the group whose turn it is wishes [to rent and] cultivate the land, then it may be rented to someone in one of the other groups. If there is nobody in the whole society who wants to rent the land, it may be rented to someone outside the society. The rent must be fully paid by the tenth day of the twelfth month. If it is not fully paid, then the tenancy can be transferred to someone in another group or to someone outside the society who has money and wants to rent it. No one is to make objections to this.[84]

If this type of organization was able to develop stably over the long term, each of the individual shareholders would become an inheritance or control-subordination lineage. For example, the Zou lineage had two plots of land endowed in the name of Guandi. "The surplus of rental income remaining after the taxes have been paid to the local granary is to be used by *the descendants of those who originally registered for the society and made donations,* the branches of Liheng, Lisheng, Jun, Jie, Zhenmeng, Wanglu, and Zhongyuan, to meet the

expenses of the procession once every four years." Thus, regardless of
the initial organizational form of a contractual lineage, with the passage of several generations it was inevitable that it would come to consist of a number of inheritance or control-subordination lineages.

*   *   *

Because a contractual lineage was based on ties of common interest
between the members rather than consanguinal or territorial ties, it
was the most flexible type of lineage organization, and so it could
develop in many different areas of social life. The records in the genealogy of the Tong surname of Liancheng County describe the following contractual lineage organizations:

> 1. The society of the estate (*hui*) for the spring sacrifice at the grave
> of the founding ancestor, which was established in 1679 with sixty
> members. "Each paid five mace (*qian*)," which was used "to purchase
> twelve *mu* of land, earning a rent of one hundred silver dollars." The
> members were divided into three groups that conducted the sacrifice in
> rotation.[85]
> 2. The society of the estate for the fall sacrifice at the grave of the
> founding ancestor, which was established some time prior to 1679 with
> sixteen members. It purchased property earning several dozen boxes
> (*tong*) rent, and its members were divided into eight groups that con-
> ducted the sacrifice in rotation.[86]
> 3. The society for the Lantern Celebration at the Lantern Festival
> in the ancestral hall of the founding ancestor, which was established
> some time prior to 1773, with twenty-seven members. It purchased two
> shop premises, the rental of which was administered in rotation by the
> members divided into nine groups.[87]
> 4. The society for the God of the Soil (*tudigong*) of the ancestral
> hall of the founding ancestor, which was established in 1758 by twenty-
> one members "each of whom contributed two boxes of tax-grade rice,"
> which was used "for the purchase of fields earning 19.1 piculs rent."
> The members were divided into seven groups that conducted the sacri-
> fice in rotation.[88]
> 5. The society for the sacrificial estate for the spring and autumn
> sacrifices at the grave of the second-generation ancestor, which was
> established in 1730 with twenty-six members, who "used the annual
> rice to purchase" fields earning twenty piculs rent. "Later the rent from
> the fields was used to purchase a shop, which earned fifteen thousand
> mace in annual rent, and sacrificial [fields] which earned 10 boxes
> rent." This society was not divided into groups.[89]
> 6. The Lantern Society of the Upper Street Branch Hall of the fifth-
> generation ancestor, which was established in 1681. It originally com-
> prised seven members. "Each contributed two boxes of rice, and relied

on Changjiu and Shiyu to lend this out for interest. Land was purchased that was used to support the annual sacrifice and celebratory lamps in the ancestral temple at the Lantern Festival." Later the number of members grew to fourteen, who were divided into seven groups that managed affairs in rotation.[90]

7. The society for worship at the altar to the God of the Soil of the Ward (*bai tu she*) in the hall of the seventh-generation ancestor Shenzhai. It is not known when this society was established, but it purchased fields earning a total rent of forty-nine boxes and had forty-nine members who were divided into seven groups that conducted the sacrifice in rotation.[91]

8. The Esteeming Righteousness (*shangyi*) society of the hall of Shenzhai, established in the Xianfeng period (1851–1861). It had fifty-eight members and purchased three premises of shops, "earning a total rent of 20.7 thousand cash," as well as "sacrificial [fields earning] 45 boxes in rent." Each year, the surplus after payment of property rents and a contribution of four thousand cash toward expenses of candidates for the civil and military examinations was spent on the "sacrifice in the hall on the night before the Winter Solstice. The sacrificial meats are distributed according to the register."[92]

9. The Clear and Bright (*Qingming*) Society of the eighth-generation ancestor Zilu. It is not known when this was established or how many members it had. "In order to provide for spring and autumn sacrifice by our branch every year, those who were willing to esteem righteousness donated funds, and their bounty extended to the relatives. Everyone's efforts were relied on for the administration of the property." Each year, sacrificial meat was distributed according to a register of members.[93]

10. The Charitable Granary Society of the hall of Zilu, which was established in 1873 with 132 members, who donated nearly one thousand boxes in all. "Every year the grain was sold [at reduced prices] in the spring and repaid once the fall harvest was in." Four managers of the society were collectively selected each year.[94]

11. The Decorated Lanterns Society of the hall of Zilu, which comprised thirty-six members. It is not known when it was established. This society purchased land which was rented out and was administered by four groups in rotation.[95]

12. The Society of the Sacrificial Fields of the eleventh-generation ancestor Shisong, which was established in 1823 with twenty-five members. "It was agreed that each should donate one box each year. Those who have new sons pay an additional box of tax rice." The management of this society was not divided into groups.[96]

Most of these contractual lineage organizations within the Tong lineage were established by the gentry stratum. This may have been because the Tong's control-subordination lineage organization, though large, was functionally limited. According to an early Qing account:

Sixteen generations have passed from the founding ancestor, whose taboo name was Shisan, to myself, Wang. Initially, the whole lineage sacrificed in the hall, and there was no one who did not go to the graves to worship one after the other. Later the members of the lineage gradually grew more numerous. For the worship of the founding ancestors we divided into groups, and those who were not in a group did not participate. For this reason, only the heads of the different groups went to the graves to sacrifice, so that there were descendants who belonged to the gentry but who did not belong to a group, and for their whole lives did not know the location of the graves of their ancestors. . . . So the gentry members of the lineage who were all of the same mind gathered to make a plan and decided that, on the first day of the eighth month, they would each contribute a sum of money to conduct the autumn sacrifice. Those who contributed were to go to the graves personally to sacrifice and sweep the graves.[97]

The record of establishment of a sacrificial estate in the name of the second-generation ancestor also indicates that:

We reflect on the fact that our family has a tradition of being famous scholars of the School of Principle. The founder of this tradition was in fact second-generation ancestor Jingzhai. . . . He was buried at Bai-keng. The sacrificial estate was insufficient, so only several dozen representatives participated in the annual sacrifice. The road was very long, and when it rained it was muddy. Sometimes the sacrifice was not completed. We participate in this scholarly [tradition]. How can we fail to commemorate our origins? Everyone agreed, so funds were collected to conduct this sacrifice.[98]

The various functions performed by contractual lineages within the Tong lineage, such as the celebration of the Lantern Festival, the sacrifice to the God of the Soil in the sixth month, sacrifices in spring and autumn to "lineage relatives with no posterity," support for examination expenses and the establishment of a charitable granary to stabilize prices, could all originally have been performed in principle by a control-subordination lineage, but in the Tong lineage they were performed by contractual lineages. Indeed, even the major and minor ancestral halls of the Tong lineage were constructed through collection of funds according to shares and therefore had some of the characteristics of a contractual lineage. For example, the ancestral hall of the founding ancestor, which was constructed in 1693, was funded by donations from 123 "distant descendants," each of whom contributed "two taels of silver." For the reconstruction of the Upper Street Branch hall in 1683, funds were raised from more than sixty descendants, each of whom contributed three taels. For the reconstruction of the branch hall of Zilu in 1827, there were in all 244 "heads and supervisors of the construction." These lineage members who contributed funds for the construction of a hall and thus held the positions of "heads and supervisors of the construction" had the right to obtain sacrificial meat to "requite their contribution" (*baogong*) in accordance with the actual amount contributed. This right could be transmitted through inheritance to their descendants or transferred in other ways. By the Republican period, twenty-two of the original 123 shares acquired by contributing to the construction of the hall of the founding ancestor in 1693 had been transferred through sale or other means.[99] This suggests that the control-subordination lineage of the Tong was incomplete, or imperfect, and so the contractual lineage was an organizational form that the lineage members could not do without.

* * *

A contractual lineage was usually the largest-scale lineage organization in a residentially concentrated lineage where no control-subordination lineage had formed or where a control-subordination lineage had already formed but was on the verge of disintegrating. A contractual lineage could take over the performance of some of the functions of a control-subordination lineage, as is illustrated by a group with the Ge surname, whose ancestors had settled in Huangxi in Ouning in the late Yuan. By the late Qing, the Ge had still not formed a control-subordination lineage. The "Regulations of the Collective Sacrificial Estate of the First- to Fifth-generation ancestors" records:

> Because our ancestors self-assuredly sought to do good [in their own lifetimes], not only did they fail to accumulate much property to leave to the descendants, they did not even establish sacrificial property themselves. Reflecting on the nurturing merit and desiring to requite their origins, the descendants later gathered 119 like-minded men and collected sacrificial funds that were used to purchase lands [the income from which] was used to meet the expenses of the annual sacrifice. . . . Later people observed and were moved so they organized an additional group.[100]

Such a sacrificial organization formed on the basis of shares was usually highly exclusive, but it could occasionally allow the participation of new lineage members. Thus the "Preface to the Sacrificial Property of the Sixth-generation Ancestor Fotong" of the Ge records:

> This sacrificial [property] was originally established through subscription of shares in order to increase the glory of the ancestors. Those

whose ancestors had not subscribed for a share always regretted that they were left facing the corner [i.e., out in the cold]. . . . Those who now have the intention to participate in the sacrifice must contribute 25 *jiao* of silver per share, which will correspond to one share.[101]

In this situation, the original contractual lineage could continually expand and gradually transform into a control-subordination lineage (see Chapter 4).

On the other hand, it was also possible for a control-subordination lineage to disintegrate for various reasons and be replaced by a contractual lineage. In the Yuan dynasty, the Chen of Kaoting in Jianyang County constructed a grave shrine, "established fields and mountain lands," and hired a monk to look after it. In 1581, the shrine was converted by "an evil Daoist" into a temple. The Chen brought a lawsuit, and the local magistrate decided in their favor "and allowed them to bring in Zhu Mingfu and Zheng Zhitong to look after the grave." The ownership rights of the hall and property were altered in the process. Thus:

It has already been collectively decided that those who contributed funds for the fighting of the lawsuit shall collect the rental income of the sacrificial property. Those who did not spend their money or exert themselves are never to enjoy this right and may not interfere. In all, there were twenty-nine men who expended their money and toil in this matter. This is a fixed number. The rental income of the hall is not to be collected by the branches in rotation in order, but rather will be collected in rotation on the basis of these twenty-nine shares alone. This is established as a permanent rule.[102]

Grave lands belonging to the Zhan surname of Pucheng in the name of their ancestor Yuanshan, which earned fifty piculs rent, were illegally sold off by a lineage member. In the Qianlong period, a lawsuit ended in a judgment ordering them to pay for the redemption of the land. But because "the hall did not have corporate funds, the matter dragged on for over fifty years without the property being redeemed." In 1816,

because the land had not been redeemed, there was no money to pay for the expenses of the sacrifice. So forty members of the lineage united [and redeemed the land]. They are divided into five groups named Ren, Yi, Li, Zhi, and Xin. Each group has eight members and is responsible for one year in rotation. Each year, the rental income and interest is used to prepare sacrificial items at the Winter Solstice, to respectfully sacrifice to the generations of ancestors and the descent-line. The descendants also feast together on the surplus sacrificial items and meat. If there is any surplus left over after the sacrifice is conducted and the taxes paid, it is divided evenly among the forty men. They are known as the Winter Solstice society. These written regulations and the register of the rotation have been in force for over seventy years already.[103]

These examples show that in a residentially concentrated lineage, control-subordination lineages and contractual lineages often had similar functions, and could even be interchangeable.

*   *   *

Most residentially dispersed lineages throughout Fujian in the Ming and Qing were contractual lineages. This was because the members of a residentially dispersed lineage had no links of common locality or reliable inheritance relations, so relations of common interest were the only ties that could link them together. For example, members of the Li lineage of Liuqiao, Yangjiafang, and other villages of Liancheng County, who successively established a "Joint Hall for Collective Sacrifice" (tongci heji) in the prefectural seat of Tingzhou and the provincial capital of Fuzhou, allocated the rights and responsibilities of these project according to shares and specified these in contractual documents. One such is the "Contract between the Ziyuan and Zirong branches," dated 1676:

> The makers of this contract are the descendants of the Li surname of Chengnan. In order to sacrifice together to the ancestors in the same hall, we have discussed and come to an agreement in the matter of sacrificial ritual. Our founding ancestor, Gentleman Shiqi (Seventeen), came to Liancheng and settled in the Song. [His line] was transmitted to the fifth generation, in which there were the brothers Ziyuan and Zirong.
>
> [The descendants of] Ziyuan lived for generations below Wenchuan Bridge in Chengnan. [His line] was transmitted to the eighth generation, in which there were the brothers Zongzheng, Zongrun, and Zongzhi. Their descendants flourished and prospered, and first divided into the three major branches. The selection of the site at Shiziping, the construction there of the beautiful and striking ancestral hall for the respectful sacrifice to the ancestors, and the establishment of sacrificial fields to provide for the spring and autumn sacrifice, were all righteous deeds performed by the three main branches comprised of Ziyuan's descendants.
>
> Zirong moved to and settled at Yangjiafang, and [his line was transmitted through] generations of descendants. They were known as a notable lineage of Liancheng. They also built an ancestral hall in their locality and established sacrificial fields to provide for the sacrifices.

The [descendants of the] two brothers [Ziyuan and Zirong] have since long ago lived in different places, which though in the same county are eighty *li* apart. Even though they now worship their ancestors separately in separate ancestral halls, whenever descendants of the lineage run into one another, they still retain the sentiments of sharing common origins, still venerate the venerable, treat as kin those who ought to be treated as kin, and do not muddle the generational order. Now, the descendants of Zirong have chosen an auspicious day and come to the [Wenchuan] ancestral hall to meet with the three branches. It has been agreed that the ancestral tablet of Zirong will be installed in the ancestral hall below Wenchuan bridge. [The branches] of the two brothers can sacrifice together and worship the generations of ancestors together. The ancestral tablets of the eighth-generation ancestor Yuangui[104] and the three ancestral tablets of Zongzheng [and his two brothers] should also be placed together. This sincere gathering and mutual understanding of the whole lineage, which will comfort the dead and bring good fortune to the living, is a momentous event whose effects will be felt for a thousand years. The ritual regulations are the most important thing to be stressed in uniting an ancestral hall. Establishment in advance of a fixed plan for the sacrificial ritual must involve the participation of the three branches. The descendants of Ziyuan and Zirong are now organized into two main branches. There ought to be fixed specification of the respective rights. The descendants of the four brothers of the eighth generation are organized into four branches, to take responsibility for the sacrifice and to preside over the sacrifice in rotation. These rules have been established in the spring of 1676. Each year the spring sacrifice will be held at the Clear and Bright festival, and the autumn sacrifice on the fourteenth day of the seventh month. Responsibility for all matters, including preparation of the sacrificial items and the feast, dividing the meat, etc., will rotate through the four branches, each having their turn once every four years, one after the other, with the rotation starting anew once it is completed.[105]

The Li of Wenchuan and the Li of Yangjiafang consisted of the two branches descended from the fifth-generation ancestors Ziyuan and Zirong, respectively. In principle, responsibility for sacrifice in their joint hall should have rotated between these two branches. But in practice, there was "fixed specification of the respective rights," and responsibility rotated among four branches, each named for a member of the eighth generation. This must have been in order to take into account the different rights of ownership. Three-quarters of the shares in the hall were held by the Li of Wenchuan and only one-quarter by the Li of Yangjiafang. The division into two branches at the fifth generation, or into four at the eighth, may well have been entirely fictive, for the Li of Wenchuan Bridge compiled their genealogy a total of seven times in Ming, Qing, and Republican times, but never once compiled it together with the Yangjiafang Li, and the prefaces, compilation principles, and records of the ancestral halls in the early editions of the Wenchuan Bridge genealogy contain detailed descriptions of segmentation and out-migrations, but never once mention the Yangjiafang Li. Thus the establishment of the "Joint Hall for Collective Sacrifice" by the Li of the two places was probably only an alliance formed for the sake of practical common interest and was not based on any common inheritance relations.

In 1753, the Li of Wenchuan Bridge and Yangjiafang joined together and made another joint investment for the construction of a collective ancestral hall in the prefectural city of Tingzhou. This was originally an endeavor of the educated elite members of the Li, whose main purpose was to provide accommodations for members who went to Tingzhou to take examinations, and also for the convenience of other members of the lineage who traveled to Tingzhou for whatever other reasons. The "Preface on the Construction of the Yinjiang Ancestral Hall" of 1751 recounts:

> In the fall of 1750, our friend Xu Huaiqi of Yinjiang came to Liancheng to tell us about an auspicious site. We asked who was the owner of this land and it emerged that it was someone named Yu. We discussed the price, and he said that about 800 taels would be enough. In 1751, several members of our lineage went to Tingzhou to take the examinations, and so they went together to check out the geomantic situation. . . . In all there were three halls and more than twenty rooms on the side, with a study above. There remained plenty of open space, with a garden and a well, and to either side of the main gate were shops that could be rented out and the income used to pay the costs of sacrifice. After these scholars of the lineage had written the examinations and returned home . . . they gathered the members of the lineage to discuss [purchasing this house for the use of lineage members taking] examinations. It was decided to use 300 taels from the corporate account of the ancestral hall, with the remainder to be met by collective donations. All those of our surname, living or dead, may [purchase] the right to receive sacrifice with a donation of 1,200 cash per name. From small amounts a large sum can be raised; many hands make light work; great affairs can be accomplished. Not only will impoverished scholars taking the examinations obtain the blessing of a quiet place to live, but members of the lineage who ordinarily go [to the prefectural city] will also have the convenience of a peaceful place to stay.[106]

After the hall was built, the two Li lineages drew up a further contract which specified anew the rights and responsibilities of each:

Altogether 1,200 taels were spent on all of the expenses. Now we have
gathered in the Chengnan hall to report this to the ancestors and allocate rights. The two main branches are divided into four sub-branches,
each receiving an equal share. The Ziyuan branch contributed 900
taels, and the Zirong branch 300. . . . The numbers of names who may
enjoy sacrifice are therefore divided evenly among the four shares. The
three branches descended from Ziyuan are assigned 330 names; the
branch descended from Zirong is assigned 110. In addition to these 440
names, additional names may enjoy sacrifice on payment of 12 taels
for each name. The money was collected by the two branches together,
to meet the public expenses of the prefectural hall. The rooms in the
hall are also to be allocated evenly to the [members of the] four
branches to occupy when the examinations are held. From now on, the
hall in the county seat will continue to adhere strictly to the old regulations, rotating the sacrifice according to shareholding, and the hall
in the prefectural seat will forever uphold these new regulations. This
matter is thus handled with the utmost sincerity.[107]

A clear distinction was made between the regulations for the county
hall and those for the prefectural hall. This is because the county hall
originally belonged to the Wenchuan Bridge Li, and the Yangjiafang
Li only participated in the rotation of sacrificial responsibility but
had no ownership rights. The prefectural hall, however, was constructed from the collective investment of the two branches, so the
rights to its ownership were distributed among the lineage members
from the two villages according to their share in the investment.
Moreover, the unit that held ownership of the prefectural hall was
nominally the branch, but in fact it was actually the individuals
within each branch whose tablets had been installed to receive sacrifice, since the main source of funds had been donations to pay for the
installation of a tablet. Members of the lineage who had never made
a donation naturally enjoyed no share of the rights.

In the late Qing, there was another residentially dispersed Li lineage in Liancheng County besides the Li of Wenchuan Bridge and
Yangjiafang which was oriented around county and prefectural ancestral halls. This lineage was known as the West Hall, and the Wenchuan Bridge and Yangjiafang Li were known correspondingly as the
South Hall. In 1873, these two large residentially dispersed lineages
joined together to build a joint hall in the provincial capital, Fuzhou,
thus forming a residentially dispersed lineage of an even higher order.
According to the records of Li Wenlan, who led the construction of
the hall:

> The branches of the two halls, West and South of our Li surname, from Song to Yuan to Ming to Qing, have become numerous and divided into many sub-branches over these several hundred years. . . . But previously at the county and prefecture there have only been separate halls. Constructing a general hall together was repeatedly discussed, but a site was never found. At the time of the examinations in 1873, I stayed at Zhirenpu on the broad avenue of the Examination Office. There happened to be a residence owned by the Yang surname which I estimated could accommodate several dozen people. I asked about the price, which was only 600 taels. . . . After the examinations were over, I informed Jiancheng, Maocai, and all the gentlemen of the two halls who had come to write the examinations. . . . Because they encouraged me, and I felt this was a responsibility that should not be avoided, I took it upon myself. Thus I returned home to solicit donations, and after a month returned to the provincial seat to draw up the deed. Several years later, many [wished] to send their ancestral tablets to the provincial seat. I again tried hard to encourage donations for the erection of the buildings, construction of the niches, and installation of the tablets. Thus the matter was accomplished.[108]

Clearly, the formation of this residentially dispersed lineage oriented around the provincial hall was also initiated by the educated elite. But in the process of construction of the Li provincial hall, merchants also played an important role. "At that time the merchants Changqi, Chang'en, Boyuan, and Zongcheng were at the provincial capital doing business. Responsibility for all the matters connected with the provincial seat hall was given to them to fulfill."[109] The Hall regulations prescribed: "In those years where there is no examination, in the middle of the seventh month, the managers shall prepare sacrificial offerings and music, and invite those merchants in the capital doing business to gather in formal attire for the sacrifice."[110] Because gentry members of the lineage went only rarely to the provincial capital, merchants may well have been the chief participants in hall activities.

The organizational structure of this residentially dispersed lineage was also characterized by share investment. The relevant contract explains:

> The makers of this contract are Shantang and Youfeng and others, of the West and South Halls. Our two halls have many descendants and many cultured men. In the county and prefectural seats we already have branch halls. We have often reflected that, as the provincial seat is an important place, we [ought to] unite together to construct a gen-

eral hall there, to solicit the efficacy of the ancestors and to provide
for the convenience of descendants who go to take the examinations
and need somewhere to stay. At the time of the provincial examinations
of 1873, Yang Pingsun and his brothers had a residence for sale. . . .
The cost was about 1,000 taels. So we gathered the two halls to discuss
and agreed that the cost should be divided among three equal shares,
with the West Hall paying for one of the three shares and the South
Hall paying for two of the three. It was agreed that anyone who
donated seven mace could place one tablet in the main niche, and those
with a good heart donated accordingly as they desired. . . . As for the
rooms, it is not necessary to spell out precisely which rooms can be
occupied by the descendants of each of the two halls when examinations are held, and rented out annually. This shows that we are all kin.
But the annual expenses for the repair of the hall, the acquisition of
furniture and utensils, the salary of the hall keeper, and all the expenses for lanterns and incense should be evenly allocated among the
three shares. Any income naturally is also to be divided evenly among
the three shares. So we have established this contract to serve as evidence in perpetuity.[111]

In this contract, the right to install tablets was not distributed among
the two halls according to a predetermined share ratio, probably
because the shareholding structure was originally determined on the
basis of individual donations for the installation of tablets. Though
the West Hall and the South Hall appear to be the direct investors in
the provincial hall, the funds actually came from lineage members'
individual donations, so shareholding rights had to be allocated to
individuals according to their donations. In other words, the West
Hall and South Hall were only the shareholders' representatives, and
not the actual shareholders themselves. The investment and ownership relations are expressed graphically in Figure 3.4

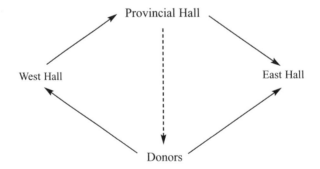

Figure 3.4. Organizational Structure of the Li of Liancheng

In this figure, solid lines reflect investment and the dotted line reflects ownership. The model reveals that, in this sort of residentially dispersed lineage, the basic participants were whatever lineage organizations were represented by the installed tablets, and not other intermediary organizations. This structural model is generally applicable to any residentially dispersed lineage at the county level or above.

Because each of the different levels of ancestral halls belonging to the Li had its own investors and amounts of investment, the ownership rights associated with each hall were independent of one another. In order to clarify the rights of lineage members to the different levels of ancestral halls, the Li of Wenchuan recorded in detail in their genealogy the "names of those who have made donations in order to receive sacrifice" at each of the county, prefectural, and provincial halls. In all, these numbered more than three thousand, which have been divided by type in Table 3.1.[112]

Within the Wenchuan Li surname, entry of a certain type of ancestral tablet, original or additional, into a particular ancestral hall required donation of a fixed amount, and therefore the rights and responsibilities associated with all of the tablets of a particular type were identical. For example, "According to the old regulations for receiving sacrifice, thirteen taels must be paid for each name [on a tablet]. Each year at the spring and autumn sacrifice in the hall, [the representative of each name] receives a chit that can be used to obtain one box of rice."[113] Because these rights could be inherited by the descendants of the person in whose name the donation was made and the tablet installed, each tablet could represent a separate and independent lineage organization. These lineage organizations could through further donations enter the various contractual lineages at different levels. Their rights and responsibilities in each were determined by share donations, and not by the genealogical position of their members. Theoretically the Wenchuan Bridge Li had 2,138 lineage organizations that belonged to the county hall, 753 that belonged to the prefectural hall, and 402 that belonged to the provincial hall. Of course, these figures include some tablets that may have been donated by a single lineage organization to more than one hall, and some tablets represented a share in some other lineage property. The majority of the tablets represented simultaneous donations to each of the ancestral halls. These tablets thus demonstrate the complicated interrelationship between residentially concentrated and residentially dispersed lineages. They do not suggest that residentially dis-

Table 3.1. Tablets Entered into the Ancestral Halls of the Li of Wenchuan

Type of Ancestral Hall:	County Hall		Prefectural Hall	Provincial Hall	
Generation	Original Number	Additional Donations	Original Number	Original Number	Additional Donations
9	10	0	0	0	0
10	16	0	13	0	0
11	16	0	11	12	0
12	23	0	11	21	0
13	34	0	15	17	0
14	31	0	18	13	0
15	36	1	17	10	0
16	58	1	27	15	0
17	90	2	57	21	0
18	131	2	86	17	1
19	181	3	122	25	2
20	202.5	5	121	30	6
21	194	28	88	49	5
22	168	48	59	49	17
23	151.5	87	43	36	15
24	102	136	30	17	13
25	43	151	15	0	11
26	4	110	12	0	0
27	0	65	8	0	0
28	0	8	0	0	0
Totals	1,491	647	753	352	70

persed lineages could form independently of residentially concentrated lineage organizations.[114]

Besides the ancestors who had purchased the right to have tablets installed, all ancestors above the eighth generation of the Wenchuan Bridge Li also received collective sacrifice in the county hall, and those above the tenth generation received collective sacrifice in the prefectural and provincial halls. Regulations specified that such tablets of collective sacrifice "did not require additional donations, and the tablets should be engraved according to the genealogy."[115] These tablets were thus merely symbols of identity for the residentially dispersed lineage, and not symbols of the actual basic participants in that lineage.

Within a contractual lineage, relations of consanguinity and common locality had only symbolic importance, and relations of common interest were the essential ties. The Daoguang edition of the Jianyang County gazetteer complains:

> In our county, the majority of the genealogies of the various surnames are unreliable. In many cases in order to gain notoriety and numbers, they try anything to link up. . . . Even when [their ancestors] are separated by a difference of several hundred years or a distance of several thousand *li*, they can all be persuaded they were fathers and sons or elder and younger brothers. Even the famous surnames and prominent lineages all fall into this trap.[116]

This custom of compiling joint genealogies uniting descent-lines that were not constrained by relations of consanguinity or locality reflects the widespread development of contractual lineages. However, joint genealogies uniting descent-lines were not compiled recklessly or at will, but invariably depended on some kind of common identification and cooperation, and were established on the basis of common interest.

In the Kangxi period, the Zhu surname of Beiluo in Jianyang claimed to be the descendants of Zhu Xi and demanded to participate in the sacrifices of the Zhu Xi ancestral hall of Shaowu. The "descendants of the descent-line heir" in Kaoting opposed this, brought a lawsuit, and rejected their bid. The reason for this was that the Kaoting Zhu had a "virtuous registration" (*xianji*), which bestowed special privileges such as hereditary tax exemptions and teaching appointments. The Beiluo Zhu were registered as commoners and enjoyed no such special privileges. When the Beiluo and Kaoting Zhu compiled a joint genealogy uniting their descent-lines, it was inevitable that the issue of "attempting to obtain the special exemptions and dodging the state tax and the various service levies" arose.[117] In his detailed account of this case, the magistrate of Jianyang wrote:

> Muddling [people] of different origins and falsely claiming registration as descendants of Zhu Xi is strictly forbidden and cannot be accepted under the laws of the state. Moreover, this is a time when [the state] is burdened by many matters. The service exactions are numerous. If [the Zhu of Beiluo] are allowed to flee and evade, then who would fulfill the needs of the military? So this violation is even more unacceptable. Furthermore, the *lijia* tax and service levy amounts are fixed. If the Zhu of Beiluo are allowed to claim that they belong to the household of the sage of Kaoting [i.e., Zhu Xi], then who is to pay the

tax in Beiluo? Thus the gentry and the commoners of the whole county will not accept this. It is not just the descendants of Zhu Xi who are sure to resist and not accept this.[118]

This example demonstrates that where there was no common interest there was no possiblity of the formation of a contractual lineage.

*   *   *

The contractual lineage was an organization based on common interest, and was a necessary supplement to the inheritance lineage and the control-subordination lineage. Especially where the commercial economy was relatively highly developed and social mobility relatively high, neither ties of consanguinity nor ties of common locality could provide sufficient basis for the development of lineage organization. Contractual lineages therefore developed widely in these settings, becoming the chief form of lineage organization. Most of the lineage organizations in the early immigrant society of Qing Taiwan, for example, were contractual lineages based on common interest (see Chapter 4, part 3). It was precisely the fact that contractual lineages were able to transcend the natural limits of ties of consanguinity and common locality which gave lineage organization its broad adaptability and extensive potential for development.

4

The Development Process
of Lineage Organization

In the history of Fujian, the basic pattern in the development of lineage organization has been one of gradual transformation from inheritance lineages to control-subordination and contractual lineages. In exceptional circumstances such as migration or unrest due to warfare, however, the development of lineage organization could diverge from this model, and other patterns might appear. In this chapter, I investigate the process of development of lineage organization in three regions of Fujian—the northwest, the southeast coast, and Taiwan— and discuss the effects of these distinct social environments on lineage development.

The Development of Lineage Organization
in Northwestern Fujian

Northwestern Fujian consists of the upper reaches of the Min River and the Ting river basin. During the Ming and Qing, this area was divided into four prefectures *(fu)*, Jianning, Yanping, Shaowu, and Tingzhou, and one department *(zhou)*, Longyan. This is a mountainous region with little arable land. Because it was relatively poor in natural resources, the scale of development of residentially concentrated lineages was relatively small. In addition, communication was difficult and social mobility low, so the development of lineage organization was relatively stable, with few dramatic fluctuations.

The residential pattern of lineages in northwestern Fujian is described in several late Qing and Republican county gazetteers, but most of these lack sufficient detail to be useful. The 1941 *Chong'an County New Gazetteer* provides a relatively detailed account of this issue. It explains: "In this county, the large surnames and lineages are

143

first the Zhou, Wu, Wang, Li, Chen, Zhang, Huang, and Xu. . . . Next, the Peng, Qiu, Yang, Lin, Yu, Zhong, Zheng, Weng, Zhu, Lian, etc. are the most flourishing surnames."[1] The total number of households belonging to these eighteen surnames was close to ten thousand, giving an average of about five hundred per surname. But in terms of residential patterns, each surname was highly scattered. The distribution pattern of the first ten surnames is shown in Table 4.1.

The table illustrates that, among these ten surnames, there are only seventeen cases where more than one hundred households belonging to a single surname lived within the boundaries of a single township *(xiang* or *zhen),* and the largest residentially concentrated lineage had only 278 households. Among the surnames listed eleventh to eighteenth, there are only a further five cases of a single residentially concentrated lineage numbering more than one hundred households. The other sixty-nine small surnames in the county mostly numbered only a few households, and it is unlikely that they formed influential residentially concentrated lineages.

In his discussion of "the fortunes of each lineage," the author of the *Chong'an County New Gazetteer* pointed out that the development of local lineages was quite unstable: "Those which flourished of old decline in the present; those which flourish in one place decline elsewhere. They cannot be all lumped together." For example, "the Liu flourished in the Song and the Qian in the Qing, but now there is no one [with these surnames]. Caodun was named for the Cao surname; Xiaotun for the Xiao, and Aidun and Ailinghou for the Ai, but now there is no such lineage [in these places]."[2] The author related this situation to the turmoil of the Yuan, early Qing, and late Qing and Republican periods. In fact, this explanation is misguided. Although there have historically been periods of turmoil in northwestern Fujian, these were on the whole shorter in duration and less destructive than similar periods in southeastern coastal Fujian, where hereditary families and powerful lineages were certainly not completely enfeebled. Moreover, in northwestern Fujian there were many hereditary families and powerful lineages whose long history has endured into recent times. But because of ecological restrictions, these lineages were unable to maintain a residentially concentrated form over the long term and were forced into continual out-migration in order to relieve population pressures. As a result, the older powerful lineages of northwestern Fujian are generally residentially dispersed rather than residentially concentrated lineages.

Table 4.1. Distribution of Households by Surname in Chong'an County

Locale/Surname	Zhou	Wu	Wang	Li	Chen	Zhang	Huang	Xu	Peng	Qiu
Qingxian	40	50	78	55	49	41	56	39	35	46
Chishi	14	23	29	18	42	18	27	17	19	17
Anqing	14	82	83	33	93	32	55	32	3	18
Xixia	4	51	33	16	12	0	7	35	5	19
Wudun	60	69	32	40	40	52	60	30	48	12
Fenggu	120	18	61	17	101	30	30	16	200	10
Likou	151	30	18	18	86	4	68	31	10	54
Shuangmei	33	152	145	39	54	84	22	39	26	15
Wufu	30	56	133	25	45	104	27	5	79	14
Dajiang	8	21	97	11	24	67	42	2	104	29
Baishui	141	83	42	16	34	10	20	1	1	16
Xingcun	54	101	29	90	110	77	84	31	35	28
Huangbo	9	91	96	30	38	6	13	9	2	7
Liyuan	278	87	56	251	59	90	48	32	28	20
Xingtian	0	0	0	120	0	0	0	210	0	120
Wenxian	38	53	25	54	37	39	24	11	1	6
Totals	994	960	875	833	874	654	584	560	496	491

Source: *Chong'an xian xinzhi*, 1942.

Because the scale of the residentially concentrated lineage in north-western Fujian was relatively small, its organizational form was relatively simple. The available sources suggest that it was only beginning in the mid-Qing that most residentially concentrated lineages in the area began to construct ancestral halls and compile genealogies. Of six ancestral halls in the community of Wufuzi in Chong'an, the Wang hall was first built in 1860, the Peng hall in 1861, the Zhang hall in the Tongzhi period (1862–1874), and the Liu hall in 1880. The two other halls, those of the Lian and the Zhan, were built only in the early Republican period. Prior to this, each lineage had generally gathered for collective sacrifice to their ancestors in an ancestral home or in a monastery or temple. However, the incomplete development of certain organizational forms within residentially concentrated lineages in the region does not imply that they were not tightly organized. In our fieldwork we have discovered many preserved registers of sacrificial property *(jichanbu)*, population registers *(rendingbu)*, contracts *(hetong)*, documents of household division *(fenguan)*, and other documents in popular hands. In residentially concentrated lineages, such documents served as effective tools for the internal administration of the lineage. The following section is a case study of the Zu lineage of Xietun village in Ouning County that analyzes the organizational form and development process of a residentially concentrated lineage in northwestern Fujian.

The Zu's first-generation ancestor was one Xixi, who emigrated to Xietun, also known as Tunshan, from Shanghu village of Pucheng County in the late southern Song.[3] Prior to Xixi's arrival there were already a number of residentially concentrated lineages in Xietun, including the Cheng, Jiang, Zhan, Long, Xie, Wu, and Guan. But as the Zu's numbers grew, its members infiltrated the residential areas of each of these lineages, and the Zu gradually came to hold a position of local dominance. In the 1820s, a member of the lineage described the situation thus in a "Preface to the Geomantic Map of Tunshan":

> Our town is located between the hills and the lowlands; though it cannot be compared to a big city, still it is quite prominent in [the local area]. . . . From antiquity it has been passed down that Shangdun neighbourhood *(fang)* is where the Cheng used to live long ago. Above Lord of the Soil *(tuzhu)* Road was the home of the Jiang. The local granary used to be the market where the Gu lived. Xiatang used to be the alley where the Long lived. Youfeng neighborhood was divided into [the residences of] the Front Xie and the Rear Xie. The Wu of Central Neigh-

borhood used to be divided into the Upper and Lower Branch. The large marketplace by the temple of the Lady by the Water *(linshui furen)* was where the Guan used to live. [The different lineages] were distributed according to the lay of the land like stars in the sky or pieces on a chessboard, and together they made up this locale. I suspect that the village may be called Xietun because it was the Xie who first lived here, or perhaps because the Xie were relatively numerous. There is no way to know all this for sure. Our lineage first moved here in the southern Song, chose a good site beside the Temple of the Lord of the Soil, and built a house. Later, the local people called the neighborhood where we lived QianPu [Prior Pucheng], to indicate that our founding ancestor came from Pucheng County, thus referring to our origins. Our lineage has consistently developed to the present without interruption, and there are people of our surname living in every corner of the village.[4]

By the turn of the twentieth century, the descent-line of the Tunshan Zu had passed through twenty-seven generations, and its members numbered more than two hundred resident households with over one thousand individuals. Over time, a significant number of lineage members had also migrated elsewhere; "the cases of the branches having divided and the descendants scattering in different places are certainly numerous."[5]

For the first five generations after their settlement, the Zu remained small in numbers, and most individuals left no posterity. In the late fourteenth century, the members of the sixth generation divided into two branches, the Qian and the Kun. At the time, the Zu may have already been organized into inheritance lineages centered on the graves of successive generations of ancestors and certain sacrificial property. According to their records, the Zu "conducted sacrifices at the graves for each ancestor" beginning with the founding ancestor.[6] "In the Song, Yuan, and Ming, in spring and autumn our ancestors sacrificed at the graves and then feasted at home."[7] In the late Qing, the collective property of the Zu included the hills on which were located the graves of these first five generations of ancestors. In 1820, one portion of these hills was given to a certain lineage member to construct a grave, in exchange for sacrificial land earning twenty baskets rent, which "belonged to the [estate of the] grave of the founding ancestor, to serve in perpetuity for the spring and autumn sacrifice."[8] The Zu also had a temple to the deity Yangong, which was said to be part of "the bounty inherited from Xixi."[9] But, aside from this property, prior to the mid-Ming none of the generations of the Zu had established lineage property specifically dedicated to the expenses of ancestral sacrifice. Thus:

> Since Xixi settled here, there have never been sacrificial fields. Perhaps this is because at that time our foundations were not yet established, and our numbers were few, so the establishment of sacrificial property had to wait for Rong [a descendant of the eleventh generation]. . . . The previous generations conducted sacrifice at the graves, but did not establish sacrificial fields.[10]

It was only in the sixteenth century that the Qian and Kun branches first established sacrificial fields for the founding ancestors of their respective branches. These were collectively inherited over the generations by the descendants of each branch. After this, each generation of the Zu also began to set aside some amount of sacrificial property, and so inheritance lineages grew continually stronger.

It was probably in the late Ming that a control-subordination lineage began to form among the Tunshan Zu. In this period, a number of large landlords and lower-level degree-holders appeared in the lineage and began to take on a leading role in local social life. In 1557, the "good men and devout women" of Xietun, responding to the request of the chief monk of Lingyun temple at Qianshan, collected funds and formed into a religious society (shenming hui) for the performance of Buddhist rituals.

> The recital [of sutras] began in the middle of the spring and only ended in the fall. The surplus funds remaining after the expenses of the ritual of confession (chan) were lent out for a year, at which point the funds totaled eighteen taels. This was used to purchase [surface rights to] three plots of land leased to tenants at Kuzhukang valley. Each year, sixty piculs of rent remain after the bottom soil rent has been paid. This is enough to pay the annual living expenses of the monk and his novice. Because of this, the incense and candles [of the temple] can be maintained forever.

Of the fifty-one male and female members of the society, eleven were surnamed Zu. The man responsible for initiating the project, and for writing the commemorative inscription, was the Zu lineage's first Government Student, Zu Ying, known as "the Man of Sunny Crag Mountain."[11] In 1583, the residents of Xietun formed a second society for the recitation of sutras and the performance of rituals, and used the surplus funds to purchase two plots of land. This society also had over fifty contributors, of whom nine were surnamed Zu.[12]

In the same period, members of the Zu lineage were attempting to consolidate the internal organization of the lineage. This is shown in the following contract:

> Zu Yi and others of Qianpubao . . . have inherited from the ancestors one plot of hill land with various pine, fir, and other trees, located before our lineage gates on Xiantinglin. . . . [The trees] had previously been sold to Wu Gui of this locality to cut down for firewood. Lineage members Zu Chuize, Zu Chuixian, Zu Huai, Zu Rixin, Zu Sheng, Zu Ming, and others reflected that this hill was an important geomantic site opposite our gates. If the trees were cut down, this would harm the geomancy. So they gathered the sum to redeem [the rights to the trees], in order that they be retained in common, to shade the geomantic hill forever. In 1583, Yi etc. pointed out that, though the lineage had collectively redeemed the trees on the hill, the deeds to the hill itself still belonged to them [personally], for it was property that their grandfather Zu Lu and father Zu Chun had themselves established. So they asked the lineage to pay them a subsidy. At that time, it was collectively discussed and agreed that Chuize etc. would pay 1.5 taels to purchase the hill belonging to Zu Yi, his grandfather Lu, and his father Chun, which would become corporate property, so that the trees would forever be preserved, to protect the geomancy of the hill opposite our home.

Dated 1583 . . .

According to the terms of this contract, certain land and trees that had originally belonged to a particular segment of the lineage became the corporate property of the whole lineage. Note that this step was taken to protect the geomancy of the lineage from harm by outsiders, and this concern for geomancy illustrates how the Zu's activities were shaped by shared interests that grew out of their ties of common residence. A small number of lineage members, who considered the local interests of the residentially concentrated lineage as their personal responsibility, interfered in the internal affairs of another lineage segment. This led to the formation of a control-subordination lineage.

It is also recorded that in the late Ming the Zu compiled a genealogy, which "recorded the ancestors from the twelfth generation and above."[13] This is also a symbol of the formation of a control-subordination lineage. However, the turmoil of the Ming–Qing transition prevented the stable development of this control-subordination lineage, and it disintegrated. "On September 7, 1649, the roaming bandit Fan Yanru led his band of over a thousand to pillage the Tun[shan] area. The buildings were all burned, and the genealogy turned to ashes. So there are no records for the thirteenth and subsequent generations."[14] Thus the unified lineage organization of the Tunshan Zu surname no longer survived, and the different segments within the lineage developed independently of one another.

During the Kangxi period, the two main branches of the Zu used the construction of ancestral halls and establishment of lineage fields to strengthen control over their respective branch membership. This led to the transformation of inheritance lineages into control-subordination lineages. Descendants of the eleventh-generation ancestor Rongliu first discussed the construction of an ancestral hall at the ancestral sacrifice of 1669. One of them recorded:

> In the seventh month of 1669, we sacrificed [to our ancestor]. All the descendants were present. Uncles Yicheng, Yijie, and Wanmao shame-facedly said: "a person has no closer kin than his ancestors; in ritual there is nothing more important than sacrifice in a hall. . . . Not having an ancestral hall is no way to express respect [to the ancestors]. You nephews should do your utmost to find a way. . . ." This task was begun in 1670 and the hall was completed in 1672. . . . One thousand was spent on the construction of the hall. The funds were obtained from the surplus income [from the estate of] our ancestor and from donations by his descendants. In the future, each year in the middle of spring and autumn, a lucky day is selected to conduct the sacrifice. The ritual in the hall is to be attended to first, and then the worship at each of the graves.[15]

Originally, this ancestral hall, known as the Hall of Hereditary Virtue *(Shide Ci)*, was used only for the worship of the lineal ancestors of the senior branch, the Qian, from the sixth-generation ancestor Yong-ning to the eleventh-generation ancestor Rongliu. But since the construction of the hall was paid for by the income from Rongliu's sacrificial estate and contributions made by his descendants, the hall was in fact a private hall *(sici)* for Rongliu. Later, other descendants of Yongning attached or subordinated themselves to the hall, which thus gradually evolved into a collective ancestral hall for the entire Qian branch. For example, in 1899, the branch descended from Deng-san, a direct descendant of Yongning but not of Rongliu, became part of the hall in the following way:

> Since their predecessors did not establish their own dedicated hall, they worried that the spirits of the ancestors had nowhere to dwell. So they specially discussed placing their ancestors' tablets in the hall to be worshipped with the descendants of Rongliu of the Hall of Hereditary Virtue, in order that the spirits of their ancestors should have an appropriate place.

In order to accomplish this, the descendants of Dengsan donated four plots of land, earning thirty-six piculs rent, to the Hall of Hereditary Virtue.

After the construction of the Hall of Hereditary Virtue, the descendants of the founding ancestor of the Kun branch, Yongming, constructed their own branch hall, the Hall of Enduring Good (*Jishan Ci*). Planning for this hall began in 1698, construction in 1702, and the hall was finally completed in 1727. In the course of this thirty-year period, "several hundred was spent, all of which came from the surplus from the income from the sacrificial property and per capita donations willingly made by the members of each branch."[16] Yongming's branch consisted of a single line of descent from the sixth to the tenth generation, but beginning in the eleventh generation, "the descendants grew numerous." The builders of the hall were descendants of the fourteenth and fifteenth generations. The corporate sacrificial property of the Yongming branch was first established by Minyi of the eighth generation, and added to by Tunjing of the ninth and Yangyan of the tenth. Most of the funds for the construction of the hall came from these sacrificial properties. Thus, from the time of its establishment, the Hall of Enduring Good was the collective ancestral hall of the Yongming branch.

Once the Yongning and Yongming branches had each separately constructed its own ancestral hall, their sacrificial property was no longer managed by rotation through the sub-branches. Instead it was transferred to the unified management of the respective ancestral hall. This pattern of management under the leadership of directors (*lishi*) is typical of a control-subordination lineage. For example, the "Sacrificial Regulations of the Hall of Enduring Good" prescribe:

> 1. The descendants of the branch are to select one honest and fair man to be the general manager (*zongli*) of the sacrificial property that was originally inherited and sacrificial fields that were established later, all of which are recorded in the register. He is to collect the rent, pay the tax, determine on which day the Grain Rains (*guyu*) solar term begins [approx. April 20], post a notification in advance, draw up the register of adult male members, and select twenty men to officiate over the [grave] sacrifice.
>
> 2. All descendants of [the ancestor buried in] this grave, regardless of their age, are permitted to attend the feast and enjoy the sacrificial foods.

3. 160 cash must be paid for each newborn male descended from the [ancestor buried in this] grave.

4. The managers are responsible for the corporate accounts, and they are required to use deeds [to their own land] as a guarantee.[17]

The general manager of the Hall of Enduring Good had to use his own property as a guarantee for his management of the sacrificial estate, so he must have belonged to the wealthiest stratum of lineage members. Although other members of the lineage had the right "to attend the feast and enjoy the sacrificial foods," they were required to pay a fee as a condition of being allowed to participate in the sacrifice. The Hall of Hereditary Virtue had similar regulations: "The sacrificial capital consists of over one hundred strings of a thousand cash, the annual interest on which is used for the distribution of sacrificial meat. . . . Only the descendants of Rong[liu] may register their names and obtain a share." The registration of names actually refers to the payment of a fee.

During the Qianlong period, in order to establish sacrificial property for sacrifice at the winter solstice, both the Hall of Hereditary Virtue and the Hall of Enduring Good encouraged members to make further donations in exchange for the right to participate in the sacrifice and to have tablets installed in the hall. The 1784 "Preface to the Autumn Sacrificial Register of the Hall of Hereditary Virtue" reads:

Although the hall's appearance is splendid, the funds for the sacrifice are still insufficient. Although the spring sacrifice is already performed, the autumn sacrifice has not been held. . . . This was reported to the lineage head and discussed with the members of the lineage, and a regulation has been specially established. Descendants of the branch of Rongliu who install tablets in the hall to receive sacrifice must pay 10 taels of silver for each tablet. The descendants who register to participate in the sacrifice must pay 400 copper cash each. The manager is in charge of this money and may lend it out to earn interest or use it to purchase property. In this way, it will become unnecessary to collect funds whenever there is a sacrifice, and arrangements can be made for the utensils for the sacrifice. Moreover, when repairs to the ancestral hall are needed in the future, it will be as easy to carry them out as it is to put one's hand into a bag.[18]

In 1792, the Hall of Enduring Good implemented a similar policy:

The funds donated by individuals amount to over four hundred [taels] which is to be lent out to earn interest to meet the expenses of the autumn sacrifice. In the future, tablets of [members of] each of the branches may be entered into the temple in *zhaomu* generational order

to receive sacrifice. For each tablet it is agreed that five taels must be
paid to the sacrificial estate. This is to serve as the permanent rule.

By 1822, thirty-four tablets had been entered into the Hall of Hereditary Virtue on payment of a donation, and sixty into the Hall of Enduring Good. Between the early nineteenth century and the Republican period, a further 545 tablets were entered into the former, and
239 into the latter. By requiring payments for participation in the
sacrifice and for the installation of tablets, the two halls accumulated
a sizcable estate, the income from which was dedicated to the autumn
sacrifice. These sacrificial properties belonged in principle to the hall
as a whole, but in practice they were more or less independent of the
general estate of the hall. Both halls established special registers for
these properties and appointed an administrator responsible specifically for their management. The "Regulations for Participation in the
Autumn Sacrifice" of the Hall of Enduring Good prescribes:

> The sacrificial estate, which has been purchased successively, has been
> paid for out of the funds collected for registration [for sacrificial par-
> ticipation], the funds paid for the entry of ancestral tablets into the
> hall to receive sacrifice, and the interest earned over the years, which
> has accumulated gradually. . . . The managers are in charge, one after
> the other, for a three-year term. . . . In the year when the responsibility
> is passed on, the old and new managers and general manager, sixteen
> in all, must gather to audit the accounts and immediately transfer the
> money.[19]

Only the descendants of people whose tablets had been entered into
the hall at some point could participate in the sacrificial activities
funded by this sacrificial property, and each generation of participants
was required to make a further donation. "Those who contribute to
participate in the sacrifice must first pay 400 cash, which is to be
loaned out for interest, and may attend the feast and enjoy the sacrificial foods only in the following year." On the surface, this lineage
organization seems to have had some of the characteristics of a contractual lineage. But because the distribution of ownership rights of
the individual participants was not definitely specified, and the relevant income could be used for various other collective purposes such
as repairing of the halls and compilation of genealogies, this was basically still a control-subordination lineage.

Members of the Zu lineage tried repeatedly to establish a single,
unified lineage organization on the basis of the halls of Hereditary
Virtue and Enduring Good. In the late Qing, a control-subordination

lineage organization that encompassed the whole lineage gradually developed. According to the 1808 "Preface to the Sacrificial Register of Founding Ancestor Xixi":

> Our ancestors separately established two halls, the Hall of Hereditary Virtue and the Hall of Enduring Good. Each year at the spring and autumn grave sacrifice, they sacrificed jointly to the founding ancestor and the ancestors of the first six generations. They were able to express their shared respect and joint love because, relying on the sacrificial property and the sacrificial registers, sacrificial leaders were selected to conduct the sacrifice together, and to assess the male population and increase the corporate funds. These registers were held in rotation, passing on from one to another and, just like a genealogy, were wrapped up in many layers like a precious object. . . . [Our lineage] has passed through more than twenty generations, and there have been more than eight hundred male members. Although a genealogy has not yet been compiled, [the genealogical lines in] these registers are already accurate.[20]

The first six generations of the Zu ancestors left behind no sacrificial property, and there is no clear record describing when property collectively belonging to the whole lineage was first established. But inferring from the above, this occurred only after the construction of the two branch ancestral halls, and through the collection of per capita levies on the males of the lineage. It is also not known when population registers for the whole lineage were first compiled after the destruction of the lineage genealogy in the late Ming. But it can also be deduced that such a register was probably compiled on the basis of the separate registers of the two branches, which suggests that the unified organization of the Tunshan Zu probably developed gradually only after the Yongzheng period. In the late eighteenth and early nineteenth centuries, the Zu went on to construct a collective ancestral hall for the whole lineage, and to compile a complete genealogy of all lineage members who had resided in Tunshan. In 1818 the Zu chose a site for the "family temple of the founding ancestor" *(shizu zhi jiamiao),* which was completed in 1830 and was known as the Hall of Classic Ritual *(Dianli Ci).* Over this thirteen-year period, "expenses amounted to about one thousand, all of which came from the donations of the various gentlemen and their descendants." "Various gentlemen" refers here to lineage organizations established in the name of particular ancestors, the most important of which were the Halls of Enduring Good and Hereditary Virtue.[21]

In 1822, at the time of the collective sacrifice to the founding ancestor, the Zu agreed to compile a unified genealogy. Those who took responsibility for the compilation relied on the historic registers of sacrifice, "used the written records of each household as a reference, examined the grave inscriptions of each branch, and consulted what the elders had to say. All of this was brought together and compiled, and workers hired to carve the printing blocks. It depended on the efforts of the group, and after several months was completed."[22] The expenses of the compilation were also met by donations. "The leaders in this matter not only fully exerted their hearts and energies but also spent their own money, going from house to house to solicit donations, experiencing misfortunes and difficulties." After the genealogy was compiled, the Zu of Tunshan continued to maintain population registers for the whole lineage, and used them as the basis for collection of contributions and distribution of sacrificial goods after the sacrifice. Thus, in terms of the practical control of lineage members, these population registers were even more important than a genealogy.

*   *   *

In the Qing, besides the three large control-subordination lineages symbolized by the halls of Hereditary Virtue, Enduring Good, and Classic Ritual, the Tunshan Zu lineage organization also consisted of a great many other lineage organizations oriented around ancestors of different generations. Most of these were inheritance lineage organizations that had formed when household estates had been divided; but some of these inheritance lineages had gradually transformed into control-subordination lineages, and there were also organizations that had been control-subordination lineages from their initial formation. Several examples will illustrate this point.

In the early Qing, the descendants of Chuifan, an eleventh-generation member of the Yongming branch, and the descendants of four twelfth-generation members of the Yongning branch collected funds to support sacrifice to these ancestors, and thus formed separate control-subordination lineages oriented around their respective lineal ancestor. A document of 1754 illustrates the first of these cases.

> Longyan had five sons, but only Chuiqing and Chuifan [had descendants and] divided into two branches. Our [ancestor] Chuifan had two sons, the eldest Youjie and the second Youyi, who divided into the Qian and Kun branches. Thus Chuifan is also the ancestor from whom our two branches Qian and Kun descend. Now then, why did the descendants of the two branches not conduct sacrifice specifically for Chui-

fan? It must have been because no sacrificial fields were established in the past, so [Chuifan] only received accompanying sacrifice when the two branches sacrificed separately to their ancestors. . . . Therefore, we arranged a meeting in the hall, assembling the elderly and the venerated of each branch. It was agreed that fertile land earning twenty baskets' rent should be set aside from the sacrificial estate of Youjie and Youyi in order to meet the expenses of sacrifice and feasting in honor of Chuifan. Everyone was enthusiastic about this. . . . For this reason a register has been established listing the property that has been provided by the two branches and the rules for the sacrifice that have been decided on, to serve as a guide forever.[23]

Chuifan lived in the late Ming, "a time of turmoil, when all under Heaven was bubbling with disorder. At that time he served as tax captain *(liangzhang)*, so he had to take the tax money to the capital. He died and did not return." As a result, Chuifan had neither grave nor dedicated sacrificial fields, so the two segments descended from him, the Qian and Kun, had no resources with which to conduct collective sacrificial activities dedicated to him. Instead, each of the two branches sacrificed to him separately at the same time as they sacrificed to their own respective branch ancestor. Thus from the time of his death in the late Ming to the mid-eighteenth century, there was no lineage organization oriented around Chuifan. Only in 1754 did the descendants of the two branches establish sacrifice specifically dedicated to him, thereby creating a lineage organization associated with this sacrifice. From its inception, this was a control-subordination lineage. Its "Sacrificial Regulations" include such regulations as a three-year term of service for the manager, and a required contribution of thirty cash due from each new male member.[24] These are definite indicators of a control-subordination lineage.

Not long after this, four branches descended from Rongliu of the Yongning branch also formed similar lineage organizations to support particular sacrifice at the graves of their ancestors of the tenth generation and above. The 1815 "Preface to the Newly Established Population Register of the Han Branch Sacrifice to Yongning" records:

Xixi's line was transmitted eleven generations to Rong[liu], whose descendants were extremely flourishing, and divided into four main branches named Huai, Si, Han, and Ji. They erected a hall and established a sacrifice, and each generation had sacrificial property. But sacrificial fields were not established for those ancestors such as Degui, Guoer, and Zhusan, from after the sixth generation when the lineage divided into branches. In the past, at the sacrifice to Rong[liu] in mid-spring and autumn, his direct predecessors also received sacrifice. In 1762, our four branches agreed to hold a particular sacrifice for them. Rice was collected on a per capita basis, and then the money divided up according to branch and lent out to earn interest. . . . But unfortunately not everyone's heart is alike. In the spring of 1786, when it was the time for the management responsibility to be passed on, the sub-branches of the Huai branch refused to take on the job. The result was that the corporate funds were distributed evenly to individual male members, and each of the branches conducted the sacrifice and cleaning of the graves separately. Since that year, our Han branch has selected a manager to take responsibility [for these funds], to manage the terms by which they are loaned out. More than thirty years have since passed, and the previous regulations have been strictly observed. . . . Now since the old register is completely full, a new register has been begun.[25]

The four branches descended from Rongliu had originally formed a single inheritance lineage oriented around his estate, on which basis they later constructed the Hall of Hereditary Virtue and became a control-subordination lineage. The collection of funds in 1762 for particular sacrifice at the graves of the generations of ancestors preceding Rongliu merely meant the addition of a new sacrificial unit within the Hall of Hereditary Virtue and did not actually imply the formation of a new lineage organization. But when the relevant sacrificial funds were evenly distributed in 1786, this meant the formation of four new lineage organizations, each comprising a different branch descended from Rongliu. Because the relevant sacrificial property and sacrificial activities of these organizations were supervised and administered by a manager, each of them was a control-subordination lineage.

Each of the four branches had previously held separate branch sacrifices and thus also comprised four separate lineage organizations. The division of the funds in 1786 might thus appear not to have resulted in the formation of new lineage organizations. But in fact the sacrificial property that had originally belonged to the four branches had been managed through rotation by their sub-branches. Thus, these were all inheritance lineages. The organizations formed in 1786, by contrast, were control-subordination lineages whose affairs were controlled by a manager. The two organizational forms were quite distinct and did not simply duplicate one another. For example, once the Si branch received its share of the sacrificial funds, a manager was charged with loaning the funds out to earn interest and holding a separate sacrifice. By the Daoguang period, over sixty strings of cash had been accumulated. "Every year on the day after the sacrifice to Siwu, our fourth branch conducts its own sacrifice and, as of old, holds a feast in the hall."[26] But as each of the original inheritance lineages itself transformed into a control-subordination lineage, the distinction between the two forms disappeared, and ultimately it was possible for the two to combine into a single organization. For example, after the sacrificial property of the Han branch ceased to rotate through the sub-branches, it was administered together with the sacrificial property dedicated to the preceding five generations of ancestors. The 1822 "Preface to the Sacrificial Register of Hansi" records:

> This small amount of sacrificial funds was accumulated coin by coin. Now we transfer it to the managers of Degui's estate to manage it in rotation and loan it out for interest. Whenever the time comes to sacrifice to Degui, sacrifice is also to be made to Hansi. At present more than 70,000 cash has accumulated. Everyone agrees that in the future there need not be an additional sacrifice [to Hansi]; rather we should wait till the sacrificial funds have grown even more and then purchase sacrificial fields. If there remains a surplus from the income of this land after the sacrifice, sacrificial meat should be distributed according to the payment of the individual fee.[27]

The income from the property originally owned by the Han branch was used in the eighteenth century to meet the costs of a lawsuit and of repairs to graves, "so the distribution of sacrificial meat was suspended for more than twenty years." As a result, the income could no longer rotate through the branches. In the longer term, all the sacrificial property that had originally belonged to each individual branch went from being administered in rotation to being centrally administered. Ultimately, then, in each case the inheritance and control-subordination lineages were incorporated within a single control-subordination lineage.

The inheritance lineages formed by the members of the Zu in the early Qing were by the middle of the dynasty turning into control-subordination lineages. The basic indicator of this process was change in the practices by which sacrificial property was managed, and the appearance of a stratum of managers.

> The makers of this contract are the descendants of the seven branches. The income from sacrificial property earning over 600 baskets' rent

and a mill in the name of Yonggeng has for a long time been collected by the branches in rotation. Now among the descendants some are good and some bad, some are rich and some poor. It has come to the point where the sacrifice is delayed, tax payments are overdue, and shame is brought to the ancestors. It is now decided that from the sacrificial land, two plots at Wukengban and Dongduo, earning a total rent of 90 baskets, as well as the mill, are to be set aside, and the rent in cash and kind is to support the collective sacrifice. Each branch is to select one manager. The collection of the rent, payment of the [bottom-soil] rent, and tax payment are to be taken care of by the managers. The branch whose turn it is in the rotation simply collects the 500 baskets of rice and has no other responsibilities aside from providing dishes, cups, and chopsticks on the day of sacrifice. . . . The mill is already managed in common. In future, the dike-passage subsidy paid by the lumber merchants to repair the dikes should also be retained for common use.[28]

Yonggeng was a fourteenth-generation member of the Yongming branch who lived from 1631 to 1687. The inheritance lineage comprising his descendants must have formed in the late seventeenth century, just under a century prior to the drawing up of this contract. The contract indicates that there was already clear economic differentiation between the members of the lineage, which made it necessary to transfer control over some of the sacrificial property and the affairs of ancestral sacrifice to the centralized administration of a group of managers, which therefore meant the formation of a control-subordination lineage.

In fact, even in the absence of clear differentiation among the descendants, various problems arising from the expanding numbers of participants in the rotation could lead to changes in the way sacrificial property was administered. For example, the 1815 "Preface to the Newly Established Sacrificial Register of Li'nan" records:

The so-called sacrificial estate earns not less than roughly 500 baskets in rent. After the tax is paid and the sacrifice performed, there is still a considerable surplus.[29] . . . Now the descendants in this branch have become extremely numerous, so the rotation lasts more than a dozen years before one gets a year's turn. Not only does this make it difficult to discover when the limits of the land are being gradually encroached upon, there are even cases where whole plots have disappeared without anyone knowing. The dikes around the plots by the water's edge or in the terraces collapse, and nobody comes forward to repair them. The tenants pay less than half the rent in cash and kind that is owed. Moreover, the rent may be collected but the tax is not paid, and those

who are blameless get implicated. What a way to disappoint the fine
hopes of the ancestor! Therefore the branch heads together have discussed and decided to draw up a contract to set aside . . . three plots
of land and the rent from the tenants. From each branch, two honest,
upright, and straightforward men are to be collectively chosen to come
forward and take responsibility for management, collect the rent, pay
the tax, pay the [bottom-soil] rent, and conduct the sacrifice. The surplus is to be retained to meet such common expenses as repairing the
fields by the water's edge, the irrigation channels, and the boundaries.
The rent from the plots that have not been set aside for this purpose
will continue to be collected in rotation by the branches.[30]

Zu Li'nan was an outstanding member of the fourteenth generation of the Yongning branch, with a reputation as "the model for the
village, and a representative for the county." His descendants divided
into four branches, which over time produced a number of examination candidates. In the Yongzheng period, "those who entered the
County School numbered more than ten, and those who were selected
by tribute eight or nine." They were known as "a renowned lineage
of personalities of the age."[31] But even in such a flourishing inheritance lineage it was difficult to avert the long-term trend toward disintegration. Inheritance lineages within the Tunshan Zu in the Qing
were generally only maintained for a maximum of three to five
generations. Once beyond the limits of mourning obligations, there
was a definite tendency for an inheritance lineage to transform into a
control-subordination lineage. Two examples suffice to demonstrate
this point. The first comes from the "Preface to the Sacrificial Register of Binyan," a member of the Yongming branch in the twelfth
generation:

In 1660 when the household estate was divided, sacrificial property
earning a total rent of 160 baskets was set aside in Binyan's name. At
that time the brothers were extremely fond of one another and the
household got along smoothly. In each rotation [eldest brother] Xiong
was given an extra turn to collect the rent, to repay him for his great
contributions in supervising the family. Thus, although we are divided
into the Tian, Di, and Ren branches, there were four shares in the rotation.[32] The taxes due were evenly divided among the four shares within
the three branches and paid by each household. So the branch whose
turn it is in the rotation to collect the rent only had to pay for the
sacrificial meat and organize the feast. As the population grew more
numerous, there was concern that this was not a method that could be
maintained for long. So in 1755 the three branches discussed and

agreed to suspend the distribution of sacrificial meat temporarily. Each branch was to select two capable branch heads, to take charge of loaning out the accumulating funds to earn interest. The interest and capital were to be saved up together. When about one hundred [taels] of sacrificial funds had accumulated, two plots of land at Wengkengzai and Rongshulong were purchased. The annual rent from the land was also accumulated in the corporate account. All those descendants who enter the County School are to be given ten taels of silver, to meet their expenses in reporting [their success] to the ancestors.[33]

The "Preface to the Register of Sacrificial Fields of Yihua," a thirteenth-generation member of the Yongming branch, provides a second example.

> In 1685, being old and weary, he divided his estate among his sons, first setting aside property for a sacrificial estate earning rent of 280 baskets. The tax responsibility was divided among the households of the four branches, so the branch whose turn it was to collect the sacrificial rent had only to pay the bottom-soil rent on the four plots of land, conduct the sacrifice, and divide the sacrificial meat. . . . Now the population has become numerous, and the expenses also increasingly complicated. It is feared that it will be difficult to maintain this in the long term. In the spring of 1822, the branch heads together discussed and agreed to draw up a contract in four copies. Beginning in 1825 the distribution of the rent of more than 200 baskets will be temporarily suspended for one year and saved. . . . Each adult male, young or mature, is also to pay 120 cash, and in addition the ten baskets of rent from [the land at] Caifenhou and Youqian are to be set aside. Each year the manager will collect and save the money to prepare funds for the repair of the fields and graves.[34]

In the first example, it took approximately 95 years from the division of the household estate to the formation of a control-subordination lineage, in which time the descent-line passed through no more than four generations. In the second example, the period was 137 years and the number of generations five. In both cases, there was a transition period in the process of transformation from inheritance to control-subordination lineage during which the original inheritance lineage had not yet completely disintegrated but continued to survive in a different form, coexisting with the newly formed control-subordination lineage, the two mutually reinforcing one another. Because most of the available documents concerning the Zu date from the early nineteenth century or earlier, there is little evidence to describe the later stages in this process of development in the late Qing, after this period of transition was over. But it can be deduced that, given the continually increasing population, the corresponding weakening of consanguinal ties, and increasing economic differentiation and polarization of wealth within the lineage, these inheritance lineages would eventually completely disintegrate and be replaced by control-subordination lineages. The Yanzong branch had, by the mid-nineteenth century, already implemented centralized management of all their sacrificial and educational fields, which had formerly been managed in rotation. "Every year those who attend the sacrifice and register their names receive a share of sacrificial meat. This is not to be violated in any way."[35] Thus this branch had become a control-subordination lineage. Yanzong belonged to the thirteenth generation of the Yongning branch and lived in the late Ming and early Qing, less than two hundred years and not more than eight generations prior to the mid-nineteenth century. These examples show that the transition period in the transformation from an inheritance to a control-subordination lineage generally took no longer than two or three generations.

By the early nineteenth century, the line of descent of the Tunshan Zu had already passed through twenty-two generations, and considerable property in the form of grave sites, sacrificial fields, tax fields, educational fields, shops and dwellings, and money that could be loaned out to earn interest had been left behind by or endowed in the name of ancestors from the eighth to the eighteenth generation. This property was collectively inherited by the descendants of each branch, which meant that inheritance lineage organizations continued to exist and develop more extensively. At any given time, even as some inheritance lineages were transforming into control-subordination lineages, or otherwise dividing or disintegrating, new inheritance lineages were simultaneously being created. This led to the formation of a pyramid-shaped structure in which the various lineage organizations of different types occupied different levels and were mutually linked. The lineage organization of the Tunshan Zu at this time is expressed graphically in Figure 4.1

We have up to this point provided a detailed analysis of the organizational forms and development process of the Tunshan Zu lineage. To this must be added the supplementary remark that the high level of development of control-subordination lineages and the limited development of contractual lineages among the Zu may be con-

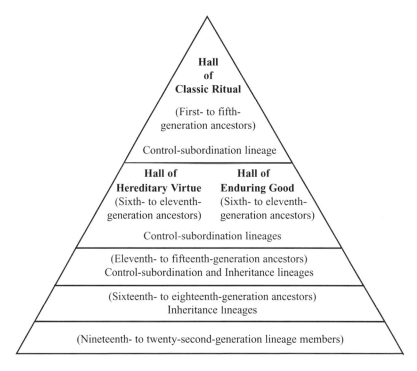

Figure 4.1. Organizational Structure of the Zu of Tunshan

nected to the relative abundance of lineage property endowed in the name of different generations of ancestors, as well as to the continued presence of an educated elite in the lineage. According to rough calculations, the total annual income from the sacrificial land in the name of ancestors from the eighth to eighteenth generation that rotated among their descendants was over 4,000 baskets, or roughly 1,000 piculs. Adding the income of lands held by the various halls brings the total to more than 1,500 piculs. There was also a significant quantity of unreclaimed land, shops and houses, and capital that could be loaned out to earn interest. This amount was sufficient not only to meet the expenses of the different kinds of lineage affairs, but it also left a considerable surplus that could be divided among the descendants.

For example, the sacrificial fields of Li'nan, which were managed in rotation, earned an annual income of almost 500 baskets. In 1815, the portion of income devoted to "managing the collection of rent, payment of the tax and [bottom-soil] rent and conduct of the sacrifice," plus that "retained collectively to meet common expenses such as repairing fields by the water's edge, irrigation channels, and boundaries" came to only 167 baskets. The remainder was distributed in rotation to the four branches, and did not need to be used for any collective expenses whatsoever. Similarly, the total annual rental income earned from Yonggeng's sacrificial properties came to more than 600 baskets. In 1784, the portion of rental income devoted to "collective sacrifice," "receiving and returning the [bottom-soil] rent, and paying the tax" came to only 90 baskets, and the remainder went to the branch whose turn it was in the rotation in that year. These funds did not have to be used for any "other expenses aside from providing dishes, cups, and chopsticks on the day of sacrifice." Thus there was clearly sufficient financial basis for the development of control-subordination lineages, and therefore little pressure for the development of contractual lineages.

*   *   *

From another point of view, the relative abundance of lineage property from different generations of ancestors played an important function in nurturing degree-holders within the lineage, and the ongoing presence of this educated elite encouraged the development of control-subordination lineages. The educational fields belonging to the Zu, which were dedicated to the nurturing of examination talent, earned an annual rent totaling over 420 baskets, which was divided among six different branches. Even branches that had not established educational fields usually gave their degree-holding members special rights to the rental income from sacrificial property. For example, "Cuanhou's Deathbed Exhortation to Use the Sacrificial Estate as Educational Fields," dated 1765, instructs:

> My great-great-great-grandfather devoted himself energetically and frugally to study, accumulating savings and advancing his household. As for my grandfather, he further enlarged the estate, but did not establish educational fields. My father Duoxian and my brother Shenghou were both Government Students; even I, though without talent, was [a Government Student] as well. I always reflect that inheriting the intentions [of the ancestors] and transmitting their affairs is a major principle of man. . . . After my death, when you [divide the estate] and live on your own, you need not establish educational fields. But if there are those among my descendants who have the desire to exert themselves

at study and who are able to continue the scholarly tradition [through examination success], then regardless of which branch's turn it is in the rotation to collect the rent, the income from my sacrificial estate should be yielded to them to collect for one year, to meet their expenses when they dress in formal attire to report to the ancestors.[36]

According to this will, whenever a descendant passed an examination, the principle of distribution by rotation through the branches had to be adjusted. This practice, which appears to have been universal among the segments of the Zu, encouraged the transformation of inheritance lineages to control-subordination lineages. Members of the educated elite were able to take advantage of this special right at any time. For example, a 1783 agreement for the provision of educational expenses prescribes:

> Now the Xing branch has a most glorious son Shirong who has become a Government Student. Naturally, we ought to recognize the intentions of the ancestors, and assist him in accomplishing his affairs. Would this not be [an opportunity] to establish a scholarship for books and lanterns? But the sub-branches within our branch are numerous, and assessing and soliciting donations would be difficult. So the only thing to do is to bestow on [Shi]rong the right to collect the rent from the sacrificial fields of our ancestor Yinxia for one year, in order that he will have funds to undertake his studies. If he goes on to become a Provincial Graduate, he will be allowed to collect the rent for three years in succession, and if he becomes a Metropolitan Graduate, he will also be allowed to collect the rent for a further three years.[37]

In addition, beginning in the late Ming, the branches of the Zu also established a number of official residences *(xiewu)*, also known as examination hostels *(kaoshi yusuo)*, in the prefectural cities of Jianning and Yanping, for the specific use of literati taking examinations.

> In the Chongzhen period (1628–1644), branch ancestor Li'nan of the Hall of Hereditary Virtue purchased and established an official residence on Xingfang road running by South Gate Street [in Jianning]. . . . In the Kangxi period the descendants of branch ancestor Yihua of the Hall of Enduring Good used the accumulated collective funds to purchase and establish an official residence to the left of the Examination Hall in Xinghua neighborhood [of Jianning]. . . . In the Kangxi period, Yonggeng established an official residence beside the Dragon gate to the left of the Examination hall in Xinghua neighborhood [of Jianning].

In the late Qing, the village was transferred to the jurisdiction of Shangyang Subprefecture of Yanping Prefecture, so some branches established similar hostels in the Yanping prefectural city. For example, the two branches descended from Shirong, a seventeenth-generation member of the Yongning branch, established a "hostel with five compartments" in Kaiping ward of Yanping city, the estate of which earned an annual rent of 16,000 cash.[38] The rights to use and collect income from such hostels belonged to the educated elite stratum within a lineage, which meant that these lineages transformed from inheritance to control-subordination lineages.

According to records in the genealogy compiled in the early years of the Republic, over 230 members of the Zu lineage obtained a degree or honorary title from the mid-Ming to the late Qing. These included eighty-five Civil Government Students, nine Military Government Students, one military Provincial Graduate, fifty-seven Tribute Students and seventy-seven recipients of honorary positions or titles, as well as a few lineage members who held minor posts such as Assistant-Magistrate, Instructor, and Registrar. Although none of these members obtained a high degree or title, they were active in different areas of local life and played a decisive role in the formation and development of control-subordination lineages. They initiated and oversaw the successive efforts to construct ancestral halls and compile lineage genealogies, and the establishment of lineage regulations and the maintenance of different sorts of internal and external relationships of the lineage were also doubtless the responsibility of this group (for further details, see Chapter 3, part 2).

After the mid-Qing, the role of the gentry members of the Zu in local issues, sometimes extending to those involving people of other surnames, became ever more prominent, which led to their control over the lineage membership also becoming ever stronger. In 1765, in the name of protecting the local geomancy, the gentry members of the Zu demanded that members of the Wu lineage yield up a plot of hill land. "They assembled the descendants of all the surnames [and agreed that] all the hillsides and plateaus, and the saplings growing to either side in front of and behind the road, and all the various trees that have been cultivated . . . should serve forever as the protective barrier for the village." Of the fifteen contracts drawn up in the course of this affair, nine were in the hands of members of the Zu lineage, and only six of members of other lineages. In 1815, gentry members of the Zu lineage initiated the reconstruction of the local temple to the Lady by the Water, whereby "the site was expanded, the temple built higher, and the wall lengthened. The intention was to hold in the surrounding dragon and protect the veins in the earth. Within, we rely on the temple to aid and protect; without, we use the trees and woods as a shield. The gate to this place is thus closed more firmly. It is truly a great site of the Tunshan area."[39]

In the Xianfeng period, Taiping forces entered northern Fujian. Local officials "ordered the military training of the community self-defense forces." Gentry members of the Zu initiated the organization of five "associated societies" *(lianshe),* which helped government troops to "clear up the whole area around Yangyuan, Jibin, Dicai, and Wuguo" and also undertook to "close the roads and clear the wilds" in the immediate vicinity. As a result, "one has only to speak of Xietun and the red-haired bandits stick out their tongues [in distaste]." In this period of great turmoil, the village was occupied briefly by Taiping troops, and was later looted by government forces. The local society and economy were severely damaged. However, the control-subordination lineages of the Zu of Tunshan did not disintegrate as a result, but on the contrary were further strengthened by these developments. According to the 1860 "Preface to the Sacrificial Register of Founding Ancestor Xixi," after the turmoil of 1858,

> not only were the poor unable to perform sacrifices, even the wealthy found it extremely hard to get by. If one tried to find a buyer for his land, one could only get a few hundred cash for each basket in rent [that could be earned from the plot]. If one tried to mortgage land, one had to mortgage land earning eight baskets in rent in order to borrow a thousand cash. There was land that no one would [rent and] cultivate, and debtors did not repay their debts. For this reason it was difficult to conduct the spring sacrifice of 1858. . . . We discussed and agreed with the rest of the lineage that the managers should conduct the sacrifice themselves, the sacrificial meat should not be distributed, and the distribution should resume the following year. . . . So two new registers were specially created.[40]

The local gentry played an important role in this process of readjustment, and the new managers were chosen from among them. In the late Qing, with the support of local officials, the gentry members of the Zu went even further in establishing their special leadership rights in the territorial lineage. According to the 1907 "Preface on the Tunshan Community Granary":

> Our humble village is in a remote part of the township, with limited land and dense population. When the harvest is poor, it is hard to avoid calling out to all sources [to borrow grain]. So in 1878, Magistrate Kong of Shangyang Subprefecture ordered the establishment of a com-

munity granary. The local gentry *(xiangshen)*, Zu Chunji, Chunxi, Zu Bishou, Biwen, Zu Hongsheng, etc., gathered to solicit donations from the wealthy of their surplus. Forty households were willing to make donations totaling over ten thousand catties. . . . For the last thirty years, this has been temporarily stored in the Hall of Hereditary Virtue of the Zu surname. Whenever the harvest is bad, and the people haven't enough to eat, they are permitted to come to the granary to borrow rice in summer, and in the fall repay it with interest. The amount that can be borrowed depends on the number of adult males [in the household]. . . . The grain that has previously been donated may be added to but may not be withdrawn. In the future, it is hoped that further donations will continously increase the amount.[41]

The authors of this preface were Zu Xiang, a County Student, and Zu Yuren, a Tribute Student. The document shows that in the process of establishing and managing the community granary, the gentry stratum acquired a certain legal authority. This authority was not only based on the wishes of local officials but, even more important, was reinforced by control-subordination lineage organizations such as the Hall of Hereditary Virtue. According to records in the genealogy, during the period from the late Qing to the early Republic, the gentry-directed Tunshan community granary became the community's paramount authority structure. Allocation and collection of dike fees from the local lumber merchants,[42] construction and management of new-style schools, and other matters all fell within the scope of the functions of the community granary. Naturally the basis for the power by which the Tunshan community granary fulfilled these functions remained the different types of lineage organizations at various levels.

*   *   *

The Tunshan Zu's significance as a case study has been to illustrate systematically the process of development of control-subordination lineages in a relatively stable environment. But, as was pointed out above, the formation and development of the control-subordination lineages of the Zu were closely connected to the relative abundance of lineage property and the continual presence of degree-holders in the lineage. What would be the characteristics of the process of development of a residentially concentrated lineage in the absence of these two factors? The Ge lineage of Huangxi, also in Ouning County, provides a useful example for the purpose of comparison.

Xingwu, the first-generation ancestor of the Ge of Huangxi, moved to Fujian from Henan in the late Yuan, "settling in Yuxi township of Jiyang, Ou[ning] County, Jianning."[43] There was a single line of descent through the second and third generations, but the fourth generation consisted of three members, and the descent-line split into three branches. Only one of the three remained in the area, and the other two moved elsewhere. The fifth generation further divided into three branches, of which one left descendants and the other two were cut off. In the sixth generation, there was a further split into five branches, each of which left descendants, and the lineage began to expand. By the early years of the Republican period, the Ge lineage had passed through twenty-two generations, and "there were more than five hundred hearths,"[44] but they were never able to form a unified lineage organization. The Huangxi Ge genealogy, compiled for the first time in 1921, records:

> The early ancestors originally had no sacrificial fields for the spring and autumn sacrifice. It was always the descendants who collected donations of money to establish property, which was used to meet the various expenses of the sacrifice and other expenditures. Regardless of generational position as recorded in the genealogy, whoever belongs to the branch descended from a particular ancestor may not participate [in the sacrifice] if he has not previously contributed funds.[45]

In other words, lineage members' rights of participation in lineage activities depended on their individual shares in the sacrificial estate of particular ancestors.

The lineage organizations of the Ge of Huangxi at the time can be divided into three levels. Those lineage organizations oriented around ancestors of the first to the fifth generation were typical contractual lineages; those oriented around ancestors of the sixth to the ninth generation had already gradually transformed into control-subordination lineages, and those oriented around ancestors from the tenth generation and later were basically inheritance lineages. The analysis here will focus on the first two of these three levels of lineage organizations, those oriented around ancestors from the first to the ninth generations.

The founding ancestors of the Ge had left no sacrificial estate, as we saw in Chapter 3. Later, two groups of descendants known as the Old and New Groups *(jiuban xinban)*, whose members were known as Names *(ming)*, contributed funds for the purchase of sacrificial fields. The Old Group prescribed the following regulations:

Each year, the Head of the Sacrifice *(jishou)* calculates the total income and the total expenditures for such items as tax payment and then determines how many pigs are to be sacrificed. If there is a surplus, it is distributed to each table [at the feast] and then at each table to each Name [i.e., to each individual representing the Name of an original donor to the estate]. The accounts for each year should be cleared each year; funds are not to be accumulated, nor should expenses exceed income.[46]

The Old and New Groups, which sacrificed to the first five generations of ancestors, were obviously contractual lineages organized on the basis of share ownership. They could not possibly have included all the members of the Ge lineage. The above regulations required that "the accounts for each year should be cleared each year," with any surplus being distributed to the Names, in other words to the shareholders. This meant that funds could not be used for any other lineage affairs. The regulations of the New Group were never recorded, but the genealogy shows that it had fifty-six members, property earning an annual rental income of 1,990 catties, and that its expenses were also calculated separately. The ancestral hall on which both groups relied "was originally the home of [the sixth-generation ancestor] Fotong, which the descendants had converted to a family temple." Thus it was simply a private hall belonging to Fotong's descendants, and not a public hall belonging to the full lineage membership. Fotong's descendants were divided into four branches, the Wen, Xing, Zhong, and Xin, the most flourishing branches of all the Ge lineage. All of the lineage organizations described in the genealogy were essentially centered on these four branches. Fotong is said to have lived from 1470 to 1553, and though "his wealth was the greatest in the locality, he cared not for material things but esteemed righteousness." Fotong left to his descendants a grave monastery *(zhong'an)*, his ancestral home, and a roadside pavilion, but he did not establish dedicated sacrificial fields. His descendants accordingly adopted the method of "accumulating [investment] shares" *(jigu)* to establish a contractual lineage. According to an 1835 "Preface on the Sacrificial Property of Sixth-Generation Ancestor Fotong," "This sacrificial [estate] was originally established through subscription of shares in order to increase the glory of the ancestors. Those whose ancestors had not subscribed for a share always regretted that they were left out in the cold."[47] Rights and interests in this estate were thus clearly allocated according to the principle of share ownership.

Prior to this, the ancestral home left behind by Fotong had already been converted to an ancestral hall. No records have been found concerning this process of reconstruction, but it was probably also linked to a contractual lineage that sold shares to pay for the costs of sacrifice. After 1835, the nature of this lineage organization underwent a change: "It has been decided that beginning this year, each adult male member must willingly contribute one string of cash, with which several plots of sacrificial fields will be purchased. The total rental income will be several dozen piculs, to be used for the expenses of the spring and autumn sacrifice." At the same time, it was also decided: "Those whose ancestors did not subscribe shares but who now have the intention to participate in the sacrifice must pay twenty-five *jiao* in small silver coins, which will match [the value of] one share." There was thus a per capita collection from the male membership, and those who had not previously held shares were also allowed to purchase them. After this change, the rights and interests of each member of this contractual lineage were no longer determined by his individual shareownership, but rather by his personal status. Thus:

> Descendants who have attained the age of sixty, or who become County Students or who obtain any official title whatsoever, may all register to be included in the group that performs the sacrifice. They must first pay one *jiao* in small silver coins to the head of the sacrifice three days in advance, to facilitate the arrangement of the tables for the feast of sacrificial foods. . . .
>
> Each year, four heads of sacrifice are to be chosen collectively, to administer all matters connected with the rental income that fall, and the spring sacrifice in the following year. . . .
>
> If the ancestral hall, the Hall of Chastity and Filiality, or the Shangchong monastery are damaged or leaking, or if the fields have irrigation problems, the heads of sacrifice must take responsibility for repairs, and must not delay.

These sorts of regulations obviously characterize a control-subordination lineage organization, not a contractual one.

*   *   *

Numerous lineage members of successive generations after Fotong each left differing amounts of sacrificial property, which were collectively inherited by their descendants. These lineage organizations were all initially inheritance style lineages. For example, the "Sacrificial Regulations for [Sacrifice to] Tenth-Generation Ancestor Guoche and Eleventh-Generation Ancestor Mingji of the Xing branch" records:

In every year containing the *you* character,[48] our branch and the Lun branch collect the income from the sacrificial estate of [seventh-generation ancestor] Tianlu. Our branch owns half the share, which rotates between the Ming and Kui branches. The Ming share further rotates between the Shun and Bi sub-branches.

In every *hai* year, our branch and the Lun branch collect the income from the sacrificial estate of [eighth-generation ancestor] Longhan. Our branch owns half the share, which rotates between the Ming and Kui branches. The Ming share further rotates between the Shun and Bi sub-branches.

In every *mao* and *you* year, our branch collects the income from the sacrificial estate of [ninth-generation ancestor] Jishui. . . . This share rotates between the Ming and Kui branches, the Ming in *mao* years and the Kui in *you* years. The Ming share rotates between the Shun and Bi sub-branches.

As for the sacrificial property [in the name of the tenth- and eleventh-generation ancestors], only the descendants of Mingji may participate in the sacrifice and enjoy the feast. The descendants of Kuiji long ago divided their share [of the property in the name of these ancestors] and established their own estate, so they are not included here.[49]

These sacrificial regulations record the rights of the Shun and Bi branches, formed by Fotong's descendants in the twelfth generation, to the sacrificial estates of their ancestors from the seventh to eleventh generation. The genealogical history of their lineal ancestors is shown in Figure 4.2. Seventh-generation ancestor Tianlu, founder of the Xing branch, had a single descendant, Longhan. Longhan's four descendants divided into four branches, the Jing, Chun, Xi, and Zhong. In the next generation, the descendants of the Jing branch further divided into six branches, the Fu, Ren, Shi, Che, Lun, and Yue. In the tenth generation, the descendants of the Che branch further divided into the Ming and Kui branches. In the eleventh generation, the descendants of the Ming branch further divided into the Shun and Bi branches.

The regulations specify that the principle of rotation through the branches remained consistent regardless of whether the branch's share in the rotation of rights to the sacrificial estates of ancestors of different generations was held separately or in common with other branches. The Xing branch also had a share in other sacrificial fields dedicated to sacrificial activities in the ancestral hall. These no longer rotated between the branches but rather were managed together by a head of sacrifice. Thus, the "Sacrificial Regulations for the Hall Sacrifice to the Seventh- and Eighth-Generation Ancestors of the Xing

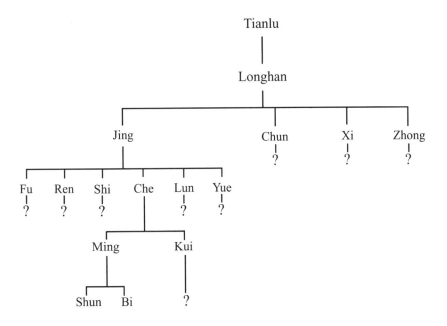

Figure 4.2. Genealogical Chart of the Ge of Huangxi

branch" and the "Sacrificial Regulations for the Hall Sacrifice to Jishui, the Ninth-Generation Ancestor of the Xing branch" both clearly specify that "Each year two heads of sacrifice are to be chosen collectively to administer all matters connected with the rental income that fall and sacrifice in the following spring." At the same time, the rights of lineage members to participate in these sacrificial activities were also restricted. "Three days in advance, each descendant who has attained the age of fourteen should bring one *jiao* in small silver coins to the home of the head of sacrifice to register his name and pay the registration fee, to facilitate the arrangement of tables for the feast. . . . The names of people on the list who have already died should be investigated and removed; they should not be retained."[50] In broad terms, this was a lineage organization that was in the midst of transformation from an inheritance to a control-subordination lineage.

*   *   *

As was discussed above, inheritance lineages began to form among the Ge of Huangxi in the late Ming, and control-subordination lineages in the mid-Qing. By the early Republican period, no control-subordination lineage organization encompassing the whole of the lineage had formed. In the late Qing, the lineage organization on the largest scale was a contractual lineage oriented around the first- to fifth-generation ancestors, the chief function of which was to conduct sacrificial activities. I believe that the chief reason why the Huangxi Ge were unable to form a large-scale control-subordination lineage was that their lineage property was insufficient. The total annual rental income from all the sacrificial fields in the name of all the different generations of ancestors was only about 246 piculs, roughly one-fifth the amount of the Tunshan Zu, which had about the same total number of members. The absence of a powerful gentry stratum within the Ge was another important factor behind the failure of a control-subordination lineage to develop. According to the genealogy, in the whole history of the lineage, only Ge Rihui and four other lineage members obtained degrees or titles, all of them between the eighteenth and mid-nineteenth century, and all of them members of the Xing and Xin branch descended from Fotong. These degree-holders made possible the formation of a control-subordination lineage within their own branch, but were not able to go further and establish a control-subordination lineage encompassing the whole lineage.

In the late Qing and early Republican periods, Fotong's tenth-generation descendant Zanxin and eleventh-generation descendant Daojun and others initiated the compilation of a genealogy. This might have been of some use in systematizing the relationship between the different branches, but due to the lack of financial support from collective lineage property, they too were unable to construct a unified organizational structure. It was said that, during the compilation of the genealogy, "Zanxin family's wealth was not even of the middle rank, but he donated two thousand cash, and Daojun's granary had no accumulated grain, but he assisted to the tune of five hundred silver coins."[51] In other words, the collective economy of the Ge lineage was impoverished. It would have been extremely difficult to take on collective affairs involving the whole lineage on this kind of foundation, and this made the formation of a control-subordination lineage impossible.

*   *   *

In northwestern Fujian, residentially concentrated lineages like the Tunshan Zu or the Huangxi Ge would have been considered relatively large and well-established. Most of the residentially concentrated lineages in the area developed only after settlement in the Ming and Qing, later than the Zu and the Ge. The *Jian'an Gazetteer*, compiled in the Guangxu period, lists thirty-five major residentially concentrated lineages, of which only five had been settled for more than twenty generations. Twenty of the thirty-five had been settled for less than ten generations.[52] Thus more than half of the residentially concentrated lineages of Jian'an had settled no earlier than the late Ming. For the most part, these residentially concentrated lineages of relatively recent settlement had not yet formed control-subordination or contractual lineages, and their organizational forms were basically all inheritance lineages. For reasons of space, I will not develop this point further.

Many members of those lineages whose founders had settled in northwestern Fujian prior to the Ming were later forced to migrate to various places, forming separate residentially concentrated lineages in each place. After the mid-Ming, some members of these residentially dispersed lineages used the compilation of joint genealogies, joint repair of ancestral graves, joint construction of ancestral halls, and joint establishment of lineage property to construct different types of dispersed lineage organizations. Most of these dispersed lineage organizations were contractual lineages, and they could transcend county, prefectural, and even provincial boundaries. The development of the residentially dispersed lineage of the Wuwei Liao of western Fujian provides a good example.

The Wuwei Liao consider Chongde to be their founding ancestor. His descendants are divided into two chief branches, named for Shifan and Gaofeng, who are considered the founding ancestors of all the Liao in Tingzhou and Longyan Prefectures, respectively. There are different accounts of when the founding ancestor of the Wuwei Liao first came to Fujian, and it is impossible to verify these, but it was probably at some time in the Tang–Song transition. It is said that when the Liao's ancestors first arrived in Fujian, they wandered for a long time without settling down, and this is what is behind the dispersion of lineage members in different places. According to an account in the Liao genealogy, "founding ancestor Shifan set off in the mid-Song because of turmoil. He went first to Xiayang market of Shunchang in Yanping and stopped there. . . . His descendants followed a single line of descent until the third generation, in which there were three brothers, each of whom moved to a different place."[53]

In such circumstances, the development of stable lineage organization was naturally most difficult.

By the Yuan–Ming transition, people of the Liao surname had already settled in different places in western Fujian in succession and gradually formed their own residentially concentrated lineages. A document from the Liao of Tianduan in Yongding County records that "back when the Mandate of Heaven was being transferred from the Yuan to the Ming, our eighth-generation ancestor Chengmin moved from Taibian in this county and settled in Tianduan . . . building a house beneath Yuan hill."[54] The Liao of Gutian in Shanghang County are said to have been using their ancestral home to sacrifice to their first ancestor who migrated, "Sixth-Generation Ancestor Gentleman Qianwu," by the late fourteenth century. This home was later converted to a "Hall of Offerings to the Descent-Line" *(Zongxiang Ci)*. In 1405, another ancestral home was converted to a "Hall of Glorious Thousands" *(Rongqian Ci)*.[55]

In the late Ming, members of the Liao lineage dispersed in different places began to discuss compiling a joint genealogy and worshipping their collective ancestors together. In 1609, a sixteenth-generation descendant of the Shifan branch named Menglin compiled the first genealogy of his branch.[56] In the same year, he also initiated the repair of the graves of the first- and second-generation ancestors in Guofang in Shanghang County and conducted sacrificial activities to them together. His "Inscription Recording the Repair of the Grave of Hua, [the founding ancestor of the] Shifan [branch]" proclaims:

> The founding ancestor of our lineage, Hua, with his wife née Feng, first moved from behind Heyang Market in Shunchang County of Yanping Prefecture and settled in Tingzhou Prefecture, Fujian, in the Song. He is the founding ancestor of all the Liao in [Shang]hang and Yong[ding]. He had one son and three grandsons, who up to the present day have flourished and divided into more than twenty [registered] households *(hu)* in Shanghang and Yongding. Our population is so numerous; how can we dare to forget our origins? Hua is buried at [place-name]. In ancient times, people esteemed simplicity and frugality, so his grave was made of mounded earth. Now because there were expansive slopes roundabout the grave, people have gradually opened them up for cultivation. This could not be borne. It was repeatedly discussed among the different households, all of whom heartfeltedly desired to requite their origins and trace their distant roots. Menglin assembled the lineages of [registered] households *(huzu)*, solicited donations, selected an auspicious day, and ignoring the distance hired workers to repair the grave. Though I don't dare use this endeavor to justify requesting pro-

tection and good fortune from the spirits of the ancestors in the hidden
world, still it is in accord with the principles of nature, and the hearts
of men can be at peace. Moreover, gathering the generations of the
different households and lineages and articulating their distinctions will
all have the virtue of bringing us relatives closer together.[57]

The terms "household" and "lineages of [registered] households" in
the inscription refer to individual residentially concentrated lineages
registered as households in the *lijia* system. Thus, the participants in
this grave reconstruction project included more than twenty residentially concentrated lineages from Shanghang and Yongding counties.
After the reconstruction of the grave, it is said that regularly scheduled
sacrificial activities at the grave came to be held. Every year on the
ninth day of the second month, collective sacrifice *(heji)* was conducted at the grave of the founding ancestor, and on the tenth day at
that of the second-generation ancestor.[58] However, a single unified
lineage organization encompassing all the lineage members from the
two counties had not yet formed at this time. In the Chongzhen period
of the late Ming, Liao lineage members in Shanghang and Yongding
separately erected general ancestral halls *(zongci)*, the Hall of One
Root *(Yiben tang)*, and the Hall of Eternal Reflection *(Yongsi tang)*,
in their respective county seats. These served as organizational structures linking all the lineage members from different places within
each county. But until the late Qing, these two general ancestral halls
in the two county seats remained independent of one another.

The general ancestral halls of the Liao surname in Shanghang and
Yongding were both seriously threatened by events of the Ming–
Qing transition, and their activities were temporarily suspended. But
from the Kangxi period onward they revived and developed further.
The "Brief Record of the Hall of One Root in the Shanghang County
Town" records:

> In the late Ming, [the hall] was occupied by rebel troops, so it was im-
> possible to gather the lineage to uphold the strict sacrifices of the lin-
> eage temple. Once the Qing dynasty had been established, County Stu-
> dent Minxian, whose taboo name was Jue, of Tianduan in Yongding,
> went and petitioned the governor, who issued a proclamation forbid-
> ding the seizure of the hall. The situation went back to how it had
> been in the beginning.[59]

In 1737, in order to raise funds for repairs, the Hall of One Root first
allowed the entry of ancestral tablets on payment of a fee. In all, nine
"households" participated. In 1682 the Liao of Yongding con-

structed another hall, the Hall of Knowing Roots *(Zhiben Tang)* in the county seat. It was repaired in 1735, with eleven "households" participating. In 1760, funds were raised for the reconstruction of the Hall of Eternal Reflection in Yongding using the method of "collecting donations for the entry of tablets of scholar members of the family" *(tijuan jiaxue paiwei),* and eight "households" participated. In the mid-Qing, these organizations also solicited donations to pay for purchases of land property, as is shown in the following document dated 1820:

> Guofang in Shanghang is where our founding ancestor first settled. The descendants later divided into branches and scattered in all four directions. Our ancestors reflected on the way to venerate the ancestors and respect the descent line, and gathered the lineage members to construct a general hall in Shanghang. . . . But there was no joint estate for the annual spring and autumn sacrifices. When the lineage members from different places came to Shanghang to perform the sacrifice, they called this performing the sacrifice, but in fact they might just bring a pig's foot or a vessel of wine, or they might just prepare a few sacrificial items and send children and youths to perform this ancient ceremony. . . . If someone asks about the so-called way to treat kin as kin and gather the lineage, this is not it.[60]

To deal with this unacceptable situation, the Hall of One Root again solicited donations for the entry of tablets. "Each branch was exhorted to make donations for a total of 334 tablets. Land earning a total of 29.672 piculs rent, which was given the name Treating Kin as Kin *(qinqin)* sacrificial estate, was established." Other records show that the management of the Hall of Knowing Roots also used the argument that there was no estate to support the autumn sacrifice to ancestor Yanji to call on "each household to organize themselves to [pay for the] conduct of this venerable sacrifice." In all, thirty-two lineage organizations purchased shares in support of this endeavor, and the "funds donated were let out to earn interest, with which sacrificial fields were purchased." After the Hall of Eternal Reflection was reconstructed in 1770, the surplus from donations was used to purchase property earning 114.62 boxes rent.

   Funds to meet the costs of construction of each of these three halls and for the establishment of estates associated with each were raised by collecting donations by household, by tablet, or by share *(gu),* depending on the hall. So the basic participants in each hall were either households, tablets, or shares. Generally speaking, in these documents the term "household" refers to a residentially concentrated lineage with a single household registration in the *lijia* system, and the term "tablet" refers to a branch segment of a residentially concentrated lineage, represented by an individual ancestral tablet. The term "share" varies in meaning, referring at times to a household, at times to a tablet, and at times to a family or an individual. Exploring the constitution of these various units will help our analysis of the organizational form and developmental processes of the residentially dispersed Liao lineage.

*   *   *

When the Hall of Eternal Reflection was built in the late Ming, sixteen hall heads *(cishou)* made donations for the installation of "tablets for scholars in the family." Four hundred taels were collected, and tablets were allocated to eight "households." The Fuxing household was allocated three tablets; the Zhenzong household one; the Xihang household one; the Jiayin household four; the Nanyang household one; the Tianyou household three; the Shigui household two; and the Rongqi household one. In this case, the basic participants represented by the tablets must have been branch segments of residentially concentrated lineages rather than the residentially concentrated lineages, represented by the term "household," themselves. This is the only possible explanation for the different rights and interests allocated to each household.

In 1770, when the Hall of Eternal Reflection was rebuilt, aside from the original "tablets for scholars in the family," donations were made for the installation of an additional sixty-eight tablets. The Fuxing household was allocated ten tablets; the Zhenzong household seven; the Xihang household sixteen; the Yuxing household eleven; the Nanyang household nine; the Jiayin household six; the Shigui household eight; and the Qimou household one. Thus, from the late Ming to the mid-Qing, the number of residentially concentrated lineages represented in the Hall of Eternal Reflection increased from eight to ten, and the number of participating branches within these lineages increased from sixteen to eighty-four.

*   *   *

The basic units of participation in the construction of the Hall of Knowing Roots in 1682 appear initially to have been households, that is, entire residentially concentrated lineages. After the hall was

rebuilt in 1735, its constituent rooms were allocated to the households, with different shares being given to each household. The
records indicate that:

> Of the eleven rooms on the left corridor, two are allocated to the Xihang
> household; two to the Nanyang household; two to the Qimou house-
> hold; two to the Zhenzong household; one to the Yuxing household;
> one to the Zaixing household; and one is to serve as the slaughterhouse
> for the sacrificial animals. On the right there is the shrine of Good
> Fortune and Virtue [the shrine to the God of the Soil] consisting of
> one hall and one room; one room for the kitchen, and ten connecting
> rooms, of which one is allocated to the Zhenzong household; one to
> the Qimou household; one to the Zhenghu household; one to the Ciji
> household; one to the Longtian household; one hall and two rooms to
> the Zaixing household; one room to the Fuxing household; and one
> hall to the Yueshan hall of the Fuxing household.

Aside from those rooms assigned special functions, such as the slaugh-
terhouse and the shrine to the God of the Soil, the list allocates rooms
to ten separate residentially concentrated lineages. We can only assume
that the differences in the number of rooms allocated to each household were connected to differences in the share of investment. In
other words, the share structure of this organization should really be
calculated in terms of rooms and not in terms of households. Yue-
shan was a sub-branch of the Fuxing lineage, which acted independently as a basic unit of investment and share allocation. In fact, the
other households named in the list may also have represented particular sub-branches within each residentially concentrated lineage, and
not the whole lineage. It is hard to imagine that each of these lineages
had already formed into a single united lineage organization, but,
owing to the absence of records, we can come to no definite conclusions on this question.

   By the Qianlong period, when the Hall of Knowing Roots solicited donations for the sacrificial estate of their ancestor Yanji, the
basic participants were definitely no longer households but different
branches within households.

> The households formed into groups (ji) to uphold the sacrifice.[61] In all
> there were thirty-two shares. In the Fuxing household, Yueshan had
> ten shares and Wenjin one. In the Xihang household, Meishan, Ting-
> zhong, Yuzhai, Shangyuan, Bolun, and Yuli had six shares altogether.
> In the Shigui household, Nianyi, Tianhuang, Yongxing, and Baiyi had
> five shares altogether. In the Wanquan household, Yunxi, Yongxiang,
> and Riwang had three shares altogether. In the Qimou household,

Zongzheng, Chengyi, and Chaoji had three shares altogether. In the Zhenzong household, Qianer'lang had three shares. In the Zhibin household, Weisi'lang had two shares.

This record indicates that the basic units of participation in the sacrificial estate of Yanji were twenty branches within seven residentially concentrated lineages. It is also possible that different kinds of organizations may have formed within these branches because of differences in the actual amounts invested. For example, the 1801 "Preface to the Seasonal Sacrificial Estate of the Great Ancestral Hall of the Qimou Household of Tianduan in Yongding" records:

> We Wuwei Liao built a great ancestral hall in the Yongding county seat. We have already assembled the descent-line branches of the different households and together perform impressive sacrifices to the ancestors in the hall. However, although the sacrificial foods are offered together, the sacrificial properties continue to be separately established. Each household has its own sacrificial estate in addition to the collective sacrificial estate, in order to express fully the desire to requite their origins. In the Qianlong period, the lineage ancestor of our Qimou household, Chanyan, suggested and took charge of organizing us into a group consisting of eighteen shares. Each share contributed one share's worth of money, which was lent out to earn interest, and then sacrificial fields earning 96.3 baskets rent were purchased. [The eighteen shares] were divided into six lots (jiu). The group is known as the Great Ancestral Hall Group (dazongci ji). Each year, on the fifth day of the second and eighth months, the income from the group's estate is collected, and the surplus after the tax is paid is used to prepare sacrificial items for the tablets that are to receive sacrifice. Everyone dresses in formal attire, comes to the hall, and conducts the sacrifice.[62]

The implication of this document is that only those members of the Qimou household who belonged to the Great Ancestral Hall Group had the right to participate in the annual sacrificial activities of the Great Ancestral Hall in Yongding. They were able to invest shares and organize this group because tablets of their ancestors had already been installed in the Hall. Lineage members who had not invested funds or whose ancestor's tablets had not been installed in the hall were naturally excluded from participation in the activities of this type of lineage organization.

* * *

The organizational form of the Hall of One Root of Shanghang at the time of its construction in the late Ming is unclear. When the hall

was repaired in 1737, funds were collected according to a formula
based on the tablets already in the hall. "For the tablets [of ances-
tors] of the third to eighth generations, the sum for each tablet is
three mace." Eighty-two taels was raised at this time, so there must
have been around 270 tablets in the hall, but the exact details are not
recorded. In 1820, when funds were raised for the Treating Kin as
Kin sacrificial estate, donations were made for the installation of 334
tablets, which roughly doubled the number of participating units.
Even more important, some residentially concentrated lineages that
do not appear in the original list of households also installed tablets
at this time.

> The Fuxing household had fourteen positions [for tablets], and in addi-
> tion its Youqing branch, twenty; the Dinghua household had four; the
> Qimou household twenty-four; the Xihang household thirty; the Nan-
> yang household seventeen; the Zhibin household seventeen; the Jiayin
> household six; the Shengji one; Yulin one; Shigui one; Qingxi thirty-
> seven; Yunzhong ten, and in addition its Yanbo branch, four. The Zhen-
> zong branch did not participate. In all there were 204 spaces.

In this list, there are a total of seven new lineages, which contributed
funds for a total of eighty-six tablets. Moreover, the Fuxing, Qimou,
Xihang, Jiayin, Nanyang, Zhibin, and Zhenzong households that
appear on this list were also participants in the Halls of Eternal Reflection and Knowing Roots. Thus, by the mid-Qing, the participants
in the main halls of the Liao surname in Shanghang and Yongding
counties had come to form a residentially dispersed lineage organization that transcended county borders. The relevant details have been
assembled in Table 4.2, which gives a general view of the basic structure and development trends of the residentially dispersed lineage of
the Liao surname in Shanghang and Yongding counties in the Ming–
Qing period.

After the mid-Qing, the Wuwei Liao of Western Fujian constructed
general ancestral halls in the prefectural cities of Tingzhou and Longyan and the provincial capital of Fuzhou, thus forming a residentially
dispersed lineage organization that transcended prefectural as well as
county lines. Aside from sacrifices to ancestral tablets, the main
purpose of these general ancestral halls was to serve as temporary
accommodations for gentry members of the lineage, for their convenience when taking examinations. In the Daoguang period, a lineage
member wrote to commemorate the construction of the Ancestral
Hall and Hall of Linked Adornment (*Zuci Shaocai tang*) in Tingzhou:

Table 4.2. Structure of the Liao Residentially Dispersed Lineage
in Shanghang and Yongding Counties

	Residentially Dispersed Lineage (Hall)				
	Yongding Hall of Eternal Reflection		Yongding Hall of Knowing Roots		Shanghang Hall of One Root
Residentially Concentrated Lineage (household or branch)	Tablets Donated (1628–43)	Tablets Donated 1770	Rooms Allocated 1735	Shares Acquired (1736–95)	Tablets Donated 1820
Fuxing household	3	10	3	11	14
Zhenzong household	1	7	3	2	unclear
Xihang household	1	16	2	6	30
Nanyang household		9	2		17
Jiayin household	14	6			6
Shigui household	2	8		5	13
Tianyou household	3	1			
Rongqi household	1				
Yuxing household		11	1		
Qimou household		1	3	3	24
Wanquan household				3	
Zhibin household				2	17
Zaixing household			3		
Zhenghu household			1		
Longtian household			1		
Youqing household					20
Shengji					1
Minlin					1
Qingxi					37
Yunzhong					10
Yinbo branch					4
Dinghua household					4
Totals	16	68	19	32	204

I have come more than once to the prefectural city and observed that
friends who come to write the examinations must immediately upon
arrival find accommodation to rent, or borrow a dwelling place and
temporarily rest their feet. Rushing around in this way is extremely
tiring. But for us of the Liao surname, arriving here is like coming home.
I have always sighed at the depth of the ancestors' bounty to their
descendants.

In the Guangxu period, the "Preface to Encourage Donations for the
Repair of the Family Hall of the Liao of Eight Counties" of the Liao
surname of Tingzhou Prefecture proclaimed:

> Now for each county we plan to set up a volume [to record] donations.
> Fair and upright men are chosen from each lineage to assist in this great
> matter. . . . If there is a surplus from the money collected, it can be used
> for construction in the remaining area behind the hall [containing the]
> tablets. Not only will this mean that the ancestors' spirits will have an
> appropriate place, it will also provide more spaces for examination can-
> didates to stay.[63]

The expenses for the construction of these general ancestral halls were
mostly met by raising donations for the installation of tablets, but
because the scale of these halls was so large, the basic units of participation in daily management and the allocation of rights and interests were not individual residentially concentrated lineages or their
branches but rather the other general halls at lower levels. The 1812
"Contract for the Jade Forest Hall *(Yusen Tang)* in the Fujian capital"
reads:

> The makers of this contract for the establishment of the Jade Forest
> Hall are the descendants of Liao Shifan and Gaofeng: Liao Bichu and
> Liao Jijia and others of Longyan, Shanghang, Yongding, and Ningyang.
> In 1812, with one heart our two branches exerted themselves to pur-
> chase by deed one residence belonging to Chen Xiaoqun and others in
> the Nanying neighborhood in the provincial capital [Fuzhou], and
> established it as a hall for examination candidates and for the worship
> of the ancestors. The amount paid was 3,000 taels. Another dwelling
> was purchased by deed, for which the amount paid was 60 taels. The
> two branches did this together. In all fifty-five land deeds, new and old,
> were entrusted to the charge of the director from the Longyan [branch]
> each year, to be passed on from one to the other. Besides the cost [of
> the purchase] and the expenses for repair, there remained some funds.
> These are to be used to mortgage property from 1812 to 1865, for
> which there are in all four deeds, which are also kept in Longyan. The
> remainder is let out for interest. Two volumes of registers have been
> set up, in which [the accounts] are recorded clearly. Out of concern that

in the future it will be hard to make an accounting, we have drawn up a contract with six copies to make it easier to do so.

As for the examination quarters in the provincial capital, when examinations are held, the rooms running in a row on the lefthand side, the study on the right, and the small study to the left of the main gate should all be rented out to earn money. The front and back chambers of the main hall and the rooms in the rear building are to be allocated to the two branches according to the arrangements of the spirit tablets: the descendants of Gaofeng staying in the rooms on the left, and the descendants of Shifan staying in the rooms on the right. But the numbers from each branch who participate in the examinations will vary; if there are too many people from one branch to be accommodated, the other branch must adjust accordingly. The standard is that four people should stay in each large room, two in each medium room, and one in each small room. One branch's rooms must all be fully occupied before it can ask the other branch to yield some of its rooms. It is not permitted to use the pretext that everyone belongs to the same lineage to demand that each person should have his own room. Nor is one allowed to bring in one's friends and relatives to stay out of friendship. Where violations are discovered, a fixed punishment should be collectively applied.

In normal circumstances, [all of the rooms] are rented out. Regardless of whether they are on the left or the right, the rent is collective income. The person who looks after the hall may not secretly put it aside. Because we are concerned that there is no evidence for what has been discussed orally, we have drawn up this contract to serve forever as proof.[64]

The contract shows that for the purpose of allocating rights and interests in the Jade Forest Hall the basic units were the Shifan and Gaofeng major branches. Daily management was handled by a stratum of directors. The contract contains other related addenda: "It is decided that every year at the Winter Solstice, the two branches shall fully assemble in the Hall of Common Roots in Long[yan] city to clear up the accounts." Naturally the participants in this sort of administrative activity would be the directors of the different ancestral halls; the statement could not possibly refer to all those lineage members who had ever made donations. Another addendum reads: "The contract is made with six copies, [which are distributed] one to Long[yan] prefecture, one to Yong[ding] city, one to Tianduan, one to Ningyang, one to the Changling household, and one to Juefang." This suggests that the members of the Jade Forest Hall did not include all of the branches descended from Shifan and Gaofeng, but rather these six major branches. Of course, within these six branches, only those lineage members who had made donations for the entry of tablets enjoyed a share in the relevant rights, such as the right to stay in the examination quarters or to participate in sacrificial activities.

In summary, lineage organizations in mountainous northwestern Fujian in the Ming and Qing generally underwent the complete process of transformation from inheritance to control-subordination and contractual lineages. In residentially concentrated lineages, inheritance lineages could be maintained and developed with some stability, and so these lineages were the dominant form of lineage organization in the area and the basis on which other forms developed. Where a residentially concentrated lineage had considerable corporate lineage property or many gentry members, the development of control-subordination lineages tended to be relatively comprehensive, and there was less scope for contractual lineages to develop. Where these circumstances did not obtain, the development of control-subordination lineages was restricted, and contractual lineages were correspondingly better developed. Most of the residentially dispersed lineages of northwestern Fujian were contractual lineages. The development of this sort of lineage organization usually began in a single county and then expanded to include several counties, prefectures, and even provinces. Most residentially dispersed lineage organizations at the county level or above were connected with examination taking and the political activities of the gentry.

I believe that this process of development of lineage organization in northwestern Fujian was natural in a context in which the scale of residentially concentrated lineages was small and the social environment relatively stable, and so the process basically reflected trends internal to the lineage. In other mountainous regions of the south where a similar social ecology obtained, such as southern Anhui, eastern Zhejiang, eastern and northern Guangdong, and the mountainous regions of Hunan and Jiangxi, the development of lineage organization was probably similar.

The Development of Lineage Organization in Eastern and Southern Coastal Fujian

Eastern and southern coastal Fujian consists of the lower reaches of the Min River and the drainage systems of the Jinjiang, Jiulongjiang, Mulan, and Huotong Rivers. In the Ming and Qing period this area was divided into four prefectures, Fuzhou, Quanzhou, Zhangzhou, and Xinghua, and two departments, Funing and Yongchun. The region includes the alluvial plains at the mouths of Fujian's four major rivers, which contain dense population and residentially concentrated lineages on a relatively large scale, conditions that were conducive to the emergence of large, powerful lineages. In the late Ming and early Qing, this region was shaken by Japanese pirate *(wokou)* attacks and coastal evacuation, which deeply affected the normal pattern of development of lineage organization and gave rise to a number of variant forms.

Late Qing gazetteers of Minxian and Houguan Counties provide a relatively detailed record of the population and lineage structure of these two counties and illustrate the general situation of residentially concentrated lineages on the plains of coastal Fujian. Aside from a small number of villages whose development was relatively late, the villages of these two counties were mostly either single surname villages or villages in which a small number of surnames predominated. There were very few villages in which people of many different surnames lived interspersed together. The Houguan gazetteer describes the population distribution with respect to surname for over five hundred villages. These are classified by type in Table 4.3.[65]

The table indicates that among the 649 villages of Houguan County in the late Qing, about 30 percent were single surname villages; 28 percent were villages where one or two surnames predominated; and 21 percent were multiple surname villages. If the 138 villages for which the surname structure is unclear are removed from the calculations, single surname and predominant surname villages account for 74 percent of the total, and multiple surname villages only 26 percent. Single surname and predominant surname villages tended to have been settled for longer than multiple surname villages, so their populations tended to be larger. In other words, in late Qing Houguan the vast majority of the population lived in single surname and predominant surname villages. Residentially concentrated lineages were extremely common.

The gazetteer of Minxian County provides details on the first migrant ancestor and date of settlement of the major lineages of the county. The relevant details of the first fifteen surnames that appear in the gazetteer have been arranged in Table 4.4. Generally speaking, each founding ancestor represents a single residentially concentrated lineage, which is why more than one founding ancestor is listed for most large surnames. There are nine ancestors listed for the Lin sur-

Table 4.3. Village Surname Structure in Houguan County

District	Total Number of Villages	Single-Surname Villages (no.)	(%)	Predominant-Surname Villages (no.)	(%)	Multiple-Surname Villages (no.)	(%)	Surname Structure Unclear (no.)	(%)
Ganzhe	19	11	58	3	16	4	21	1	5
Zhuqi	21	2	10	2	10	15	71	2	10
Baisha	28	8	29	4	14	11	39	5	18
Guanyuan	52	17	33	18	35	3	6	14	27
Damu	14	7	50	0	0	4	28	3	22
Muyuan	45	26	58	5	12	13	29	1	2
Wenshan	17	6	35	5	29	4	24	2	12
Hongtang	18	7	39	3	17	5	28	3	16
Duxun	22	5	23	9	41	5	23	3	13
Xiyuan	36	8	22	0	0	8	22	20	55
Pudong Xi	22	3	13	9	41	5	23	5	23
Fenggang	40	14	35	20	50	3	8	3	8
Nanyu	31	15	48	8	26	5	16	3	10
Xianban	22	10	45	6	27	4	18	2	9
Shangdu	17	4	24	3	18	7	41	3	18
Dahu	63	12	19	9	13	0	0	42	67
Xiyuan	34	5	13	18	53	9	26	2	6
Fulin	29	5	17	16	55	8	28	0	0
Dabeiling	49	12	25	18	37	8	16	11	22
Xiaobeiling	48	15	31	20	42	2	4	11	26
Xihu	22	2	9	6	17	12	55	2	9
Totals	649	194	30	182	28	135	21	138	21

Source: *Houguan xian xiangtuzhi*, 1903.

name, eight for the Chen surname, and so on. The table indicates that of seventy-one founding ancestors belonging to the fifteen largest surnames, 56 percent had settled prior to the Song; 17 percent in the Song and Yuan, and only 25 percent in the Ming and Qing. Under the next fifteen surnames in the gazetteer are listed twenty-five founding ancestors, of whom 60 percent had settled prior to the Ming, and 40 percent in the Ming and Qing.

In the late Qing, the largest residentially concentrated lineages in different parts of Minxian County could number several hundred or even several thousand households, frequently extending over several villages or even several dozen villages. In the Baihu area:

Table 4.4. Founding Ancestors of the Major Surnames of Min County

Time of Settlement:	Han	Three Kingdoms	E. Jin	Southern Dynasties	Tang	Five Dynasties	Song	Yuan	Ming	Qing	Totals
Ancestors											
Lin			2		1	1	2		1	2	9
Chen			1		1	4			1	1	8
Huang			1		1			1			3
Zheng		1		1				1	2	2	7
Zhan	1				1	3		1			6
Qiu				1						1	2
Hu		1	2								3
He	1						2			1	4
Wang			2			1			3		6
Liu			2			3					5
Zhang	1					1	1				3
Li	1				1				2		4
Zhao	1						2				3
Yang			1		1		1	1			4
Wu				1			1		1	1	4
Totals	5	2	11	3	6	13	9	4	10	8	71

Source: *Minxian xiangtuzhi*, 1906.

As for the population of the lineages in each village, the Huang, Zheng, Lin, and Chen are the largest surnames. Among the Huang surname, the single lineage of the Huang of Yixu has more than two thousand households. There are two thousand households in Yixu, and Shangbaodun and Bantian have three hundred households each; Xingdun and Chidong have one hundred households each. All of these have the Huang surname and belong to the same lineage as Yixu. Lianban and Shaoqi also have over two hundred households each, also of the Huang surname. Among the Zheng surname, in Huangshan, aside from a few dozen households of the Liu surname, there are about five hundred households. There are three hundred households in Luxia; three hundred in Yangxia, and over one hundred in Chengshan. In Yutou and Yexia, [the Zheng] live interspersed with the Lin and Xu, and in each number several dozen households. Among the Lin surname, the Chengmen lineage is the largest, with eight or nine hundred households. The more than one hundred households in Aoli, and the several dozen in Shanjiaocheng, are all of the same lineage as Chengmen. Next there is the Lin of Linpu, with seven or eight hundred households.[66]

In Minxian County in the late Qing, residentially concentrated lineages numbering over one thousand households were common, and the gazetteer even describes those with only several hundred as interspersed *(zaju)* with other surnames or scattered *(sanchu)*. The scale of residentially concentrated lineages in the Fuzhou area would have been inconceivable in the mountainous regions of northwestern Fujian but was very common in the coastal plains regions. The relatively greater scale of residentially concentrated lineages in the coastal regions of Fujian was not simply a function of the more favorable natural ecology but was also closely tied to the high level of development of the commercial economy. In the villages of the Fuzhou region in the late Qing, a significant proportion of the residents made their living not from traditional agriculture but from commerce, industry, and commercial agriculture. For example, in the Waiqili district of Minxian County: "The villagers mostly work at ceramics and stonecutting. The three hundred families of Tangyu village are all stoneworkers; the six hundred families of Huangshi village all work making porcelain. They mainly produce the Dengxincao brand."[67]

In Shati in Houguan County, "there are over a thousand households of the Zhao surname, which work in agriculture, weaving and commerce." In Zemiao, "there are over a thousand households of the Zhang surname, which work in agriculture and commerce. The village produces mainly oranges." In Chencuo, "the residents are surnamed Chen and number more than nine hundred households, which work at the four occupations. The local products are oranges and plums." In Dawenshan, "there are about six or seven hundred households, all of the Chen surname. There is little land for fields, so they all make earthenware. There are about eighteen earthenware kilns." In Ganzhe, "the local residents number over three thousand households, with the Cheng the largest surname, and there are also Zhang, Zou, Lin, and Zheng. Some are scholars, some work in the fields, some pull carts and work as merchants. . . . On Xiazhou island, mostly olives, mulberry, and sugarcane are grown. This can certainly be said to be a prosperous place."[68] This sort of multifaceted economic structure not only provided ample material basis for residentially concentrated lineages but also had a powerful influence on the pattern of development of lineage organization.

Many large and powerful lineages were found in the coastal regions of Fujian even prior to the mid-Ming. As early as the northern Song, Cai Xiang wrote: "The people of the prefectures of Quanzhou, Zhangzhou and Putian must pay a head tax in copper every year . . . [the poor cannot afford it] so the powerful descent-lines and prominent lineages exert themselves to take over [their land], and the dissipate or lazy peasants are forced into vagrancy."[69]

Large and powerful lineages clearly already dominated the socio-economic structure of coastal Fujian at that time. But the documentary record suggests that, in the Song, lineage organizations throughout Fujian were mostly oriented around specific local temples and monasteries, and were associated with the special political rights of prominent scholars or senior officials. Their social character was complex, and it would require a separate work to do justice to the subject. But after the southern Song, lineage organizations throughout Fujian gradually split away from temple and monastic systems and began to develop independently. By the Yuan and Ming periods, residentially concentrated lineages in coastal regions were building ancestral halls, establishing lineage property, and compiling genealogies, and successively forming control-subordination lineages led by the gentry stratum. During the Ming and Qing, *wokou* piracy and the coastal evacuation caused most coastal lineage organizations to undergo a process of disintegration and subsequent reconstruction. After the mid-Qing, residentially concentrated lineages on the coast recovered and developed further, and different types of residentially dispersed lineages gradually formed. This section analyzes the characteristics of the different stages in the development of lineage organization in the coastal region.

*   *   *

The spread of control-subordination lineages in the coastal regions prior to the mid-Ming was mainly expressed in the proliferation of offering halls or ancestral halls *(citang)*. Lineage ancestral halls in Fujian often originated in ancestral residences *(zucuo)*, which were later rebuilt and converted to dedicated shrines *(zhuanci)* for ancestral sacrifice. In the genealogies, the ancestral home left behind by an ancestor is often simply described as an offering hall, making it easy to make the mistake of thinking that ancestral halls were established much earlier than was in fact the case. The use of the term "ancestral hall" to mean a structure specifically dedicated to ancestral sacrifice was an innovation of Zhu Xi in the southern Song. Prior to this, "offering hall" usually referred to a spirit shrine—that is, a place where the gods or spirits received sacrifice. But the offering hall advocated by Zhu Xi was simply a chamber attached to a private residence, in which only the most recent four generations of ancestors, from father to great-great-grandfather, received sacrifice. Thus the meaning of the term was similar to the later terms "private dwelling" *(sishi)* or "common hall" *(gongting)*. It did not describe a freestanding dedicated shrine independent of a residence.[70]

Distinguishing between these terms is essential to understanding the development of lineage organization. The ancestral home, private dwelling, common hall, and the offering hall advocated by Zhu Xi were all confined within a residence and were not easily adapted to sacrificial activities on a large scale. In contrast, the dedicated shrine that emerged after the Song was a sacrificial structure independent of any residence, and hence the size of the structure did not necessarily limit the scale of sacrificial activities, which could thus be endlessly expanded. In the process of development of a residentially concentrated lineage, the construction of a dedicated shrine is a crucial marker of the formation of a control-subordination lineage. In the coastal regions of Fujian, dedicated shrines independent of a residence appeared by the Song and Yuan at the latest. This is clear from an inscription composed by Huang Zhongyuan, probably from the late thirteenth century:

This hall is called a shrine *(ci)*; it is the family temple *(jiamiao)* of antiquity. It is also known as an image hall *(yingtang)*. It is the place where the Dongli lineage of the Huang surname sacrifice to the ancestors in spring and autumn, and pay their respects to one another at the seasonal festivals. Why is the hall named Respectful Intention *(Sijing)*? The intention of sacrifice is chiefly to express respect. Why is there this hall? The hall is the former public hall in the residence of our lineage uncle Tongshou, whose taboo name was Shi. I, Zhongyuan, and my younger brothers Zhonggu, Rixin, Zhigong, and our nephews Xianzu and Yuqian inherited it, and not wishing to divide it into private property, desired to convert it into a hall, to sacrifice to all the ancestors descended from the ancestor from whom our lineage began, Censor Tao, and also all the ancestors who have inherited the greater and lesser descent-lines and branches of Case Reviewer She, with their connections up, down, and across [the descent-lines] clear, [their tablets] arranged in *zhaomu* generational order, thirteen generations in all. It is said that all the things born under Heaven share one origin. Sons have grandsons; grandsons have sons of their own. Because kin are treated as kin, the ancestors are venerated. Because the ancestors are venerated, the descent-line is respected. Because the descent-line is respected, the lineage is gathered. Without an ancestral hall, how could the genealogical lines be determined, the agnates linked, the cultural tradition passed on, and the collective maintenance of the system of ritual be ensured forever? . . . It has been said that funds for the renewal of this hall came from saving up the income of the sacrificial fields for the four annual sacrifices and clarifying the ownership of hill and forest lands. Some of the brothers and nephews of the lineage also gave money to assist, and though the amounts were small, they have still been carved on a stone record, so they are not recorded here. Should the walls and rooms later require repair, or the implements require protecting, the illustrious or good-spirited members of our descent line [must] repair or protect them, restoring [the hall] to its present condition, so that it does not decay. If [their names] are already recorded, they need not be recorded again.[71]

Huang's inscription shows that the Hall of Respectful Intention was originally the residence of an ancestor that came to be used for sacrifice to thirteen generations of ancestors beginning with the founding ancestor.[72] Its expenses were met largely by income from lineage property. Because the Hall of Respectful Intentions was a lineage shrine founded by a small number of gentry and used for sacrifices to all generations of ancestors beginning with the founding ancestor, it can be deduced that a control-subordination lineage led by members of the gentry and encompassing the full membership of the lineage was formed when the hall was built. A mid-fifteenth century account shows that this hall continued to serve as a center for the Huang lineage members living in that locality at that time. "The lineage members and descendants of the surname gather annually to pay their respects, sacrifice, and enjoy [a feast]. [Their sentiments] grow stronger with the passage of time."[73] Thus this control-subordination lineage enjoyed very stable development.

At around the same time the Huang constructed their hall, another large established lineage of Putian, the Jiumu Lin, also constructed a hall and established sacrificial fields. But this hall was said to be "poor and small in scale, insufficient for intercourse with the spirits." So in the early Ming, "on the site of the ancestral residence a chamber with three compartments was constructed, protected by an outer gate."[74] Obviously the Lin ancestral hall was also converted from an ancestor's former residence.

From the Southern Song to the early Ming the construction of ancestral halls had not yet become widespread, nor was there a single accepted standard of construction. The gentry stratum of the early Ming had considerable doubts about the construction of halls, and for a long time there was an ongoing debate over whether or not they were appropriate (see Chapter 5, part 1). Gentry attempted both to provide theoretical justifications for the halls and to expand their scale even further. As a result, dedicated halls in which distant ancestors received sacrifice became increasingly standardized. In the mid-fifteenth century, the Putian gentryman Weng Shizi wrote in his "Memorial Inscription on the Descent-line Shrine of the Zhou Surname of Qingjiang":

> The Zhou are a prominent surname in our town of Qingjiang. . . . Their family records for the time before the Song dynasty moved south have already been destroyed. There is nothing to rely on [to recover them]. They live in Qingjiang and are considered the indigenous residents. Thus the term Zhou Family Lane *(Zhoujia xiang)* has been around for a long time already. . . .
>
> Annual ancestral sacrifices are conducted regularly in the main chamber [of the home]. Some have offering halls, which only extend to four generations of ancestors. At present, the real descent-line heir and descent-line grandson desire to use sacrifice to promote harmony among the members of the descent-line, to lead their kin so as to ensure that the worship of their ancestors is maintained forever. So this hall for [sacrifice to] distant ancestors *(tiao)* has been built. Although this is not entirely in accord with the classical rites *(Li),* their intention

to requite their ancestors and treat their kin as kin is not unworthy of being recorded. I am a maternal relation of the Zhou, so they have asked me to write this epigraphic record. *Note:* the [earliest] ancestor which the Zhou know about was Gentleman Shiqi (Seventeen). His line was transmitted to Gentleman Yijiao. Their portraits are still extant. The clothing and hats are in the Song style. Yijiao's sons were Gentleman Sansan (Three-three) and Gentleman Sansi (Three-four). Gentleman Sansan lived in the main chamber; Gentleman Sansi lived in the rear hall.[75] In front of the hall of the main chamber was a corridor that was used to distinguish venerated from base and young from old. Other residences did not have this, so [the residence] was given the name Upper Corridor. . . . According to the genealogical records, Gentleman Mengren was the direct descent-line [heir] of the Zhou. Mengren's wealth and property were considerable. He left around 300 *mu* of sacrificial fields. His grandsons and great-grandsons saved up the surplus left over after the sacrifices and cleaning of the grave and the payment of the household tax in order to construct this hall for distant ancestors. Construction began in 1467 and was completed in 1481. In the center was built a hall. In the north of the hall five niches were arrayed. In the middle niche an ancestral tablet for the sacrifice to the ancestors from Gentleman Shiqi down to Mengren was installed. Those lineage members who have no descendants or no private dwelling to which they can return also receive supplementary sacrifice there. Every year at New Year's, there is a sacrifice for which the whole lineage gathers.

In each of the other four niches is installed an ancestral tablet for the sacrifice to the ancestors of each of the four branches descended from Gentleman Mengren. The names of all the deceased descendants of the branch are written [on the tablet]. At the customary festivals when seasonal offerings are made, these receive [sacrifice] first. Because this temple to distant ancestors is the [source] from which all the descendants of Mengren originate, extending upward as far as the beginnings of the descent-line is to requite one's origins, and extending downward clarifying all the divisions of the line is to treat kin as kin. Requiting one's origins is to consider that there is no one in the whole lineage who should not be treated with the appropriate sentiment. This is to have unity in [the practice of] benevolence. Treating one's kin as kin does not mean that all kin are treated equally. This is to have discernment [in the practice of] righteousness. To extend benevolence and to establish righteousness, is this something that what are now called hereditary lineages *(shizu)* can also accomplish? . . .

In the center of the ancestral hall [the sacrificial objects] are arranged. To the south are two sets of steps surmounted by doors. When there is no [ritual], they are opened and closed according to schedule. When there is a ceremony, whether they are closed or opened is strictly [regulated]. At the bottom of the steps is another hall where the descendants perform the rituals. Because the descendants are nu-

merous, and their status and order should not be muddled, outside the
rooms there is an open-air stage to accommodate them all. To the east
and west of the hall are two side rooms. The room in the east is called
Reflecting on Success, which is where the sacrificial items are prepared.
The one in the west is called Comfort of High Office, which is where
the feast is held. When there is a feast, the men eat in the Reflecting on
Success room, and the women in the Comfort of High Office room.
Outside each room there are two more chambers, which is where the
cooking, slaughtering, and cleaning is done. South of these two chambers are two long corridors. The east is called East Promenade. The
west is called West Promenade. Outside . . . is a large gate that serves
as the gate to this hall. There is a placard reading "Cassia Garden" . . .
I admire this, and desire to relate it to my sons and grandsons.[76]

The inscription reveals that the Zhou originally sacrificed to their
collective ancestors in "the main chamber [of the home]." Some
branches had "offering halls, which only extend to four generations
of ancestors." This shows that there was already some clear differentiation within the lineage. The branch descended from Mengren,
representing the main descent-line of the Zhou, used the income
from sacrificial fields to construct a descent-line "hall for distant
ancestors" in order "to promote harmony among the members of the
descent line." This was a structure independent of any residence.
This ancestral hall was used to sacrifice to the collective ancestors
prior to and including Mengren, and also to "the ancestors of the
four branches descended from Gentleman Mengren." In other words,
it could be used for sacrificial activities of groups organized at a
number of different levels. Additional facilities such as a meeting
hall, kitchen, and banquet room made it a comprehensive facility for
lineage activities. Although Weng Shizi recognized that "this is not
entirely in accord with the classical rites," he still heartily approved
of "their intention to requite their ancestors and treat their kin as
kin." He described in detail the structure of the ancestral hall, claim-
ing this was in order "to relate it to my sons and grandsons" and
even asked, "is this something that what are now called hereditary
lineages can also accomplish?" In the conflict between ritual theory
and practice, the literati ultimately submitted to the latter.

   In the hope of legitimating the construction of dedicated shrines,
some members of the gentry went so far as to manipulate the terminology of the imperial ritual system, describing such shrines as a
form of the legitimate family temple (jiamiao). For example:

   Our dynasty referred to the [practices of] antiquity in deciding the
   [ritual] regulations, following the Yili [Book of ceremonial], but

authorizing [the proposals of] the Cheng brothers and Zhu Xi to replace the [family] temple with the [ancestral] hall, according to which those who now hold official position [may worship] four [generations of ancestors], and scholars two [generations]. According to the regulations, in the center should be the hall, outside the hall a gate house, on either side staircases, and an encircling wall surrounding. There should be a storeroom for inherited books and sacrificial utensils, and a place for slaughtering the sacrificial animals, separated by an external door. There is also to be an outer door to close it off. These [regulations] are so strict and careful. How could one even discuss ritual with those who would [consider them so presumptuous as to be] comparable to someone without his own state taking on the practices of feudal princes, or someone without his own district taking on the practices of Grand Masters?[77]

In fact, the Ming temple regulations did not allow even serving officials to sacrifice to more than four generations of ancestors. These regulations were thus in accord with the ancestral hall system established by Zhu Xi. But the popular dedicated shrines in which distant ancestors received sacrifice were a different matter altogether. In the late Ming, the Tong'an gentryman Lin Xiyuan wrote detailed regulations for an ancestral hall for sacrifices to founding ancestors in his "Family Injunctions," but he also pointed out that, "although this is not the old [system] of Zhu Xi, it does arise out of righteousness."[78] This shows that in implementing the "veneration of the descent-line and the gathering of the lineage," Ming gentry had already developed theories of the descent-line system that went beyond those of the Song Neo-Confucians (for details see Chapter 5, part 1).

* * *

Because the social environment of coastal Fujian was relatively stable in the early Ming, residentially concentrated lineages underwent rapid development. As lineage populations grew ever greater, the scale of ancestral sacrifice grew ever larger, and the construction of ancestral halls became ever more common. For example, the West Village branch of the Baitang Li of Putian built and rebuilt their ancestral hall three times from the Zhengtong to the Chenghua reign periods, about once every ten years. According to their records:

In the Yongle period, the main hall of the Assistant Director's old residence burned down. So the descendants sacrificed to their own ancestors in their homes, each according to the generational limits of the lesser descent-line. The sacrifice by the whole [lineage] to Zhigan and the early ancestors was simply done each year in a temporarily borrowed location. In 1437, the lineage head was fourth-generation ancestor Dewen of West Village, who constructed an ancestral hall on the site of the main hall of the old residence. It was 3.6 *zhang* long and over 4 *zhang* deep. In the center was installed a large niche where the spirit tablets of the ancestors of distant generations received sacrifice together. As for the system of rituals, it was not comprehensive or complete. In 1464, subsequent lineage head Dehuai also built a front chamber, in which feasts could be held after the sacrifice to the ancestors. In the middle was a main gate; outside a corridor encircled it; the access route was paved with stones; there was a stairway to enter the hall. The collective sacrifice continued as before. In 1466, late lineage head Mengyin, who was virtuous and esteemed the rites, eliminated the central niche in the name of righteousness and had an altar built of stone. It was 1.2 *zhang* long and one-third as deep, and divided into five niches. In the center Zhigan, the Assistant Director, and the other ancestors received sacrifice. To the left, Yizhai and his father, who had donated land and earned merit, received sacrifice. Because they were old and had no posterity, they received dedicated sacrifice. To the right, and to the extreme left and right, were the ancestral tablets of the descendants of Wensen and his two brothers. For each brother there was a niche. Though they are more than four generations distant, they contributed to the renewal of flourishing of this family, so they receive sacrifice through the generations. The sacrifice to the most recent four generations of ancestors is still done in private residences, and their [tablets] are not entered in the ancestral hall. The old regulations are followed with respect to the sacrificial items. The descendants of the three branches each year collect the annual income from the sacrificial estate to provide them. As for the graves, there are sacrificial fields to pay for the sacrifice and the feast at the grave on the taboo dates of the ancestors, and at the Winter Solstice, New Year's, and other customary festivals. In addition, the ancestors should be greeted every month on the first and the fifteenth.[79]

These three episodes in the history of the Li's ancestral hall demonstrate not only the expansion of the hall but also its increasingly strict regulation. "More than ten generations of ancestors" are said to have been worshipped in the hall, so it was clearly being used for the sacrificial activities of a control-subordination lineage. "Sacrifices to the most recent four generations of ancestors" in "private residences," in contrast, refer to the sacrificial activities of inheritance lineage organizations.

Not long after this, the Li of West Village together with the Li of East Village constructed an East Village Hall, whereupon a unified lineage organization including all the Li of Baitang was formed. According to a Jiajing era record by a lineage member:

> The East Village hall is the former residence of our ancestor Yuxuan. . . . Yuxuan's line was transmitted through four generations to Zhigan,

so the house was [part of] the inheritance of his eldest son, the Director. He demolished the chamber to construct the ancestral hall. He built another house in West Village for his second son, the Assistant Director. Mengxian, the ninth-generation descendant of the Director, sold the house to the He [surname]. As a result the ancestral hall became fouled and indecent. The person responsible for the hall was brought to the attention of the authorities. The gate was moved, and this ancestral hall was first dedicated to ancestral sacrifice. In 1505, the roof collapsed and [the wall] leaned. At that time, Prefectural Assistant of Yanzhou Guyu; Clerk of Yong'an Leyuan; Office Attendant of Guangdong Zhongzhou; and my father, Sheng'an, promoted to the title Military Erudite, led the lineage members to reconstruct it. . . . In the middle of the spirit board images of the King of Jiang and Consort Xiao were painted, and [the ancestors from] Yuxuan down to the three sons of Zhigan were arranged in order, males on the left and females on the right. In front of the spirit board were set five wooden ancestral tablets, on which were written in black the lines of descent and names. They were divided among the branches. Though the wooden tablets are numerous and some are already worm-eaten and cannot be fully read, they are all ancestors of one generation or another.[80]

This ancestral hall became a facility for collective ancestral sacrifice by the whole of the Li lineage of Baitang. Thus, "for the annual sacrifice by the descendants, the East Village [Hall] is used for the greater descent-line *(dazong)* and the West Village [Hall] for the lesser descent-line *(xiaozong)*. All others are sacrificed to individually in the chamber [within the residence]."[81]

Some members of the Li also constructed private shrines *(sici)*. In 1526, the Putian literatus Lin Jun wrote:

Earl Li Ting'an . . . built a new dwelling, first making an offering hall in four chambers, to sacrifice to his great-grandfather Qiyang County Magistrate Long, his grandfather Yangtang, who did not serve in office, and his father, Director of the Board of Revenue Ti, who was awarded the title of Gentleman for Fostering Virtue, each of them being placed in order in the hall. The left chamber remained vacant to serve as the place for his own sacrifice [after his death]. . . . When the hall was completed, his two sons Cai and Zhi requested a record. His great-grandson Jiufeng, who is my son-in-law, explained [the circumstances], so I wrote this record.[82]

Such a private ancestral hall, constructed specifically for ancestral sacrifice, was quite uncommon before the mid-Ming, and probably few gentry built one. So Lin Jun compared it to a family temple and offered a special explanation for it: "The Earl was further promoted to Grand Master *(dafu)*. In accordance with the [ancient rules of] ritual, he could erect temples to three generations of ancestors. His method was to use the same hall divided into different chambers, which does not transgress the current regulations, and thus it can be called appropriate."[83] This permanent ancestral hall was in fact quite different from an official family temple, which could be constructed only when one held office and had to be destroyed on leaving office.

In the early Ming, ancestral halls in coastal Fujian were constructed mostly by the gentry, perhaps because of their special rights to construct shrines. By constructing ancestral halls, individual gentry strengthened their control over other members of residentially concentrated lineages, which in turn encouraged the development of control-subordination lineages. For example, in the early Jiajing period, the Lin surname of Kuilin ward in Putian constructed a Hall of Beginning Predecessors (Kaixian ci). Lineage member Lin Jun then drew up a set of "Lineage Regulations for the Lin Surname" which were written in the hall and read annually at the ancestral sacrifice, "in order to commend them and bestow them on the lineage members." They read, in part:

> Among all the descendants of the Lin, fathers should be loving and sons filial; elder brothers friendly and younger brothers respectful; husbands upright and wives obedient. The distinctions between affines and agnates must be maintained; the status of elder and younger should be in order. Ritual, righteousness, modesty, and shame should all be cultivated simultaneously. Scholars, farmers, artisans, and merchants should all keep to their own occupations. Spirits should be upright; hearts good; affairs conducted fairly; expenditures frugal; study serious; behavior proper; speech careful. In serving one's superiors, one should be loyal and respectful; in serving in office one ought to be honest and restrained; while at home one should maintain the peace. Do not have dealings with men who are not good. Do not pursue things which are not righteous. If rich, do not be arrogant. If poor, do not be unrestrained. Do not allow trusting the talk of women to harm family relations; do not let gossip about the mistakes of others encourage a spirit of unkindness. Do not harm men or damage affairs out of jealousy of virtue and ability; do not collude with officials so as to enrich oneself and inspire the hatred of others. Do not act licentiously, steal, conspire, gamble, or bring lawsuits. Do not be proud, ignore warnings, or act carelessly in small matters. Do not ruin your reputation and sacrifice your own principles, harming yourself and bringing shame to the ancestors. Good people should be appreciated, and those troubled by poverty and worries, deaths, funerals, or sickness should be helped and relieved. Those who do evil should be admonished, and if they do not reform, they should be cast out by the group and not allowed to enter the ancestral hall. This is in order to maintain our tradition of cultivation and virtue. Respect! Take heed! Do not ignore![84]

Lin Jun was the most prominent member of the Lin lineage, a senior official who served as the President of the Board of Punishments in the early Jiajing period. His "Lineage Regulations" were not purely educational but also served effectively to strengthen gentry control over the rest of the lineage. His son Lin Da had them carved on a stone inscription after his death, "to be transmitted long and far."[85] Historically, the gentry stratum was very highly developed in coastal Fujian, so this type of control-subordination lineage was also very widespread.

*   *   *

In the mid-Ming, as a consequence of the proliferation of ancestral halls, control-subordination lineages became common throughout coastal Fujian. In large residentially concentrated lineages, the ancestral hall had already come to be seen as an indispensable tool for social control. The "Note on the Decision of the Lineage to Reconstruct the Ancestral Hall" of the Huang of Gongxi in Putian proclaimed:

> How would not rebuilding the ancestral hall harm the ancestors? But the living uncles and brothers would then have no place to gather in their formal attire at the time of the seasonal festivals. Then when they ran into one another in the lanes and villages, they would simply pass by ill-manneredly without adjusting their clothing, just like strangers. As unworthy descendants got used to this state of affairs, they would get angry and lose control in a conflict over the smallest benefit, leading to unspeakably shameful actions. The cause of all this would lie in the collapse of the ancestral hall. If there were still an ancestral hall, those who belong to the branches of the lineage could periodically assemble in formal attire, [and their conduct] could be investigated. Elders could educate [juniors] and peers mutually admonish one another. As for those whose hearts could not be purified, surely would they not still be afraid of being cursed to their face and looked down on? In this way, they could probably be reformed. This is an obvious consequence of whether or not there is an ancestral hall.[86]

In this example, it would be inaccurate to describe the purpose of constructing an ancestral hall as ancestral sacrifice. Clearly, the ancestral hall was seen here as a means of controlling lineage membership.

Of course, not all ancestral halls were constructed with such an obvious political intention. To build their hall in the Yongle period, the Hong surname of Yingshan in Nan'an County "set aside one plot of riverine land at Xiawei, earning an annual rent of 230 *lao*, which the descendants of the eight branches collected in rotation to pay for the spring and autumn sacrifices."[87] After the Su surname of Taijiang in Longxi built their ancestral home in the Xuande period, "[the income from the] sacrificial fields and the prepared implements were used by the descendants to conduct the sacrifice."[88] These ancestral halls were doubtless used for sacrificial activities by inheritance lineages, and not for the purpose of controlling the lineage members. But as internal differentiation in the lineage membership increased, the political functions of an ancestral hall tended to become stronger, and it tended to become the political instrument of a control-subordination lineage.

*   *   *

In the late Jiajing period in the mid-sixteenth century, coastal Fujian was disrupted for a decade by the activities of the *wokou* pirates, with extremely destructive effects on local society. This led to the appearance of a number of variant forms of lineage organization. In his 1563 "Memorial Requesting the Establishment of County Governance," the Haicheng gentryman Li Ying described the turmoil as follows:

> Zhang Lian and Hong Dizhen led forces in the millions to cause turmoil in Zhejiang and South Zhili. The wealthy region of Jiangnan was upset for six years, because of which state taxes had to be reduced. In recent years, the followers of twenty-four generals and the soldiers of twenty-eight barracks have followed one after the other, filling up the borders between Fujian and Guangdong, with Fujian being poisoned worst of all. In these ten years, one guard garrison *(wei),* two battalion garrisons *(suo),* one prefectural seat, six county seats, and not less than twenty walled forts *(chengbao)* have all fallen. There has been such a slaughter in the towns that for a hundred *li* no hearth smoke can be seen, and the smoke of burning houses endures for a year. Men cry and ghosts weep; the sun and moon are dimmed; even the wild grasses are crying.[89]

According to the calculation of Zhu Weigan in his *Draft History of Fujian,* between 1555 and 1563 one prefectural seat, eleven county seats, four guard garrisons and four battalion garrisons in the coastal regions of Fujian were captured by the pirates, and a further twenty-two provincial, prefectural, or county seats and other local defense centers were besieged.[90] These figures include several places that fell more than once, such as the provincial capital of Fuzhou and Tong'an, which fell four times each; Quanzhou, three times; Funing, Changle, Zhangpu, and Qinyu Fort, twice each. The Ningde county seat fell four times in three years, and the Yongning guard fort twice in one year. These figures illustrate that, as a result of the pirate incursions in the Jiajing period, the coastal regions of Fujian suffered extensive repeated invasion and harassment.

Because the *wokou* were economically motivated pirates, their goals in capturing cities and taking territory were to loot property and kidnap people for ransom. The damage they inflicted on society and the economy was thus particularly severe. In 1562, Censor Lin Run wrote in his "Memorial Requesting Relief for Three Prefectures":

> Up to the present, the period in which the pirate turmoil has affected this area has lasted eight years. Those who have died beneath the knife number two or three out of every ten; those who have been kidnapped for ransom number four or five of every ten; the number of those who have become vagrant and fled to other places is beyond counting. Recently, moreover, serious plague has arisen in every prefecture, and is especially serious in the towns. In a ward with several dozen families, five or six are dead; in a family with several dozen members, seven or eight of every ten are dead, and there are even cases of families being completely exterminated. The sounds of weeping are heard from door to door and the corpses are piled up in the wastes. Even beyond the city walls, for a thousand *li* all is empty. Weeds grow up in the paddy fields and brambles in the marketplaces. Subcantons *(li)* that used to consist of ten wards now have only one or two; wards that used to consist of ten *jia* now have only one or two.[91]

Lin Run was writing about the prefectures of Xinghua, Quanzhou, and Zhangzhou, but the destruction was just as serious in Fuzhou and Funing. In the course of this catastrophic period, the residentially concentrated lineages along the coast came under violent attack. Many lineage organizations virtually disintegrated and were unable to resume normal activities for a long period. In 1585, Shi Lishou of Putian wrote in his "Record of Suffering from the Pirates":

> In 1550, I was responsible for the sacrificial ritual. So many lineage members came to participate in the sacrifice that it was difficult to count them; the descendants young and old numbered over eight hundred in all. Who would have expected that in 1558 the pirates would enter Fujian? At first they attacked Hanjiang. People worried that they were not safe. They observed the smoke from the burning and were warned. In 1559 and 1560, the pirates repeatedly invaded our land, but we could still flee behind the walls of the coastal forts, so for the most part our lives were protected and saved. Then, by 1561, the pirates occupied a stockade on the coast, assembled together, and did not disperse. On November 5, they took the Shenhu police office, capturing

and killing more than half the people. On March 12, 1562, they took
Yongning guard garrison, and only a few remained from our whole
lineage. Everyone cried out beneath the knives and scurried about amid
the swords. Ransoms had to be paid to recover the living; money had
to be paid to recover the corpses of the dead. Bodies and skeletons lay
scattered in the wilds; dwellings were burnt down. Luckily, the site of
the ancestral hall survived, but the images of the four early ancestors
were all broken. Furthermore, pestilence arose at the same time. Those
who had been lucky enough to escape the hands of the fierce brigands
now passed away one after the other morning and night. . . . I was
besieged in Aocheng. Of the ten members of my family only two survived; of my four younger brothers only one survived; of our dozens of
young servants, not a single one remained. In the senior branch there
were only sixty odd people, and in the second branch only fifty odd. . . .
    Now, in 1585, I am sixty-one years of age. Observing how the
population of the lineage is ever increasing, I wish to compile the genealogy, but the research is difficult. Luckily, Shiyu and Guangbiao, great-
great-uncles of the second branch, had a genealogy they had taken to
Quanzhou, which has been brought back and shown to me. This indicates that Heaven does not intend to destroy the transmission of our
lineage. So I have written this record to show to the later generations,
to let them know the reasons for our decline at that time, and also to
show the descendants of later generations the circumstances of our
suffering then.[92]

The Shi genealogy was recompiled less than twenty years after the
period of turmoil, but their ancestral hall was not reconstructed and
lineage sacrificial activities revived until the Chongzhen period of the
late Ming, some eighty years later.

    There are many similar records in the genealogies of lineages
throughout the coastal regions. For example, a genealogy from a lineage from Xunxi, in the Quanzhou area, records: "When the pirates
attacked Quanzhou city, it was even more serious in Xun[xi]. [Our
village] was besieged several times, and torched repeatedly. The flourishing lineages were destroyed, and they were cast among the wastes
and grasses. This was the case everywhere."[93] A genealogy jointly
compiled by two lineages in Yongchun County records:

> During the Jiajing period of the Ming, the pirate bandits invaded the
> interior. Our lineages united to defend Yushan fort to the death. We
> fought with the pirates for several days and nights running. Because
> our water supply was cut off, and we did not get relief from outside,
> we were defeated in the end. All the houses of the village were ruth-
> lessly burnt. Only the members of three families, men and women,
> young and old, remained. The disaster we suffered was most pitiful.[94]

Some lineage organizations completely disintegrated because of the flight of large numbers of lineage members. The *Fuzhou Guo Surname Branch Genealogy* records:

> In 1558, the chief pirates attacked the interior. The brothers of my uncle's generation all moved one after the other to the provincial capital. Only Dayou, Lu, and Qian remained to look after the old place. When these three gentlemen died, the houses fell into ruin. They were lent out to other people to live, and the planks, doors, and windows were completely destroyed. . . . So I sighed and said: "If there is not a major change in the situation, there can be no major renewal. The estates of the brothers have all been moved to the provincial capital. The wood from the ancestral home is being stolen by robbers. Conflicts arise frequently, and there is the expense of going back and forth. It would be better to give up the old to start anew." So my younger brother Ruiwu and I decided to sell off the wood and bricks. In all we obtained less than six taels.[95]

The Guo had originally lived in Zelang in Fuqing. When the lineage members fled in succession to Fuzhou city, the original residentially concentrated lineage no longer existed, and so even the old ancestral home was sold off.

The pirate attacks weakened control-subordination lineages all along the coast to varying degrees, and contractual lineages developed accordingly. The "Preface on the Reconstruction of the Family Temple" of the Zhu of Qianjiang, in Xianyou, dated 1573, records:

> In 1322, Wenyi first constructed this shrine in three halls, to serve as the site for the descendants to venerate and requite [the ancestors]. But he worried that without funds to support the sacrifice, the descendants might slide into lack of respect. So he left behind fields, orchards, mountain land, and [land that could be reclaimed from the] sea. . . . In the late Jiajing period of the current dynasty, the barbarians swarmed up, destabilizing Fujian and Guangdong, doing evil in the localities, and treating people's lives like they were no more than weeds. The bodies piled up and the blood flowed. The descent-line and community altars were laid waste. The people were unable to live together and bring order to their locale.
> Only now in 1573 has peace returned. Fathers and sons who were formerly separated live together, flourish, and know the joys of life. Still, after the turmoil and flight, we live in peace but reflect on that dangerous time. We care not for profit, and our striving for righteousness is like a thirst. But if no one takes charge, there is no way to get things started. . . . Therefore it has been decided that for the fund-raising for the meritorious [re]construction [of the ancestral hall], the initial unit [of donation] shall be twenty taels. We do not dare to allow

less than twenty, for less would be insufficient to accomplish the matter.
We do not dare to ask for more than twenty, for more would frighten
men's hearts and would lead to the task being abandoned. In this way,
everyone came to an agreement. The date was February 20. It was also
decided to draw up a register, to record the names and branches of all
those descendants of the four branches who are included among the
donors. This will be used to restrain people's hearts,[96] and will also
have the sense of creating a blood oath between them. Next, the record
can be used as the standard [for collecting funds] and people will
ready the money so that their names are marked off. . . . In this way,
our efforts will harmonize and our hearts link, and we can then accomplish this meritorious matter.[97]

Obviously, in the process of reconstructing their ancestral hall, the
Zhu surname gathered funds through share investment, which led to
the formation of a contractual lineage.

In residentially concentrated lineages with a relatively well-devel-
oped gentry stratum, a prior control-subordination lineage could
usually be maintained, but its social functions were bound to be
affected by the great losses in population and property. In 1565,
Putian Government Student Cai Boshou wrote:

Since coming to Dongsha, [the lineage] has passed through fourteen
generations up to myself. The sacrifice is enjoyed annually and [the lin-
eage] united by the feast. Among the different branches there are not
less than three hundred men. The genealogy has also been repeatedly
compiled; the descendants preserve it like a treasure. In the last seven
or eight years, the pirate barbarians caused turmoil. Of all the disasters
in Fujian, those in Putian were the most serious. Of all the disasters in
Putian, those in our Dongsha were the most serious. It was not just
the lives of the young and the elderly that were troubled, but even
among the adult males more than half died. The dwellings were all
burned down. How could there still be a genealogy? It happened that
there were those who had taken [a copy] to Putian town. In 1562, the
town fell, and it was completely burnt. . . .

   In the winter of 1563, I fled to Xianyou. Xianyou town was also
surrounded by the pirates, and the siege only relieved on the last day
of the year. In the middle of the first month of the spring of 1564, I
first left the city. The annual sacrifice [to the ancestors] in that year had
originally been my responsibility, but in the end the sacrifice was suspended. Over the spring and summer, the pirate turmoil gradually
subsided. In fall and winter, I began to plan a restoration. I suggested
to the lineage head that we repair the front hall of the ancestral hall in
order to place the [tablets] of our ancestors there. The next year we
resumed the annual sacrifices. The young and adults who assembled
for the feast numbered only just over one hundred. The sentiments of

sadness at separation and joy at reuniting were many times deeper [than in previous years]. I asked around about the genealogy, but not one copy survived. . . . I also asked all the younger brothers of the lineage and the branch, and out of the ashes was able to obtain one genealogical chart. On the basis of it, I questioned the old family heads closely and subjected it to a close analysis, in an attempt to recover our origins from the branchings, as one searches for the roots from the leaves. I restored and reconstructed a genealogy in order to link all those who belong to our family within a matter of three or four years.[98]

The Cai of Dongsha were a classic control-subordination lineage. They were said to be the descendants of Cai Xiang, a high official in the Northern Song period. Over the years, the lineage had produced a number of famous scholars and officials, and their lineage organization had been highly organized. In the early Ming, they had rebuilt their ancestral hall twice, compiled their genealogy four times, and repeatedly repaired ancestral graves.[99] Cai Boshou was anxious to rebuild the ancestral hall and recompile the genealogy in order to revive and restore the original hierarchical moral order. But at the time, not everyone in the lineage agreed with Boshou's project. His elder brother Gongyi, returning home from official duties in 1575, wrote in a preface to the genealogy:

> Moreover, my younger brother's concern for the ancestors and the descent-line was not limited to the compilation of the genealogy. The ancestral hall was falling apart, and there was no place for the spirits of the ancestors. My younger brother led the reconstruction. He first accumulated rents [from sacrificial property] and then loaned the money out to earn interest. For a dozen odd years, he was repeatedly wronged and mocked, but he neither regretted nor ceased his efforts. . . . Now the hall has a new appearance for all to see. Although the lineage head was [nominally] in charge, the planning and management should all be credited to my brother.[100]

The recovery and reconstruction of this control-subordination lineage was obviously due not only to Cai Boshou's strenuous efforts, but also to the existence of corporate lineage property.

* * *

As Zhu Weigan has pointed out, the gentry stratum was weak and ineffectual during the pirate turmoil of the Jiajing period. At the first warning of danger they fled, abandoning their native places. But they still suffered more than anyone else during this period. After the fall of the Xinghua prefectural seat, the casualties included over four hundred members of the gentry, including 19 Metropolitan Graduates, 53 Provincial Graduates, and 356 County Students.[101] By the time the situation had returned to normal, the control-subordination lineages which they led had been greatly weakened.

Another consequence of the pirate incursion was that lineage members were encouraged to construct forts for their own defense, thereby strengthening the military functions of residentially concentrated lineages. In the Wanli period, Lin Jiechun, a gentryman from Zhangpu county, wrote in an essay entitled "General Account of Military Defense":

> When the pirates first arrived, they brought with them their fearsome reputation from Zhejiang and South Zhili, and committed poisonous acts of burning and killing at will. At that time, whenever the people heard they were coming, they abandoned their villages and forts. Puwei alone was able to rely on a small fort to resist the rampaging evil enemies. Though the bandits encamped in the surrounding area, and attacked for days on end, they finally departed without having been able to bring it down. . . . After this, people knew that walled forts could be relied on. Every few dozen families gathered to build a fort. You could see from one stone wall to the next. The arrow-holes were lined up one after the other. Every time a warning came, drums and gongs were beaten, and the clamor was unceasing. Even if the brigands numbered in the tens of thousands, and passed repeatedly through the area, they actually did not dare to look up and attack a single fort. This is clear evidence of the effectiveness of local forts.[102]

This kind of defensive fort was not new in the mid-Ming, but previously it had been found mostly in very remote areas, and mostly for the purpose of defense against local bandit gangs. According to a 1517 inscription:

> In the past several decades, rascals hiding in their remote lairs have gathered and made trouble in the villages, turning them into barren wilds and cutting off the hearth fires. In the gloom the ghosts moan, and the authorities are troubled by this. So where the people are gathered densely in places distant from the prefectural and county seats, they petition the authorities [to allow them] to build forts themselves for their own protection.[103]

This suggests that in the early sixteenth century state approval was required for the construction of walled forts, and there cannot have been many of them. Later, as the pirate threat became increasingly serious, walled forts proliferated throughout the coastal region. In his *Record of the Virtues and Deficiencies of all the Prefectures and*

States under Heaven, Gu Yanwu wrote that "Walled forts in Zhang-zhou used to be very uncommon. Since 1561, the people have built walled forts and walled buildings in ever-increasing numbers, especially in the regions along the coast."[104] In Quanzhou Prefecture, privately constructed forts were called *sai.* Gu wrote that

> The southeastern part of Quanzhou prefecture is on the coast, near the island barbarians. In the counties of Jinjiang, Nan'an, Tong'an, and Hui'an, *sai* have been constructed for defense against the pirates. . . . In the Jiajing period, the pirates were everywhere. Where the *sai* were reinforced and the people strengthened, the populace of the villages mostly avoided harm.[105]

Forts also became extremely common in northeastern Fujian:

> In 1555, the pirates entered Fujian from Zhejiang, ravaging throughout the locale. All the places all along the coast and on the bays, such as Shage, Zhuyu, and Nanping in the south; Houshou and Qinghao in the west; Qidu and Sansha in the east; and Zheyang in Xilin in the north, all began to build walled forts. There were at least twenty such places.[106]

In 1559, pirates besieged Zheyang fort but failed to capture it, and walled forts became even more widespread. "Along the coast fifty-seven forts were built in succession."[107]

At the same time as forts were being constructed to defend against the pirates, people began to organize local defensive militia. According to Lin Jiechun, "The strategy for maintaining defense and avoiding capture lies in building forts and training the local militia *(xiang-bing).*" Clearly the two measures were seen as complementary. Local militia relied on the forts for their base. They were armed forces organized by the people of territorial lineages themselves. In Puwei, Yangxia, and elsewhere in Zhangpu County, once forts had been constructed, "next the lineage members gathered to study the arts of fighting. One man taught ten men, and ten taught one hundred. . . . Whenever the bandits arrived, the troops assembled at a single call, waving their banners and distributing their armor, uniting just like the clouds gathering."[108] In Houpu in Tong'an County, local militia had already been trained prior to the construction of forts. In 1560, when there was word of a pirate attack, "within a period of a few weeks, 103 *sai* were constructed, and sixty [militia] groups assembled, protecting the area they oversaw and providing mutual assistance."[109] In some areas, local militia became the main defense force on which state officials relied. The magistrate of Tong'an, Tan Weiding, once personally led local militia forces against pirates who had attacked the county seat, capturing their chief E Shiji and others, and forcing the pirates to lift the siege and disperse.[110] The militia of Gao'an fort in Changtai County numbered over a thousand men, who were not only used for defending the local area but were also repeatedly despatched to Anxi, Longxi, and elsewhere, and won every battle they fought. The Qianlong period *Changtai County Gazetteer* records:

> Once the pirate slaves achieved their objectives in the interior, the authorities gathered visiting troops, who assembled as numerous as ants and ate as ravenously as silkworms. If they saw the bandits they scattered and fled, and furthermore they looted and plundered us. Only the local militia of Gao'an united for self-protection. They did not burden [the state] with demands for rations, and wherever they went they defeated their enemies. Like a high mountain, they served as protector for the whole of Zhangzhou. . . . So they are specially commemorated, to demonstrate that it is better to [rely] on local people than to gather state troops.[111]

The effectiveness of local militia in defense against the pirates should not be underestimated. But it must also be pointed out that the development of this kind of territorial lineage fighting force frequently also led to intervillage or interlineage feuding, intensifying social contradictions within localities. The genealogy of the Su of Haicheng County records:

> In 1561, groups of local lawbreakers took advantage of the turmoil caused by the barbarians to organize into gangs in order to attack the Su's fort. They killed over ninety men, including Yuelun, Yuezhen, and others, then burned their homes, plundered their property, destroyed their descent-line temple, and [took over] cultivation of their fields. Five hundred years [of settlement by the lineage] was transformed in an instant into a wasteland. At the time when the bandits were still flourishing, Shifen brought a lawsuit to avenge his father. But in the end he was charged with inciting turmoil and beaten to death in custody. After that, those who were willing to risk death to get revenge came one after the other, but in the end no one was able to clear up the situation.[112]

The term "local lawbreakers" *(xiang bugui zhitu)* obviously refers to territorial lineage military forces, and the official charge that Su Shifen was responsible for inciting turmoil shows that this incident must have been connected with interlineage feuding. I believe that the interlineage village feuding that was so common in southern coastal Fujian in the Qing can be traced back to the organization of such militia.

In another manifestation of the contradictions within local society, local militia in Nan'an County were used to suppress a peasant uprising. According to the genealogy of the Furong Li of Quannan,

> In 1559, [pirates] entered our Quanzhou region and remained through 1560, 1561, and 1562. The people's homes beyond the city walls became empty wasteland. Pestilence arose repeatedly. Nine in every ten families were exterminated. In Nan'an, Yongchun, and Anxi, construction of forts began. . . . Previously, in 1560, Lü Xiangsi of Yongchun, and Chu Duo and Lin Geng of this county, had also caused disturbances, bringing hoes, shovels, and spears to attack the town. At that time, the governor heard of [Li] Xi's reputation and bestowed on him a red flag to command over eight hundred local militia. These formed into a single unit to assist in the fighting. They captured more than ten members of Chu Duo's gang, and not long after this the chief leaders were also destroyed.[113]

The disturbance led by Lü Xiangsi, also known as Lü Shangsi, was actually an uprising of starving peasants, said to have included in their numbers several Village Heads *(lizheng)*. The suppression of this uprising by the militia led by Li Xi can thus be seen simply as a violent conflict between different territorial lineages *(xiangzu)*.

The territorial lineage militias that had formed throughout Fujian persisted even after the pirate threat subsided, and in some places developed further. The Meiling area of Zhao'an County was said to be an old pirate lair. Once the area was pacified in the late Jiajing period, the remaining armed bands were converted into legal territorial lineage militias. A long-term rivalry developed with the militia of the Yunxiao area. Lin Jiechun's "General Account of Military Defense" records:

> The fierce brigands were based in Meiling. Under the pretext of accepting the amnesty, they enjoyed the favor of investiture with imperial office. They tricked the officials above and gathered their hordes to oppress and threaten the local residents below. They took no notice of southern Zhao'an, running wild in the extreme. But they were always worried that the local militia of Yunxiao would attack them from behind, and repeatedly sent proclamations of war, pretending they were spoiling for a fight. We were unmoved, and they did not dare to cross the boundaries and spy on us. Though their troops repeatedly came onto the roads to steal people's grain and meat and tie up their saddles and stirrups, as soon as they saw someone from Yunxiao, they lowered

their heads and concealed their traces, and did not dare to act in the least way willfully. . . . This is clear evidence of the reliability of local militias.[114]

Such long-term military rivalry promoted the cohesiveness of territorial lineage organizations and encouraged a social atmosphere in which bravery and ferocity were highly esteemed. As a result, feuding in this area was particularly common from the late Ming, and the oppression of weaker lineages by stronger ones particularly severe.[115]

*　　*　　*

Coastal Fujian was relatively stable from the mid-sixteenth to mid-seventeenth century, and lineage organizations revived and developed. But the residentially concentrated lineages of coastal Fujian were soon threatened once again, by the violent turmoil and the coastal evacuation of the early Qing. Yu Biao's *Record of Incidents in Pu[tian]* describes the changing circumstances of lineages during this period:

> Our county is hemmed in by mountains, extensive in the plains, and stretches out into the sea. In the mountains there is one village every several *li* and each village may have only a few families. In the plains the residents live in close proximity, distributed like stars in the sky or pieces on a chessboard. The larger [villages] may have several hundred families, and the smaller ones several hundred people. This is also the case on the coast. . . . One surname may have two or three thousand adult males, and one village one or two thousand people. Since the pirates created disturbance for ten years, there were considerable losses in population. In the roughly one hundred years of peace between 1562 and 1644, the numbers increased. There is no knowing about other [places], but as for Xialin, which is my mother's natal village and so I visited there often, each year as many as several dozen new sons were reported. If one surname was like this, the situation in other surnames can also be imagined. If one village was like this, the situation in other villages can also be imagined. Thus in our locality the population has never increased at the rate it did in the Chongzhen period.
>
> After the change of dynasty . . . as soon as the official troops came out, be it to do battle or to pacify forts, not even a chicken or a dog remained in the villages. It is estimated that more than half the populace died in this period. In the autumn of 1662, the coastal evacuation order was issued. Those who survived on the coast fled and roamed about. All over was heard the mournful call of wild geese. It was impossible to put things in order. Moreover, in 1664 and 1665, there were the disasters of flood and drought, and innumerable service levies were imposed simultaneously. Among the people within the bounda-

ries [of the evacuation], some died fulfilling the service levies, some of hunger, and some from tax pressures. It came to the point where there were lanes with no residents and roads on which no one walked.[116]

This description of the Putian plains broadly holds for the whole of coastal Fujian. The coastal evacuation policy implemented in the early Kangxi period, in particular, led to the total disintegration of many residentially concentrated lineages. The purpose of the coastal evacuation was to facilitate an economic blockade of Zheng Chenggong's anti-Qing strongholds; it was intended to sever links between Zheng's followers and the interior. As early as 1660, a small-scale coastal evacuation was implemented in Tong'an and Haicheng Counties in the Xiamen area. The residents of eighty-eight coastal settlements were forced to evacuate to the interior.[117] In 1661, the populations of coastal Jiangsu, Zhejiang, Fujian, and Guangdong were all ordered to move to the interior.[118] The evacuation was implemented along the entire coast of Fujian in 1662. The evacuation order was partially repealed in 1669 and only fully repealed in 1680.[119] Du Zhen, an official specially despatched in 1683 to handle the consequences of the repeal, reported on the extent of the coastal evacuation and the amount of land that fell out of cultivation in Fujian in precise detail.[120] Du's report is summarized in Table 4.5.

The evacuated settlements are divided into two categories, those "in the sea" *(ruhai),* referring to peninsular and island settlements, and those "by the sea" *(fuhai),* referring to settlements on the mainland. Because the topography of coastal Fujian is so complex, the scale of the coastal evacuation was larger than it might appear. According to documents from the period, the evacuation was imposed thirty *li* from the shoreline.[121] But, as the boundary of the evacuation region was drawn across the map of Fujian, it covered many settlements more than thirty and as far as ninety *li* from the coast. The list of settlements affected is not comprehensive; only the most important ones that fell outside the boundary are included. For example, in Putian County, over seven hundred villages fell outside the boundary as it was defined, but Du Zhen lists only six. Furthermore, according to Zhu Weigan's analysis, Du Zhen's calculations of the amount of land that had fallen out of cultivation were made after the partial repeal of the evacuation in 1669. Land records from individual gazetteers yield a figure of over three million *mu* for the amount of land lost to cultivation after the initial evacuation, much higher than Du's figure of two million.[122]

Table 4.5. Coastal Evacuation of Fujian in the Early Qing

Prefecture and County		Number of settlements outside boundary of evacuation		Cultivated Acreage Affected (qing = 00 mu)
		rubai (in the sea)	fubai (by the sea)	
Zhangzhou	Zhao'an	30	30	409
	Zhangpu	60	74	1,163
	Haicheng		36	784
	Longxi		50	382
Quanzhou	Tong'an		45	1,941
	Nan'an	30	10	372
	Jinjiang	110		1,252
	Hui'an	105		1,909
Xinghua	Xianyou		33	81
	Putian	110	28	4,430
Fuzhou	Fuqing	250	7	4,634
	Changle	75		913
	Minxian		25	389
	Lianjiang	180	20	234
	Luoyuan	110	60	266
Funing	Ningde	210	60	160
	Fu'an	110	30	484
	Funing	220	10	1,797

Source: Du Zhen, *Yue-Min Xun shiji lue.*

The methods used to force the residents of coastal Fujian to evacuate to the interior were extremely brutal: "On the day of the order,
men carried their wives and supported their children, and took to the
roads and exposed places. Fires were set to destroy the houses. . . . It
is estimated that the men despatched by the governor to burn down
homes numbered 1,300."[123] According to the *Record of Incidents in
Pu[tian]*: "Those who did not move within ten days were savaged by
service levy troops. . . . Once [the order] to evacuate was transmitted,
large numbers of people were enlisted to assist the officials in coordinating the evacuation. Residences were destroyed and walls torn
down. Some people were crushed to death."[124]

After the court issued the evacuation order, the governors-general
of the affected regions were ordered to "make immediate arrangements for the migrants, and allocate fields and dwellings to them."[125]
In fact, no such measures were undertaken. Xue Rong of Fuqing wrote
in his "Preface to the Tonglin Genealogy":

> In 1662 the order came to move to the interior, to burn the residences
> on the coast and turn it into wasteland. The people were allowed to
> carry whatever foodstuffs they wished, supporting the men and women
> who were old and the sick. They simply went in one direction until they
> halted. Not only was the situation unlike Gu Rang's proposal, whereby
> an amount equal to several thousand years of water-control expendi-
> tures was given to the migrants to be their estates, it was also unlike
> the time of the initial enfeoffment when the [people of] DongOu and
> MinYue were settled on the lands of Jiang and Huai. They had neither
> lands nor estate to enrich them.[126] Those who did not die scattered
> over the distant and nearby localities, even to other counties and prefec-
> tures, as well as to Hubei, Henan, Jiangsu, and Zhejiang. Some went
> as far as several thousand *li* from their homes.[127]

Under such conditions, no residentially concentrated lineage in the
areas affected by the evacuation could avoid total collapse and dispersal. This is made clear in many genealogies, including the following, from Zhao'an: "In the early Qing, [Zheng Chengkong] used the
sea as his pirate's lair. The dynasty ordered the coastal evacuation to
cut off his connections. The residences of the lineage were all on the
coast, and as a result we became vagrants, fleeing and scattering. The
graves and ancestral tablets were completely lost."[128]

Another genealogy records:

> In 1664, Tong[shan] was subject to the evacuation order. Provincial
> Administration Commissioner Xi Ping led a large body of troops to
> Tongshan to enforce the evacuation. They toppled the walls and burned

the dwellings. The residents all fled. It was miserable beyond words. The ancestral shrine was burned to the ground; the houses were turned into wasteland, and the graves were once again cold and desolate. It is impossible to record fully how many members of the lineage were scattered all over the place.[129]

By the time the coastal evacuation order was finally rescinded, lineage populations had been devastated, and virtually all ancestral halls, ancestral homes, ancestral graves, and genealogies in the affected areas destroyed. The original lineage organizations had disintegrated completely and had to be rebuilt anew.

Reconstruction of residentially concentrated lineages after the coastal evacuation generally followed one of two basic patterns. In the first, a small number of officials or local powerholders rebuilt a control-subordination lineage. In the second, lineage members returning in succession to their native place willingly organized themselves into contractual lineages. The Shi lineage of Yakou in Jinjiang County provides a good example of the first pattern. According to their genealogy, the Shi first settled in Yakou in the early years of the Song, became powerful in the mid-Ming, compiled a genealogy in the Jiajing period, constructed an ancestral hall in the Chongzhen period, and by the end of the Ming had developed into a residentially concentrated lineage of considerable scale.[130] In the early Qing, lineage member Shi Lang became prominent for his contribution to the pacification of Taiwan, but during the coastal evacuation his fellow lineage members were nonetheless made homeless. Early in the evacuation, Shi Lang is said to have taken various steps to comfort his fellow lineage members and limit their losses. "He was concerned about the troubles suffered by the lineage members, so he established fields and residences for them in the interior and gave them draught animals with which to cultivate. He also worried that their old homes had fallen into ruins, so he built an ancestral hall in Qingyang, to unite the members of the lineage."[131] But the majority of lineage members did not actually benefit from his efforts. "They wandered hopeless and miserable, unable even to look after their closest relatives."[132] After the coast was reopened, Shi Lang took great pains to care for the refugees as they returned home. "Several hundred families of the lineage relied on him for their livelihood." He also promoted the recompilation of the lineage genealogy, rebuilt the ancestral hall, restored the ancestral graves, and expanded the amount of lineage property. This enabled the prior control-subordination lineage to revive quickly and develop further. In 1683, Shi Lang wrote in a preface to the new genealogy:

> Since the evacuation in 1661, in the great lineages and powerful descent-lines, countless numbers have sunk under the pressure of the military imprecations and become refugees. At present, although the ridge-poles and beams of the ancestral home have all been destroyed, the site yet survives. The lineage members have been scattered but now gather anew. The scholarly tradition of old has declined and now flourishes anew. . . . Though busy with official duties, I gathered all the lineage elders to reconstruct the shrine, and even went so far as [to recompile] the genealogy.[133]

In 1689 the Shi ancestral hall was completed and the ancestral tablets installed. Again Shi Lang personally wrote an essay in celebration:

> The great ancestral hall was constructed in 1640, and only a little over twenty years later we were troubled by the pirates. In 1661 the villagers along the coast were all evacuated to the interior, and as a result the hall was destroyed. . . . I was busy with affairs on behalf of the state, but worried that the spirits of the ancestors had no fixed abode. In the winter of 1687, this ancestral hall was rebuilt on the ancestral site. It was completed in the following fall. Now, on April 15, 1689, the tablets have been installed in the temple. The mantels and the tables are all new. In this way our intentions will be transmitted to the descendants.[134]

Shi Lang also made numerous efforts to expand lineage property. After his death, his sons went on to establish a charitable school, expand the charitable fields, establish lineage regulations, and recompile the genealogy, thus further strengthening this control-subordination lineage.[135] In 1715, a lineage member wrote in a preface to the genealogy: "now lineage members who have funerals to conduct receive aid, and those who have weddings to hold are provided with funds. The descendants who are poor scholars receive support for their expenses when the provincial examinations are held."[136] All of this was credited to Shi Lang and his sons, and to honor his memory a special particular sacrifice to Shi Lang was held on the anniversary of his birthday.

The development of the residentially concentrated Shi lineage at this time was linked to the special prerogatives they enjoyed from the state. These gave the lineage an obvious capacity to expand and made them a significant threat to other residents of the locality. As early as 1683, Shi Lang sealed off the hills around the lineage's ancestral graves, forbidding "indiscriminate burials" by other local residents.[137] The lineage estate that he established also consisted of many tax collection privileges obtained by virtue of his high position. This is made clear in the "Memorial Inscription on the Rental Incomes from the Sacrificial [Property]" composed by his son Shi Shilun:

> Alas! Our father Imperial Tutor [Shi Lang] received the protection of the ancestral line and was rewarded with the hereditary title of marquis. His respectful restoration of the sacrificial rites and plan to pass this project on to his grandsons, and his establishment of rental properties, the income from which provides for the sacrifice, ensuring that it can be enjoyed without interruption, can be praised as thorough and complete. Although there exists a register in which the amounts of rental income are recorded, with the passage of time this may be lost. Accordingly, the annual amounts to be collected for each of the five sources of income, rent in rice, the grasses tax, the lake tax, the sea tax, and the tax on shops are recorded in detail on the reverse face of this stone, which has been erected in the temple of the great descent line, to be known in the future and transmitted forever.

> The amounts of sacrificial property:

>> The rent on the orchards of Yakou, Xupozhuang, and other villages: 15,054 catties per annum
>> The grasses tax to be paid by Xizhou, Puzhai, and other villages: 143 taels per annum
>> The lake tax to be paid by Wengcuo, Longhu, and other villages: 33.8 taels per annum
>> The sea tax to be paid by Xunmei, Ludong, Putou, and other places: 30 taels per annum
>> The annual rent on shops and residences in Yakou: 24.025 taels.

> Recorded on the day of Grain Rains, in the second month of spring, 1699, by the seventeenth-generation descendant Shilun.[138]

The items in this record were in fact extralegal impositions forcefully extracted from the local population on the basis of special political status. Control over the tax revenues from Longhu lake was restored to the state in 1725, in commemoration of which the local residents erected a "Memorial Inscription on Being Washed in [Official] Bounty":

> Our villages are situated on the shores of Longhu lake. All our fields and properties depend on the lake to prosper. Some take the grasses from the lake to be used as fertilizer; some take the fish of the lake to fill their bellies. This lake is indeed something that we poor villagers of

the lakeshore cannot do without. Formerly, from the Song to the present day, the people of the lakeshore paid an annual lake tax of 4.26 piculs, as recorded in the official tax records. Lately the people of the Shi lineage, relying on their power, force us to let them pay the tax on our behalf and then collect money from us indiscriminately. All those who wish to go down to the lake must, according to their instructions, first request a licence from them, each licence costing 3 mace, in order to be sure of their own safety. If there are foolish or stupid villagers [who don't obtain the licence], the powerful bullies [of the Shi] act like tigers, tie them and beat them, and apply all sorts of tortures. So the local people have no choice but to bow their heads and obey. In all, more than six or seven hundred licences are issued each year, and the total amount of money brought in each year is over 200 taels.... We who are thin, weak, and afraid originally did not dare to report them. It is just that their unrestrained tax collection is without limits. The oil from our lamps is exhausted. Though we are still alive, we are no better than dead. But we hope to escape from death back into life. So we have gathered and agreed [to request] that the tax rice for this lake should be allocated according to the old practice and everyone should pay immediately. In this way, the brutal illegal tax collection can be avoided.

As a result, Magistrate Ye ordered: From now on, once the tax has been paid according to the old practice, you are permitted to go to the lake and collect the plants and animals. The Shi family may not continue to lord over this lake and demand licences and collect tax without restraint. If they dare to violate this, you who have brought this suit are permitted to report it to the county [magistrate], who will definitely strictly investigate and deal with this, and will certainly not be soft on them.[139]

Clearly, the growing power of the Shi aggravated contradictions within local society.

There could have been few lineages as powerful as the Shi. However, the role of the gentry stratum in the process of reconstruction of many residentially concentrated lineages of the coastal region after the repeal of the coastal evacuation order should not be underestimated. The sources suggest that in most cases the establishment of ancestral halls, ancestral estates, and so on was either initiated by the gentry or funded by the personal donations of individual gentry. The lineage organizations that developed on this basis were thus usually control-subordination lineages headed by the gentry stratum. For example, in the Ding lineage of Chenjiang in Jinjiang: "The great descent-line shrine was rebuilt by Wuting. It collapsed in 1685, and the original shape cannot now be discerned. Yanshui donated one hundred taels to encourage the lineage members to reconstruct it, and completed the main chamber."[140] Wuting was one of the names of the Ming gentryman Ding Rijin, a secretary of the Board of Revenue, who in 1600 rebuilt an ancestral hall that had been destroyed by pirates in the Jiajing period, thereby greatly strengthening the Ding lineage organization. His tablet was entered into the ancestral hall, where it received sacrifice from the full membership of the lineage.[141] Yanshui was the Kangxi-period gentry Ding Wei, who held the office of Judicial Commissioner of Huguang. In 1685 he initiated the reconstruction of the main chamber of the ancestral hall, and in 1704 he organized eleven managers *(dongshi),* each of whom donated forty taels, to undertake the complete reconstruction of the hall. The lineage members then "requested that [the tablets of] Yanshui, the eleven managers, and their fathers, grandfathers, and wives [be installed] to receive sacrifice" and "set out tables and sacrificed collectively to them."[142] The identity of these eleven managers is not clear, but they were probably either powerful individuals or members of relatively powerful branches within the lineage. The recipients of sacrifice in the ancestral hall were said to have originally all been members of the local gentry, whose tablets were installed specifically "to encourage the descendants by giving special treatment to the gentry." But in 1704, "Because it proved impossible to collect funds from each individual, the whole lineage discussed and agreed that anyone who paid forty taels in order collectively to accomplish this undertaking could enter [the tablets of] his grandfather, his father, and their wives into the hall, to enjoy sacrifice at spring and autumn.[143]

This challenged but did not completely undermine the special position of the gentry in the Ding lineage. The following year, the branches of the Ding announced, in a "Contract on the Installation of Tablets," that the policy had been "a temporary expedient. After the matter is accomplished, it is not to serve as a permanent rule."[144] Thus, even after the tablets of donors had been installed, the Ding lineage continued to be a control-subordination lineage led by the gentry stratum.

*   *   *

The reconstruction process of other residentially concentrated lineages depended on allocating subscriptions from lineage members, and so these were control-subordination lineages from their inception. For example, in 1688 a member of the Cai surname of Dongsha in Putian County wrote:

> Now we are grateful for the imperial order that we can return to our native place, and are able to avail ourselves of temporary grass shelters. All the members of our lineage rely on the old sites left by the ancestors and reflect that [the spirits of] the ancestors have nowhere to live. Can the descendants face them without feeling afraid? . . . In the spring of 1686 we decided together to build an ancestral hall for sacrifice to Zhonghui, in which all the ancestors of Dongsha can also enjoy the sacrifice. We came together and were able to accomplish this. In the summer of 1687 there was unusual weather, and the hall almost collapsed again. That fall, funds for reconstruction were collected from each individual. The managers of this were grand uncle Dangyin, uncles Shuting and Angsou, and brothers Yiquan and Huishan.[145]

That funds were collected "from each individual" implies a certain control over lineage members. Because there had been degree-holding members of the Cai lineage continuously from the Song to Ming period, the position of control enjoyed by the gentry in the lineage was relatively stable. The revival and reconstruction of the control-subordination lineage therefore proceeded relatively smoothly in this case. In fact, the managers named in the above document were all "surviving elders from the previous dynasty," that is, men who had obtained official titles in the late Ming.[146]

A lineage that was reconstructed entirely through donations by a small number of gentry members was a classic control-subordination lineage. In 1686, Huang Xingzhen, a gentry man of Zhangpu County, used his own personal funds to establish "a fort for security, a family temple, a charitable school, sacrificial fields, educational fields, and charitable fields," all of which he donated to the lineage, thereby forming a functionally comprehensive control-subordination lineage. It is said that in 1559 the Huang had "constructed Meiyue fort, to protect the lineage gathered in the locality, in order to defend the ancestral sacrifice." In 1648, the fort was "destroyed in an incident with the neighbors [i.e., a feud], and the lineage members moved to Huxi." Later, gentry members of the lineage had tried and failed to construct an ancestral hall. Moreover, all of the lineage property had disappeared, so "the talented members of the lineage had nothing with which to pay for their education; the impoverished had nothing from which to obtain relief; the dispersed had nothing to draw them back together, and those who had settled had nothing with which to make themselves secure." Huang Xingzhen's efforts to respond to this situation were thus intended to "make arrangements for the spirits of the ancestors and to fund education and relief," in other words, to give the lineage members a safe haven. A stone inscription he composed records:

> Prior to the construction of the fort, there were only a few dozen households of our lineage living here, and all the remaining land around was misty wasteland over which weeds spread. Now, because of the righteous [objective] of unifying the lineage members, though I had built the fort on my own, I did not dare consider the land as my own property. I accepted the lineage heads' assessment of the price of all the land owned by others and purchased it fairly. After the land had been purchased, I first built an ancestral temple and a charitable school. Because I was worried that there was little to protect them in front and behind and to both sides, I further constructed a hall for the lesser descent-line, residences, and a study. I also built a temple to the Guangping King [Chen Yuanguang], so that the village could perform the annual rituals of prayers for a good harvest. I measured off and handed over the remaining land for the people to build their own dwellings. The six branches and I drew lots to allocate it. Everyone together constructed homes. So as to express my collective sentiment, I did not selfishly take an extra inch. I am concerned that with the passage of the generations the descendants will gradually become distant from one another and may try to purchase the land back or make up the excuse that they wish to redeem the land they have sold. So I have converted all the land that I purchased and divided for the construction of houses into sacrificial land. Each year, a rent of two cash is to be paid on each room. This is to be used in rotation by the branches for the performance of the sacrifice. Once the rotation is complete it starts again at the beginning. This will prevent disputes. I also purchased sacrificial fields on which can be planted twenty piculs, to pay the costs of the sacrificial items; educational fields on which can be planted twenty piculs, to meet the living and educational expenses of students; and charitable land on which can be planted forty piculs, to support those members of the lineage who because of poverty or suffering are unable to perform marriages or funerals. Whether or not [particular individuals] should receive assistance must be evaluated. The wealthy are not to make a claim on these funds. [The lineage] should collectively appoint branch heads and people with a virtuous reputation to manage these affairs in succession. [The managers] must make payments and collect income in a timely manner, so as to prevent embezzlement. In this way, [this system] can be maintained for a long time.[147]

This stone was erected in 1688, when Huang Xingzhen was Administrative Commissioner of Hunan. Two years later, he established more sacrificial land in the name of his father, grandfather, and great-grandfather, and erected a stone inscription which read:

> I reflect on the fact that there are more than a hundred of my close relatives with whom I share a mourning-grade relationship who participate

in this sacrifice together. So I have made a plan that takes into account the filial sentiments of the fathers and brothers within the five mourning grades. I have established sacrificial land in the name of my great-grandfather on which ten piculs is planted; land in the name of my grandfather on which twenty piculs is planted, and land in the name of my father on which forty piculs is planted. These are to be administered in rotation by the relevant branches and sub-branches. The annual income is to be used to pay for the seasonal sacrifices, and to pay the tax and service levy on this land. Any surplus that remains goes to the person in charge of the rotation, to supplement his income and allow him to make a bit of profit.[148]

Here Huang Xingzhen was constructing inheritance lineages restricted to the mourning grades, organized on the principle of the lesser descent-line.

Such a comprehensive and systematic lineage organization must have been very rare in the immediate aftermath of the coastal evacuation, and probably would have been possible only at the hands of a high official like Huang Xingzhen. But the example does illustrate the widespread gentry belief that lineage organization should ideally be organized at both the level of the greater descent-line and the lesser descent-lines, which correspond to the control-subordination lineage and inheritance lineage of our typology. Of course, if it was not possible to organize both, gentry men might treat the establishment of the greater descent-line lineage organization as their first priority, assuming personal responsibility for regulating the whole population of the residentially concentrated lineage.

*   *   *

In residentially concentrated lineages where the gentry stratum was not highly developed, the reconstruction of lineage organization usually depended on share investment, leading to the formation of a contractual lineage. The Zhu of Qianjiang in Xianyou provides an example.

The makers of this contract are Jinkui of the Xiating branch, Feichuan of the Xiaotou branch, and others. The descent-line hall with three chambers, in which the ancestors are worshipped, was built in the Zhizhi period of the Yuan (1321–1323) by Wenyi. He also donated rent-earning lands to pay for the sacrifice and sweeping. In the past the Xiating and Xiaotou branches had no claim on the site of the three chambers of the ancestral hall or the sacrificial property. Because of the coastal evacuation, the hall was destroyed by fire. Now that the borders have been reopened, the lineage unites to restore the hall. We reflect that all share the same origins. So the Xiating branch descended

from Jiheng and the branch descended from Jike ought each to pay an
equal share of the costs [because these are the two main segments of
the lineage], just as the Wenyi and Xiaotou branches should also [pay
the same amount, because they are equivalent segments in the genealogical chart]. But the members of the Xiating and Xiaotou branches
are few in number, weak and insufficiently wealthy. So [a system] of
six branches [has been set up] to collect funds and assist in the construction. [These two weak branches] will each comprise one [branch in
the system]. Yuanhuang and Yuantai are responsible for paying the
money owed by the Xiating branch. They may not transfer this responsibility without notice. In the future, when the whole hall has been restored and its appearance renewed, the right to conduct sacrifice in the
front chamber will be shared evenly by the six branches. The site of the
hall is still owned by the four branches descended from Wenyi, but they
are not permitted to collect rent or to demand a purchase price. . . . In
the lineage village there is also rent-earning property left behind by
Mianzhai and sacrificial property collected from the six branches. This
is also to be managed in rotation by the six branches.[149]

The Zhu ancestral hall was originally owned collectively by the
four branches descended from Wenyi. When it was previously reconstructed in 1573, funds were solicited only from the descendants of
these four branches. But on this later occasion ownership was vested
in six branches. The so-called six branches were actually created in
the process of raising funds for the reconstruction and really refer to
six shares of ownership in the hall. This is evident from the genealogical chart of the Zhu, shown in Figure 4.3. The line of descent divides
after the founding ancestor Mianzhai into two branches, Jiheng, also
known as Xiating, and Jike. The Jike branch is subdivided into the
Wenyi and Xiaotou branches. The Wenyi branch is further subdivided into the senior and second branches, each of which is further
divided into two sub-branches. The contract shows that the four
branches of the Wenyi segment paid for two-thirds of the cost of construction of the hall, while the Xiating branch and the Xiaotou
branch took responsibility for one-sixth each. As a result, shares of
ownership in the hall could not be allocated strictly on the basis of
genealogical structure, which would have assigned half-ownership to
the Xiating branch as one of the two main segments, and one-quarter
ownership to the Xiatou branch as one of the two segments making
up the Jike branch. Instead the four sub-branches descended from
Wenyi were each assigned a share equal to that of the other two contributors, for a total of six shares. The six shares thus represent not
kinship segments but shares of ownership in the hall. The corporate

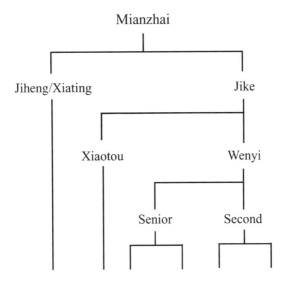

Figure 4.3. Genealogical Chart of the Zhu of Qianjiang

property "left behind by Mianzhai," which is mentioned at the end of the contract, was also taken over by the six shares at this time, and management rights to this property rotated between the branches along with the newly established property. According to the Zhu genealogy, the property "left behind by Mianzhai" had actually been established in 1578, when at the behest of one Ruohui it was agreed that "2.8 taels should be raised by an assessment on adult males. This was used to purchase .7 *mu* of land to secure the geomancy [of the ancestral graves]. The income was collected in annual rotation, and used for the sacrifice and cleaning of Mianzhai's grave."[150] This shows that in the late Ming the Qianjiang Zhu had formed a control-subordination lineage centered around the estate of Mianzhai. But this control-subordination lineage did not survive the coastal evacuation, and its position was taken over by the contractual lineage made up of the six branches.

In the aftermath of the coastal evacuation, the Cai surname lineage of Dongsha in Putian reconstructed a control-subordination lineage headed by gentry members, but by the Yongzheng period (1723–1735) it too had given way to a contractual lineage. A biography in their genealogy describes a dramatic incident connected to this development:

In his life [great-grandfather Zhong] often accomplished things when he was roused to do so. In the Yongzheng period, our lineage had many troubles, such that the sacrificial property was wasted and diminished, and as for the annual sacrifice to the ancestors of the descent-line, even if it was not cut off, it hung on by only a thread. No one who had a heart was not worried. One day [Zhong] said to the lineage members: "Now it is extremely urgent that we recover the sacrificial property. I propose that every household which is willing should contribute one picul of grain.[151] This can be used to recover some of the sacrificial land, and the members of these households may participate in the sacrifice. Those who are unable [to pay] will surely be ashamed that they do not participate in the sacrifice, and will be encouraged to try to do so."

Lineage uncle Yizuo said, "This will be difficult. [The households of the lineage members] are not equally wealthy, nor are they all of equal size. If you are indeed able to persuade fifty households, then I will give you 3,000 cash to participate in the sacrifice. If you are unable to do so, then you must pay me twice this amount." [Zhong] said, "If you really mean this, we should draw up a contract." So lineage uncles Jiansou, Tianren, Xiezhen, and others agreed to serve together as guarantors [for the contract] which was given to great-grandfather, and the outcome awaited. Great-grandfather used his righteousness to move people, and more than sixty names wanted to contribute. Unfortunately, in that year the fall harvest was disappointing, and only 60 percent of them actually paid. [Zhong] spent many days and much energy, but he did not reach his goal. He bravely decided that he would pay on behalf of each of the lineage members, one after the other, allowing them to repay him and clear their debt as they could. . . . After this, the accumulated [funds] were gradually revived, first by a few, then by many, and finally the complete [amount was raised].[152]

The direct result of this affair was that the original control-subordination lineage was replaced by a contractual lineage comprising the sixty-odd households that had contributed. On the surface, the transformation appears to have been the consequence of insufficient sacrificial property. The real underlying cause was the decline of the gentry stratum within the Cai surname. According to the genealogy, members of the Cai began to succeed in the examinations and hold official posts only in the mid-Qianlong period. Prior to this, no member of the Cai was appointed to office under the Qing.[153] In the mid-Kangxi period, there were still many prominent and respected "surviving elders" of the Ming dynasty, and under their leadership it was still possible to reconstruct the ancestral hall by collecting funds from each individual member. But by the late Kangxi period, these elders had all died, and the original control-subordination lineage was disintegrating. In the previous chapter, I argued that the formation and development of control-subordination lineages usually depended on the presence of considerable lineage property and powerful gentry figures. In the period immediately after the restoration of the coastal areas, most lineage property had disappeared, so the gentry served as the chief support for control-subordination lineages. In residentially concentrated lineages that did not have a highly developed gentry stratum, reconstructed lineage organization generally took the form of contractual lineages.

*   *   *

The inheritance lineages of coastal Fujian were also severely damaged by the coastal evacuation. When the evacuation was rescinded, lineage members were scattered, ancestral residences, ancestral graves, and sacrificial fields were lost, and most inheritance lineages had disintegrated. In response, some local gentry and other powerful individuals tried to reconstruct these original inheritance lineages through the repair of ancestral graves, the construction of lesser descent-line ancestral shrines, and the establishment of sacrificial property for ancestors of different generations. The case cited above of the Huang surname of Xihu in Zhangpu is a typical example of one such effort. However, in the chaotic situation in the immediate aftermath of the evacuation, reconstructing inheritance lineages was not seen as the most pressing concern. In most cases, the reconstruction of inheritance lineages in the coastal areas occurred only after the reconstruction of control-subordination and contractual lineages. As a result, through the eighteenth century we find many examples of prior inheritance lineages being revived.

Cai Jingwu, a merchant from Tong'an, traveled widely as a youth. "Starting off owning a single set of clothes, his name came to be known widely at home and abroad." In the early Qianlong period he returned home, "constructed the lesser descent-line hall at Heshan, and established sacrificial property for successive generations.... For the ancestors from Puliang, the first-generation ancestor of the Heshan hall, to Ci, [he established], in all, sacrificial fields for five generations [earning rent] totaling over six hundred piculs. He did not dare to leave more than this amount to his sons."[154]

Wu Luo of the Yanzhi Wu of Quanzhou returned from Taiwan in the early eighteenth century and devoted himself to rebuilding his lineage organization. In 1771, he wrote, in a foreword to the genealogy he personally compiled:

In 1707 I returned from Taiwan. I selected an auspicious time to re-construct the ancestral hall, which occupied the whole of the old site and was on a grand scale. It cost about two thousand taels. I also undertook the repairs of the graves of the generations of ancestors since the founding ancestor. For each of the ancestors of this branch I established sacrificial property, at a cost of another one thousand taels.[155]

When a rich or powerful individual constructed a hall, established sacrificial property, repaired graves, and compiled a genealogy, the original inheritance lineage could be revived and rebuilt. But for most ordinary members of the lineage it would have been difficult, if not impossible, to restore an inheritance lineage to its original form, and the lineage might rather disintegrate completely. This may explain why, according to recent figures, the proportion of lineage corporate land in coastal Fujian was lower than in northwestern Fujian.[156] But because, as we have seen, inheritance lineages form naturally as a result of household division, this type of lineage has strong reproductive potential. As soon as order was restored, new inheritance lineages would reappear. Zhao'an magistrate Chen Shengshao wrote in the nineteenth century:

When an ancestor first divides his estate, a certain area of fields is set aside for the descendants to collect the rent in rotation and to provide for the sacrifice. These are known as fields for the spring and autumn sacrifice *(zhengchang tian)*. Later, when [the descendants] have divided into branches, it may take several years before one gets one's turn in the rotation, sometimes more than a decade and sometimes several decades, before one first gets one's turn. The rental income varies from several hundred or several thousand piculs down to a few dozen piculs. The surplus after the expenses of the sacrifice have been provided is retained to be enjoyed by the rota holder.[157]

The inheritance lineage thus remained the basic form of lineage organization for the people of the coastal regions in the late Qing.

                              *   *   *

After the turn of the eighteenth century, the situation in coastal Fujian gradually stabilized. Residentially concentrated lineages grew ever larger, and each of the different types of lineage organization developed to some degree. From this point on, the trends in the development process basically resembled that of the residentially concentrated lineages of northwestern Fujian, so we need not consider it in detail again.

But the pattern of development of residentially dispersed lineages in coastal Fujian during the Qing remains to be examined. There may have been some residentially dispersed lineages in coastal Fujian as early as the late Ming. In the Chongzhen period, with the shrine of the founding ancestor of Huang Alley *(Huang xiang)* in Putian on the verge of collapse, Huang from all over Putian county "discussed and decided to repair and reconstruct it. All those who come from this hall should be notified."[158] Huang Alley was said to be where the first Huang migrants to Fujian had lived, and by the Ming, their descendants were distributed throughout southern coastal Fujian. If this reconstruction effort had succeeded, it would have meant the formation of a residentially dispersed lineage on a massive scale. But even had this kind of residentially dispersed lineage existed in the late Ming, it could not possibly have survived into the early Qing.

Some residentially dispersed lineages began to revive in the early Qing. For example, according to one genealogy:

> The Longsun branch is made up of the descendants of Yunmao, Duke of the Qingyuan [Quanzhou] Commandery. It is called Longsun to indicate that we belong to the *Long*shan branch, and that we have lived for generations at *Sun*jiang. Thus we do not forget our origins. In our Zeng surname, after Yanshi entered Fujian, his line was transmitted through seven generations to Mu, whose four sons, nine grandsons, and twenty-eight great-grandsons all served in office. In the Song, this flourishing of officeholders was foremost in Fujian. So the lineage multiplied and dispersed throughout Quanzhou, Zhangzhou, Xinghua, and Yongchun. But all were kin sharing the same origin. The division into branches occurred when the ancestral hall repair was completed in the Kangxi period of the Qing. It was decided that for the spring and autumn sacrifices, one branch in rotation should take responsibility for the spring sacrifice and one for the autumn sacrifice. In all, there were forty branches. Lots were chosen in front of the ancestral tablets to determine the order. Once the rotation is complete, it starts again at the beginning. The names of each branch were determined at this time. Probably, the [first ancestor of the] Longsun branch being placed in the sixty-fourth generation also occurred at this time.[159]

In the Kangxi period, people of the Zeng surname from Zhangzhou, Quanzhou, Xinghua, and Yongchun built a common hall and organized collective sacrifice, and at the same time arranged a division into branches. Sacrifice was conducted in rotation, and a genealogical order arranged on the basis of the branches. Each of these so-called branches actually represents a different residentially concentrated lineage. The Longsun branch of Sunjiang was one such lineage. Thus the participants in this residentially dispersed lineage were some forty residentially concentrated Zeng lineages from all over southern Fujian. No clear evidence has been found that explains when this residentially dispersed lineage first formed, or when their collective hall was first built. But since the hall required reconstruction in the Kangxi period, it must have been first constructed some time prior to this, probably not later than the late Ming. The reconstruction of the hall and the organization into branches must have taken place after the coastal evacuation order had been rescinded, probably in the late Kangxi period.

In around 1690, the governor-general of Fujian-Zhejiang, Xing Yongchao, implemented a tax reform known as "allocating tax households to the descent line" *(lianghu guizong),* which led to the formation of a large number of residentially dispersed lineages oriented around particular household registrations. The basic content of the policy was to allocate tax-bearing households and service levy responsibilities according to lineage. It was intended that this system would replace the original *lijia* organization. According to the Qianlong *Haicheng County Gazetteer:*

> At the beginning of the dynasty there were the *dadang* and *xiaojia* service levies. [For the *dadang*], the households of the *li* were divided into ten groups *(ban),* and each group was responsible in rotation for the collection of all tax, service levy, and miscellaneous expenses for one year. The *xiaojia* was set up on state farms and operated in the same way. . . . Later, Governor-General Xing Yongchao went on to implement the system of unifying household registration according to descent lines *(guizong hehu),* eliminating the groups within the *li,* and permitting the *jia* households to unite together.[160]

The *lijia* system had historically generated severe problems in the coastal region, so the populace welcomed the new policy. According to the *Zhangpu County Gazetteer:*

> The custom in Zhangzhou is that those who do not have registration as a *li* head household are considered minor families *(xiaojia*[a]*).* Powerful people always seek out a ward whose *li* head is weak and powerless in which to register their household. This is known as taking over the group *(dingban).* Powerless people, even if they have a hundred thousand *mu* of land, cannot avoid being controlled by others, and it is not necessary to spell out how things are for the poor and isolated small surnames. Because of this problem in Fujian of local tyrants within the *li,* in 1690 an order was received permitting the people to unite their household registration according to descent line, whereupon all those who were registered [in the subordinate position] of affiliated house-

holds *(zihu)* sought *li* heads who had the same surname to affiliate with. This made it possible for them to avoid the distinction between *li* heads and affiliated households.[161]

In response to the policy of allocating the tax households to the descent line, many residentially dispersed lineages affiliated to and oriented around a single household registration developed in coastal Fujian. Lineage members with the same household registration might spread across several counties, or even prefectures. The magistrate of Zhangpu complained in 1697:

> The registered males of Zhangpu [who actually live] in nearby counties are indeed numerous, and in counties as distant as Minxian and Yongfu in Fuzhou, and Nan'an in Quanzhou, there are also men with Zhangpu registration. Their household head goes annually to collect [tax]. If they are not able to fulfill his demands then he always reports them and asks to have them arrested. When asked when they moved away, [the answer] may be a hundred years, or two hundred years, and the more recent ones [are too numerous] to mention. Moreover, nearly one-third of the people who actually live in Zhangpu pay their head tax in other counties.[162]

These lineage members living in different places may not in fact have previously belonged to a single unified lineage organization. Rather, they had simply renewed a descent-line connection in order to "unify the households." In 1692, the Chen surname lineage members of Anxi County wrote a "Contract on the Unifying of the Household Registration" that proclaimed:

> Recently, in 1691, Governor-General Xing, an official who, like a parent, gives life to the people, issued the order [allocating the tax households] to the descent line. He held them close when talking with them and penetratingly investigated their problems. In our county, about half the people hurried to implement the order, and about half did so with some delay. Is this not what is meant by the passage in the *Yijing* (Book of Changes): "The noble man acts upon something as soon as he becomes aware of its incipience and does not wait for the day to run its course"?[163] We returned to [the registration under the name of] the household of Chen Tianzu in Ganhua, to amiably fulfill the *lijia* service levy, so as to flourish for ten thousand generations. Although the ex-penses of the transfer of household registration were considerable, coming into [the new registration] we wished to get along like a fish in water, and leaving [the old one] we recall its good governance. So we have done what we ought to do.[164]

According to their genealogy, the founding ancestor of the Chen moved from Zhangping to Anxi and first registered his household in the Yongle period of the Ming. His descendants spread to Shuiche,

Feiya, Xiaoshi, and Luhua in Anxi; Nancheng in Dehua; and Liuzhen in Yongchun. Originally each of these groups of descendants had its own household registration, and they maintained no relations with one another. But after the "allocation of the tax households to the descent line," they developed into a residentially dispersed lineage "to amiably fulfill the *lijia* service levy."[165]

In theory, the existence of a descent-line was a prerequisite for "unifying the households." In other words, a single household registration could only be shared by a single descent-line. But in practice, people often deliberately fabricated genealogical links, establishing false descent-lines, in order to "unify the households." The Ye of Daguan in Haicheng provide an example:

> The first-generation ancestor is Jicheng. . . . This is a false name that has been assigned. According to the genealogy from Haomen, the founding ancestor was Jiancheng, and his personal name was Changfa. Jiancheng [constructing *(jian)* a base in Haicheng] is a name that means the same thing as Jicheng [establishing a base *(ji^a)* in Haicheng]. [Jicheng] had five sons, who split up and lived in different places but registered together as a single household under the name Ye Hongyuan, in the registers of the second ward of sector 3 of Haicheng County. The eldest son was Haoshan, whose personal name was Ren. He lived in Haomen and registered his own household under the name Ye Fang. The second son was Lushan, whose personal name was Yi. He moved away and became the ancestor of [the Ye of] Neixi and Zhang[zhou] city, registering his own household under the name Ye Hongjue. The third son was Runshan, whose personal name was Li. He moved away and became the ancestor of [the Ye of] Xin'an and Xiawei in sector 3, registering his household under the name Tingchun. The fourth son was Huashan, whose personal name was Zhe. He settled with Runshan at Xiawei, registering his household under the name Cai'an. They are known as the Upper and the Lower Ye. The fifth son was Guanshan, whose personal name was Xin. He lived at Qingkoushe on the slopes of Guanshan, registering his household under the name Ye Jia.
>
> In 1678, Shiyuan wrote a preface for the Haomen genealogy, which also records the preceding. Now we rely on it for the compilation of our genealogy, for it is believable and has a [reliable] basis. . . . Let this serve as [explanation for our origins] for the time being. But in the future this must be investigated in detail.[166]

The inheritance relations between the general household *(zonghu)* under the name of Ye Jicheng and the affiliated or sons' households *(zihu)*, were obviously fabricated. The genealogical records of the Ye had been lost long prior to this account, and for each of the first five generations of ancestors there was "a false name that has been assigned."[167] The first person to come up with these fictive ancestors was Ye Lian, known as Shiyuan. In 1679, because "the genealogy has no basis and there is no record of [our] distribution," he began to compile a genealogical record. But at that time the "allocation of the tax households to the descent-line" policy had not yet been implemented, so his genealogy was limited to his own village and did not include Ye from any other village.

> In our descent-line, for all ancestors prior to [sixth-generation ancestor] Wenhui, the details of births, deaths, burials, and sacrifices have all been lost. . . . The ancestor who branched off and came to [Hai]cheng has been given the name Jicheng after the name of the county. He is the ancestor of the Upper and Lower Ye of this locale, and all the Ye of Gaofeng and Kangnei as well as Shanbei and Xiawei. He was the first-generation [ancestor]. Then our ancestor branched off [and settled] on the slopes of Daguanshan. Because of the name of the place, he has been given the name Guanshan. He was the second-generation ancestor and the founding ancestor of Qingkou. After this there was Qixiang, the third-generation ancestor, who is the founding ancestor of our village. After the founding ancestor came Yuan and Kai, who were the fourth-generation ancestors. The descendants of Yuan and Kai each split into four branches, namely, ancestors Ge, Zhi, Cheng, and Zheng, and Xiu, Qi, Zhi, and Ping, who were the fifth-generation ancestors. As for Wenhui's generational position, it is in the sixth generation.
>
> To make a genealogical record in this way is like starting from the end and looking for the source, and then following the branchings from the source. If we were to record only what can be verified as true, then we would have to start with Wenhui as the first generation. I do not dare to pass on false evidence irresponsibly and recklessly to the descendants.[168]

The Ye of Gaofeng, Kangnei, and Shanbei, mentioned in this preface, were not included in the later account that linked the general household registration to the affiliated households. On the other hand, the Ye of Haomen, Neixi, and Zhangzhou city, which are included in that account, are nowhere to be found in the genealogical chart compiled at the time of this preface. Obviously, the inheritance relations between the general household and the so-called sons' households were completely fabricated, in response to the new tax policy of "allocating the tax households to the descent-line."

In Zhao'an County, Dongshan and elsewhere there were even cases of people with different surnames uniting under a single household registration. According to Chen Shengshao, in Zhao'an, "several surnames unite to establish a single household, such as the Li,

Lin, and other households that are united [under the name] Guan Shixian, or the Ye, Zhao, and other households that are united [under the name] Zhao Jianxing."[169] Such households, comprising different surnames united for registration purposes, frequently had common "ancestors" or ancestral temples and used a system of branches or segments to allocate responsibilities associated with the registration. In terms of organizational form, such organizations closely resembled residentially dispersed lineages. For example, according to the "Collectively Erected Memorial Inscription on Guan Yongmao" at the Guandi temple on Dongshan Island:

> We have heard that in Zhao'an County there are military households with no descent-line who together venerate Guandi as their ancestor and who have applied to register a household under the name Guan Shixian for the payment of land and head tax. This is considered very convenient. In 1711, when the tax registers were recompiled, we discussed this case together, and also expressed [the wish] to register a household under the name of Guan Yongmao. Everyone agreed it could be done. So we applied to County Magistrate Wang requesting that we be allowed to establish a household. Permission was obtained for Guan Yongmao to take on the payment of land and head tax for the ninth *jia* of the sixth ward of sector 17. . . .
>
> Recently it has been learned that in the county, prefectural, and provincial registers of households there is a record of one household under the name "Guan Yongmao, which consists of Huang Qitai and others." We are concerned that there is a danger of the flowers being replaced with wood and the head concealed but the tail revealed.[170] It is only three years [since the establishment of the household] and there are already such discrepancies. How can we ensure that in future there will not be tricky people who will create problems in order to take advantage of our descendants? Therefore, in front of the deity, everyone has collectively drawn lots to divide into seven branches. Small problems can be resolved by the branches; for larger matters, everyone should gather together to divide the responsibilities evenly. All of us are uncles and cousins, so we treat one another like brothers, and there are no distinctions like those between *li* heads and the *jia* households. There will never be distinctions between large and small; the noble are not to humiliate the base, or the powerful bully the weak. If some look down on others thereby giving rise to evil attitudes, it is permitted for everyone to gather to the sound of drums and attack them. This is the way [to ensure that] there is no partiality or factionalism, and for there to be complete equality and complete prudence. So we have erected a stone to commemorate this matter forever without decay.

> Senior Branch: You Jiye, You Kunyu, Wu Gejiang, Ou Shaozong,
> Fan Yan, Hong Fu'an, Sang Chuanci
> Second Branch: [*sic*]
> Third Branch: Zheng Zhenji, Tang Mianfang, Li Yucheng, Liao
> Guangcai, Wu Ricai, He Xinglong, Tian Xingbang, Zhang
> Faxiang
> Fourth Branch: Chen Siming, Sicong, Siwen, Sigong, Sijing,
> Siwen, Sinan, Siyi
> Fifth Branch: Yao Jiamou, Weng Wannian, Ma Zhu, Cui Guo-
> zhen, Zhu Tianqing, Kong Yang, Zeng Xu, Guo Longhe,
> Dong Yang, Lai Zhan
> Sixth Branch: Lin Shifa, Shiqiang, Shiming, Shigang, Shiyi,
> Faxiang, Farui
> Seventh Branch: Huang Shiwen, Shiliang, Shigong, Shixin,
> Shirang
> Erected 1713. Composed by Jiang Risheng of Zhupu.[171]

Dongshan Island had originally been a Ming garrison, and its residents were mostly descended from hereditary military households. After the coastal evacuation, the garrison was abolished and the military registrations of these households accordingly eliminated. *Lijia* household registrations were first set up in 1701, but the descendants of the military households, having no descent-line to which they could affiliate, found it difficult to escape the subordinate status associated with what were called affiliated households *(bangren menhu),* that is, residents who did not belong to a registered *lijia* household. So they united to establish a shared household registration. The so-called household of Guan Yongmao was thus actually an organization uniting lineages made up of former military households. The fourth, sixth, and seventh branches consisted of people with a single surname and may have each represented a single lineage, while the first, third, and fifth branches included a number of different lineages. This phenomenon of a single household uniting people of different surnames is an indication that the *lijia* system of this period had become completely subsumed within lineage organization. This was an inevitable consequence of the policy of "allocating the tax households to the descent-line."

*   *   *

Residentially dispersed lineages with shared halls and collective sacrifice became common throughout the coastal region after the mid-Qing. Such lineages were rarely restricted to members of the same

descent-line; usually anyone with the appropriate surname was permitted to participate. For example, Guan Xianyao, a gentryman from
Anxi County, recorded in his genealogy:

> In the spring of 1740, on the way home for a holiday, I passed through
> the provincial capital and met descent-line elder *(zonglao)* Zhanyan for
> the first time. Our sentiments were most cordial. After that, whenever
> I went to the provincial capital I stayed at his house. He once brought
> out his genealogy to show me, and I learned that the people of the
> Shangguan surname in Fujian all treat Adjutant Jie as their ancestor.
> . . . In 1777, Zhanyan's son Zhuba sent a letter informing me that he
> had purchased a plot of land at their ancestral home in Pagoda Lane,
> which was suitable for the construction of a shrine for the Adjutant.
> Two years later, in the summer of 1779, he reported that the hall was
> already completed, and a date after the middle of the eighth month
> was to be chosen for the installation of the tablets. Descent-line mem-
> bers from all over who had come to [Fuzhou to] participate in the exam-
> inations could all assemble for the sacrifice in the new temple. . . . I
> ordered my two sons Xueli and Xueshi [to purify themselves] by re-
> fraining from meat and conducting themselves well, and to assist at
> the appropriate time in the temple.[172]

The ancestors of the Guan of Anxi were said to have once had the
two-character surname Shangguan. It was not known when they had
changed this to the single-character surname Guan. The genealogical
connections between the Guan of Anxi and Shangguan Jie, the first
ancestor of the Shangguan to settle in Fujian, were completely ob-
scure. Nonetheless, Guan Xianyao and his sons willingly participated
in the sacrificial activities associated with the construction of the
Shangguan hall, and the Shangguan surname lineage members were
happy to accept them. In fact, even within the Shangguan surname
of Fujian, not everyone necessarily shared a common descent-line.
According to Song records, there were two different legends about
the origins of the Shangguan surname in Fujian. One version had
some people of the surname "fleeing south in the Yongjia period of
the Jin (307–312)"; the other traced descent back to Adjutant Shangguan Jie, who had served in the Revenue Section of Fuzhou in the
Yuanhe period of the Tang (806–820): "He died in office and his
descendants were unable to return home, so they settled there." In
the Yuanfu period of the Song (1098–1100), Shangguan surname lineage members happened to discover a grave inscription for Shangguan Jie, and on the evidence from it concluded that he was the
founding ancestor who settled in Fujian.[173] After this, Shangguan

surname lineage members all over Fujian worshipped Jie as their founding ancestor, but their genealogical records were not all unified. The construction of the hall to the founding ancestor in the provincial capital simply gave lineage members from throughout Fujian who shared a common surname a shared hall for collective sacrifice. This did not require that all their genealogical records be consistent. Guan Xianyao recognized this when he wrote: "Once I talked over with Zhanyan the idea of inviting all the various lineages of Fujian to erect a general ancestral hall together in the provincial capital, to sacrifice to the migrant ancestor, Adjutant Jie. The annual sacrifice could endure for a long time, and the members of the descent-line could gather on schedule in the hall to make the sacrifice. . . . If it is not possible to know the generational order, then they should [arrange themselves] according to age."[174] In fact, in such a large-scale residentially dispersed lineage it was totally impossible to be sure of everyone's generational relationship. Even if there had been a consistent genealogical chart, it could only have been a fabrication.

In the Qianlong period, people of the You surname from all over southern Fujian erected a "General Ancestral Hall of Quanzhou Prefecture" and decided to divide into twelve branches to conduct sacrifices in rotation. They adopted a common naming pattern beginning with the twenty-second generation. But because there were no consistent genealogical records linking the different branches, they were forced to use planchette divination to determine the position of each branch in the generational order.[175]

Some residentially dispersed lineages openly proclaimed that anyone with the same surname belonged to the same line, and there was no need to distinguish genealogical origins. For example, the "Corporate Register of the Great Descent-line Hall of the Huang of Xianxi" reads:

Among us of the Huang surname in Xianyou, some have come from the provincial capital, some arrived from Putian, some have moved from Quanzhou. But, simply speaking, all of us originated in Jiangxia [in Hubei]. So, based on the imperative to treat kin as kin, we have constructed a Great Descent-Line Hall in the county town, to sacrifice to Yuanfang, the Prefect of Jinjiang Prefecture in the Jin period; Shougong, a respected man in his prefecture in the Jin; An, the prefect of Guizhou, enfeoffed as state-establishing duke in the Tang, and Investigating Censor Tao. Beneath them are installed ancestral tablets according to contributions. Property has been purchased for the annual sacrifices. This hall is known as the Hall of Respectful Inheritance (Jingcheng

Tang), to reflect the deep significance of respecting the ancestors and uniting the descent-line.[176]

The names in this document are all of famous "founding ancestors who settled in Fujian" *(ruMin shizu)* bearing the Huang surname. All of the Huang in the Xianyou area considered themselves to have originated in Jiangxia. Thus virtually anyone with the surname Huang could participate in this dispersed lineage. The organization of the Huang Great Descent-Line Hall was quite open. Regardless of whether or not he was the descendant of one of the original constructors of the hall, anyone could install a tablet at any time simply by making a donation. The hall's rules prescribe that "all those in the villages [whose ancestors] have not previously installed a tablet must now donate twelve taels [per tablet they wish to install]." "For every tablet there is a tally. . . . At the appropriate time, the sacrificial foods are distributed according to the tallies, so as to facilitate the calculations." This hall, first constructed in 1734 and reconstructed in the Guangxu period, contained 542 tablets by 1933, and these were divided among six branches "for the conduct of the sacrifice in rotation."[177] The number of tablets assigned to each branch is indicated in Table 4.6. The members of the Huang Great Descent-Line Hall were dispersed in over one hundred towns and villages throughout the whole county. The branches of the hall were determined on the basis of place of residence of the donors and the number of tablets installed, and had no real genealogical significance.

The Great Descent-Line Hall of the Lin of Xianyou contained over twelve hundred tablets in the early twentieth century. Its members were distributed over all fourteen subcantons of the county. "They take it in turns to be in charge, through [a rotation] of twelve shares *(jiu).*" The principle for the distribution of shares was:

> Each share is based on the unit of one hundred tablets. . . . If there is a subcanton with fewer than one hundred tablets, it must combine with neighboring subcantons to reach a minimum eighty tablets, which will correspond to one share. If it has more than one hundred tablets, it must have over one hundred and fifty tablets to receive two shares, and it is not permitted [that the turn in the rotation of these two shares should fall] in two successive years.[178]

It is not known when the Lin hall was first constructed, but it was repaired in the Tongzhi period and again in the early years of the Republic. This is another example of a common surname organization worshipping the founding ancestor who settled in Fujian.[179]

Table 4.6. Tablets in the Great Descent-line Hall of the Huang of Xianxi

Branch Name	Number of Tablets	Places of Residence of Branch Members
Zhongtang or Li branch	78	Zhongtang, Qiangfeng, Lingpo, Rende Donglin, Meifeng, Daban, Huixian, Pudou, Shanwei, Qianpo, Siyang, Shuigou, Xifeng, Huiyang, Tapu, Jingshan, Beimenwai Dasunxia, Nanmenwai Shiguchi, Taipingling
Houxian or Le branch	109	Houxian, Zhifeng, Xijiao Erbao, Banyang, Bifeng, Xibian, Gebi, Shili, Huangzhai, Shangong, Yunling, Shangzao, Panling, Jiutiangong, Baishiling, Xiaxincun, Houmentian, Taidouling, Lunfeng, Jinxi
Zhongfeng or She branch	86	Jinqiu, Jiafeng, Jiedai, Dongfeng, Xiafeng, Loufeng, Zhengban
Jingge or Yu branch	90	Xiatusai, Yutian, Houcai, Tuku, Yuannei, Nanmenwai, Jingtian, Batou, Yangchi, Dongzhai, Meiyang, Jipu, Fengting, Tashan, Donglin, Tangbian, Dahuang, Dahang, Beitangwei, Yuedimiao, Shaku, Houxizai, Tiezao, Shangqin, Fengjiang, Xiahu, Chitu, Luocheng, Houdai
Xingtan or Shu branch	91	Xingtan, Baxia Lianhuachi, Tieshan, Jinliange, Ganlanyang, Helingxia, Renhang, Lianqi, Cangxiang, Yangshan, Shiliu, Dongdu, Dongmen Xiacuo, Jiangzhuang, Geli, Dingxiqi, Louqian Xijin, Tiantou, Dapu, Pozhesun, Yaolongli
Donghu or Shu[a] branch	88	Donghu, Houfeng, Sanhui, Longyang, Cixiaolingfeng, Jinxi, Dongling, Batou, Songboyang, Wusong, Gedou

The development of this kind of surname organization may have been connected to intensifying contradictions within local society. In the Daoguang period, Chen Shengshao wrote that "in Xianyou the small surnames fear the large surnames more than they fear the officials. What are they afraid of? With a single call, supporters [of the large surname] respond from all directions, and they prepare to do battle."[180] With surnames vying for power on the basis of strength of numbers, distinctions between descent-lines became irrelevant. To oppose stronger surname groups, furthermore, a number of small lineages of different surnames might combine into a single same-surname organization. "At first, the large surnames oppressed the small surnames, so the small surnames combined the different surnames into a single surname in order to resist them. Previously Bao was used as a surname, and Qi as a surname. Recently Tong has been used as a surname, and Hai, and Wan."[181] In areas of fierce territorial and lineage feuding, even large surnames organized fabricated same-surname organizations. The Republican period *Tong'an County Gazetteer* records that "in 1728, the Bao and Qi assembled and fought. The large surnames like Li, Chen, Su, Zhuang, and Lin were the Bao, and various [smaller] surnames were the Qi. They inflicted casualties on one another."[182] This custom is said to have begun in the late Ming and had become common by the Qing. Jiang Risheng wrote of Pinghe County of Zhangzhou: "in the Chongzhen period the local gentry were wanton and cruel. The people suffered under them, and many of them made a plan to unite together with a common heart, taking Wan as their surname."[183]

By the Qing, local gentry had become actively involved in such activities. In the Jiuzhen area of Zhangpu County, the Chen, Zhang, Zhong, and Wu lived intermingled with one another, "treating one another as kin and with love, even more than they would have had they actually been related." In 1740, "Hanlin Examining Editor Zhang Guangji and others together worshipped the Sage Mother [Mazu], treating the temple as their ancestral [hall]. They gathered the elders and divided into four branches, arranged them into generational order, and earnestly [revived] the long neglected ceremonies." In 1924, the local elite proclaimed that "neighbors with the same surname may consider themselves brothers, thus different surnames can also share the same ancestral temple."[184] In such organizations, the distinctions between different descent-lines and even between different surnames were no longer meaningful. Any kind of social organization could potentially take the form of a lineage. The development of these kinds of same-surname lineages and multiple-surname lineages reflects the adaptability of lineage organization, and also the extent to which the entire social structure was shaped and permeated by lineage principles and organizational forms.

*   *   *

In summary, in eastern and southern coastal Fujian, the scale of residentially concentrated lineages was relatively large, so the formation of control-subordination lineages occurred relatively early. The proliferation of ancestral halls in the coastal regions prior to the mid-Ming demonstrates the widespread development of control-subordination lineages under gentry leadership. The pirate turmoil of the late Ming and the coastal evacuation of the early Qing seriously threatened the residentially concentrated lineages of the coast, and many lineage organizations simply disintegrated. Lineage organizations that were reconstructed after the turmoil subsided were initially mostly control-subordination and contractual lineages, with inheritance lineages reviving only somewhat later. The turmoil of the late Ming and early Qing shattered the existing social order, intensifying contradictions between lineages and leading to rampant feuding. The military and defensive functions of residentially concentrated lineages in the coastal regions grew stronger as a result. Residentially dispersed lineages formed by linked descent-lines, shared surnames, or even multiple surnames, also became widespread. In a sense, the history of lineage organization in the coastal areas of Fujian since the mid-Ming has been the product of specific historical circumstances, and should not be considered representative of the normal form of lineage organization development in traditional China. However, it was precisely in such exceptional historical circumstances that lineage development demonstrated the greatest potential, so the study of such contexts may help us to understand more fully the internal characteristics of traditional lineage organization. In other places with a violent history, such as the coastal regions of Jiangsu, Zhejiang, and Guangdong in the late Ming and early Qing, and the lower reaches of the Yangtze in the late Qing, lineage development may have undergone a similar process. The development process of lineage organization in coastal Fujian from the mid-Ming onward thus also has important representative significance.

The Development of Lineage Organization in Qing Taiwan

A great deal of research has already been done on lineage organization in Qing Taiwan. This section is intended chiefly to describe the

process of development of lineage organization in Qing Taiwan
based on the work of Taiwanese scholars and the documents I have
been able to consult personally.

Large-scale migration of mainlanders to Taiwan began at the time
of Zheng Chenggong's recovery of the island in 1662, when around
sixty thousand people, including troops, followed Zheng to Taiwan.
By the time Taiwan was brought under Qing control in the Kangxi
period, the total number of ethnic Han on the island was about
120,000. But because the Qing court was initially uncertain about
whether or not to retain sovereignty over the island, there were few
permanent Han settlers, the majority "returning every year to Quanzhou, Zhangzhou, Xiamen, and other places." In 1688, only a few
thousand Han had settled on Taiwan.[185] Under these circumstances
it was obviously extremely difficult for stable lineage organizations
to form. By the mid-Kangxi period, Taiwan's political status had
been decided, and large numbers of mainlanders began to immigrate,
leading to a rapid increase in population. The population of Taiwan
exceeded one million by the late eighteenth century and was 2.54
million in 1881.[186] With the ongoing increase in the population and
the expansion of Han settlement, the patterns of lineage organization
that had existed on the mainland were gradually replicated and
developed further.

Although Taiwan in the Qing was a newly opened immigrant region, the phenomenon of residentially concentrated lineages was nonetheless already quite widespread. This is because, in the early period
of migration to Taiwan, in order to respond cooperatively to the complex social ecology, mainlanders tended to migrate along with others
of their locality and lineage, and successive migrants from a common
locality or lineage mutually supported and assisted one another. Thus
from the start there was a tendency for people of the same lineage
and locality to settle together. After the mid-Qing, in certain areas that
had been opened up relatively early, feuding often arose between migrants from different native locales or different lineages. The weaker
parties were forced to flee to places where people from the same native
locality or lineage were more numerous, further expanding the scale
of residentially concentrated lineages. According to Chen Shaoxin
and Morton Fried's detailed analysis of the 1956 census data, a
considerable portion of the total population in every part of Taiwan
is made up of a few predominant large surnames. Chen Qi'nan's
study of townships in which the two largest surnames comprise 40

percent or more of the total population provides further confirmation of this pattern of residential concentration of surnames in Taiwan.[187] The results of this research are summarized in Table 4.7.

The table shows that the phenomenon of residential concentration by surname is most striking in areas settled by migrants from Zhangzhou and Quanzhou, and is less obvious in areas settled by Guangdong migrants. But because the data on which these calculations are based were compiled by township *(xiangzhen),* they do not fully reveal the pattern of lineage residence. If the unit of analysis had been the village, the phenomenon of residential concentration by lineage would be even more striking.

Moreover, the residential concentrations of certain large surnames frequently included several villages and might even transcend the limits of a single township. For example, in the Zhanghua plains:

> In central Dacun township there are seven or eight villages the population of which is made up of a residentially concentrated lineage of the Lai surname, whose native place is Xintian township, Pinghe County, Zhangzhou Prefecture. The area of Puxin township and Yuanlin town is divided among people of the Huang and Zhang surname, whose native place is Raoping County, Chaozhou Prefecture, Guangdong Province. In the region southeast of Yuanlin and northeast of Shetou township, the four villages between Kantoulin and Longtou are inhabited by the Liu lineage from Fangtou, Sheyang, Nanjing County, Zhangzhou Prefecture. South of Shetou and north of Tianzhong town live people of the Xiao surname of Shuyang, Nanjing County, Zhangzhou Prefecture. In the area lying south of Tianzhong to Ershui live the Chen lineage of Zhangpu County, Zhangzhou Prefecture.[188]

Residentially concentrated lineages in the Zhanghua plains were thus of a scale similar to that in coastal Fujian.

Most scholars of Taiwan hold that the early lineage organizations of Qing-era migrants to Taiwan were primarily contract-based lineages *(heyuezi zongzu),* which were oriented around sacrifice to Mainland Ancestors *(Tangshan zu).* They refer to these as large lineages *(da zongzu).* Once migrants had settled and undergone several generations of natural development, they gradually formed lineages based on documents of family division *(jiufenzi zongzu),* or small lineages *(xiao zongzu),* oriented around the worship of a Founding Ancestor on Taiwan *(kai Tai zu).* The former was a transplantation of a previously existing lineage on the mainland; the latter was a "classic" lineage, a product of Taiwan itself. The transition in lineage organization from the former to the latter type represents the pro-

Table 4.7. Surname Distribution and Native Places of the Taiwanese Population

District	Township	Largest Surname	% of Population	Second-Largest Surname	% of Population	Two Largest Surnames (combined % of population)	Native Place
Taibei	Wugu	Chen	42.4	Lin	10.8	53.2	Quanzhou
	Luzhou	Li	44	Chen	11.1	55.1	Quanzhou
	Dadu	Chen	24.3	Lin	15.6	39.9	Zhangzhou
	Mingjian	Chen	41.5	Wu	10.5	52	Zhangzhou
	Tianzhong	Chen	28.1	Xiao	12.7	40.8	Zhangzhou
	Shetou	Xiao	34.6	Liu	20	54.6	Zhangzhou
	Dacun	Lai	45.3	Huang	15.1	60.4	Zhangzhou
Taizhong	Puxin	Huang	26	Zhang	19.5	45.5	Guangdong
	Longjing	Chen	29.5	Lin	17.5	46.7	Quanzhou
	Xianxi	Huang	47.4	Lin	18.5	55.9	Quanzhou
	Puyan	Chen	25.4	Shi	24.8	50.3	Quanzhou
	Xihu	Yang	25.6	Chen	21.2	46.8	Quanzhou
	Fangyuan	Hong	31.4	Lin	16.8	48.2	Quanzhou
	Erlun	Liao	39.8	Li	17.2	57	Zhangzhou
	Mailiao	Xu	34.6	Lin	28.9	63.5	Quanzhou
Yunjia	Taixi	Lin	36.9	Ding	27.4	64.3	Quanzhou
	Xihu	Wu	46.2	Cai	14.9	61.1	Quanzhou
	Liujiao	Chen	23.2	Lin	22.1	45.3	Quanzhou
	Jiangjun	Wu	24.9	Chen	18.7	43.6	Quanzhou
Tainan	Qigu	Huang	23.7	Chen	22.2	45.9	Quanzhou
	Anding	Wang	30.7	Fang	9.7	40.8	Quanzhou
	Danei	Yang	32.9	Chen	11.3	44.2	Zhangzhou

Source: Chen Qinan, Taiwan de chuantong zhongguo shehui 132–133 (adjusted).

cess of nativization *(tuzhu hua)* of Qing-era Taiwanese immigrant society.[189]

The category of contract-based lineage or large lineage in Qing Taiwan, formed through voluntary share investment, corresponds to my category of contractual lineage. Shares in this kind of lineage organization could be inherited by descendants, and could be divided and transferred through sale and purchase. This is demonstrated in two contracts.

> Document recording the drawing of lots [for the division of an estate]; Liu surname of Miaoli, 1884.
>
> The makers of this document are the holders of thirty-two shares in the sacrificial estate of [ancestor] Wenda. In the Qianlong period, the ancestors together contributed seventy-two shares for the establishment of the sacrificial estate of Wenda. They purchased land in succession at three sites at Dongshanmenshou, Putouzi, and Puweizi, and also had two dwellings for ancestral sacrifice. By the Daoguang period, we retained [control] over thirty-two shares, [ownership of which] has to the present been contested in a lawsuit for several years. In the third month of 1884, we received County Magistrate Zhu's decision on the case, which ordered us to divide into two estates. Liu Bingxian is to manage twenty shares, which give the right to collect 230 piculs of sacrificial rental income: 200 piculs from Dongshanmenshou and 30 piculs from Puweizi. The sacrificial dwellings in the estate, aside from [that portion] which has been allocated by lot to the Dongchuan sacrificial society, belong to these twenty shares. Liu Tingjun is to manage twelve shares, which give the right to collect 140 piculs of sacrificial rental income: 110 piculs from Putouzi and 30 piculs from Puweizi. The field buildings in the west part of this estate belong to these twelve shares. At present, 60 piculs of rental income in total comes from Puweizi, of which each estate is to receive half. The branch heads have assembled at the site and drawn lots to distribute control [of this property]. Now because we wish there to be evidence, we have made this document of selection by lot with two identical copies, for each to take as proof.[190]

This sacrificial organization had originally consisted of seventy-two shares. Between the Qianlong and Daoguang periods, most of the shares had been transferred or sold, so only thirty-two shares remained. In 1884, the remaining shares were divided among two estates. Prior to 1884, the property of the sacrificial organization had earned rental income of 370 piculs, or just over ten piculs per share. After the division, one estate comprising twenty shares earned rent of 230 piculs, and the other estate comprising twelve shares earned rent of 140 piculs. In other words, the income per share remained constant at just over 10 piculs. This shows that ownership of the property associated with the original estate was divided purely on the basis of the number of shares held.

> Document recording the final redemption of a share by the corporate society *(gonghui)*; Lin surname of Miaoli, 1904
>
> The maker of this document recording the final redemption of my share by the corporate society is Lin Laopu. I inherited from my father, Lin Weizheng, a share in the corporate society [oriented around sacrifice to] Lin Shiling. My sons and I have discussed and agreed that we wish to sell off this share. Through a middleman, I have contacted the administrator of the Lin Shiling society *(gong)*, who has come forward to purchase the share. The three parties have agreed that the current price *(shizhi)* for the full sale of the share, originally worth seven mace, shall be sixty large silver dollars. On this day, the money has been received through the middleman and the document drawn up. Both sides are satisfied. [Lao]pu etc. agree that the rightfully owned share is dissolved, ownership returning to the corporation to control. As for the fields and houses owned by the society, and the spring and autumn sacrifices, [Lao]pu etc. will not dare to interfere with these matters. . . .[191]

The corporate society of Lin Shiling was obviously a contractual lineage formed through share investment. By the late Qing, the shares had already come to have a market value. The share held by Lin Laopu and his sons, which may have been a fraction of a full share but which represented an initial investment of seven mace, now had a current price of sixty silver dollars. It was purchased directly by the society as a whole, whereby Lin Laopu withdrew from the organization. In the early immigrant society of Taiwan, relatively high social mobility may have made the division and sale of such shares quite common, which would explain why there was an agreed market value. The practice of division and transfer by sale meant that membership of a lineage was highly flexible but changes to the membership did not necessarily influence the ongoing development of the organization as a whole. The sacrificial society in the name of Liu Wenda had lost half its shares by the Daoguang period, and later divided into two separate organizations, without ever completely disintegrating. In an unstable social environment, the contractual lineage was particularly responsive to changing conditions.

Contractual lineages played an important role in the process of opening up Taiwan in the Qing. In a penetrating analysis of the documents of the period, Zhuang Yingzhang and Chen Yundong have shown that some of the earliest land developers of Toufen in Miaoli

County were lineage organizations oriented around a Mainland Ancestor.[192] For example, the *Miaoli County Gazetteer* records that, in 1751, more than fifty households and over two hundred men opened up the area from Zhonggang to Toufen ("First share") for cultivation, "and then from there continued on to open up Second share, Third share, Fourth share, Hechun, Zhongdu, Xinwuxia, Wanggengliao, and other areas." The men named include Lin Hong, Wu Yongzhong, Wen Dianyu, Huang Rixin, and Luo Deda, all of whom were Mainland Ancestors who had never actually gone to Taiwan. Lin Hong was a tenth-generation member of the Lin lineage of Luojingdan, Zhenping County, Guangdong Province, who probably lived in the late sixteenth or early seventeenth century. It was his descendants in the eighteenth to twentieth generations, that is, eight to ten generations later, who first moved to and started to farm in Taiwan. Wu Yongzhong was a tenth-generation member of the Wu lineage of Wuzihu, Zhenping County, Guangdong Province, who probably lived in the mid-sixteenth century. His descendants from the nineteenth to twenty-third generations moved to Taiwan.[193] Thus the Mainland Ancestors recorded in the documents associated with the opening up of Toufen are actually references to a particular kind of consanguinal kinship group. We are not yet clear about the early organizational form of these kinship groups, but it is safe to say that they probably developed directly out of pre-existing lineage organizations on the mainland.

In the late Qianlong period, some migrants to Taiwan began to collect funds for ancestral sacrifice, forming contractual lineages oriented around a Mainland Ancestor. For example, the preface to the share register of the sacrificial society of Luo Deda, dated 1793, reads: "We have moved to distant Taiwan. That we are able to live in harmony and in virtue is surely thanks to the aid of the spirits of the ancestors who have come here. So the uncles and nephews in Dan[shui] in Tai[wan] enthusiastically gathered [to found a sacrificial estate]. Each share cost one picul of rice. . . . Sacrifice is conducted each year in autumn." Members of this kind of contractual lineage established in a migrant locale initially simply gathered at a scheduled time to perform collective sacrificial activities. Later, they might invest funds to purchase land, and the lineage became a land-development organization. In 1799, migrants of the Lin surname organized the Hall of Harmonious Achievement *(Muchuang Tang)* of the Sacrificial Society of Lin Hong of Toufen. At first, capital consisting of one picul of rice per share was loaned out to earn interest, and more capital gradually accumulated. "Together with the Wen, Wu, Huang, and Luo, we five surnames acquired land to be opened up for cultivation from Lin Jun of Fujian." In 1806, immigrants to Toufen of several surnames gathered funds to purchase land to develop. In 1835 they divided the land up into seventeen shares. The shareholders included contractual lineages represented by the Mainland Ancestors Lin Hong, Wu Yongzhong, Wen Dianyu, Huang Rixin, and Lin Leyin.

The sacrificial society of the founding ancestor of the Chen surname in Zhonggang was formed in 1799 with 124 shares, each share representing a contribution of one *yuan*. In 1811 the society began to purchase land to rent out. By the Daoguang period the total capital was 2,090 *yuan*, and the value of each share had risen to 12.5 *yuan*. As Zhuang and Chen have argued, these examples demonstrate that the contractual lineages formed in the course of the development of Toufen "may appear to be dedicated to ancestral sacrifice, but were actually a kind of land investment organization, which made use of kinship relations to concentrate labor and capital, and actively engaged in opening up land for cultivation." For the ordinary migrant with limited capital, joining this kind of lineage organization was an effective investment strategy. This is precisely why contractual lineages developed widely in the early immigrant society of Qing Taiwan.

Contractual lineages oriented around the worship of a Mainland Ancestor tended to be offshoots of preexisting lineage organizations from the mainland, and the names of the group and of its object of sacrifice were usually those of the original organization. Where there were many migrants from the same lineage, the existing organizational system from the mainland might be completely transplanted, along with its complete genealogical structure. For example, the members of the Xiao lineage of the Shetou and Tianzhou area of the Zhanghua plains established corporate sacrificial property for each of their lineal ancestors beginning with the founding ancestor. Most of these estates were established by assessments on all descendants and were known as societies of individuals (*dingzaihui*), but some were established through voluntary share investment, in which case they were called ancestral societies (*zugonghui*). Figure 4.4, which is drawn from the work of Chen Qi'nan, shows the organizational structure of the various organizations made up of different branches.[194]

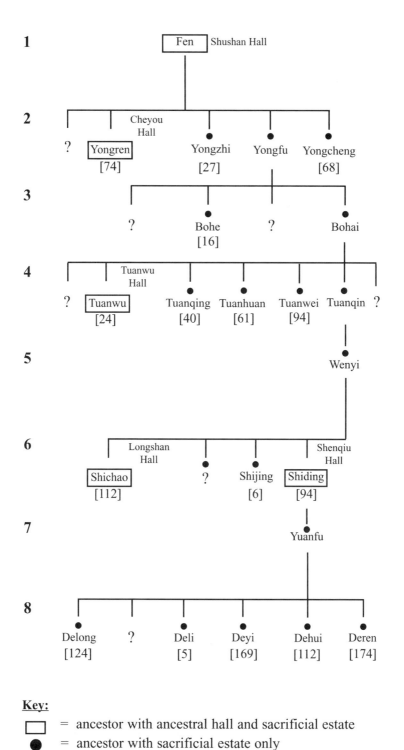

1   Fen   Shushan Hall

2   ?   Cheyou Hall   Yongren [74]   Yongzhi [27]   Yongfu   Yongcheng [68]

3   ?   Bohe [16]   ?   Bohai

4   ?   Tuanwu Hall   Tuanwu [24]   Tuanqing [40]   Tuanhuan [61]   Tuanwei [94]   Tuanqin   ?

5   Wenyi

6   Longshan Hall   Shichao [112]   ?   Shijing [6]   Shiding [94]   Shenqiu Hall

7   Yuanfu

8   Delong [124]   ?   Deli [5]   Deyi [169]   Dehui [112]   Deren [174]

Key:

□ = ancestor with ancestral hall and sacrificial estate
● = ancestor with sacrificial estate only
[ ] = number of members in sacrificial society

Figure 4.4. Estates and Organizations of the Xiao of Shetou and Tianzhou

The estates of those ancestors whose names are contained in boxes consisted of both ancestral halls and sacrificial property. Those with a circle had sacrificial property but no hall. The numbers indicate the number of individual members in the *dingzaihui* organization associated with the estate. The figure shows that there was sacrificial property endowed in the name of each of the ancestors from the first-generation ancestor Xiao Fen to the eighth generation, and in some cases a dedicated shrine. According to genealogical records and field investigation, the ancestors from the first to the eighth generation were all Mainland Ancestors. In the Xiao's native place of Shuyang township, Nanjing County, Zhangzhou Prefecture, there are lineage organizations that also worship these same ancestors. The organizational structure of lineage members on both sides of the Taiwan Straits is identical.[195] According to the legends of Xiao lineage members on the mainland, early migrants to Taiwan from the lineage redeemed their portion of the lineage collective property in Shuyang and used it to purchase land in Taiwan for ancestral sacrifice. If this legend is true, it helps to explain the process whereby mainland lineage organizations were transplanted to Taiwan. However, according to Chen Qi'nan's research, the development process of the lineage organization of the Xiao in Zhanghua essentially began through assessments on individual migrants to Taiwan for the formation of *dingzaihui* organizations, which sacrificed to recent ancestors. Later these organizations invested in shares of higher-order ancestral societies, which sacrificed to more distant ancestors. Both types of societies operated on the principle of voluntary investment. Not all descendants of a particular branch participated, and the shares owned by different branches were not necessarily identical. For example:

> The corporate sacrificial property of third-generation ancestor Bohai is divided into six shares. Each of the societies *(hui)* of the fourth generation owns one share. Of the remaining two shares, 40 percent is owned by the society of the sixth-generation ancestor Shichao and the remaining 60 percent by the five societies of the eighth generation.
>
> Furthermore, the corporate sacrificial property of the fourth-generation ancestor Tuanxin is also held by an ancestral society, which is divided into four shares in all. The senior, second, third, and sixth branches of the eighth-generation each owns one share. . . . With respect to the corporate sacrificial property of ancestor Xiao Fen's Shushan shrine, neither the society of Yongren, his second-generation descendant, which has seventy-four members, nor that of his third-generation descendant Bohe, which has sixteen members, has a share, though both of these societies are made up of his descendants.[196]

Clearly, these lineage organizations had not simply been transplanted unchanged from the mainland to Taiwan. Rather, Xiao migrants constructed them gradually on the model of the mainland original.

The branch descended from Xiao Fen joined together with another branch of the Xiao surname in the Zhanghua area, whose ancestral hall was the Doushan shrine, to build a joint hall, the Hall of Fragrant Ancestry *(Fangyuan Tang)*, in which sacrifice was offered to their collective ancestor, Jiyu. This contractual lineage acquired "corporate sacrificial property of the Eleventh *Jia*," which in the late Qing earned a rent of over one thousand piculs, managed separately by eleven "*jia* heads." This organization was organized according to the principles of individual share ownership. New shares could be added, which meant that the organization was very open, similar to the residentially dispersed lineages organized by tablets on the Fujian mainland. The membership and property registers of this organization can be used to analyze the structure of the individual shares.[197] This analysis is summarized in Table 4.8.

The table shows that the organization continued to accept new members after it was first formed, and the total number of shares

Table 4.8. Share Ownership in the Hall of Fragrant Ancestry of the Xiao of Shetou and Tianzhong

Place of Residence	Total number of *ding* (shares)	Original number of shares	Shares later added	Unclear shares
Beishan	27	27	0	0
Laohubei	56	38	18	0
Caixitou	56	56	0	0
Unknown	77	55	14	7
Dakuwei	43	32	5	6
Longtanbian	261	80	143	22
Tiandi	31	25	4	2
Houtian	10	5	5	0
Dakuweiliu	55	28	27	0
Tianzhongying	24	9	15	0
Chizhou	22	0	20	0
Chetian	29	0	29	0
Totals	691	355	299	37

Source: Materials collected by Chen Qi'nan.

eventually almost doubled. The majority of shares belonged to lineage members from Longtanbian, who increased the number of their shares on sixteen separate occasions. The shares belonging to Chizhou and Chetian all represent investments made after the initial formation of the organization. Because the relevant records use only the hexadecimal calendar and do not provide the reign periods, the formation of the organization and subsequent investments cannot be dated precisely. But the records were probably compiled in the late Qing or early in the period of Japanese occupation and describe a period of about two hundred years. Therefore, the organization was probably formed in the late Kangxi or early Qianlong period, in the first half of the eighteenth century.

The place-names that appear in the records are all locales in the Xiao native place in Nanjing County, Fujian. The term "Eleventh *Jia*" corresponds to an old term from the *lijia* system on the mainland. Through fieldwork in Nanjing, we have learned that lineage members there today also refer to their different settlements in terms of numbered *jia,* which suggests that they once belonged to the same *lijia* organization. The Eleventh *Jia* organization of the Xiao surname in Zhanghua thus seems to be a replica of a similar organization on the mainland. Fieldwork has also shown that the branches connected with the Shushan and Doushan shrines in Nanjing live in scattered settlements spread over a large area. In other words, they are actually a residentially dispersed lineage. Although the Xiao in Zhanghua are relatively more concentrated, they are still distributed over a number of villages in the Shetou and Tianzhong area, and thus can also be considered a residentially dispersed lineage. Cases like the Zhanghua Xiao allow us to comprehensively compare and contrast lineage organization on the mainland and in Taiwan, and call for more thorough investigation.

*   *   *

As the immigrant society of Taiwan gradually transformed into a settled society by the late Qing, the form and content of the contractual lineages there also changed accordingly from transplanted lineages into local, or nativized, lineages. The sacrificial society of the founding ancestor of the Tang surname of Miaoli provides an example of this nativization of early immigrant lineages. The Tang native place was in Gaosi township, Zhenping County, Guangdong. Their common ancestor was Sishiqi (Forty-Seven), who had settled there in the Yuan. A "Preface to the Register of the Sacrificial Society of the Founding Ancestor," dated 1788, explains:

> Since the Yuan dynasty, several hundred years have passed, and the members of our lineage have grown numerous, now numbering not less than ten thousand. . . . Later, the land became insufficient and the people too numerous, so some moved to other localities, and some looked to Taiwan and crossed over there. Reflecting on their origins, they collected money for an ancestral estate and created a register, to maintain forever the ancestral sacrifices. . . . Peng and others again reflected that, although we have wandered abroad from a young age, [our desire] to requite the ancestors persists. So we organized over one hundred uncles and cousins, and each person contributed one foreign silver dollar. The accumulated total was loaned out to earn interest, which was used to meet the expenses of sacrifice to the founding ancestor.[198]

The Tang must already have had a similar lineage organization in their native place in Guangdong, that is, a residentially dispersed lineage organization the members of which included some who had "moved to other localities," including Taiwan, and which had formed through investment and the establishment of an estate.[199] Later, more than one hundred individual members who had migrated to Miaoli invested funds there and formed a contractual lineage symbolized by the sacrifice to their founding ancestor. It is not known exactly when this organization was formed, but it was probably prior to the mid-Qianlong period, and its organizers were first-generation migrants who had been abroad "from a young age." When the organization was first formed, sacrificial activities were conducted every three years. By 1788, the value of each share in the sacrificial estate had grown to eight silver dollars. It was agreed that "wealth or land deeds are required to serve as collateral for loans." This indicates that some members of the organization had already settled down and established property. In the Daoguang period, the organization constructed an ancestral hall, successively increased the amount of property, and set up new regulations. Its organizational structure and social functions became increasingly complex.

> On May 10, 1837, sacrifice was conducted in the hall. All those present collectively agreed that every member of the society who goes to the prefectural seat to participate in the examinations should receive three silver dollars from the group to assist with travel expenses. If they are only going to the subprefecture or the county seat for examinations, they should not request assistance from the group.

On April 25, 1840, it was collectively agreed that, according to the old regulations of the society, anyone who wishes to redeem or sell his shares may do so at the rate of eight silver dollars per share. In 1834 we began construction of an ancestral hall, which was completed and the niches installed in the eighth month of 1836. The order [of arrangement] and the writing of names on the tablets was determined according to shares. . . . Now the uncles and nephews have agreed to establish the regulation that, in future, once a name has been written on a tablet, it may never be sold off, mortgaged, etc. In the future, because of inequalities in wealth among the descendants, unfilial descendants may wish to sell off the [share] of their ancestors in the society. The share may be redeemed at the rate of eight silver dollars, but the name on the tablet may not be removed. The purchaser is only permitted to collect a portion of the sacrificial meat in place of the original name. The seller may not claim that because the original name remains on the tablet he too is entitled to a share of the sacrifice. If the purchaser wishes to install a name on a tablet, sixteen silver dollars must be paid for the hall to conduct the tablet [installation] ritual for each tablet. If everyone agrees, a new tablet may be additionally installed to enjoy the sacrifice.

On October 7, 1875, sacrifice was conducted in the hall. The whole lineage gathered on the spot and agreed that a new register should be created in four identical copies, and also a corporate seal, which was divided into four sections. The group should collectively select four honest men to hold [the register and seal quarters]. For all corporate matters of the society, regardless of the nature of the expense record or deed, the four parts must be combined together and used to stamp the document for it to be confirmed. On the day of the sacrifice, the holders of the register and seal sections should submit them for all to see. The expenses of the sacrifice should be calculated, and on the following day entered into the registers. Once everyone has had a chance to look them over, they should be stamped as evidence of the annual audit. After that, the holders take the registers back with them. . . .

It is agreed that tenants who wish to purchase the land they cultivate must notify the holders of the register and seals, who must notify the adult uncles and nephews of the sacrificial [society] to discuss the price and the deposit and to draw up a deed as evidence. They must not keep this secret. The annual bottom-soil rent is to be retained by the tenants. If it is to be sold, the holders of the registers and seals must notify the adult uncles and nephews of that sacrificial [society]. They should gather in the ancestral hall to discuss things and determine the appropriate way to proceed. [The holders of the register] may not privately receive or disburse [the rents]. . . .

It is agreed that the descendants of those whose names are in the society may never sell or divide their share. They ought to consider the important significance of their ancestor's intention to contribute the money to establish this society. Those who do not heed this injunction

which derives from harsh [experience] and still wish to sell their share
are required to offer it to the group to take over. Neither individual
members of the society nor outsiders are permitted to take over the
share. If someone sells a share secretly, the sale should not be recorded
in the register. . . .

It is agreed that the previous regulations prescribe a meeting once
every three years. Now we have decided on a new regulation that we
should meet annually on the first day of the eighth month to decide
collectively on the expenditures for the sacrifice. In accordance with the
ancient system, the ritual of the sacrifice should not be lost.

It is agreed that uncles and nephews who become Government Students, Provincial or Metropolitan Graduates should receive a reward.
In the future there may be new regulations established, so we have a
register in which such regulations can be recorded.[200]

When their ancestral hall was completed in 1836, the organization
began to sacrifice to its own founders, the Founding Ancestors on
Taiwan, in addition to their Mainland Ancestor, and also to encourage lineage members to participate in the examinations. In 1875, the
previously triannual sacrificial activities of the organization became
annual. The management of the property, shares, and financial activities also became increasingly systematized. By this time, the members of the lineage were no longer first-generation migrants but rather
their settled descendants, and the lineage organization had changed
from a migrant lineage into a local, native lineage. The construction
of the ancestral hall in the Daoguang period can be seen as a symbol
of the nativization of the Tang lineage. Felicitous phrases on the
lintels of the Tang hall proclaimed:

> The branches of the descent-line extend to the soil of Taiwan.
> Let the descendants be hardworking and frugal to the utmost,
> Grand and imposing in this place; naturally able to extend their
>   good fortune.[201]

The implication is that the purpose of constructing the ancestral hall
had been to supersede the legitimacy of the original lineage organization on the mainland and establish a new descent-line in the new
locale.

After the hall was constructed, the tablets of the Founding Ancestors in Taiwan began to receive great attention:

Last year (1839) one called Lanliang came to Taiwan. He audaciously
wished to scrape his father Longrui's name off the ancestral tablet,
hoping to sell off his share in the family's society in Taiwan to someone
else. His own close relatives were unable to purchase it, so he had to

ask Dingsheng to purchase the share and obtain the portion of sacrificial meat in his place. He was not permitted to erase the name on the tablet.[202]

The following year the organization formalized the rule that, even if a member of the lineage sold off his share, the name of his ancestor on the tablet could not be erased. This measure was not taken to protect the rights of particular founding ancestors, but rather to demonstrate the esteem in which the Founding Ancestors in Taiwan were collectively held. In fact, it was precisely because the Tang hall served as the site where all the founding ancestors received sacrifice collectively that the hall could become the center for veneration of Founding Ancestors in Taiwan for all lineage members living there.[203] The organization also provided support only for examination candidates who registered for the examinations in Taiwan. The regulations of 1877 state clearly that, "Among the uncles and nephews of the hall in Taiwan, Government Students who cross over to the provincial capital [Fuzhou] to participate in the examinations are to be assisted with six silver dollars for expenses. Provincial graduates who go to the national capital for the metropolitan examinations are to be assisted with twelve silver dollars for expenses. Those who do not belong to the hall, or those who belong to the hall but are on the mainland, are not entitled to request assistance." Thus lineage members who remained on the mainland were perceived as being equivalent to non-lineage members. One's current registration was the essential marker of identity. So even though the sacrificial society of the Founding Ancestor of the Tang in the late Qing continued to be a large lineage symbolized by the worship of the Mainland Ancestors, it had been nativized to no less a degree than "small lineages" that were oriented around sacrifice to Founding Ancestors on Taiwan.

In Qing Taiwan, lineages based on documents of household division, or small lineages, to use the terminology of Taiwanese scholars, typically grew out of inheritance lineages formed in the process of household division. The formation and development of this sort of lineage organization have not previously been studied systematically. Some scholars believe that the formation of small lineages in Qing Taiwan only became possible a minimum of three to four generations after migration. Therefore they deduce that this sort of lineage must have developed mainly only after the mid-nineteenth century. For example, Zhuang Yingzhang writes: "the six large lineages of Linpipu were all formed prior to 1825. The other six small lineages were all formed after 1854."[204] He defines the criterion for the establishment of these small lineages as the construction of an ancestral hall. But if we consider the establishment of sacrificial property to be the essential criterion of the formation of a small lineage, most of these small lineages actually formed prior to 1850. Zhuang's book provides details of the processes by which these six lineages were established.

1. Corporate sacrificial property in the name of Ye Chu: Ye Chu's native place was Pinghe County, Zhangzhou Prefecture. He lived from 1707 to 1790. In 1740 he built the Jiangyaliao dike near Linpipu, to irrigate more than eighty *jia* of fields. Ye Chu had a single son, but his grandson's generation was divided into six branches, all of which settled in the locality. "The land property and water rights to Jiangyaliao dike left behind by Ye Chu were managed in rotation by the six branches." Thus this organization developed when the six branches were formed through household division, which must have been no later than the end of the Jiaqing period (1820).

2. Corporate sacrificial property in the name of Chen Chao: Chen Chao moved from Zhangpu County, Zhangzhou Prefecture to Nantou, Taiwan, in the Yongzheng period. His son Chen Ji opened up land around Linpipu. "Chen Ji left behind land around the first *jia* to serve as corporate sacrificial property. Over the years, managers administered the property and used the income for sacrifice to the common ancestors." Since this property was established by Chen Ji himself, this sacrificial organization must have formed no later than the end of the eighteenth century.

3. Corporate sacrificial property in the name of Zhang Chuang of Sheliao: Zhang Chuang moved from Longxi County, Zhangzhou Prefecture to Sheliao in the mid-Qianlong period. He had three sons. His grandsons settled in Sheliao and Zhongliao and thus developed into a residentially dispersed lineage. "Zhang Chuang's lineage divided into three branches. They had corporate sacrificial property that was cultivated in rotation by the three branches, which also took responsibility for the expenses of the ancestral sacrifice." The origins of this sacrificial property are not clear, but since it was cultivated in rotation by the three branches, it was probably set aside when the three branches divided their household estate no later than the early nineteenth century. In 1833 the organization went on to construct a common hall *(gongting)*.

4. Corporate sacrificial property in the name of Chen Fozhao: Chen Fozhao moved from Nanjing County, Zhangzhou, to Sheliao in the late Qianlong period. In the late Jiaqing period, he invested jointly with local people surnamed Zhang to construct a dike. His six sons inherited his estate. "Chen Fozhao left behind three *jia* of property, which was cultivated in rotation by the six branches. Each branch cultivated the land for one year in six, and the branch whose turn it was to culti-

vate the corporate land was responsible for the expenses of the sacrifice in that year." This shows that a lineage organization must have formed when the six sons divided their estate, which would have been in the first half of the nineteenth century.

5. Corporate sacrificial property in the name of Chen Gao: Chen Gao lived from 1677 to 1728. He moved to Taiwan from Haicheng County, Zhangzhou. His fourth-generation descendant Chen Yi opened up land in Linpipu. "Chen Yi's grandson Lianchi was given the title Gentleman for Good Service in 1854, whereupon he established corporate sacrificial property [in the name of] Chen Gao." The structure of this organization is not clear, but it does not seem to have formed as a result of division of the household estate.

6. Corporate sacrificial property in the name of Liao Meng: Liao Meng was from Yongding County, Tingzhou. He moved to Tainan in the Yongzheng period, and later relocated south of Linpipu, where he "made his living by producing ceramics." His descendants remained there. "They had early genealogical records. . . . In 1925 they constructed the Hall of Martial Authority *(Wuwei tang),* which was known as the Common Hall of the Liao surname." It is not known when this organization first established corporate sacrificial property, but the mention of genealogical records indicates that they had previously formed some kind of unified organization.[205]

Of the six small lineages of Linpipu, then, the date of formation of one is unknown, four were formed between the late eighteenth and early nineteenth centuries, and one in the mid-nineteenth century. The six large lineages of the area also formed in this period, the earliest in 1781 and the latest in 1825. Thus, in terms of the timing of establishment there is little to distinguish large lineages from small lineages.

The documents of household division which I have seen suggest that migrants to Taiwan generally divided their household as early as the first generation after settlement, at which point they already began to set aside corporate property *(gongye)* or corporate expenses *(gongfei),* thus forming inheritance lineages that operated on the principle of rotation through branches. Every one of the twenty-four documents of household division dating from the Qianlong to Daoguang periods found in the *Reference Materials Appended to the Common Law of Taiwan,* compiled during the Japanese occupation, records the setting aside of corporate property. In a more recent compilation of several dozen documents of household division, the majority of documents dating from prior to 1850 also mention the setting aside of corporate property.[206] Of the sixty-nine documents of household division in these two works, a total of sixty-four describe the setting aside of corporate property or corporate expenses in one form or another. The documents describe household estates and corporate property of varying sizes, indicating that the practice was common across different strata of society. Because the place of origin of most of the documents is not known, it is impossible to come to any firm conclusions about geographic distribution, but it would be safe to deduce that in the plains of southern and west-central Taiwan, which were developed relatively early, the formation of inheritance lineages may date back to the early eighteenth century, and they had spread to the rest of Taiwan by the early nineteenth. So-called small lineages were clearly very important in the early migrant society.

*   *   *

The corporate property of inheritance lineages in Qing Taiwan mainly took the form of corporate sacrificial property established in the name of an ancestor. But such property could have multiple functions besides ancestral sacrifice. For example, a document of household division of the Zheng surname, dated 1795, records:

> As for the sacrificial property, the autumn harvest each year should be used to pay the bottom-soil rent, and any surplus is to be used to meet expenses for sacrifices on the taboo days of the ancestors; annual festivals; temples and roads; the head tax; personal affairs [i.e., marriages and funerals]; and candles and incense for the spirits of the ancestors.[207]

In Qing Taiwan, retirement estates *(shanlao ye* or *yangshan ye),* property retained by or given to parents to provide them support in their old age, usually also became a sort of functionally comprehensive lineage property after the death of the parent. For example:

> The retirement property was originally set up to provide for the support of Mother and two others. It is also appropriate that it should later become rotating corporate property to be used for corporate matters. If we are fortunate and Mother lives to an old age, the branches will not dare to suggest that it start to be managed in rotation and used to pay for group sacrifices on taboo days and festivals and for taxes. It should be used entirely for Mother's personal needs. If by misfortune Mother should die, once her funeral is paid for, this property should be managed in rotation. In all matters concerning the whole group, the rota holder must fully respect the old regulations.[208]

This document illustrates that, after division of the household estate, many collective matters might be undertaken by an inheritance lin-

eage. In early immigrant society, where a stable social order had not
yet developed, there were probably many unanticipated corporate
expenses, which would have tended to strengthen the inheritance lineage. Even some inheritance lineages that had little corporate property had rules like the following:

> All corporate debts, borrowings, affairs, and expenses are to be
> divided among the 3.5 shares. It is not permitted to shirk one's share.[209]
>
> With respect to the property and sites belonging to the three shares,
> payment of the bottom-soil rent, as well as any expenses arising from
> unexpected matters such as disputes with other people, are to be allo-
> cated evenly among the three shares.[210]

In this case, even though no lineage property had been established,
the lineage members still had indivisible shared responsibilities, so a
functional lineage organization might still form.

In inheritance lineages with considerable lineage property, it was
common to establish different kinds of corporate property, each with
a specific function. For example, the 1736 Document of Household
Division of the Lin surname records:

> The rotating corporate property consists of one plot of unirrigated land,
> known as Haifengzhuang and Geyuanzhuang, a sugar mill 3.5 *zhang* in
> size located in it, and thirty-eight head of ox.
>
> It has been verbally agreed that each person [i.e., branch] will man-
> age the property for one year, and when [the rotation] is complete it
> will start again at the beginning. The manager each year earns the sur-
> plus [rent] left over after the bottom-soil rent has been paid to the
> Zhang family. The other three do not have any claim on a share. The
> land tax and the expenses of submitting the tax to the *yamen*, the
> songs and dances in spring [i.e., the annual village festival], the house-
> hold tax, etc. are all to be paid by the holder in that year. He is not
> permitted to [illegible] the other three.
>
> The annual rental income from the sugar mill is 47,100 catties of
> sugar. From this, 7,850 catties should be used by the rota holder to
> square accounts with the Zhang family. For the remaining 39,250
> catties, the conversion rate regardless of the market price of sugar is
> fixed at seven mace per hundred catties, which comes to a total of
> 274.75 taels. Out of this amount 25 taels is to be paid to the cartmen
> and the tax collector, leaving a remainder of 249.75 taels. This is to be
> divided into four equal shares, each share consisting of 62.43 taels.
> [Each branch's share] is to be obtained from the rota holder for that
> year on the day on which the income for the mill is fully received. Dif-
> ficulties should not be created. . . .
>
> The retirement property is listed in another register. You all should
> collect the income in rotation and hand it over to me for my use. In
> the future it can be added to the sacrificial property.[211]

Thus the rotating income from the corporate property of the Lin was used to meet certain collective expenses. The income from the retirement property was mainly used to meet the expenses of the elderly parent, and would later pay for the ancestral sacrifice. Rent from the sugar mill was divided directly among the four branches.

There were many wealthy and powerful households in Qing Taiwan.[212] They left behind considerable lineage property when they divided their household estates, and this served as a strong material foundation for the development of inheritance lineages. One 1793 document of household division describes an estate valued at 64,280 taels. At the time of division, 3,209 taels were set aside "for the enjoyment [of the sacrifice] in the name of the group"; 250 taels for "the installation of tablets into the lesser descent-line [shrine]"; 1,639 taels as the retirement estate for the primary wife; 441 taels as retirement estate for concubines; and 3,415 taels for educational fields. The total of these five items comes to 13,660 taels, about one-fifth of the total estate.[213]

A contract of 1797 records:

> While our late father was alive, he established several plots of fields and land at Rende North Subcanton and elsewhere as charitable land. The descendants of Youde and his four brothers manage it in rotation. This permits them each to have some security. He also established rental property at Dapulin and elsewhere, with a value of more than 100,000 taels, and endowed this under the name Yuan corporation *(Yuanji dagong)*. All the descendants of the Yuan corporation, regardless of whether or not they earn a reputation in the examination system, can take a turn in the rotation according to their position [in the genealogical charts] to collect the rent and handle the corporate affairs of the lineage. He also purchased fields in the area of Guangzhu East Subcanton, which contains a grave site with excellent geomantic properties. He ordered that he be buried there after his death, and the property should serve as sacrificial fields, to meet the expenses of sacrifice and sweeping. . . . Now our father has died. We brothers declare that we wish to inherit his ideals and fulfill his ambitions. Out of the retirement estate with a total value of forty thousand taels that he established while alive, once the funeral expenses have been paid, there remains rental property [as follows]: topsoil and bottom-soil rents from Kanglangbao and Daqiutianbao, 80 percent of the sugar income, the sites of two shops, and the dike, with a total value of 10,500 taels. We have discussed and agreed that this property should serve as educational fields, and it is given the name Jie estate *(Jie ji)*.[214]

The total amount of lineage property was over 150,000 taels, or more than 50,000 taels for each of the three branches into which the descendants of the Yuan corporation were divided. Such a well-endowed inheritance lineage would have had a major impact not just on the economic lives of the lineage members but also on the entire local social and economic structure.

*   *   *

In Chapter 2, I showed that there were many multiplex households resulting from multiple inheritance in Qing Taiwan. When a multiplex household divided its estate, several separate inheritance lineages were usually formed simultaneously. This 1838 partition document provides an example:

> Eldest brother Chengzhang, second brother Yuxi, third brother Baoqing, and fourth brother [Bao]zhuan, etc. reflect back to when our parents were still alive. Because uncle Jielin had no posterity, they ordered third brother Baoqing to go over and serve as his son. Because uncles Chengye and Chengyan also had no posterity, they ordered fourth brother Baozhuan to go over and serve as their designated grandson. Later Father and Mother died. . . .
>
> The plot of land purchased together with Dai Liangui from Lin Laixi of Zhipa Subcanton at Waigang belongs in perpetuity to Chengzhang and Yuxi, and is to serve to meet the expenses of the annual spring and autumn sacrifices to Father and Mother. The descendants of Baoqing and [Bao]zhuan must not interfere with this. Also, the plot of land at Chiniuzhou at Waigang, as well as the property acquired by extending a mortgage, is retained as the corporate property of all four shares, to meet their annual corporate expenses. Any collective surplus remaining after these expenses are paid is to be lent out to earn interest, and the income divided evenly among the four shares. A register has been drawn up with four copies, and in it are recorded all these items, as well as detailed explanations.[215]

In this example, the first and second branches, which inherited the descent-line of the birth father, together with the third and fourth branches, which inherited other descent-lines, together comprise a single inheritance lineage based on the corporate property inherited collectively by all four. At the same time, the branches also form three separate inheritance lineages, each one symbolized by the inheritance of a different descent-line.

Sons who were adopted out sometimes also inherited from their original descent-lines, so their descendants belonged to a number of different inheritance lineages simultaneously. This is the case described in one 1868 document of household division. There were four brothers in the family, "but second brother Ying was adopted out to serve as the designated grandson of an ancestor of the preceding generation. So among the four branches there was one that had no posterity." Ying had three sons. "When he was dying, he reflected: a tree has its roots, and a stream its source. He had his second son Hou return to [serve as posterity of] the second branch [of his original family]." As a result, when his own household divided, "the rent from two plots of land, one redeemed and the other newly acquired, was set aside to serve forever as the sacrificial estate, to rotate through the four branches to pay the costs of the sacrifice." Ying's second son returned to the original inheritance lineage, while his other two sons formed another inheritance lineage oriented around the ancestor for whom Ying served as the designated grandson.[216]

There were also cases of multiple inheritance of different surnames in Qing Taiwan. One such case is described in a household division document dated 1817: "Stepmother Yang . . . reflected repeatedly on the happy sentiments of her first marriage, and desired to have her own fifth son serve half as posterity for the Huang. From that day on, the sons would sacrifice separately to the two families, and were not to falsely substitute for one another."[217] Because the fifth son served "half as posterity" for another surname, his descendants would be divided between the two surnames, and would therefore belong to separate inheritance lineages. This dilemma of multiple inheritance of two descent-lines or two surnames was frequently handled by having the descendants of the adoptee alternate inheritance with each generation. This led to the development of multiple-inheritance lineages with extremely complex inheritance relations. In Taiwan there are many multiple-surname lineages, such as the Zhang-Liao-Jian and the Lin-Cai, which formed as a result of this kind of multiple inheritance.

Many surviving early deeds from Taiwan involve corporate property being divided, sold, and purchased. These inevitably resulted in the disintegration of an inheritance lineage. However, with the gradual transition from the early immigrant society to a settled society, the development of inheritance lineages became more stable. Some such lineages that had formed in the early period had become highly developed by the late Qing. The following three deeds, dated 1866, 1879, and 1886, provide examples:

The corporate sacrificial estates of our grandfather, great-grandfather and great-great-grandfather [have been inherited]. When it is our turn in the rotation, the three large branches must go together to the tenants and together collect [the rent] and together spend it to meet expenses. Any surplus is divided evenly among the three branches.[218]

It has been decided that the plot of irrigated field at Gongcuobian mortgaged to Chen Wei, earning a topsoil rent of thirty-five piculs; the two small plots of irrigated field inherited by the fifth branch, earning topsoil rent of ten piculs; the plot of unirrigated land at Gongcuobian, earning five silver dollars rent; and the [property of] the sixth branch at Jiuzili, earning topsoil rent of 3.6 piculs are all to be used to meet the collective expenses of the sacrifice. The three large branches will manage them in rotation, one after the other, and are not to try to shuffle their position.[219]

When it is the turn of our branch in the rotation, the rent from the rotating sacrificial income of the estate of Fuxing at Dashuke and of Minkuan at Xinzhuang Shanjiao, together with the orchard rent and the tea rent, should be rotated among the six [sub-]branches.[220]

These inheritance lineages had all developed to the third or fourth generation, and each generation had established new corporate property, forming a multilevel segmented system. In the cases with the greatest number of levels, there might be several dozen segments, which meant that the lineage was already approaching the limits of its potential development. Because the inheritance lineage was organized on the principle of management by rotation through the branches, once the branches grew too numerous, it became impossible to sustain the rotation, and the lineage either disintegrated or changed into a control-subordination lineage. This, recall, is why inheritance lineages in mainland Fujian rarely survived for more than three to five generations.

The first of the three deeds above also contains the prescription that the estate of the parents should be managed in rotation, but the sacrificial estates endowed in the name of the three generations prior to the parents were to be "collected together and disbursed together to meet expenses" when it was the lineage's turn in the rotation. That is, this income did not rotate between the three sub-branches. This suggests that there were already many branches with a claim on these estates, so the period of rotation had grown too lengthy for the practice of rotation to be maintained. Generally speaking, when income from lineage property was collected and dispensed collectively, rather than rotating through the branches, the lineage was in the process of changing from an inheritance to a control-subordination lineage. But because I have not had the opportunity to study complete and accurate genealogical records from Taiwan, I am not able to analyze this process of transformation further.

In the late Qing, residentially concentrated lineages in parts of Taiwan had already attained considerable scale, and in some areas intralineage or intersurname feuds broke out.[221] In the larger residentially concentrated lineages, control-subordination lineages led by local gentry or strongmen formed. Zhuang Yingzhang has found that by the time of the Japanese occupation eight of the twelve large and small lineages of Linpipu had already built ancestral halls.[222] The construction of these halls was closely linked to the formation of local control-subordination lineages. For example, according to the early records of the Lin surname Hall of Venerating Roots *(Chongben Tang)*:

> In 1788, after the uprising of Lin Shuang[wen], the Lin of Linpipu gathered funds and constructed the Lin Hall of Venerating Roots, to commemorate the merit of the opening up of Linpipu. In 1802, led by Lin Shiping, they collected subscriptions by household from the Lin households in the Linpipu area for its reconstruction. In 1855, the Lin lineage members again collected funds for reconstruction. Every year, aside from the spring and autumn sacrifices, minor sacrifices were held at the Clear and Bright, Double Five, Winter Solstice, Middle Origin, Double Nine, New Year's Eve, and other festivals. The supervisors were chosen from the important members of the Lin lineage and held their position for an indefinite period. There was no post of Master of the Incense Burner *(luzhu)*, but only a Head of Affairs *(shoushi)*. The five neighborhoods of Wanzi, Jieziwei (Lower Street of Linpipu), Zhuweizi, Zhutouzong, and Xiapu each selected one man to hold the office, and the responsibility for supervising the affairs of the sacrifice rotated among these five men.[223]

This document indicates that the collection of funds for the construction of the ancestral hall was initiated by a small number of lineage members, and its organizational structure was based neither on household nor on shares, but rather on the selection of a small number of managers who took responsibility for administration and supervision of all matters connected with the hall. The ordinary membership of the organization included all the local residents who were surnamed Lin: "All those of the Lin surname who lived in the Zhushan area could participate. Those who migrated away from Zhushan lost their eligibility."[224] This lineage organization, in which a small number of members controlled lineage affairs and in which ties of common locality served as the unifying link, is a classic example of the control-subordination lineage.

In some cases, contractual lineages formed by migrants in the early period had also gradually changed into control-subordination

lineages by the late Qing. For example, the Zhong lineage of
Neipuzhuang established property with funds originally invested
through share purchase for the construction of a port. The port
project did not succeed, so the money was entrusted to a certain
lineage member to lend out to earn interest. By 1804, the capital
had grown to 462 *yuan,* which was used to establish the Venerating
Literary Classics *(chongwendian)* educational estate. According to
rules established in 1827, "civil and military Government Students
. . . twice every year divide among themselves a scholarship of sixty
piculs from the Venerating Literary Classics educational estate."[225]
The rights to this estate were thus no longer allocated according to
the original investment, but rather according to the personal status of
the participants. In other words, the organization had transformed
into a control-subordination lineage. We as yet know too little about
the formation and development of control-subordination lineages in
Taiwan in the late Qing, and this is an important topic for further
research.

*   *   *

In summary, when migrants from the mainland first crossed over to
Taiwan, people from the same native place and the same lineage
frequently provided one another mutual assistance and therefore
attracted subsequent migrants. Thus from the start there was a tendency toward the residential concentration of such groups. After the
mid-Qing, feuding among people from different native places encouraged further expansion in the scale of residentially concentrated
lineages. The lineage organizations of the early migrants were mostly
contractual lineages symbolized by the worship of Mainland Ancestors. The formation of this kind of lineage organization was usually
related to lineage organization in the original native place, and in
some cases the lineage in Taiwan was simply a reconstruction of the
lineage in the original native places. Because of the relatively high
social mobility of early immigrants, this kind of lineage organization
was most unstable. Its members could freely join or withdraw from
the organization, and the organization might have no fixed property.

Once immigrants became settled, this sort of lineage organization
gradually stabilized and began to construct ancestral halls, establish
property locally, and collectively worship the Founding Ancestors in
Taiwan. In this way, it changed into an independent nativized lineage. At the same time, inheritance lineages, also oriented around

worship of Founding Ancestors in Taiwan, began to develop among the descendants of the migrants. The formation of this sort of lineage organization was usually associated with collective property set aside at the time of the division of the household estate, so it tended to have considerable economic power and occupied an important position in the economic structure of local society. In some lineages, corporate property was set aside by each generation, leading to the development of multilevel inheritance lineages. By the late Qing, control-subordination lineages led by gentry or local strongmen had also formed in the larger residentially concentrated lineages. Some lineage organizations may have had the character of control-subordination lineages from the time of their establishment, but most control-subordination lineages developed out of inheritance or contractual lineages. My access to documents on the history of the lineage in Taiwan has been limited, so my aim in this section has been merely to present some hypotheses for further investigation. Due to limitations of space, I have only attempted to show that the typology of lineage organization introduced in this work may also be applicable to Taiwan. It also seems likely that the characteristics of the development process of lineage organization in Qing-era Taiwan would share similarities with other immigrant areas in that period, such as Sichuan and Northeast China.

5
Family Lineage Organization and Social Change

Serving as a form of organization that played a structural role in society, family lineage organization adapted to meet changing political, economic, and cultural circumstances. The development and transformation of family lineage organization therefore went on in parallel with broad, fundamental social changes. In this chapter I shall discuss the relationship between family and lineage organization and social developments in Ming and Qing Fujian from three different perspectives: descent-line ideology, social control, and property relations.

The Popularization of Descent-Line *(Zong)* Ethics

The basic meaning of the term "descent-line system" *(zongfa)* is the system of inheritance of ancestral shrines to recent ancestors *(zong)* and to distant ancestors *(tiao)* of the descent-line. The term can also be extended to mean the principles of lineage organization. The *zong* and the *tiao* together refer to all sites where ancestral sacrifice is conducted. In the strictest sense, the lineage *(zongzu)* is the group of patrilineal consanguinal kin oriented around such sites—that is, the group described by the expression "those who have the same surname, belong to the same descent-line, and unite as a lineage." The *Bohu tong* (Comprehensive discussions in the White Tiger Hall, a work of Confucian exegesis attributed to Ban Gu [32–92 C.E.]) provides the following gloss for the term "lineage" *(zongzu):* "What does *zong* mean? *Zong* means to honor. He who officiates as host to the ancestors is honored by the members of his lineage."[1] The *Erya* (Examples of refined usage, c. 3 B.C.E..) offers the following definition: "The father's group is the lineage."

In antiquity, veneration of ancestors was seen as a fundamental human sentiment, and sacrificial activities as an effective means to unite kinsmen. According to the *Book of Rites:* "The way of humanity is to treat the kin [with the sentiments appropriate to] kin. Because the kin are treated [with the sentiments appropriate to] kin, the ancestors are venerated. Because the ancestors are venerated, the descent-line is respected. Because the descent-line is respected, the lineage is united."[2] This is the classic expression of descent-line ethics. "Venerating the ancestors and respecting the descent-line" has remained the essential condition for cohesive lineage organization up to the present day. The widespread development of lineage organization among the populace can thus be seen as a reflection of the popularization of this descent-line ethics.

The right to erect temples for the worship of ancestors has historically been a marker of status distinction.[3] Every dynasty placed strict controls on this right, which resulted in a strictly hierarchical lineage system. Prior to the Qin, there were distinct temple regulations for the ruler and the ranks of the nobility. The common people were not permitted to erect shrines to worship their ancestors, "but sacrificed to their fathers in the chamber *(qin)* [inside the residence]."[4] In the nobility, the shrines to ancestors recent and distant were inherited generation after generation solely by the descent-line heir *(zongzi),* the eldest son of the principal wife in each generation. He performed the sacrifice of the great descent-line *(dazong),* which was "maintained without interruption for a hundred generations." Other sons were permitted only to establish lesser descent-lines *(xiaozong),* in which sacrifice was maintained for five generations only, and were subject to the authority of the descent-line heir of the great line.[5] This sort of lineage system, in which "the great descent-line is able to lead the lesser descent-lines, and the lesser descent-lines are able to lead the groups of younger brothers,"[6] was suited to the feudal system of hereditary ranks and emoluments. Its purpose was to safeguard the hereditary dominance of the aristocratic class. After the Han, the disappearance of the system of hereditary ranks and emoluments led to changes in the descent-line system. But the distinction between aristocrats and commoners, and between the descent-line heir and other descendants, persisted. According to Ming regulations, only officials above a certain rank were allowed to erect an ancestral shrine for sacrifice to four generations of ancestors, and commoners were only allowed to sacrifice to their parents inside their homes.[7]

According to Qing regulations, both officials and commoners could sacrifice to four generations of ancestors, but only officials could erect shrines to sacrifice to their ancestors. Commoners were still restricted to "sacrifice in the chamber [inside the residence]."[8] Ming and Qing law also prescribed that the right to sacrifice to the ancestors should be inherited in the first instance by the eldest son of the principal wife, and only if this was not possible by sons of other spouses or younger sons. Thus, in principle, the descent-line heir alone inherited the right to sacrifice to the ancestors, and other sons had no right to interfere.[9] This strictly hierarchical descent-line system discouraged the development of lineage organization among the populace and even limited the possibilities for officials to "venerate the ancestors and unite the lineage."

Some scholars believe that there were significant changes to the descent-line system after the mid-Ming. Commoners, they argue, were given permission to erect ancestral temples and extend sacrifice back to founding ancestors, and these changes encouraged the spread and development of lineage organization among the populace.[10] This view is incorrect. Although beginning in the early Ming a number of officials proposed such changes, they never became formal laws. The development of popular lineage organization in the Ming and Qing was not based on the official model of the descent-line system. Rather, demolishing the restrictive official system was the essential precondition for this development.

A popularized version of descent-line ethics, which provided the essential ideological condition for the spread and development of popular lineage organization, gradually took shape beginning in the Song, under the influence of Cheng Yi, Zhu Xi, and other neo-Confucians. Cheng Yi believed that "the great-great-grandfather falls within the mourning grades, so it would be extremely wrong not to sacrifice to him. From the Son of Heaven down to the common people, there are no distinctions in the mourning grades; this should also be the case with sacrifice." He therefore advocated eliminating the distinction between aristocrats and commoners for the conduct of sacrifice and relaxing restrictions on the number of generations of ancestors to which the common people could sacrifice. He also suggested that, although ancestors prior to the great-great-grandfather did not fall within the mourning grades, they should still be sacrificed to annually, in order to demonstrate respect for origins and to repay the favor of distant ancestors.[11] Zhu Xi expanded on this argument.

He wrote: "When a gentleman builds a house his first task is always to set up an offering hall *(citang)* to the east of the main chamber of his house. Four altars are made for offerings to the ancestral tablets of his earlier ancestors."[12] The offering hall envisioned by Zhu Xi was a niche for tablets set up in the main hall of the residence, so it did not conflict with the ancient principle that "the common people sacrifice in the chamber [inside their residence]." But because this sort of offering hall allowed for the worship of four generations of ancestral tablets from the great-great-grandfather down to the father, in practice it meant permitting the common people to perform the sacrificial practices of a lesser descent-line. As for sacrifices to founding ancestors and other ancestors more distant than the great-great-grandfather, Zhu Xi believed "these did not exist in antiquity. [Although] Cheng Yi's suggestion [that common people perform these sacrifices] arises out of righteousness. . . . I regard this as a transgression. At present I do not dare [to recommend] this sacrifice."[13] But he did instruct that sacrificial land established to meet the expenses of the offering hall, "is to be converted to grave fields after the mourning grades have been exhausted. . . . The descent-line heir should manage the property to provide for the costs of sacrifices."[14] This indicates that although Zhu Xi excluded founding ancestors and distant ancestors from the sacrifices in the offering hall, he approved of offerings to them at the gravesite. In other words, he sanctioned popular performance of the sacrificial practices of a great descent-line, "maintained without interruption for a hundred generations," at the graves.

In the late Southern Song, the Cai brothers, neo-Confucian philosophers from Jianyang County, "together investigated the offering hall system described in Zhu Xi's *Family Rituals (Zhuzi Jiali).*" The Cai of Lufeng were a famous lineage of northeast Fujian, of whom it was said, "in four generations they had nine Confucian scholars; to the Six Classics they added three commentaries."[15] Their ancestral hall regulations state that there should be an offering hall for the worship of four generations of ancestors, and that, "after the mourning grades are exhausted, the tablet is removed and buried behind the grave. Every year the lineage members are led to sacrifice there once. This is to be continued without variation for a hundred generations."[16] This was an organic integration of offering-hall sacrifice and grave sacrifice, which combined the implementation of the major and minor descent-line sacrifices. The practical consequence was that the restriction on the numbers of generations of ancestors to whom sacrifice could be offered was effectively lifted.

The sacrificial ritual developed by Cheng Yi, Zhu Xi, and other neo-Confucian philosophers, it was said, "is not based on the Way of the [Ancient] Kings, but arises out of righteousness." Their goal was to extend the methods of "venerating the descent-line and uniting the lineage," which had originally been applicable only to the nobility and official classes, into a common standard of behavior for all levels of society. Their popularized version of sacrificial ritual, although never formally enshrined in law, nonetheless became an important ethical justification for the popular practice of venerating the line and uniting the lineage, and thus played an important role in stimulating the widespread development of lineage organization after the Song. In 1489, Putian literatus Peng Shao wrote, in the "Inscription on the Reconstruction of the Ancestral Shrine of the Li of Baitang":

> In the past, Master Cheng Yi once sacrificed to the founding ancestor and the early ancestors. Master Zhu Xi on this basis included [this sacrifice] in the *Family Rituals*. Afterward, he had doubts because he was unsure, and he [wrote] no more. In the early years of the Hongwu reign of our founding emperor, the gentry and the commoners were permitted to sacrifice to their great-grandfathers, grandfathers, and fathers. In the Yongle period, the *Xingli daquan* (Great compendium of nature and principle) was compiled, and the *Family Rituals* promulgated all over the empire. So sacrifice to distant ancestors become the common rule.

As the influence of Cheng-Zhu neo-Confucianism spread, sacrificing to ancestors of distant generations became accepted practice. But the Song neo-Confucians' stress on the distinction between greater and lesser descent-lines still limited the development of lineage organization. As a result, in the popular practice of ancestral sacrifice, the ritual system of the Song philosophers was superseded in many new ways. In particular, Zhu Xi's ideas about the offering-hall system underwent significant changes. Erecting a dedicated shrine outside the home, and sacrificing there to ancestors more than four generations distant obviously represented a new development in the ancestral hall system. Although the Hongwu emperor had sanctioned sacrifice to four generations of ancestors, Peng Shao continued:

> there was not a dedicated hall for the placement of tablets. At present, most of the prominent lineages of Putian have such [a hall]. Each

family has its own system for the number of ancestors and their arrangements in the niche. Some divide [the niche] into five chambers, sacrificing to the ancestors descended from the great-great-grandfather and the great-grandfather on the left and right; others, though also dividing [the niche] into five chambers, arrange the descendants by branch on the left and right, and each branch sacrifices to its own great-great- and great-grandfather. In both cases, they use the central chamber to sacrifice to the early ancestors. Some who follow the *Family Rituals* distribute the four most recent generations of ancestors among the different chambers, with the most venerated to the west, and sacrifice to the early ancestors only at the tombs. Some people question this. The old scholars who discuss ritual have still not come to a common opinion. This is certainly because people's deepest emotions cannot be controlled or unified. At present, in the ancestral hall at Baitang, more than ten generations of previous ancestors receive sacrifice. According to the intentions of the system of ritual, this is not appropriate. But the members of the lineage are numerous and their relationships distant. If this is not done, then their hearts will be dispersed, and there will be nothing with which to tie them back together. If one desires to ensure that the lineage sacrifice will endure without interruption, and the tradition of the ancestors be transmitted without end, won't this be very difficult?[17]

Zhu Xi's original intention was that an ancestral hall be used for the sacrifices of a lesser descent-line only, and the tablets removed after five generations. Thus each generation was to eliminate the sacrifice to their ancestor in the fifth generation previous. This set narrow limitations on the possibilities of "respecting the line and uniting the lineage," and greatly impeded long-term lineage organization. But once sacrifice in ancestral halls was extended to ancestors more than four generations distant, lesser descent-lines were effectively transformed into greater descent-lines. This made it possible for lineage organizations to be maintained with stability over the long term and to grow ever larger in scale. Even more important, the practice of establishing dedicated shrines for ancestral sacrifice outside the home implied that the regulation that "the common people sacrifice in the chamber" had been superseded. Class distinctions in the conduct of ancestral sacrifice were being effaced.

In early Ming Fujian, such changes in ancestral halls had not yet been standardized. As Peng Shao wrote, "each family has its own system." While some gentry objected to this, from the mid-Ming the construction of dedicated shrines and sacrifices to distant ancestors became common social practice. In the Qing it grew even more prevalent. Thus, in the Quanzhou area, for example, "in a lineage of only one hundred members, or as soon as one member is appointed to office, they immediately make plans to erect a hall and establish sacrificial lands." In Shaowu, "in the villages the people assemble together and dwell as a lineage. They erect descent-line shrines and conduct annual sacrifices, in which custom they are just like the people of antiquity."[18] In Putian County, "the various hereditary lineages all have great descent-line halls and lesser descent-line halls. They hold feasts and make offerings annually, and without regard to distinctions between noble or base conduct these according to seniority. One-fifth of all the land inside the city walls is occupied by ancestral halls. Whenever a house is built, the ancestral hall is built first. This is indeed the custom."[19] In Zhao'an County of Zhangzhou, "even if all they have is a small space in which to live, still they all have ancestral shrines, descent-line halls, and branch halls. They carve the beams and engrave the pillars, and do not regret the expense."[20] In such halls, not only the First Ancestor who Settled or the First Enfeoffed Ancestor of the lineage received sacrifice, but often also the First Ancestor of the Surname to Migrate to Fujian or the First Ancestor to Obtain this Surname. This meant that "respecting the line and uniting the lineage" could extend beyond county or prefectural and even provincial limits. The spread in popular construction of ancestral shrines demonstrates that the official descent-line system was already a dead letter, a meaningless abstraction, and the descent-line theory of the Song neo-Confucians no longer had any practical significance.

Aside from sacrifice in ancestral halls, the sacrificial practices of the people of Fujian from the Song onward also included sacrifice in the ancestral home *(zucuo)* and at the graves.[21] Because the latter two forms were the easiest to practice, they were historically the fundamental forms of popular sacrifice. The popularization of descent-line ethics inevitably led these kinds of sacrifice to flourish as well. The ancestral home refers to a corporately owned hall that was excluded from successive household divisions and was used primarily for sacrifice to the branch ancestor of each branch or sub-branch within the lineage. Setting aside the ancestral home at the time of household division was common social practice throughout Fujian, which itself reflects the flourishing of family sacrificial activities. The lineage regulations of the Li of Baitang prescribe that the ancestral hall is to be used only for sacrifice to ancestors five generations distant or more. "Sacrifice to those within four generations should be maintained for each in the private dwelling *(sishi)*; [their tablets] are not to be brought into the hall."[22] The term "private dwelling" here means the ancestral home of each branch. The regulations of the Shimei Wu lineage of Fuzhou prescribe that, while collective sacrifice to all the generations of ancestors is conducted in the ancestral hall, each branch must still "conduct their own sacrifice in the chamber [inside the residence]" for their direct ancestors.[23] There must therefore have been an ancestral home for each branch. The genealogy of the Guan lineage of Yongchun describes in some detail the changing fortunes of the lesser descent-line shrines, that is, the ancestral homes of each branch. These were clearly seen as a symbol for the cohesiveness of each branch:

> Residence *(ju)* is truly important. It is the basis for gathering what is dispersed. Now the descendants of our surname are prospering. Large halls face one another, [too numerous] to be recorded completely. But the great descent-line hall of the earliest ancestor, and the lesser descent-line shrines *(xiaozong shiyu)* of each branch should be recorded in broad detail as we are compiling the genealogy, so that the descendants will know that their founding was not easy, and so that the rising and falling fortunes of each branch can be understood. . . . The ancestral hall of the pioneering ancestor is in the middle of our village. [His descendants] divided into three branches. Our lineage is a sub-branch of the third branch. In the ninth generation, it further divided into three sub-branches. . . . Since that time, there has been a lesser descent-line shrine called Shantou. It was originally the home of Siqi (Four-seven), the eldest son of Erba (Two-eight). His line was transmitted to the sixteenth generation, in which Yiqi and Yize were unable to maintain the sacrifice. So it was sold to the descendants of the West branch. There is also a shrine called Shipantou. It was originally the home of Shiliu (Sixteen) of the Tianzhong branch. Now [his descendants] have moved to Weiyuan, so this house has also been abandoned. There is also a shrine called Yanjiaoshan. It was originally the home of Xibin of the East branch. His descendants have now placed the ancestral tablets in the main hall, and each year at the festival of Middle Origin, when the sacrifice is complete they gather for a feast. This shrine has a most imposing appearance. . . . There is also a shrine called Andou. It was the home of Xinliu and Xinshi of the West branch. It still exists. Some of the ancestral shrines of the earlier ancestors of the whole lineage discussed above have survived and others have been abandoned. For those which have survived, the villagers generally use the name of the shrine to identify the lineage branch. This is just like the old meaning of the terms Dongli surname and Dongmen surname in the *Spring and Autumn Annals* or the *Zuo Zhuan*.[24]

The shrines of the lesser descent-lines were actually branch halls that had developed out of the residences of the founding ancestors of each branch. The objects of sacrifice in such halls were clearly not limited to four generations of ancestors. Many ancestral halls throughout Fujian in the Ming and Qing similarly developed out of ancestral homes. For example, in the early Ming, the Li of Baitang in Putian sacrificed to their ancestors in the main hall of an old residence. As we saw in Chapter 4, this site was destroyed by fire, so the descendants sacrificed to immediate ancestors in their homes, and to their founding ancestor Zhigan in a "temporarily borrowed location." In the Zhengtong period, they constructed an ancestral hall on the site of the former residence for large-scale collective sacrifice.[25]

Some lineages were able to sacrifice to successive generations of ancestors even though they never constructed an ancestral hall, because they maintained an ancestral home for generations. For example, in the Li lineage of Huqiao in Yongchun, "from the Ming to the Qing, through two dynasties, [our lineage] was transmitted through more than ten generations, each of which maintained the old ancestral home of our ancestor, and an ancestral hall was never constructed."[26] Thus, in the course of the development of lineage organization in post–Song Fujian, sacrificial activities in an ancestral home could play an important function in generating lineage cohesion.

Many documents of household division from Qing Taiwan make reference to ancestral homes. For example, one document of 1835 describes: "a plot of land and one dwelling inherited jointly from grandfather, who purchased it from Lin Jiao. . . . Because the brothers [have divided the household estate] and dwell separately, this property will be retained and held in common. The central chamber will be used to sacrifice to the collective ancestors, and for the spirit tablets of the four brothers."[27] An 1856 contract of the Zhang surname records: "The central chamber that is used for sacrifice to the spirits of the ancestors . . . will be retained as corporate property, with the three main branches managing it in rotation."[28] An 1879 will records: "The central chamber is set aside to serve as the hall of the collective offering hall *(gong citang).*"[29] An 1892 contract prescribes: "The central chambers in the front and back of the second hall in the main residence belong to the original ancestral home. They are used to worship the gods and ancestors."[30] An 1898 Chen legacy makes the following request: "Half the main hall, the general altar, and one plot of land at Leiwei have been collective property since previous generations. You ought to retain it as collective property."[31] The practice of setting aside the ancestral home at the time of family division was thus clearly also common in the immigrant society of Qing Taiwan. For the most part, in the early period of immigrant settlement, when there were neither ancestral halls nor ancestral graves, the ancestral home was the only possible site for ancestral sacrifice. So ancestral homes were particularly significant in the development of immigrant lineages.

*   *   *

Sacrificial activities at ancestral graves flourished already in the Song. The twelfth-century *Sanshan (Fuzhou) Gazetteer* records:

> The people of the prefecture perform obeisances below the graves at the spring sacrifice at the time of the Cold Food festival. The rich households and great surnames own land property to support the grave-yards. When the sacrifice is over, the agnates assemble. They may number as many as several hundred people or as few as several dozen. Because of this [event], they hold a feast, arranging themselves in order and treating one another with familiarity. This is the way to honor the ancestors and encourage warm feelings among the agnates.[32]

It is possible that already at this time sacrifices were being made at the graves of ancestors of each generation beginning with the founding ancestor, and that grave sacrifice was thus the most systematized form of sacrifice practiced by lineage organization. In the Ming and Qing, as the sheer number of ancestral graves grew ever greater, lineage members found it impossible not to make distinctions between them and pay attention to only some of these graves. To ensure the maintenance of the sacrifices to each generation, some lineages drew up plans for the order of grave sacrifices, regulating the dates of sacrifice at each grave.

> Our lineage conducts grave sacrifice for all the ancestors. Each person feels closest to his own relatives, so on the day of the Clear and Bright Festival, he sacrifices to the ancestors of his own branch. So the grave of the founding ancestor is sacrificed to last of all. . . . Now the two halls have agreed that the total [income from] the sacrificial fields of the founding ancestor must be used to pay the tax due by the end of the year, and [the remainder] converted to cash, to prepare for the expenses of sacrifice and the distribution of sacrificial meat in the following spring. The schedule of the sacrifice is fixed at ten days prior to the Clear and Bright Festival. In this way, the grave sacrifices can be conducted in the appropriate order, and there will not be scheduling conflicts for the people who have registered to participate.[33]

Within the lineage, grave sacrifices were a type of sacrificial activity that was organized individually, so their organizational form was different from that of sacrifice in the home or hall. Sacrifices in the home or hall were collective sacrifices, in that generations of ancestors received sacrifice simultaneously, while grave sacrifice was particular sacrifice *(teji)*, in that only a single ancestor received sacrifice at a time. Thus, even if home sacrifice and hall sacrifice were conducted for all the generations of ancestors, it was still necessary to perform grave sacrifice at the individual graves of each ancestor. "It is the responsibility of the descendants of each branch to recarve the inscriptions and personally repair the graves of their branch; they must not be remiss in sacrificing or sweeping, nor may they have outsiders do so [on their behalf]."[34] "As for [the graves] of the generations of ancestors, each branch is to conduct the particular sacrifice, which is performed twice, in spring and in autumn. Within the branch, responsibility is to be taken in rotation, and it is not permitted for anyone to omit the ritual."[35] Because each sacrifice was directed at a particular ancestor, grave sacrifice served to divide the members of the whole lineage systematically into sacrificial groups whose degree of kinship was clearly articulated. This served to maintain the distinct existence of the internal segments of the lineage.

*   *   *

As the practices of ancestral sacrifice spread and developed, the system of inheritance of the descent-line shrines also underwent a fundamental change. The crux of this change was that the descent-line heir lost his monopoly on sacrifices to all the previous generations of ancestors. In the classical descent-line system, the descent-line shrines were inherited by the descent-line heir alone, which implied a system of authority in which "the great descent-line is able to lead the lesser descent-lines, and the lesser descent-lines are able to lead the groups of younger brothers,"[36] that is, the descent-line heir had authority over the heads of the lesser-descent-lines, who in turn had authority over the descendants as a whole. The Song neo-Confucians did not eliminate this distinction between greater and lesser descent-lines precisely because they wished to maintain the system of sole inheritance of the sacrificial sites by the eldest son of the principal wife, in the hope of reconstructing and expanding a structure of authority along the lines of the descent-line system and based on the power of the descent-line heir. The restrictions of the descent-line system could be effectively challenged only by eliminating these special rights of the eldest son of the principal wife. This change is evident in the "Family Admonitions" of the late Ming Tong'an gentry Lin Xiyuan:

According to the *Family Rituals* of Master Zhu Xi, the ancestral hall is to be constructed with four niches, for sacrifice to the ancestors back to the great-great-grandfather. At present the descent-line system is not practiced, so there is nothing to control the members of the lineage or to restrain the younger descendants. I fear that after five generations, when the mourning grade of the great-great-grandfather is exhausted, the descendants of the lesser descent lines will each sacrifice to their own ancestors, and will no longer have anything to do with the ancestral hall. Now we have discussed and decided that the first founder of our family, and those who have arisen through holding official positions, should be [treated as] founding ancestors, and [their tablets] should remain for a hundred generations. For other ancestors prior to the great-great-grandfather, [the tablet] should be removed and stored in another niche.

According to the *Family Rituals* of Master Zhu Xi . . . it is appropriate to sacrifice in the residence. But some people's ancestral halls are not located in the east of their residence. For example, the ancestral halls of the Lingxia Ye and the Li of Qianjie are located where the members of the lineage are most densely settled, at some distance from the residences. Those who are responsible for the sacrifice are also dispersed in all four directions, forty or fifty *li* from the ancestral halls. At present the system of the descent-line heir is not practiced. In some cases the descent-line heir is impoverished and unable to sustain himself, or has dispersed to the four directions, and there is no chamber which can accommodate the sacrifice. If the instructions on sacrificing in the chamber are to be followed but there is no residence, what is to be done? So it is now decided to fix an ancestral hall system in which the hall shall have a chamber of two beams, divided into five rooms, in order to hold the five niches.[37]

Lin Xiyuan summarizes these changes to the ancestral hall system with the penetrating remark that "at present the descent-line system is not practiced." Because no descent-line heir was designated, the distinction between great and lesser descent-lines had essentially disappeared. Retaining ancestral tablets in ancestral halls forever rather than discarding them after five generations could now become the norm. From another perspective, it was precisely because there was no descent-line heir that there was no obvious chamber inside a residence in which to conduct sacrifice in accord with classical principles. This made it necessary to erect a dedicated shrine independent of any residence. In the absence of a descent-line heir, this sort of ancestral hall could only function if the right to sacrifice to previous generations was inherited collectively by the descendants who sacrificed together to the generations of ancestors. Some lineages retained the title of descent-line heir or descent-line grandson, but the holders of these titles had only symbolic importance, and certainly did not inherit the sole right to sacrifice to previous generations of ancestors. According to the 1554 "Collective Oath on Arrangements for the Sacrificial Clothing of the Descent-line Heir" of the Su lineage of Tong'an:

> We have read in the *Rites* that the descent-line heir regulates the lineage, maintains the family [estate], and thus follows the way of the ruler. If the sacrificial garments are not prepared, he does not dare hold the sacrifice. For this reason, in antiquity sacrificial land was established for the descent-line heir to preserve through the generations, in order to stress the importance of origins. Our ancestor Yuweng first moved to Taijiang, establishing an estate to transmit the tradition. He performed all the rituals and practices of righteousness, but he hadn't time to see to this matter of land. So the descent-line heir's responsibilities were light, and he was not responsible for the complete ritual. But descent-line grandson Ding's household was so poor that he was unable to live to an old age, and his orphan Shouzai had to rush about in order to find food and clothing. The rituals were in greater danger of being abandoned. At that time he had no posterity, so the members of the lineage proposed that Ding's distant nephew Ji, who understood the classics and whose conduct was refined, should serve as Ding's heir, to regulate the lineage and maintain the sacrifice. But Ji was also poor, and unless the sacrificial garments were prepared for him, he would have found it difficult to face the ancestors and announce the ritual [on behalf of] the lineage members. The lineage heads and the members therefore collectively agreed to extend our ancestor's intention to esteem the origins and respect the sacrifice, and set aside thirteen piculs of rice from the annual rental income of the Nourishing Prosperity *(Zifu)* sacrificial lands originally established by our ancestor. Regardless of the success of the harvest, the full amount is to be given to descendant Ji on schedule. This income is to be used in perpetuity to pay the expenses of the sacrificial garments. It shall not be transferred to other purposes, for this would disappoint everyone. . . . This is corporate property. Descent-line heirs of later generations may not consider it their own private property, or look for ways to take it over or make changes that would cause conflict. The descendants of the branches must also not rely on their strength and struggle to take it over, thereby ruining these regulations which have been made.[38]

In theory, the lineage member who held the position of descent-line heir or descent-line grandson had authority over the lineage in maintaining the sacrifice, but in practice this translated only into the responsibility to serve as the lineage's ritual representative. A descent-line heir who could not even afford to prepare the appropriate sacrificial garments was a far cry from the descent-line heir of antiquity, who "regulates the lineage, maintains the family [estate], and thus follows the way of the ruler." Even the oath above simply gave the heir the right to draw on the corporate estate to pay the costs of the sacrifice. The estate itself was still inherited collectively by the descendants.

The fundamental cause of all of these changes is, I believe, that individual social and economic status became more unstable after the disappearance of individual hereditary ranks and emoluments and lineage hereditary status. There would invariably be cases where the eldest son by the principal wife was too poor to perform the necessary sacrifices. This led inevitably to changes in the way the rights to sacrifice were inherited and made it impossible for the descent-line heir to retain stable and permanent special rights.

＊　＊　＊

The various kinds of sacrificial sites used by the people of Fujian in the Ming and Qing were usually collectively inherited by the descendants of a given line, to ensure that, even after household division, lineage members would continue to maintain collective sacrificial activities. As the first part of Chapter 3 showed, under such conditions, the spread and development of inheritance-type lineages were inevitable. But in the process of the development of lineage organization, practical territorial ties or ties of common interest could lead to corresponding adjustment or manipulation of the inheritance of rights to perform sacrifice. Documents from the Cai lineage of Lufeng provide an example that demonstrates this:

> The Cai of Jianzhou originated in Yiyang and developed in Masha. Over several hundred years up to the present day, the line of descent grew ever more proliferating and flourishing, and the spring and autumn sacrifices at the shrines and graves of the Nine Sages have never been interrupted. . . . The ancestral hall in our hometown, the [sacrificial] land, and the hill where the founding ancestor is buried are recorded in the old genealogy. All of these are now preserved for successive generations by the branch descended from Wenqin. Wenchang is the ancestor of the branch in Guangze. All the hills where ancestors are buried, the ancestral hall, and [sacrificial] fields at Lufeng have been maintained by them for generations. The branch descended from Wenbi

lives at Pengyuan in Chong'an. The Jiufeng and Esteeming Worthies shrines in Chong'an, and the graves, [sacrificial] fields, and shrines of Mutang and Wensu have been maintained by them for generations. The other branches are dispersed all over, living in different places. They have not ever been concerned about the halls, fields, and graves. Why is this so? Xishan had four sons. Yun died young, and only the descendants of Yuan, Chen, and Kang grew numerous. Yuan and Kang moved away at the time to other prefectures. Only the descendants of Chen lived close to the graves of the ancestors. So the hills in which the ancestors were buried and the fields were mostly maintained through the generations by them. They also established some themselves. Those who lived close by made the largest contribution to the management and recovery [of lost property]. . . . We are concerned that as the branches in the lineage grow ever more numerous not all are equally virtuous or intelligent. There may be some who use the pretext of unifying the genealogy to convert the graves and fields into corporate property, violating the corporate rules of the Nine Sages and confusing the excellent regulations that endured for many generations. Not realizing that this [property] has been added to by those living nearby, they might look on it hungrily from the outside, contrary [to our expectations that the compilation of the genealogy would] serve to venerate our origins. Now we make these restrictions, in order to strictly maintain the ancestor's system. Every year in spring and autumn, we will assemble together in the Houshan Academy to worship the ancestors. In addition, the grave hills, halls, and fields of local lineage members are to be transmitted through the generations and [the income used for] sacrifice according to the old regulations. It is not permitted to encroach or to bury secretly there. Only in this way will the descendants of each branch under the bounty of the ancestors be able to enjoy peaceful relations, and the spirit of the Nine Sages will be preserved through the generations.[39]

In the southern Song, Cai lineage members had built an ancestral hall, compiled a genealogy, and established lineage lands, forming a cohesive lineage organization. The political misfortunes of the Song–Yuan transition led to the dispersal of lineage members and the disintegration of the organization. But in the Ming and Qing, with strong official support, the Cai lineage organization in Jianyang, Chong'an, and other places recovered and further developed.[40] In the mid-Qing, they went on to establish a residentially dispersed lineage organization, linked by a joint genealogy and collective sacrifice in a joint ancestral hall. In an enormous dispersed lineage like this one, it was naturally impossible for collective sacrificial sites to be collectively inherited on the basis of predetermined inheritance relations. Rather, such sites could only be inherited on the basis of territorial links and ties of common interest. Thus, although the descendants of Xishan, whose name was Cai Yuanding, were divided into three branches, only the members of the one branch descended from his son Chen were able to inherit the sacrificial sites, and the other two branches had no rights to them. This is because the descendants of Chen remained settled in the original native place, and it was they who maintained the sites, adding some new property and contributing to the recovery of other property. But even those members of the Cai lineage who remained in their original native place did not all collectively inherit the relevant sacrificial sites. Rather, these were monopolized by a minority of lineage members. In 1747, Chen's seventeenth-generation descendant, Cai Chong, in his "Handwritten Record of the Sacrificial Fields of the Xishan Spirit House *(jingshe)* and Lufeng Academy," declared:

> The old genealogy records [property earning rental income of] three hundred baskets. After the Yuan–Ming transition, some of it was either boldly seized by local strongmen or illicitly sold by unfilial lineage members nearby. . . . In 1723, I rebuilt the Lufeng Academy; in 1741, I restored the Xishan Spirit House, and then revived the sacrificial property. Without regard to family concerns, without regretting the spending of my own capital, without fear of strong opposition, I exerted myself to clear up matters, preparing funds to redeem the property that had been illicitly sold. As for the [property belonging to] the Xishan Spirit House, which had been boldly seized, I brought a lawsuit before the officials and obtained its return. . . . Each year I collect the rent, conduct the sacrifices in spring and autumn, pay the taxes, and sacrifice and sweep the graves. Throughout the year, I pay careful attention to the Spirit House and the Academy, without taking the least amount for myself.[41]

Here, Cai Chong was asserting his monopolistic rights over lineage sacrificial sites on the basis of his own efforts to restore them.

In 1750, the descendants of the Wenbi branch of Chong'an recorded:

> The Academy of Esteeming Worthies and the Jiufeng shrine were originally built outside the western gate, two *li* from the town. In the early years of the dynasty, they were burned by the military and destroyed. After peace was restored, our ancestor Guozhang and his younger brother Guolian rebuilt the two shrines inside the western gate, within Chong'an town. They specially established eighty *mu* of sacrificial fields for the Academy of Esteeming the Worthies, . . . and entered the Academy in the household registration records. The sacrificial fields of the Jiufeng shrine earn rent of 25.2 baskets and bear a tax burden

of 1.08 piculs, the obligation for which is registered under the ancestral household registration. During the military turmoil of the Ming, we lost control over [property earning] 4.7 baskets. Since then, the remaining 20.5 baskets of rental income has always been used to meet the expenses of the two shrines. It is sufficient to provide the sacrificial vessels and offer the sacrificial foods forever. . . . Through the special favor of the imperial dynasty, which esteems learning and stresses the Way, respects the rites and promotes the virtuous, all those descended from [those who have been honored with] a Shrine to the Worthies are awarded official position to support the sacrifice. The Academy of Esteeming the Worthies and the Jiufeng shrine have been awarded [the right to appoint] two Shrine Students *(cisheng)* [i.e., two Government Students by virtue of association with a Shrine]. This branch having been specifically awarded the right to select the Shrine Student, it is decided that an outstanding descendant of the branch descended from Xishan's principal wife should be selected. Those of the same surname but belonging to a different descent-line have no right to participate.[42]

Here again, the members of this branch had, in the process of reconstructing the shrines and restoring its sacrificial estate, asserted rights of sole inheritance over the relevant sacrificial sites.

*   *   *

In the Ming and Qing period, the general attitude toward descent-line inheritance relations was realistic and practical. Official regulations and the strict demands of the neo-Confucian philosophers became almost irrelevant. In Chapter 4, I discussed the Huang of Gongxi in Putian, who declared in a document concerning the reconstruction of an ancestral hall in the Jiajing period:

The expenses of the present [reconstruction of] the ancestral hall should be raised by the members of the lineage who should make donations according to their own calculations of their numbers. . . . What need is there to argue over who has given more and who less, comparing amounts, leading to an uproar of troublesome remarks? . . . Whether or not a man is righteous depends on many things. Which is to be the measure? For this reason, those who wish to participate in the construction should do so; those who do not can do as they please.[43]

The gist of these remarks is that the construction of the ancestral hall and the worship of ancestors were ultimately in the service of the practical interests of lineage members. Whether or not lineage members participated in these sorts of activities was entirely a matter of individual preference. Under these conditions, descent-line inheritance relations could be manipulated at will. Anyone who wished to could establish a descent-line. A Fuzhou branch genealogy prescribes:

> Each year, sacrifices are held in the hall five times. Each household may send one male to participate in the feast. . . . In the past, people took pity on the descendants of Shicheng of the senior branch because of their decline in numbers, so it was decided to permit one man from among his direct descendants to participate in the sacrifice. The other members [of this branch] are not to come to the hall to participate in the sacrifice. Why is this? This is because the ancestral hall was established together by the descendants of Shiji. The descendants of Shicheng have no claim on it.[44]

The Shiji branch's rights of inheritance of the descent-line were determined by their involvement in the raising of funds for the construction of the hall. According to the relevant official regulations and the principles of the Song neo-Confucians, the right to sacrifice in the Wang ancestral hall should have been inherited by the senior branch, that is, the branch descended from Shicheng, the eldest son of the founding ancestor. But because this branch had not participated in the construction of the hall, its members lost their right to inherit the descent-line and were allowed to send a representative to participate in the sacrifice only on the sufferance of the Shiji branch.

Some lineages that were attempting to expand in scale went so far as to invent an ancestor in order to facilitate the manipulation of descent-line inheritance rights. Recall the Daguan Ye of Haicheng, discussed in Chapter 4. Their first-generation ancestor was given the name Jicheng (i.e., establishing a base [*ji*] in Hai*cheng*), of whom it was written, "this is a false name that has been assigned." The same phrase was attached to the account of the second-generation ancestor, Guanshan. The account of the third-generation ancestor, Zhaoxiang, reads: "His ancestral tablet and the details of his spouse[s] have been lost. His name, and [the location] of his grave are unclear. So this is also a false name that has been assigned."[45] Only beginning with the ancestors in the sixth generation was there a factual basis for the records of the Daguan Ye; the preceding five generations in the genealogy were all invented. The purpose of this was obviously to facilitate the compilation of a joint genealogy of all the Ye lineages of the county and to establish collective inheritance relations for the descent-line.

The fragmentation and manipulation of descent-line inheritance relations opened up all sorts of possibilities for control-subordination and contractual lineages, because sacrificial arrangements in such lineages were organized on the basis of practical relations of common locality or common interest. Naturally these diverged from predetermined descent-line inheritance principles. To bring this type of activity into line with the general principles of traditional kinship organization required making adjustments in the descent-line inheritance system. The various examples from the Lufeng Cai, cited above, all reflect adjustments to suit the requirements of control-subordination and contractual lineages. Most control-subordination lineages permitted only respected, "righteous," and wealthy members to take responsibility for sacrificial activities and the management of sacrificial sites. Most contractual lineages permitted only investors and subsequent shareholders to participate in sacrificial practices and in the management of sacrificial sites. Both of these patterns represent divergences from the system of predetermined descent-line inheritance rights. They reflect efforts to adjust and manipulate this system, to make it appropriate for dealing with practical ties of common locality or interest while at the same time conforming to the general rules of traditional kinship organization practice.

In summary, the sacrificial activities and methods of descent-line inheritance in Fujian after the Song violated both the official descent-line system and the principles of the Song neo-Confucian philosophers. Descent-line ethics in the post-Song period was characterized by sacrifice to many generations of ancestors, failure to designate a descent-line heir, elimination of the distinctions between elites and commoners and between greater and lesser descent-lines, and the fragmentation and manipulation of descent-line inheritance relations. Because the modification of descent-line ethics was conducive to the development of popular lineage organizations, it can be considered the popularization of descent-line ethics. This popularized ethics transcended the restrictions of traditional kinship categories. In this sense, it reflected a trend toward the permeation of society by lineage ideology. Because this ideology became applicable to many different kinds of social relations, its historical and cultural implications were profound.

The Rising Autonomy of Local Society

Two broad systems of authority and control can be distinguished in traditional China, the public *(gong)* and the private *(si)*. These correspond to state control and control by the territorial lineage *(xiangzu)*. State control over society was potentially either direct or indirect. It was only when state power was highly developed that direct control could actually be exercised. When the state was weak, only indirect control was possible. Indirect state control was reflected in varying degrees of local self-regulation or autonomy *(zizhi)* by territorial lineages. Thus the weakening of state authority and the strengthening of territorial lineage power can both be considered as evidence of the rising autonomy of local society. In the Ming and Qing periods, central government authority evolved from direct to indirect control, and the degree of autonomy of local society rose constantly. In Fujian, by the mid-Ming at the latest, the state *lijia* system merged with lineage organization, the two together making up the basic local political structure. In this section I consider the role of family lineage organization in the administration of the population registers on which taxation was based, and the actual allocation and collection of tax and service levies, in order to illustrate the trend toward greater autonomy of local society in Ming and Qing Fujian.

*   *   *

There were basically two aspects to household registration in the Ming: the occupational register, which divided the populace into commoner, military, artisan, or salt worker household; and the registers connected with the *lijia* system, which identified households as *li* heads, *jia* heads, or other households. Both registers served as the basic units for the allocation and collection of taxes, but their social function and the policies associated with them were different, and they must therefore be discussed separately.

Let us consider first the occupational registers. In the early Ming, military households, artisan households, and salt-worker households were ordered to provide specific services to the state. Descendants of these households were not permitted to register as separate households, out of concern that they might try to use new registration as a means to evade their service levy. As a result, occupational household registrations were effectively hereditary from the outset. In Ming Fujian, the largest hereditary occupations were commoner households *(minhu)* and military households *(junhu)*. "There are about one-third as many military households as commoner households, and the number of individual members is about half the number of those in commoner registration."[46] Because military households had a hereditary obligation to provide military service, the descendants of these households inherited a collective obligation. This led naturally to the development of a system of corporate service fulfillment in which the basic unit was the lineage. According to the genealogy of the Zheng of Rongfang:

> In the early years of the Hongwu period there was still turmoil all around. . . . At court and in the provinces, peace and stability had not yet been regained. The government sent for our ancestor to be conscripted into the army. He was posted to the Nanjing Regency Left Guard, to serve as a barracks guard. Our third-generation ancestor Tian'er personally took on the responsibility to serve. His name in the military register was Zheng Kuilao. Fourth-generation ancestor Renliu also went to serve in the Guard. There were in all five men, including the seventh-generation ancestor of the senior branch, Wenxuan, whose name in the military register was Zheng Wenzi, and the ninth-generation ancestor of the second branch, De'er, whose name in the military register was Zheng Dezai, who went to serve in the Guard in Nanjing according to a rotation. Each branch of the lineage collected funds that were sent each year to the Nanjing Guard to compensate them for their onerous labor and suffering.[47]

Over the course of the Ming dynasty, the Zheng met their ongoing obligation to provide military service by rotation through the branches of the lineage. Those who did not serve personally were responsible for providing financial support for those who did. According to the genealogy, in 1530:

> The sum of 34.72 taels was collected from the lineage [registered as this] household to pay for equipment and travel expenses for the soldier. On June 6, 14.36 taels was collected from Wenzhen and Hongye of the third branch; a supplement of 9 taels from the descendants of Hongshi; a further supplement of 1.8 taels from the descendants of Honghui; and a further supplement of 9 taels from the descendants of Deyi and Zhengzhen.[48]

To ensure the supply of funds, at the time of household division some military households set aside a portion of the estate to be collectively inherited. For example, when a Li surname military household in Jianyang divided its estate in the early fifteenth century, fifty-four *mu* were set aside as a military estate *(junzhuang)*. The income from the estate was dedicated to the expenses of fulfilling military obligations. Management of the estate rotated through the branches.[49]

The law gave military households that provided military service tax exemptions of one adult male from the ordinary service levy, and of three hundred *mu* from the miscellaneous service levy. Any additional adult males and property beyond these exemptions were incorporated into the local *lijia* registers.[50] The following case shows how this worked in practice. In the early Ming, a certain military household in Yong'an County was also made *jia* head. The corresponding tax responsibilities became the collective responsibility of the whole lineage comprising the descendants of that household. Their genealogy records:

> To fulfill the current obligations of the sixth *jia,* the ancestors' system was to divide the lineage into three shares, each to take responsibility in rotation. The first share is made up of the Zhongrong and Zixin branches; the second, of the Zhongjing and Jinglu branches; the third, of the Zhongda and Zijiu branches. When the rotation is complete, it starts again anew.[51]

From their initial formation, management of the household registers and allocation of the service levy within a military household were organized by a family lineage organization, which therefore had a high level of independent decision-making authority.

The branch genealogy of the Guo lineage of Fuzhou records:

> The military [registration] of our descent line began with ancestor Jian of the Ren branch, who fulfilled his obligation serving as an archer in Zelang fort. . . . In 1405, Jian fell ill and died. There was no [member of the lineage] in the garrison to replace him, so a conscription order was dispatched to get a replacement. At the time, Yin was in poor health, so Wei of the Di branch was chosen by lot to be conscripted. The whole lineage appreciated his righteous actions, so they gave him a reward as encouragement. After he entered the army, on his own authority Wei altered the name on the registration from Guo Jian to [Guo] Guiqing. In 1416, Wei returned home to arrange for his supplies. It was collectively agreed to collect 50 taels to give him. It was insisted that he personally write a receipt, guaranteeing that he would not come back to the ancestral home to try and get more money. Wei then took his younger brother Zhen and went to Shaanxi. Zhen's descendants Biao, Yu, and Ying were registered in Xixiang County in Shaanxi. Their descendants were extremely numerous. In 1522, Wei's great-grandson Xiong and two friends from the military unit, You Jiang and Zhang Fengqi, returned to Fujian to visit their relatives. At that time, the *li* secretary regularly made trouble for us, using the excuse that the members of our lineage were required to send a conscript to fulfill our military obligations. Xiong reported that our family had members in Shaanxi who fulfilled the responsibility, so it was unnecessary to conscript someone in the place of original registration. He reported this to the county [magistrate] and brought back a certificate of proof. In 1575, Xiong's great-grandson, Jiuyu, went to Jianyang on business and took advan-

tage of the opportunity to return and pay his respects to the ancestors. The members of the lineage together collected 11 taels to give to him. Four years later, he came again. After that he did not come anymore.[52]

One branch of the lineage, represented by Wei, had elected, on condition of fulfilling the military obligations of the household, to leave that original registration and be entered in the registers in another province, thereby absolving the remaining members of the lineage in the original native place from providing military services. Strictly speaking, this was illegal, but local authorities were really only concerned that someone actually fulfill the service levy, and they would not investigate the actual circumstances of the military household. This demonstrates that, as long as its military responsibilities were fulfilled, a lineage consisting of a military household had considerable autonomy in the administration of its registration and the allocation of the service levy. The state or other people outside the lineage did not have the power to interfere.

As the state lost direct control of the management of military household registration, it became difficult to locate replacements in cases of desertion, so neighbors and relatives were often conscripted to fill the place of deserters. In the late fifteenth century, a prominent member of the Xianyou gentry named Zheng Ji wrote in a letter to Administration Vice-Commissioner Pang Dacan:

> Last year the Ministry of War issued the order to the army to replace 30 percent of all desertions. . . . Guo of the Imperial Bodyguard had just been appointed in Fujian. He hoped to make an outstanding contribution in order to raise his status. In carrying out this order, he beat anyone who had held the position of Village Elder *(lilao)* in the last ten years nearly to death. He beat them incessantly from morning to night, insisting that the 30 percent quota be met. Some households of old men and women had no adult males able to serve in the army. Their sons-in-law were made to report [for service]. These were called soldiers by virtue of being a son-in-law *(nüxu jun)*. There were cases of [someone being chosen from among] the descendants of those who had previously been registered in the military on the basis of their genealogical records. These were called soldiers by virtue of having the same surname *(tongxing jun)*. There were cases of people who had purchased the land of soldiers who had left no posterity, and other people who wanted to acquire their land reported them. These were called soldiers by virtue of having acquired an estate *(deye jun)*. People were beaten from morning till night, until the quota was met. . . . The village elders' families had no more adult males in their household, and all their property was gone before they heard the end of it.[53]

As a result of this harsh and brutal policy to obtain troops, many peasant households were converted into military households, which meant that these households too effectively passed out of the direct control of the state. Zhou Chen, a Ming official who analyzed falling population figures in the Jiangnan region, suggested that a key factor in the disappearance of households was the concealment of military or artisan households. In Fujian, as the proportion of military households was very high to begin with, and the authorities repeatedly forced peasant households to convert to military ones, the phenomenon of declining numbers of ordinary households must have been even more serious.

On the basis of this discussion, I would suggest that, under the population registration system of the early Ming, lineage organizations formed earlier and developed faster among military households than among ordinary households.

*   *   *

In the Ming, *lijia* households were originally responsible for carrying out in rotation certain public works on behalf of the local authorities. Later, these obligations grew, and *lijia* households became the objects of exploitation by official and suboffical functionaries at all levels of the administration. According to He Qiaoyuan:

> The service levy obligations of the *lijia* households originally consisted only of pressing for tax payment and assembling labor for public works. Later, they became responsible for meeting various government expenses. They had to take care of the [official] sacrificial expenses, the Village Drinking ritual, and the ceremony of Welcoming the Spring, for example. Gradually this extended to paying all kinds of miscellaneous personal expenses of the officials. All kinds of expenses appeared for which there was no basis. As soon as a single document was issued, there was immediately no way to avoid it. Moreover, the secretaries and *yamen* runners also demanded bribes and money in this manner. The *lijia* [households] were pushed into bankruptcy.[54]

In the early Ming, it was ordered that the households with the largest number of adult males and the most property in each *li* and *jia* be selected as the *li* and *jia* heads. Every ten years, when the Yellow Registers were recompiled, these registrations were updated and the *li* and *jia* heads selected anew from the current largest and wealthiest households. But as the obligations on *lijia* households grew heavier and more complex, people tried to conceal the size of their households by any means possible. The state-compiled population registers became so inaccurate as to have no practical significance. Beginning in the early fifteenth century, the number of households registered in the *lijia* began to decline precipitously, and the organization itself began to disintegrate. In Xianyou County, for example, sixty-four *li* were set up at the beginning of the Ming. In the early fifteenth century, "the tax burden was increasingly heavy, and tigers and epidemic disease brought disasters in quick succession, so the population decreased by eighty to ninety percent. In the Zhengtong and Jingtai reign periods (1436–1456), only twelve *li* remained. In the Tianshun period (1457–1464), migrants from other counties were entered into the registration, so the number of *li* went up to fourteen."[55] This decrease in the number of *lijia* households and the disintegration of the organization indicate that official control over the *lijia* registrations had been lost, and it had become impossible to conduct the decennial recompilation of the registers accurately. To deal with this situation, by the Chenghua and Hongzhi reign periods (1465–1505) at the latest, officials in many different places simply imposed a system of fixed tax and service levy obligations on the current *lijia* households. In effect, this meant that the ongoing reassignment of *lijia* households on the basis of changes in the population and property of individual households ceased.

In 1471, Kang Fucheng and his brother migrated from Anxi to Yongchun and registered for tax payment in the ninth *jia* of sector 6–7.[56]

> We took on the household registration of Chen Focheng, whose household was extinguished [i.e., he had died without descendants], taking over responsibility for land in the *jia* that earned 120 piculs rent. At the same time, [properties associated with] the registration of [*jia* head] Huang Bosun, whose household was extinguished, consisting of land at Mei'an and mountain lands behind the abandoned monastery at Yuannei, were also obtained as a result.[57]

They also came to an arrangement with the *li* head:

> When it is the turn [of this *jia*] to fulfill the service levy, we agree to provide two months of labor. The expenses incurred by the person fulfilling the levy in traveling to transmit the tax will be paid from an assessment based on the land and head tax assessment of the members of the group. In intervening years, we will contribute .8 taels to cover miscellaneous exactions. We will not dare to regret this later. If we do not come forward to fulfill our obligations, or if the descendants are unable to fulfill the service levy, thereby adding to the burdens of the *li*

head, the property will be returned to him. We will not dare to sell it off. If it turns out that we have sold it off, this contract can be used as the basis for laying an accusation before the officials.[58]

In 1474, the *li* head drew up an additional contract, proclaiming:

> I willingly transfer the rent-earning ordinary land registered under the name of the *jia* head Chen Focheng, whose household has been extinguished . . . to *jia* head Kang Fucheng, who will come forward to take charge of the decennial obligations, and to collect the annual service levy on the basis of the property [assessments]. If the service levy equalization *(junyao)* is implemented in the future, he will help the *li* head to meet the additional expenses of tax allocation at that time. Furthermore, he will also bear responsibility for unallocated tax in the amount of .5 piculs.[59]

These documents show that, in practice, the allocation of taxes associated with the *lijia* system in Yongchun at that time was the responsibility of the *li* head, who in turn transferred the responsibility to the *jia* heads. In this situation, the position of *li* and *jia* head households simply became permanent, and the rights and obligations of these households were also fixed. In other words, the *lijia* system had become hereditary, and tax and service levy responsibilities had become fixed.

Another description of the fixing of *lijia* obligations during this period comes from Zheng Ji's "Preface to the New *Lijia* Registers" of Xianyou:

> This year my younger brother prepared to serve as *li* head *(lizheng)*. He assembled all those who were involved in the matter, so they could devote themselves wholeheartedly to thinking things over. They agreed that, in order to meet the exactions on schedule, they should gather and prepare this register. All of the obligations from [the ceremonies on] the Emperor's Birthday and the Village Drinking ceremony down to the most trivial of corvee services, and the various troublesome exactions, have been assessed and classified by type. . . . Altogether, the total annual expenses are just under 500 taels. So the annual obligations of each *jia* come to between twenty and thirty taels, only one-seventh or one-eighth of the amount that used to have to be paid [when the obligations were distributed by rotation]. After the register was compiled, it was presented to the *yamen*. The one hundred and forty households of this *li* have collectively vowed to uphold it, so it will become the rule by which the annual exactions are met.[60]

Records indicate that the miscellaneous service levy obligations of the *lijia* in Xianyou had previously been allocated by each *jia* taking responsibility for one day in rotation. But as the exactions differed from day to day, this kind of allocation of responsibility by rotation was inequitable. This document suggests that the annual exactions due from each *li* had become fixed, and under the new system described by Zheng Ji, these annual exactions were now distributed equally amongst the *jia*. Thus, the obligation of each individual *jia* was both equalized and fixed. The fact that it was the individual households which agreed to maintain this allocation system suggests that their individual responsibilities had also become fixed. This meant that the *lijia* registration status of each household had also become permanent.

In order to relieve inequalities in *lijia* tax obligations, local officials in Fujian in the mid-Ming implemented a series of attempts to reform the method of allocation.[61] The thrust of these changes was to shift responsibility for the costs of tribute goods and local government expenses off the *li* and *jia* households in rotation and onto the head and land tax of the whole county, in the form of surcharges. But because the state had already lost control of the census registers, these new measures could only be allocated by dividing responsibility evenly among the existing *li*. The existing *lijia* registers were simply legal fictions and did not reflect the actual population. According to He Qiaoyuan:

> At present, the families of the common people recorded in the registers are known as official adult males *(guanding),* and those which are not recorded in the registers are known as private adult males *(siding).* . . . When the officials compile the registers [every ten years], the population is estimated on the basis of the amount of tax that has been collected. None of these are accurate figures.[62]

Some local officials allocated the service levy obligations as a surcharge on the registered adult males or registered land tax obligations, which effectively converted the *lijia* population registers into fixed tax obligations. For example, in 1616, the magistrate of Yong'an "requested that his superiors authorize an assessment of ten adult males per household. Regardless of whether or not the household died out, the assessment would remain fixed."[63] As late as 1686, the Dehua county government was still relying on the Ming records, allocating the head and land tax obligations evenly among the *li*. "Each *li* was assigned 630 piculs of land tax and 280 adult males of head tax. This is recorded clearly, to serve as a permanent rule."[64]

Once the *lijia* registers had become merely formulaic and *lijia* obligations fixed, when a household estate was divided, the descendants generally did not register as separate households, but rather collectively retained the original *lijia* registration. That is, the descendants inherited and fulfilled the obligations of this registration collectively. The effect was that, after the mid-Ming, *lijia* registration became basically synonymous with lineage organization. Each *jia* simply represented a single lineage. For example, the genealogy of the Rongfang Zheng of Yongchun records:

> At the beginning of the Ming, the court fixed the commoner households and tax obligations, and each household was given a registration placard. Our ancestor Renliu was *jia* head of the first *jia* of sector 4–5, with responsibility for meeting the public obligations in every year [containing the character] *ren*. At the time, the *jia* included three other households, one in the name of Liu Yu of Damao village in this sector, [whose registration is now held by] Zhang Yu of Xitou, and [two in the name of] Wu Long of Shishan and Li Zao of Jingshan, both in Dehua County, [whose registrations are now held by] Ke Shun and Ke Xinglong, respectively. In 1648, the registers were recompiled based on the Ming system. Our lineage continued to serve as *jia* heads in rotation. Thereafter, there was considerable military turmoil, and fulfilling the major supplementary obligations *(dadang)* was extremely onerous.[65] Thanks to the silent assistance of the ancestors, the income-earning property did not diminish. In fact, we received the support of a few virtuous descendants. After 1684, the officials dealt strictly with the shortcomings of the *lijia* allocations. In 1690, Governor-General Xing implemented the land tax equalization *(junmiao)* reform, whereby each group was assessed an obligation of fifty-three piculs. The number of tax-bearing adult males and the amount of tax-bearing land in our lineage was no less than before. But county officials and functionaries were bribed into falsifying the allocations, and they transferred the other households from this *jia* into another *jia*. Our lineage was still responsible for serving as one of the decennial *jia* heads of the first *jia* of sector 4–5.
>
> From antiquity to the present, every time the registers have been compiled, the amount of our tax-bearing property has changed, either increasing or decreasing, and the name of the household head has changed. It is difficult to describe this in detail. When the registers were compiled in 1721, [our lineage] was assessed over forty piculs for the purposes of the land tax obligations and the equivalent of ten official adult males for the purposes of the head tax. The household was then registered under the name Zheng Tai; later this was changed to Zheng Xiong.[66]

The Zheng lineage had been registered as a military household in the Ming, so lineage members were not allowed to divide their household and register separately. The Qing did not impose this same restriction, but the Zheng nonetheless continued to remain registered as a single *lijia* household. The Zheng themselves were unwilling to establish new household registrations, preferring to inherit collectively the original registration and the specified responsibilities associated with it. Prior to 1689, the Zheng were responsible for the other three households within the *jia* and could call on their help in meeting these responsibilities. After 1689, the various fixed responsibilities had to be met entirely by the Zheng members collectively. From the perspective of the Zheng, over the whole Ming and Qing period, *lijia* registration was in a sense simply a marker of the collective identity of the lineage membership, and administration of the *lijia* registration and allocation of the tax burden were collective responsibilities. Thus, when *lijia* registration became hereditary and service levy obligations became fixed, this naturally led to the strengthening of the lineage.

Within particular lineages, various organizational forms were adopted to facilitate collective administration of the *lijia* registration and allocation of the tasks associated with it, in order to adapt to the changing social and economic status of lineage members. A good example of how these structures could develop is provided by the records of a lineage from Yongchun County. The Li settled in Guanlin in the early Ming, and their second-generation ancestor first "registered as a household for the payment of tax." Their registration was in the fourth *jia* of sector 9–10 of Yongchun. When the third generation divided its estate, they "set aside a quantity of land earning 150 piculs rent to assist the descendants in paying the annual tax and the decennial *lijia* major supplementary obligations." From then until the Jiajing period, "the three branches took it in rotation to collect the annual tax and to pay the decennial *lijia* major supplementary obligations expenses, without any exceptions."[67] The three branches also managed the service levy estate in rotation. In this early period, then, the members of the lineage formed an inheritance lineage based on equitable cooperation for the fulfillment of *lijia* responsibilities.

In the Jiajing period, a member of the fifth generation named Hanjie, "being poor and immoral, sold land earning 150 piculs rent at an artificially low price to an official named Wang Fu of the prefecture [Quanzhou]." When this was reported to the authorities, the members of the lineage were ordered to collect the money needed to redeem the land. . . . In 1555, Hanyuan of the senior branch gathered the lineage, and it was decided that the redeemed land should be distributed to the three branches, with each branch receiving land earning fifty piculs rent. The *lijia* service levy remained the collective responsibility of the three branches, with the days and months of the year divided up for each to take responsibility. This was reported to the county government for approval and certification with an official stamp.

When the service levy estate was distributed among the three branches, the original inheritance lineage disintegrated. But because the *lijia* registration was still collectively inherited, service obligations still demanded the cooperation of the three branches. Their lineage organization did not completely disintegrate, but rather began to transform into a contractual lineage.

By the Wanli period, increasing economic differentiation among the three branches rendered this arrangement, whereby each branch was responsible for four months of the year, impracticable. It was replaced by an arrangement whereby responsibility rotated according to an assessment of the number of adult males in and amount of property owned by each branch. In a contract dated 1589, the lineage agreed that the responsibility for tax payment was to rotate through the whole lineage over a six-year period. The period of responsibility of each branch was determined by its head and land tax assessment. "The senior branch is responsible for collecting the tax for one year; the second branch for three years, and the third branch for two years." In 1618, "because the third branch owed little tax, the lineage members gathered and drew up another contract, establishing a five-year rotation system, in which the senior branch continued to be responsible for collecting the tax for one year; the second branch for three years, and the third branch for one year." This allocation of service levy responsibility on the basis of land and head tax assessments, in which tax burdens were adjusted according to the individual circumstances of each branch, illustrates that the lineage itself assessed the population and property of its constituent branches.

At the same time, the assessment of service levy responsibilities within the different branches was growing ever more decentralized, and the original contractual lineage, the basic participants in which were the three branches, also began to disintegrate. In the Wanli period, the tax estates owned by the three branches continuously diminished in size because of illicit sale and encroachment. Funds were raised to regain ownership of some of the land that had been lost. But because only a small group of lineage members was willing or able to donate to this cause, "this land is managed and controlled by those who had contributed money." In a sense, this land had become privately owned. Thus, "the land redeemed by Yongquan of the second branch was personally established as a tax collection levy estate. The rest of the lineage, and the rest of the branch, have no claim on it."

By the late Ming or early Qing, administration of *lijia* registration and allocation of service levy responsibilities had come under the control of a small number of members. The contractual lineage had transformed into a control-subordination lineage.

Since [the establishment of] the dynasty, the annual tax collection has been conducted by the second branch. In 1660, the first branch first took responsibility for the collection for one year; in 1662, Chaoxu of the third branch also took responsibility for one year. In 1672, Chaoxu and Chaojun of the third branch agreed with the second branch that the responsibility for tax collection should be based on the land and head tax assessments, and should rotate in a five-year cycle. The second branch was responsible for four years, and the third branch for one. Because the senior branch had so little land, they did not participate [in the rotation]. Instead they paid five piculs each year to the person [in charge of tax collection], to repay him for his exertions. The whole lineage also agreed that, when the miscellaneous exactions were numerous or onerous, a supplement of two mace per picul of tax should be levied and paid to the man responsible for tax collection, to repay him for his exertions. When the miscellaneous exactions were less heavy, the levy was one mace per picul of tax. This is established as a permanent rule.

As for property belonging to the whole lineage, the rent from which is dedicated to tax collection expenses, Xu Fu paid 10 taels of silver to the lineage to serve as *jia* head, and it was collectively agreed to use this money to purchase rent-earning land, the income from which should go to the person responsible for tax collection to repay him for his exertions. . . . There is also 5 taels belonging to *jia* head Lin Wang, whose household has been extinguished. Now, in the third month of 1714, this 5 taels has been used to purchase from Guangxiang land earning 2.1 piculs rent located at Qingshezi. [Guangxiang] will cultivate the land himself, and pay the rent to the person responsible for tax collection. . . . Guangmou and Shixin etc. of the senior branch also pay 5 piculs in rent each year to the person responsible for tax collection. The rental income from property belonging to the whole lineage, which is used to meet the expenses of tax collection, is 675 catties in total.

In our lineage, originally a single person took charge of the tax collection each year. When the land tax equalization reform was implemented, the tax obligations of Li Zhong of this household were transferred to the second *jia*.[68] In the first month of 1694, the lineage agreed that two people should be in charge of the tax collection to facilitate the task. The total rental income from the tax estate should be divided by them evenly. One of the two should be chosen in rotation from the branch descended from Yongquan, and the other in rotation from the branches descended from Chuanjian, Piqi, and Saise and Sairu. When the rotation is complete, it starts again at the beginning. It is not permitted to shirk responsibility.

The branch descended from Zhaishan . . . has an estate devoted to tax payment that earns a total of 1316.5 catties. Those members of the branch who are responsible for tax collection divide this income among themselves. In the years when no member of the branch is responsible for tax collection, this income should be accumulated, sold, and the proceeds used to purchase more land. Other members of the lineage who are responsible for tax collection have no claim on this estate.

In the Qing, the lineage member who was responsible for tax collection was actually personally responsible for pressing the members of the lineage to pay. Accomplishing this depended on the ability to exert effective control over the population and property of the branches of the lineage. Only a few lineage members could have had the wealth and status necessary to take on the responsibility of assuming the power to administer the household registrations and to allocate taxes in the name of the lineage. The rest of the lineage was therefore placed in a position of subordination relative to this minority.

In addition to the responsibility to collect the annual tax, *lijia* obligations in the early Qing included the decennial *dadang* supplementary obligations. In the Li lineage, this obligation was allocated according to the assessments for land and head tax. Their genealogy records:

When this [Qing] dynasty was established, the various exactions were numerous and heavy. The service levy exactions were allocated according to the land and head tax. In 1655, more than 30 taels was charged per adult male and per picul of land tax. In 1665, just under 30 taels was charged per adult male and per picul of land tax. In 1675, the surtax was less than in the past, about 7 taels per adult male. 1685 was a time when great peace was approaching, and only 3 taels was charged per adult male.... [In 1711] the whole county agreed that each year an annual surtax on the land tax should be paid for the transport of the tax receipts. The county official should collect and clear this account. This was reported for approval to the prefecture, the province, and the governor-general, and then implemented accordingly. Thereafter the major supplementary obligations were eliminated.

Once the major supplementary obligations were eliminated in the mid-Qing, *lijia* obligations consisted mainly of tax-collection responsibilities. The point to note from the Kangxi period adjustments is that, even though the tax on a portion of the Li's property was transferred to another *jia,* the Li still retained the power to collect this tax, and all the tax continued to be collected by the member of the lineage assigned that task. In other words, the Li lineage retained authority over the population and property of the whole lineage, and therefore the whole lineage comprised a corporate organization with unified household registration and tax and service levy obligations. The Li were also able to obtain additional property, such as that belonging to Gu Yonggui, and funds, such as the money saved by Lin Wang and that paid by Xu Fu. This shows that they must have been a *li* head household, which gave them a certain degree of control over the household registration and the property of the *jia* heads in the *li.*

The trend of household registration becoming hereditary and tax and service levy obligations becoming fixed not only strengthened lineage organization in general, but also caused transformations in the form of some lineages. Lin Xiyuan wrote in his "Family Injunctions":

> Within this household, in the early generations the adult males were few in number, so some adopted men were included in the registers in order to assist the household in fulfilling its [service levy] obligations. Now, this should be considered a warning. Those who have already been entered in the registration are not permitted to be entered in the genealogy.[69]

The prevalence of bond-servant adoption in Ming Fujian can be linked to these trends of household registration becoming hereditary and tax and service levy obligations becoming fixed. Although Lin Xiyuan saw adopted sons as fundamentally different from lineage members, because in practice adopted sons and birth sons collectively inherited the household registration together, they thus effectively belonged to a single lineage organization. In the Luo lineage of Hui'an, a dispute broke out in the Wanli period between descendants of adopted bond servants and descendants along the descent-line. The issue was collective inheritance of *lijia* registration. A Luo ancestor had adopted a child who had been registered so that he could assist in fulfilling the service levy. Because the adopting ancestor "worried that in the distant future a capable bond servant might usurp the position of the master, the descent-line should be strictly kept track of and carefully detailed in the genealogy." Over the course of the Ming, "the service levy obligations of the *li* head rotated between the two branches, and the *jia* heads beneath them were distributed between them." The two branches consisted of the descendants of the Luo ancestor and the descendants of his adopted bond servant. Conflict arose when members of this latter group objected to their formal exclusion from the lineage, "searched for records in the genealogy that would be useful to them, and used these to trick official families into writing funerary inscriptions in their honor." They then declared themselves the senior branch of the Luo lineage.[70]

In the Qing, while most lineages throughout Fujian had some restrictions on the adoption of bond servants, they usually allowed them to be included in the genealogy and to participate in lineage sacrifices, which meant that they were effectively recognized as regular members of a control-subordination lineage. A more relaxed attitude toward bond servants and their descendants had clearly developed. This attitude obviously brought practical benefits, but it may also be true that it was encouraged by a sense of gratitude for their historical assistance in fulfilling service levy obligations. As one genealogy put it, "having acted with laxity in the beginning, to impose great strictness later would not be judicious."[71]

Changes to the tax system could strengthen lineage organization, but they could also have the opposite effect. Even among lineage members whose consanguinal relations were extremely close, division into different household registrations could lead to the division or disintegration of the lineage organization. The genealogy of one Changting County lineage explains:

> We recall that in the past our ancestors together with uncle Yesong openly took over the registration as *li* head of the Little Zou. Later, because the Little Zou failed to fulfill the obligations of a military household [to supply a conscript], the resulting troubles almost bankrupted [our] family. Uncle Yesong and his sons stood by and watched passively, and would not even aid us with half a cash. They once said that they would always serve as *jia* heads of the tenth *jia,* but swore they

would never serve as *li* head. In 1542, Tingkui and his brothers dis-
obeyed their father's order and again said they also had a share in the
right to serve as *li* head of the tenth *jia* and wished to assume the position. They called on Government Students Ma Huiqin and Ma Xiaole
to draw up a contract for them. They held this post three times under
an assumed name. Only in 1572 did they change the name on the
household registration to Tinghuai. Our family therefore went to
serve as the *li* head of the fourth *jia* in the fourth ward.[72]

In this lineage, separate registration and other changes to the *lijia*
household registration generated insurmountable problems within
the membership. Up to the end of the Qing it proved impossible to
form a single unified lineage organization. "The territory of the
Upper and Lower ancestral halls was separate."[73]

A Huang lineage genealogy of Shaowu records:

> Our ancestor Fuwu first left Jianyang and settled in Shaowu. He regis-
> tered his household in the tenth *jia* of the fourth ward of sector 1, and
> so began [to fulfill] service levy obligations. In the fifth generation,
> Kangjiu moved to Xuntan and temporarily registered his property there
> under the registration of the Gong household of sector 5. His son
> Gongbao then changed the registration to the eighth *jia*. Those who
> remained behind in Shuiwei stayed under the original registration.[74]

As a result, "the Huang of Shaowu for many generations had two
household registrations, and so differed from other lineages." In
1659, Huang Yingbo and other descendants of the Kangjiu branch
left the registration in sector 5 and returned to the original registration, fulfilling their service levy obligations there. The lineage members who remained registered in sector 5 were unhappy about this.
They wrote in the genealogy:

> The service levy of Yingbo and his two sons, Fa and Zan, of our lineage,
> was originally in the eighth *jia*, under *jia* head Bai Luguan. Because Fa's
> tax obligations were heavy, he came back to the original household reg-
> istration in the tenth *jia* to fulfill the obligations. Having both wealth
> and power, he was able to leave the head tax assessment behind. This
> caused great trouble for [our] Huang lineage.[75]

This case demonstrates that once lineage members left their original
lijia registration they also effectively left their original lineage organization.

In the mid-Qing, the decennial supplementary exactions were
eliminated in different parts of Fujian, and the process of incorporat-
ing the head tax into the land tax was more or less complete. In prin-

ciple, this did away with the *lijia*'s role as a tax allocation unit. But as
the officials were still unable to exert direct control over the amount
of land tax due from tax-paying households, the original *lijia* registrations still had to be used as the basis for the actual collection of
tax. Chen Shengshao described Zhao'an County in the early nineteenth century as follows:

> I don't know how many thousand *mu* of land and tens of thousands
> of member households belong to the Liao lineage of Guangbi or the
> Shen lineage on the outskirts of the county town, as well as the Xu,
> Chen, or Lin. But the whole lineage is registered with the officials under
> the names of one or two general households *(zonghu)*, such as Liao
> Wenxing, Liao Rixing, Xu Lifa, or Xu Shipu. Also, in order to evade
> service levy responsibilities, several surnames combine and register as
> a single household. The Li, the Lin, and others, for example, are regis-
> tered together [as a single household] under the name Guan Shixuan.
> The Ye, the Zhao, and others are registered together [as a single house-
> hold] under the name Zhao Jianxing. Aside from taking it in rotation
> to serve as household head or chief tax collector, they also have infor-
> mal records known as alias households' *(huahu)* records. One has no
> choice but to turn to these in order to collect the tax each year. Where
> there is no household head or chief tax collector, then the job of *yamen*
> runner responsible for tax circulates among them. He also has this kind
> of record, so it is not too difficult to go from household to household
> collecting the tax.[76]

The general households referred to here were actually each lineage's
collectively inherited *lijia* registration. In some lineages, even where a
number of alias households registered for tax payment, the lineage
incorporated them into the original *lijia* registration, so these new
households did not escape lineage control. The Shaowu Huang
genealogy, cited above, explains: "Since the Yongzheng period, there
was the burden of accumulated tax arrears. In the Qianlong period,
there was also the burden of actual collection of tax in kind *(zhenggu
caishi)*.[77] As a result, many households were established." The goal
of registering a household was to avoid the tax obligations of the
lineage as a whole. But at the same time the land tax of the different tax-bearing households was still collected by the lineage
organization.

> In the past, this *jia* always appointed one man to take care of the cus-
> tomary gifts for the *yamen* runners, as well as the head and land tax
> and the local granary [contributions]. This was called the annual ad-
> ministration tax *(guannian)*. Each year everyone paid him a certain
> amount of rice, to repay him for his exertions. The position was held

for fifteen years and then transferred. . . . In 1750, there was no one
who would serve in this position. So the three main branches of the
lineage divided the task up between them, and drew up a record of the
agreement.

The Huang also specifically set aside some rental income, "to be
given to the secretary. Anyone in our *jia* who establishes a new tax-
bearing household and registers property need not pay any [addi-
tional] money."[78] Clearly, the lineage organization continued to manage matters related to the service levy even when households were no
longer registered under the lineage's registration.

Although the tax appeared to be collected by *yamen* runners,
some lineages in fact retained the power to regulate the tax-bearing
households. This is evident from the following contract:

> The maker of this agreement to undertake [responsibility for] the records
> is Lin Fangzhang. The Li surname previously purchased from Chen
> Boyan the records for administering the tax [registered in the name of]
> commoner Li Jisheng of the fourth *jia* in sector 9–10. In the past, my
> ancestor Lin Yunzi undertook with the Li to administer [the tax], and
> also drew up a contract which the Li held as a guarantee. Because a
> long time has passed, the figures are out-of-date. Now I have gone
> through a go-between and asked the branch of the Li descended from
> You to renew my responsibility to administer the tax. All of the tax-
> bearing property has been assessed by the three parties. I do not dare
> mix it up. Once this contract is established, if the items in this prop-
> erty record prove to be mistaken or deliberately altered, I will willingly
> return the property records to the Li so that they can collect the tax
> themselves, and I will not dare make any trouble or complaint. The
> salary will remain as in the old contract, that is, for each picul of tax
> collected, a supplement of ten catties will be paid. For the registration
> of new property, regardless of whether it is official land or commoner
> land, the fee will be 120 cash if the land is one *mu* or less, and ad-
> justed accordingly if it is more. It is agreed that, every ten years, I will
> compile the records for the whole lineage and for each household and
> give them to the Li to keep. Now, because we wish to have evidence to
> rely on, the records have been handed over and this contract drawn up.
>
> Guarantor Chen Yingguan
> Fifth month of 1881
> The maker of this agreement to undertake [responsibility for] the records Lin Fangzhang
> Witness Lin Fanghao[79]

Lin Fangzhang, the maker of the contract, was actually a *yamen*
functionary hired to collect tax. But clearly he had to obtain the lineage's permission before he could directly collect tax from the tax-

bearing households, and the obligations of each household had to be recognized by the lineage organization. The lineage organization still retained effective control over the tax-bearing households, and the *yamen* runner was simply the lineage's representative. The Li lineage had a regulation requiring the runner to recompile the relevant records according to a fixed schedule, and the tax-bearing property was to be assessed by "all three parties" to prevent the figures from becoming outdated. According to records in the genealogy, Lin Fang-zhang requested renewal of his appointment as administrator of the tax in 1895 and prepared a contract declaring: "I will collect and submit tax each year based on this record, and will not dare mix things up."[80] Thus we can see that the lineage remained the standard unit for land tax collection even in the late Qing.

Under normal circumstances, coordinating unified tax collection through the lineage organization encouraged lineage members to take mutual responsibility for one another's tax obligations, which helped limit tax shortfalls or resistance. This is why officials in Qing Fujian repeatedly ordered the implementation of the policy of "allocating tax households to the descent line." But when central authority became too weak, and the system of control faced collapse, this kind of tax collection system could become the basis for collective tax resistance, and the state might completely lose control of finances and the taxation base. For example, large-scale collective tax resistance broke out in coastal Fujian in the mid-nineteenth century. According to Cheng Laochun's request to be relieved from office in Maxiang in southern Fujian during the period of the Small Swords Uprising, there were several dozen villages, with "large lineages and powerful men," which regularly refused tax payment or paid only a fraction of what was owed. Their resistance was expressed in the following way:

> Slippery people emerge as leaders and take control; the tax-bearing households then look on. If there is even one gentry man in the County School, his exemption extends to the whole lineage [i.e., they all claim his tax exemption]. If there is even one man serving in the military, they tyrannize the whole township. If they are not pressed, they simply pay whatever they please. If they are hounded, they gather in large numbers at the sound of a drum to resist.[81]

When "the vile practice of stubborn people evading their taxes" arose, there was nothing a local official could do but request to be dismissed. When local autonomy developed beyond a certain point, it posed a latent danger to central authority and might even lead to decentralization and separatism. The localism that led to the Qing collapse and the warlord period can be seen as a consequence of excessive autonomy of local society.

*   *   *

Household registration in the Ming and Qing was not only the basic unit of tax allocation and payment but also an important marker of social status. According to one gazetteer account:

> In this county, those who serve as *li* heads are households with many members and much property, so they always bully the weaker households. Within the *li* head's household, young and old are all referred to as *li* head, treating the *jia* heads as if they were the households of their own children, as if they were people under their control. Even the old and white-haired members of the *jia* households have to use the [respectful] terms of address [appropriate] to a man of a senior generation *(shuhang)* when they come across the children of the *li* head household. When members of the *jia* households die leaving behind sons and daughters, the *li* head household can decide who they should marry, or even sell them off.[82]

Status distinctions like these, based on *lijia* registration, persisted up to the late Qing. The genealogy of the Rongfang Zheng lineage of Yongchun County records:

> In the early Hongwu period, ... the tax-bearing property of our lineage was many times that of other *jia*, so we Zheng were made the [*jia* heads] of the first *jia* of sector 4-5. The order to fulfill the duties was carved onto a stone inscription. At that time, the Li lineage of Jingshan were affiliated with the first *jia*. They were responsible for the spring sacrifice in every year containing the character *ren*. The Liu of Damao and the Zhang of Xitou were also affiliated to the first *jia* and were responsible for the autumn sacrifice. Our ancestors of the Zheng surname were in charge, so they had to bow before them. Later, the Li lineage was extinguished. Their registration was taken over by the Ke, who took responsibility for the spring sacrifice according to the existing regulations. The Liu of Damao were also extinguished, but the Zhang were unable to take over their responsibilities fully. So we Zheng, as *jia* head, took over the autumn sacrifice ourselves, and the Zhang lineage provided assistance. Up to the present this has not changed. In 1862, all ten *jia* heads assembled at the Community Altar and collectively appointed County Inspector Xie Chunnian to prepare a new rotation record. In this register, the Ke and the Zhang remained affiliated to the first *jia*. Who would have expected that Ke Jichun and Ke Xiaoyi would be so full of themselves? In the spring of 1867, they made a false accusation before the prefectural authorities, claiming that be-

cause they were responsible for the spring sacrifice while we Zhang were responsible for the autumn sacrifice, they were senior and we were junior. They wished that we be considered like elder and younger brother. This was like a case of slaves mocking their masters; the masters cannot accept it. . . . In the fall of 1867, our lineage requested that all ten *jia* heads go to the prefecture and together make a complete report based on the facts. So the Ke had to back down, and they agreed that they would always be an affiliated household of the *jia*. This was recorded in the register as clear evidence for the conduct of the sacrifices in perpetuity. Out of concern that with the passage of time this may be forgotten, it has also been recorded in the genealogy, that later generations should be aware of it.[83]

This conflict over family status between the Zheng and Ke lineages reflects the politicization and localization of lineage organization. This dispute was not just about different versions of history but was also a competition for real power. Because *lijia* registration was an expression of the power and status of a lineage in local society, lineages were extremely conscious of it, seeing it as the foundation of lineage survival. As the compiler of the Rongfang Zheng lineage genealogy wrote:

The territory of the ruler and the people of the ruler are recorded in the registers. Those who are numerous and have property must all pay their tribute. For this reason, our ancestor, on behalf of his descendants for thousands of years, established an estate and transmitted a tradition, using all his knowledge and effort, in order to obtain our status in the registration. The later descendants are able peacefully to enjoy his accomplishment. How could they not reflect on this?[84]

The author of the Guanlin Li genealogy also repeatedly stressed: "It is only because of the payment of tax and the fulfillment of the service levy that we have been registered and can be considered local people. . . . Because of their arrangements for tax and service levy payment and thus our household registration, how can the model of the ancestors not be considered great and distant?"[85] Within a social structure founded on imperial control of land and populace, tax payment, service levy fulfillment, and household registration were the bases for the existence of lineage organization. It was precisely the fact that household registration became hereditary and tax payment fixed which spurred the development of political authority and territorial control by the lineage.

The Ming and Qing dynasties are generally regarded as the period when autocratic power developed to its highest degree. But this may simply be a surface phenomenon of the bureaucratic government. If we look closely at the control mechanisms of the Ming and Qing periods, it is clear that the maintenance of autocratic power was only possible at the cost of allowing local autonomy. In other words, bureaucratic government in the Ming and Qing was in fact powerless: it was unable to exert effective control over society. Under these historical conditions, private control systems became increasingly powerful. Territorial lineage organizations and local gentry associations grew more dynamic than ever before and exerted complete control over the basic level of society. The growing autonomy of local society inevitably led, therefore, to the widespread development of lineage organization, and to the development of lineage political authority and territorial control, which in turn encouraged the large-scale development of control-subordination lineages. This is evident not only in the history of the household registration and tax systems, but also in other areas of social and economic life.

The Corporatization of Property Relations

Lineage property in the Ming and Qing was property owned corporately by lineage members. The appearance and spread of lineage property was a manifestation of the larger trend of the corporatization *(gongyouhua)* of property relations.

Lineage property consisted mainly of lineage fields, but it could also include mountain land, houses, sites for later construction, capital for usury, industrial and commercial capital, and irrigation, transport, and other collective facilities. The appearance of lineage property in Fujian can be traced back to the Tang and Song, but its development on a large scale occurred in the Ming and Qing. After the mid-Ming, it became common for each generation to set aside a portion of its estate to serve as sacrificial property, which meant that the amount of lineage property was constantly expanding. By the late Qing, in some parts of Fujian the proportion of land held as lineage corporate fields was equal to or greater than that in private hands.[86] This proportion grew even higher in the Republican period. Investigations during land reform found a high ratio of "village and lineage corporate land" *(xiangzu gongyou di)* to total land under cultivation throughout Fujian, reaching 50 percent or more in mountainous northwestern Fujian, and 20–30 percent in coastal regions.[87] "Village and lineage corporate land" basically refers to lineage fields. For

Table 5.1. Corporate Property in Fujian at the Time of Land Reform

Region	Total expropriated land *(mu)*	Village and lineage corporate land *(mu)*	Ratio
Nanping	197,038	128,859.6	65.39
Yong'an 1	108,371		55
Yong'an 2	74,482	49,848	66.92
Fu'an	271,938	134,702.81	49.53
Minhou	526,975.49	257,818.02	48.92
Longxi	368,099		44.5

Source: *Fujian sheng nongcun diaocha.*

example, in the first round of land reform in the Nanping area, 128,859.6 *mu* of "village and lineage corporate property" was confiscated, of which 114,744 *mu,* or about 90 percent, consisted of lineage fields. Table 5.1 shows the scale of lineage community corporate property in different parts of Fujian.

The figure for total expropriated land area is the total amount of "feudal land" *(fengjian tudi),* including village and lineage corporate property, landlord property, rich peasant property, and other property that was rented out rather than cultivated by its owner. Village and lineage corporate property was feudal land subject to confiscation, because almost all of it was rented out. In this sense, it was an important part of the structure of the landlord economy. The formation and development of lineage corporate property was therefore actually an aspect of the formation and development of the territorial lineage landlord economy.

Lineage land in Ming and Qing Fujian was originally private land that had been converted into corporate property, usually because it had been set aside at the time of household division. The purpose of setting aside lineage land when a household estate was divided was to resolve the problems generated by the division, enabling the members of the household to maintain close social relations even after division. In 1392, when Zhou Ziyuan of Jianyang divided his estate among his three sons, he told his relatives and friends:

I reflect back that our ancestors have gathered here as a lineage since the Song and Yuan dynasties. Their warm spirit has endured for hundreds of years already. . . . Now I have three sons, still young in age. . . . I worry that after they grow up each will be partial to his own

wives and children, and the sentiments and desires will be hard to
manage. If they are made to live together in a single hall, then there
will be quarrelling in the house and rifts created. This is not a practicable long-term plan. If they are allowed to split up and live separately,
then the kin will be divided, and their sentiments and mutual obligations
will be increasingly dispersed. This too is not the way to unite the
agnates. So I divide them into three branches . . . dividing the wealth
into three shares and the property into three shares. Each shall manage
his share, devote himself to his own affairs, and not interfere with one
another. In addition, I have established sacrificial fields, to meet the
expenses for the spring and autumn sacrifice at the ancestral temple
and ancestral grave, and on the taboo days. The three branches will
collect the income from this sacrificial land, one after the other in rotation, in order to meet the expenses of the sacrifice. This way, at the
annual festivals, [the relatives who share common] bones and flesh
will be able to assemble and celebrate, everyone in the hall feasting
and enjoying themselves. Thus everyone's share will be clear but their
sentiments will not be neglected. Their mutual concern will be deep
and resentments will not arise. The ancestors' estate will thus be preserved, and all the sons will all be able to stand up on their own.[88]

Zhou hoped that establishing sacrificial fields would ensure that "the
descent line was venerated and the agnates united," and thus that
household division would not cause the relationship among the relatives to disintegrate.

From another perspective, in the context of a residentially concentrated lineage, lineage members continued to share certain unavoidable common expenses even after household division, so division did
not simply bring their economic relations to an end. In 1388, Yuan
Shouba of Chong'an divided his estate between his two sons. He set
aside a piece of land earning over one hundred piculs rent, "to meet
the corporate expenses of the descendants. The branches descended
from [his two sons] are to manage the property in rotation. . . . Eighteen piculs of the income from the mill is to be used to purchase a pig
and other sacrificial items for sacrifice to the ancestors." Most of the
remaining income was to be used to pay "the various obligations
associated with the decennial service as ward head *(tutou)*."[89]

Beginning in the mid-Ming, as the social functions of lineage organization continually expanded, the varieties of lineage property also
continually increased. This was also part of the process of corporatization of property relations. Records in the genealogy of the Huang
of Jianyang prescribe:

The sacrificial property, regardless of whether it has been left behind
by one's ancestors or established by oneself, and whether it is field or

mountain land, should be recorded clearly and in detail. The ancestor and ancestress in whose name the descendants have donated the land to the ancestral hall to enrich the sacrificial property should also be recorded clearly and in detail. The property must not be encroached on, mortgaged, or sold. As for [the income from] charitable fields *(yitian)*, it is to go to poor descendants who cannot afford marriages or funerals. There are also the service levy fields, to be used to pay for the service levy obligations associated with the household registration in the *lijia*. There are also educational fields, to be used to pay the costs of the scholars' lamp oil, tuition, and expenses for taking examinations. These are each to be recorded clearly and in detail to prevent problems from arising in the future.[90]

Each type of lineage property had its unique source and function, but all belonged to the lineage members' corporate property, which is why they all had to be recorded in the genealogy, to prevent conflicts from arising.

Setting aside sacrificial land during household division was not only a way to deal with the various kinds of collective responsibilities of the descendants, but also a landlord strategy to preserve wealth and status. Beginning in the Song, the prevalence of household division meant that the size of individual private landholdings always tended to decrease. The people of Shaowu had a saying that "wealth does not last more than three generations; poverty does not last more than three generations either."[91] This old folk saying suggests the instability of personal economic status and shows that the private landlord economy had reached its historical limits. For the scale of private landownership to expand required continual expansion in the amount of land held, in order to meet the consumption needs of the ever-growing number of members. But if the household estate was divided in each generation, then the amount of land held by each household diminished rather than increased. Even if the members of each generation managed to maintain the estate they inherited, eventually bankruptcy still threatened. According to the Weng lineage genealogy of Jianyang:

> Wancheng established an estate of common rice land more than 1,280 *mu* in size, which he left to his four sons. . . . Each son was given over 320 *mu*. Boshou had two sons, . . . each son received more than 160 *mu*. Our great-grandfather Zhiyuan had three sons. . . . They each inherited the ancestral property, each receiving 53 *mu*. This was inherited by my father Zongwen, who continued the transmission of the ancestral estate. He rose up through a combination of farming and scholarship, and established 548 *mu* of common land. . . . He donated [some] to meet expenses of incense and candles, set aside some as dowry for

his daughters, and donated some of his land to serve as charitable fields. There remained over 450 *mu* of rice land, which was divided evenly among my two older brothers and me, for each to inherit separately.[92]

After three successive divisions of the estate by three successive generations, the more than 1,200 *mu* left by Wancheng amounted to only a little over 50 *mu* per household. This is a classic example of the negative consequences of fragmentation for the household economy. Had this division continued until the fifth generation, the households would have found it difficult to sustain themselves as self-cultivating peasants, let alone live off the rental income of the property. Division of the household estate with each generation was the direct cause of the fragmentation of the private landholdings of the Weng.

In Ming and Qing Fujian, an estate the size of Weng Wancheng's would have been considered a large one, but it could not survive the effects of three generations of family division. The effects of even a single division on smaller landlord households were even more serious. Weng Wancheng's sixth-generation descendant Zongwen was the sole inheritor of his father's estate, so he did not suffer the effects of further family division and was able with effort to maintain his position as a small landlord. Later, through a combination of scholarship and agriculture, his personal success enabled him to begin a new cycle of increasing wealth, and he increased his holdings to over five hundred *mu*. But his children were once again to divide the estate, so the expansion was interrupted and the process of fragmentation of private landholdings resumed. Clearly, except in the exceptional case of sole inheritance, concentration of landholdings was rarely as rapid as fragmentation, and most private landholdings ultimately disintegrated. Only if corporate property was set aside at the time of household division, thereby limiting the fragmentation of landholdings, could landlord status be maintained over the long term.

The genealogy of the Houshan Cai lineage of Pucheng explains the purpose of setting aside lineage land:

The ancestors' concern for their descendants extends long into the future, so their preparations are thorough. When the family estate is divided, even if it is worth several tens of thousands of taels, once transmitted through several generations, the estate becomes more minute with each division. The only thing to do is to set aside a great deal as retirement land, to meet one's own needs while still alive and to serve as sacrificial property after one's death, to meet the expense of sacrifice. It can be managed collectively in order to express filiality or managed in rotation out of respect for the sacrifice. Persisting forever without ceasing, it endures through the ages. If through some unfortunate circumstance the descendants are in danger of falling destitute, . . . they may use the surplus to maintain themselves.[93]

Regardless of whether property was set aside as a retirement estate or as a sacrificial estate, the goal was the same, to ensure that a certain amount of property "persisting forever without ceasing, . . . endures through the ages." This practice arose out of careful calculation by the landlord class. Chen Shengshao praised the setting aside of sacrificial land to be managed in rotation. His description of the practice in Jianyang, cited in Chapter 3, continues:

> The gentry and common people of Jianyang all have rotating rental income for sacrifice. . . . The land may never be mortgaged or sold, and it is very rare for lawsuits to arise over the mortgaging or sale. Relying on the sacrificial land left behind by the ancestors can relieve the poverty of the descendants. Facing upward, it meets the costs of sacrifice to the ancestors; facing down, it can serve as a technique to relieve the poverty of the descendants. This system is the height of excellence.[94]

Chen perceptively realized that income from corporate sacrificial property could supplement shortfalls in private landholdings, and that it was therefore a tool of the landlord class. For some landlords, setting aside corporate land was more for their own benefit than that of their descendants. In the Qianlong period, a landlord from Chong'an named Yuan Shaowu divided his estate between his blood sons and his adopted sons, declaring: "My fields are insufficient. I would feel awkward calling on you to maintain me in my retirement, so I have kept a portion of rent-bearing income, to meet the expenses of my retirement while I am still alive and of my sacrifice later on."[95]

Zu Deyao, a landlord from Pucheng, was more subtle about his intentions in establishing lineage corporate property. He instructed his sons as follows:

> In 1761, we divided all the family estate into two equal portions, to allow the two sons to manage their own finances and stand on their own. A portion of land earning 100 piculs rent was set aside to serve as the capital for my retirement estate, and later to meet the expenses of sacrifice. In 1768, my concubine Liu had another son, and he was given the name Tan. I therefore gave this property to Tan to meet his living expenses. . . . Now I again command [my sons] Nai and Xiang

to each provide land earning 10.5 piculs rent to serve as the sacrificial
estate for me and my wife. . . . They are to establish a separate household registration [for the tax on this] sacrificial land, which is to be
passed down to the descendants. When Tan has grown up and become
a man, he and his brothers are to take responsibility for the sacrifice
in rotation.[96]

Obviously, from the perspective of a living proprietor like Zu Deyao,
the larger the retirement estate the better, and retirement estates
would generally be transformed into sacrificial land after the death
of the beneficiary. To avoid privation in their old age, landlords con-
sciously retained a considerable amount of property to serve as the
retirement estate. This was an important reason for the rapid development of lineage land.

By the Ming and Qing, the practice of setting aside lineage property with each generation had become common practice among the
Fujian populace. The proportion of property set aside in this way
was also continually increasing. In a previous study of documents of
division of landlord households from northern Fujian dating from
the eighteenth to twentieth century, I showed that the proportion of
land set aside as lineage land at the time of division was never less
than 20 percent of the total property, and averaged 37 percent.[97]
Moreover, since each generation attempted to maximize the amount
of corporate land set aside when they divided the estate, the rate of
concentration of corporate land was greater than the rate of fragmentation, and the amount of corporate land snowballed. The great-
grandfather of Su Wukai of Pucheng, for example, established a sacrificial estate earning 300 piculs rent. Su's grandfather and grand-
uncles established sacrificial and educational fields earning 150
piculs, and his father and uncles land earning 400 piculs. Su Wukai
himself left sacrificial land earning 200 piculs rent.[98] Thus, four generations of household division created a total accumulation of sacrificial land earning over 1,000 piculs rent. Even though private
landholdings were constantly fragmenting through household division, accumulation and concentration occurred simultaneously at a
striking rate because of the establishment of lineage land. There was
an inverse relationship between these two phenomena. The circulation of land ownership in Ming and Qing Fujian ensured the long-
term trend of rising proportions of lineage land.

*   *   *

The development of lineage land in the Ming and Qing was also linked to occupational diversification. Lineage members working in different occupations found it impossible to manage land themselves. Lineage property was a way to practice centralized management of land property. This is illustrated by the development of the lineage property of the Huang of Shaowu, for generations a powerful merchant family. According to their genealogy, lineage member Tinghui was an extremely successful merchant in the Kangxi period. He moved to Wenjia Lane in the county town, so he yielded his land to his brother.[99] His son Dengjin inherited more than one hundred *mu* from his father, but he too traveled widely doing business, so he "abandoned his fields, took the money, and traveled to the north and south buying and selling. His profits were immeasurable."[100] While Dengjin and his father were engaged in commerce, they gave up the management of their lands, and then, when they retired, they again purchased land and lived off the rental income.

Dengjin's descendants tried various strategies of centralized land management in order to allow members of the lineage to be sure that their land was being well-managed while they pursued different occupations. These strategies included maintaining a household with collective residence and common estate, maintaining a household with separate residences but common estate, and the establishment of lineage land. Dengjin had four sons. At first he ordered them to devote themselves to study. Later he had one of his sons run the family business, and the other three each either made a living as a sojourning merchant or continued his studies. In 1740, the four sons set up their own households, but their property continued to be managed collectively. Each year, each household was allowed to withdraw forty piculs of rice from the estate. The excess was reinvested, and the interest distributed equally among the four households. Upon Dengjin's death in 1747, the brothers were permitted to withdraw a further twenty piculs per year, and a portion of the property was designated as their father's sacrificial estate. Finally, after the funeral of their mother, they discussed dividing up the property of the whole estate and shifted more property into the sacrificial estate.[101] Obviously, maintaining a household with collective residence and common estate, or a household with separate residences but common estate, as was attempted here, was not an acceptable solution in the long term.

Setting aside lineage land was the only effective means of stable

long-term collective ownership. It was recorded in the Huang genealogy that, "the law says that the private sale of sacrificial land is a
crime, and dividing it into private shares is prohibited. Thus, even if
a family has not a single picul of savings, the sacrificial property will
still endure forever."[102] The argument here, that collective ownership
of lineage property did not depend on any private ownership, is
valid. But the explanation that this had been decreed by law is clearly
false. Lineage land had such a stable character because individual lineage members pursued diverse occupations and could not personally
manage their land.

The large-scale development of lineage land strengthened the economic functions of lineage organizations, which were gradually
transformed into profit-driven economic entities. In lineage organizations rich in corporate property, most of the income from that property was not devoted to collective expenses but was divided among
the membership. In the late seventeenth century, the Zu lineage of
Tunshan in Ouning County set aside land earning 500 baskets rent to
be the sacrificial property of one Li'nan. The four branches of his
descendants took turns collecting this income, and "after the tax is
paid and the sacrifice performed, there is still a considerable surplus." In 1815, the descendants divided the property into two. A portion earning 167 baskets and ten taels rent was set aside. "From each
branch, two honest, upright, and straightforward men are to be collectively chosen to come forward and take responsibility for management, collect the rent, pay the tax, pay the [bottom-soil] rent, and
conduct the sacrifice. The surplus is to be retained to meet such common expenses as repairing the fields by the water's edge, the irrigation channels, and the boundaries." Aside from this portion, there
remained property earning 325 baskets in rent, and a hostel located
in the county town. "The right to collect this income continued to
rotate through the branches," but the income did not need to be used
to meet any collective expenses.[103] Collective expenses thus accounted
for less than one-third of the total income from the sacrificial estate,
and the remainder was distributed as income to the branches.

When successive generations set aside a portion of property to
serve as corporate land, the total income from such property could
be considerable and could have a decisive impact on the economic
life of lineage members. The sacrificial estate of Xibin, a member of
the twenty-sixth generation of the Donghai Xu lineage of Pucheng,
earned more than 100 piculs in rent, which was collected in rotation

by the two branches of his descendants. The two branches of the next generation established sacrificial estates earning a total income of 240 piculs rent. There were seven households in the twenty-eighth generation. On average, each household thus earned about 50 piculs rent from the sacrificial estates of the father and grandfather of the household head.[104] In the Zu lineage of Tunshan, the Qin and Jian branches, which had formed in the nineteenth generation, each divided a total annual income of 344 baskets from the sacrificial property of their father Shengwen. In alternating years, they earned 40 baskets from the sacrificial estate of their grandfather Shilong. Once every six years, they earned an income of 96 baskets from the sacrificial estate of their great-grandfather Changqi. Once every eighteen years they earned 221 baskets from the sacrificial estate of their great-great-grandfather Rukui. On average each branch earned more than 300 baskets per year from the sacrificial estates of their most recent four generations of ancestors.[105] From the perspective of the collective owners of lineage fields, even if a household was completely bankrupt, its members might still be able to survive on their share of the rental income from sacrificial property.

As the lineage collective economy developed, it might take over some of the functions that had previously been fulfilled within the household economy. Thus, in 1879, after Guo Weisu of Taiwan divided his estate among his sons, the estate of each household continued to be managed collectively, because "the funds were held together [in the form of] shares in the Longyishu enterprise."[106] The document of household division of a Huang surname household in Minxian County, dated 1906, records:

> We have collectively decided to evenly divide the property and business into shares and to [reinvest the shares] to establish together the Hall of Public Accumulation Corporation (gongji tang gongsi). The profit earned each year is to be reinvested in the corporation once living expenses have been distributed according to the number of people [in each household].[107]

The Huang lineage Hall of Public Accumulation continued as a profit-driven economic enterprise into the Republican period. An agreement concerning the annual rotation of its corporate property states:

> We have together discussed and come to this agreement that the total annual income from the collective property of the Hall of Public Accumulation will be managed in rotation by the five branches, Shu,

Yuan, Xiang, Li, and Zhen. Each branch will take a turn in the rotation for one year, and when the rotation is complete it will start again
at the beginning. The rota holder each year receives two hundred
silver dollars from the income of the collective property. The remainder
is used to meet the expenses of the spring and autumn sacrifice and
for the purpose of expanding the property.[108]

This lineage organization was thus a jointly managed share corporation, in which the branches were the shareholders.

Economic differentiation within the lineage membership could
lead to changes in the corporate property relations of the lineage, and
in turn to corresponding changes in its organization. This is illustrated by the following deed for the sale of sacrificial land, dated
1841:

The maker of this deed of sale, Zhang Shiyao, inherited from my ancestor a share in several plots of sacrificial land the income from which
is earned in rotation by the Ri, Yue, and Xing branches. The land is
located at the place known as Huanglong, and elsewhere. The annual
income in topsoil and bottom-soil rent is 20 piculs. The Ri branch is
further divided into the Yuan, Heng, Li, and Zhen sub-branches, and
the Zhen sub-branch is further divided into the Qian and Kun sub-
branches. The Kun branch is further divided into the Shipang, Shifa,
Shiyao, and Shiyi sub-branches. Shiyao's share earns an income in topsoil and bottom-soil rent of 3.3 pecks *(dou)*. The boundaries of this
land are all recorded clearly below. Because I have a present need for
cash, I have asked a middleman to negotiate on my behalf to sell the
rights to this land by deed to Shisen of this lineage. . . . This property
is truly the property left behind by our ancestor to the Ri, Yue, and
Xing branches. The other uncles and brothers of our lineage have no
claim on it.[109]

This deed illustrates that lineage members could leave the original
collective ownership group by dividing or selling their rights of ownership to lineage property. The sale of portions of ownership could also
lead to changes in the way rights were allocated, leading in turn to
the transformation of an inheritance lineage to a contractual one. For
example, the Yingchuan Chen lineage, discussed in the third part of
Chapter 3, had a sacrificial estate endowed in the name of ancestors
Ying and Gui. When their descendants repeatedly divided and sold
portions of these rights, the original system of allocation of ownership rights according to branch was transformed into a system of
allocation of rights according to share, and a contractual lineage
based on share ownership emerged. The descendants of the original
owners of the estate successively sold off their individual shares. Lin-

eage members' ownership rights in the lineage were thus determined not by their membership in a branch whose share in the property was passed on from generation to generation, but rather by the share of the property each individual himself had purchased.[110]

Division, sale, and purchase of rights to lineage property within the lineage made it possible for property rights to be transferred relatively freely. Any member of the lineage or any organization within it could divide, sell, or purchase lineage property. This could make for extremely complex patterns of collective landownership relations.

A 1792 contract records:

> The maker of this deed of sale of top- and bottom-soil rights to a plot of common field is He Tiansi. At present, because I am short of money, I have willingly determined to sell [my share of] bottom- and top-soil rights to two plots of land . . . which I have inherited from my ancestors, and which bear a total tax of exactly one pint *(sheng)*. This land originally belongs to three shares, which cultivate it in rotation. Now I desire to sell off the share belonging to Puliang, which my father has purchased. Through a middleman, I have been introduced to Changyan and the other five shareholders of the Boji branch of our ancestral hall, who will use their accumulated funds to purchase this land to be their own property, in order to meet the expenses of repairing the ancestral hall. Today all three parties have agreed that the price of the land is 45 taels of silver. . . . Once this land has been sold, the ancestral hall will manage it and [select tenants] to cultivate it. I will not interfere or make trouble. The tax obligation on this land is still registered under my household. When the land registers are next compiled, the obligation to meet the service levy and pay the tax will be transferred to the purchaser's registration. There are no irregularities to the sale and purchase; usury is not involved, nor has there been any coercion. Both parties engage in the transaction willingly, and neither will regret it. Now, desiring a record, we have drawn up this contract of final sale of top- and bottom-soil rights to common land. . . .[111]

The purchaser in this contract was a contractual lineage organization made up of six shareholders, and the seller an ordinary individual member of the lineage. But this had no significance for the transaction. The other two parties with a share in this property had to know who or what the third shareholder was, but it was of no import to them whether it was an individual lineage member or a lineage organization.

In most cases, sellers of lineage property were required to give members of their lineage branch right of first refusal. If the other original owners were not interested, the property rights could then be sold to members of other branches, or even other lineages. This led to the development of collective property relations between more than one lineage. For example, an 1881 contract reads:

> The maker of this deed, Zhang Youcai, inherited from the ancestors two plots of land cultivated with early ripening rice, which rotate between the three branches. . . . The descendants [of our branch] have further divided into three sub-branches, Chaike, Rongmao, and Youcai, which cultivate the land in rotation in years containing the characters *yin, shen, ji*[b], and *hai* [i.e., every three years]. Unexpectedly, while he was alive Chaike was ill-fated, and so he sold his share to the rights during those years to another branch of our lineage. Now Rongmao has died leaving no posterity, and there is no money to pay for his funeral. For this reason, I am now selling my share and Rongmao's share to Li Jinyan of this locale. . . .[112]

In this case, the sale of lineage property to a nonmember of the lineage led to the development of collective property relations transcending the single lineage. The lineage collective economy was transforming into a lineage–village or territorial-lineage collective economy *(xiangzu gongyou jingji)*. However, as some of the shares in the property were still under the control of members of the original lineage, this did not mean the complete disintegration of the lineage collective economy. In other words, lineage collective ownership was an organic part of lineage–village collective ownership, and lineage–village collective ownership was simply an extension of lineage collective ownership. The different kinds of interlineage economic structures that developed in the Ming–Qing period were thus really extensions of lineage economic structures.

Naturally, if all the shares in lineage property were transferred to members of other lineages, this meant the complete disintegration of the original lineage's collective economy, but what replaced it was often simply another lineage. For example, the Ge lineage of Huangxi in Ouning County owned certain property the income of which was used to pay the costs of "opening paths and marking fields," and for the support of the Shanchong monastery. This land had originally been lineage property belonging to another lineage. According to the Ge genealogy:

> This property was originally sacrificial land belonging to Zhang Chaolin and others, which was managed in rotation by the Ri, Yue, and Xing branches. Each of these three branches was itself further divided into three sub-branches, so in all there were nine branches in a nine-year rotation. Ge Dagao purchased the fourth branch's share and Ge Longlin purchased the fifth branch's share.[113]

The income from the share purchased by Dagao was used to pay for road and field repairs, and that from the share purchased by Longlin for support of the monastery. In this case, once the lineage land of the Zhang was sold share by share to the Ge, the land became part of the collective landholdings of two separate inheritance lineages, and each lineage managed its shares according to its own system. Together, the two lineages also formed a contractual lineage organization based on shares in the property.

Lineage members' ownership of shares in lineage corporate property was essentially still a form of private ownership, and this is what gave these shares their potential mobility. It was precisely the potential mobility of share ownership of lineage property that permitted adjustments to be made to collective ownership structures in response to changes in the economic situation of the individual households of the lineage, and thus made the long-term development of lineage collective ownership possible. Of course, this mobility also meant that all the shares in a certain lineage property could potentially come under the control of a single member of the lineage. This, too, meant the disintegration of collective ownership and the renewal of small private landholding. For example, in the Zhan lineage of Pucheng, shares in the sacrificial estate of ancestor Luo were transferred and sold by several generations of lineage members and eventually became the private property of one individual. According to the genealogy:

> This property was originally managed in rotation by the Wen, Liang, Jing, Jian, and Rang branches to support sacrifice. The Wen, Jian, and Rang branches sold their share in the sacrificial estate by deed to Shichao, a nineteenth-generation member of the Jing branch. Because Shichao was unable to fulfill his service levy obligations, in the Kangxi period he reported to the county magistrate that he wished to return his rights to Rangjun, a twenty-first-generation member of the Liang branch. . . . Shichao's son Liangzhen also sold his own share in the Jing branch, as well as the three shares that had belonged to the Wen, Jian, and Rang branches, to Rangjun.
>
> In the Qianlong period, Benkuan, a twenty-second-generation member of the Jian branch, brought a suit [to recover the rights to this property]. This led Rangjun's grandson Daoji and others to bring a countersuit to the county, prefectural and provincial authorities. The lawsuit lasted for many years. . . . Later, through outside mediation, the suit was dropped, and a report was sent to the officials settling the matter. So although the land owned by the four shares is called a sacrificial estate, in fact it is just private property.[114]

This example demonstrates that in the process of development of lineage collective economy there was always the potential of a countertendency back to private ownership. The stability of lineage collective ownership should therefore not be overestimated.

*   *   *

Strictly speaking, the lineage collective economy based on collective lineage property took shape and developed only within the landlord class. Poor peasants of the lineage could not possibly leave an estate earning rental income sufficient to maintain their descendants. Moreover, economic differentiation inevitably arose even among the descendants of landlords, and it was not necessarily possible for all of them to maintain themselves on rental income from lineage property. A certain Ye Changshou, a maker of fried cakes in Jian'an in the Qing, was so poor that "he had not even enough land to stick in an awl." After he died, his wife and children turned for assistance to a charity for widows. "All five of them were pale [with malnourishment]." But the Ye lineage to which they belonged "was a prominent lineage of the county. Their ancestor had bequeathed sacrificial property that earned one thousand piculs rent, but it took thirty years for it to rotate once through the lineage. In the year that one had the right to collect the rent, one could go from poverty to great wealth."[115] Obviously, a down-and-out lineage member like Ye Changshou could not rely on his rights in lineage collective property to become rich, and indeed probably found it difficult even to hang on to those rights. Another recipient of aid from the same charity for widows was a woman née Huang, who had married into the Deng family. "This woman had rights to a sacrificial estate, but while her husband was alive and before it was their turn, he mortgaged the rights to members of the lineage to raise money to fill their bellies. This practice was commonly called encumbering fields *(ketian)*." A contemporary observer commented:

> Rich households make use of the practice of encumbering fields to enrich themselves at the cost of impoverishing the rest of the lineage. They do not consider the intention of the ancestors in establishing a sacrificial estate to enrich the descendants. They think only of their own profit and do not consider uniting the lineage. This is an evil practice in Jianning.[116]

Encumbering fields was an exploitative form of usury somewhat similar to a mortgage. This is illustrated in the following 1909 mortgage contract:

The maker of this deed, Nephew Shanfa, inherited from the eighth-generation ancestor a [share in a] sacrificial estate consisting of top- and bottom-soil rights to one plot of common land. . . . The annual income totals 1,400 catties of unhusked rice, which is collected in rotation by the Jing, Kuan, Xin, Mei, and Hui branches. I belong to the Jing branch. I am scheduled to earn the income in 1914. Because I am now in need of money, I have arranged through a middleman to mortgage my right to collect the income in 1914 to uncle Maoyuan. Today I have received six silver dollars and agreed that the annual interest will be 20 percent. The money has been handed over in full, and it is now up to Uncle to meet the tenant and manage the land. Tax payment, the expenses for the sacrificial wine, and the miscellaneous expenses are Uncle's responsibility, and are not my affair. . . . If there is a drought [in 1914] and the rent cannot be collected fully, I will still pay the interest, but Uncle will collect the income next time it is my turn in the rotation. Until the account has been squared away, I will not complain. I will collect whatever surplus remains [after the loan and interest have been repaid].[117]

The right to income from sacrificial land was being used here as security for a loan, and the income itself was to be used to repay the principal and interest on the loan. This made the borrower's rights to the corporate property effectively meaningless, and thus effectively excluded him from collective ownership.

Some lineage members even transferred this type of right to a non-lineage member, which led to a different kind of change in the collective lineage economy, as is illustrated by this mortgage contract dated 1872:

The maker of this deed, Xu Huiyuan, has inherited from the ancestors rights in two plots of a sacrificial estate that is managed in rotation. . . . Because I am now in need of money, I have mortgaged the rights to collect the income from this property to Huang Chengti. The three parties involved have agreed that I will today receive 14,000 cash. The money has been handed over in full and received by the Shou branch [i.e., Xu Huiyuan]. Whenever it is my turn in the rotation to earn the income from the sacrificial estate, Chengti may remove the tenant, manage the land, and [select tenants] to cultivate it. The tax payment and the sacrifice at the graves remain my responsibility, and the income from the plot of land at Qiangli has been set aside to meet these expenses. These two matters are not Huang's affair. Ownership of this property is divided among the Fu, Lu, Shou, and Xi branches, and it consists of property inherited from the ancestors. Other branches have no claim on it. We have agreed in person that there is no time limit for the repayment of the principal and redemption of the land on the basis of this contract. Huang shall not obstruct this. Until I redeem the land, Huang will continue to control it.[118]

Until Xu Huiyuan was able to repay the loan and regain his rights to the land, the sacrificial estate was held collectively by the other members of the Xu lineage and Huang Chengti. These examples demonstrate that, in the face of economic differentiation within the lineage, it was very difficult to maintain stable collective ownership by the members of the lineage over the long term, and the lineage collective economy would disintegrate or change form as a result.

*   *   *

In summary, the development of lineage property in the Ming and Qing reflected the corporatization of property relations within the lineage. Lineage property was the material basis for lineage organization, and also part of a strategy to prevent private landlords from falling into poverty. To a degree, it was also a response to occupational specialization by the lineage membership. The rapid development of lineage property gradually transformed lineage organizations into profit-driven economic enterprises. The economic functions of the individual household diminished correspondingly. Lineage collective landownership, which was rooted in lineage property, was in fact a type of collective ownership by private landlords, so it was obviously affected by economic differentiation within the lineage membership. Division and sale of rights to lineage property were the chief ways in which collective ownership rights were affected. The result was not only changes to collective ownership and the lineage collective economy, but also corresponding changes in lineage organization. Within the lineage, the sale and transfer of shares in lineage property was an important factor in the transformation of inheritance lineages into contractual lineages. The circulation of these shares beyond the limits of a single lineage could also lead to the formation of multilineage lineage–village collective ownership and lineage–village organization. The corporatization of property relations thus provided an impetus for the development and transformation of family lineage organization, encouraging the further extension of lineage ideology.

6
Conclusion

Several conclusions follow from the preceding discussion. First, in a society in which the subsistence and commercial economies coexisted in a state of mutual tension, the large household had definite economic advantages because it could help sustain a diversified system of cooperation based on division of labor. This is why the large household was seen as the ideal household structure in traditional China. But the practice of household division was detrimental to the development of large households. When the estate was divided in every generation, the long-term cycle of household structure was typically one of dynamic equilibrium between large and small household phases. The domestic cycle of the traditional household meant that the cooperative division of labor within the household collapsed periodically. In response, household members needed other bases for cooperation, which made them seek out more stable, long-term forms of cooperative relations. This led naturally to the spread and development of lineage organization.

Second, different measures were adopted to alleviate the stresses generated by household division on social and economic life. These measures included dividing the household but not dividing the property, dividing the household but not dividing the household registration, and dividing the household but maintaining sacrifice in common. Each of these measures meant that certain property and responsibilities were inherited collectively, thereby enabling lineage members to maintain existing cooperation based on division of labor even after household division. This in turn led to the transformation of the large household into a lineage organization. The lineage organization that developed directly out of household division was an inheritance lineage based on ties of consanguinity. Its chief function was to ensure

325

the continued transmission of the descent-line, and so the rights and responsibilities of individual lineage members were determined by their inheritance relations. The weakening of consanguinal ties over time and growing economic differentiation within the lineage tended to lead to the disintegration of an inheritance lineage and its replacement by a control-subordination or contractual lineage. Control-subordination lineages were based on relations of common locality, and their chief function was the maintenance of the traditional social order. Thus the rights and responsibilities of the members of such lineages were determined by their position in the social structure. Contractual lineages were based on ties of common interest, and their basic function was investment in and management of collective enterprises. The rights and responsibilities of members were determined by their fixed share of ownership.

Third, where the social environment was relatively isolated and stable, as in northwestern Fujian, the general pattern of development of lineage organization began with the formation of inheritance lineages as a result of household division, followed by the gradual development of control-subordination and contractual lineages resulting from internal economic differentiation and reorganization. After periods of violent unrest, or in areas newly populated by immigrants, the development of lineage organization might follow the opposite pattern, with control-subordination or contractual lineages developing first and inheritance lineages appearing only later. The former process was a reflection of the inner logic of lineage development, so it can be considered the normal pattern. The latter processes were a reflection of particular environmental constraints; they should be considered exceptional patterns. Regardless of which process occurred in a particular area, both ultimately led to multifaceted, multilayered lineage organization. This is the most striking historical characteristic of lineage organization since the Ming–Qing period.

Fourth, the development of family lineage organization in the Ming and Qing reflected profound changes in traditional Chinese society. The spread of ancestral worship among the common people, and the diversification and manipulation of the patterns of inheritance of the descent-line, reflected the popularization of lineage ideology. The integration of family lineage organization with basic-level political authority and the hereditization of *lijia* household registration and fixing of *lijia* obligations reflected the rising autonomy of local society. The rapid development of lineage property, and the spread of share ownership as the means by which its income was allocated, reflected the corporatization of property relations. Each of these processes in traditional Chinese society found concrete expression in the development of family lineage organization, and therefore political, economic, and cultural life came to be thoroughly influenced by family lineage organization.

Finally, it should be pointed out that in the social structure of the Ming and Qing periods, family lineage organization was not the only form of social organization, but it was the most fundamental form. Other forms of social organization that transcended the family lineage were in fact ultimately based on family lineage organization or consisted of linkages between more than one family lineage organization.[1] According to Fu Yiling, the influence of family lineage organization extended to every aspect of social organization:

> In the upper stratum of the gentry it developed into political factions. In the lower strata of society, it was gradually transformed into popular societies, which united people of different surnames into a single family and had the equalization of property ownership as their goal. Among merchants and farmers, it developed into native-place associations and guilds, which aimed to ensure equitable development within individual occupations and small-scale local associations.[2]

In other words, family lineage organization contained within it the potential for the development of many different kinds of social organization. Thus, many scholars believe that family lineage organization was the foundation of traditional Chinese society, shaping and conditioning the course of Chinese history. I believe that, by the Ming–Qing period, family lineage organization had already transcended the limitations of consanguinal kinship relations and had incorporated other organizational principles capable of adapting to other social relations. Family lineage organization was inclusive and flexible, and provided the potential for the further development of traditional Chinese society. In a sense, the purpose of this study has been to consider the historical character and implications of this extension of lineage ideology.

Marx wrote that the whole history of human society is the "continuous transformation of human nature."[3] What he meant by human nature is social nature, the sum total of man's actual social relations. Historical research must identify the ways in which social relations change, for these are the essential features of the historical process. Morgan classified human social relations into kinship relations, territorial relations, and property or profit relations, and argued that the development of society is largely manifest in the transition from kinship relations to territorial relations and from territorial relations to property relations.[4] This argument remains influential to the present day. But in the history of China the development of society has not manifested itself in a linear progression from one form to another, but rather in the intermingling of all three. Any attempt to divide Chinese history into successive stages is thus extremely problematic. As Fu Yiling pointed out, traditional Chinese society developed early but never matured fully. All sorts of social formations could coexist at the same time in a highly flexible pluralistic structure.[5] Ming and Qing family lineage organization, which combined consanguinal kinship relations, territorial relations, and interest relations, clearly demonstrates this pluralistic character of traditional Chinese society. The detailed study of family lineage organization in the Ming and Qing periods can thus help us to understand the forces driving the internal development of traditional Chinese society.

Notes

PREFACE

1. Peter Laslett, "Introduction," in Peter Laslett, ed., *Household and Family in Past Time* (Cambridge: Cambridge University Press, 1972).

2. Lutz Berkner, "The Stem Family and the Developmental Cycle of the Peasant Household: An Eighteenth-Century Austrian Example," *American Historical Review* 77 (1972): 398–418; "The Use and Misuse of Census Data for the Historical Analysis of Family Structure: A Review of *Household and Family in Past Time,*" *Journal of Interdisciplinary History* 4 (1975): 721–738; Lutz Berkner and Franklin Mendels, "Inheritance Systems, Family Structure, and Demographical Patterns in Western Europe, 1700–1900," in Charles Tilly, ed., *Historical Studies in Changing Fertility* (Princeton, N.J.: Princeton University Press, 1978).

3. Olga Lang, *Chinese Family and Society* (New Haven, Conn.: Yale University Press, 1946).

4. Arthur P. Wolf, "Chinese Family Size: A Myth Revitalized," in Hsieh Jih-chang and Chuang Ying-chang, eds., *The Chinese Family and Its Ritual Behaviour* (Nangang: Institute of Ethnology, Academia Sinica, 1985). See also Arthur Wolf, "Family Life and the Life Cycle in Rural China," in Robert Netting, Richard Wilk, and Eric Arnould, eds., *Households: Comparative and Historical Studies of the Domestic Group* (Berkeley: University of California Press, 1984).

5. Liu Ts'ui-jung, "Demographic Constraint and Family Structure in Traditional Chinese Lineages, ca. 1200–1900," in Stevan Harrell, ed., *Chinese Historical Microdemography* (Berkeley: University of California Press, 1995).

6. Zhao Zhongwei, "Demographic Conditions and Multi-generation Households in Chinese History: Results from Genealogical Research and Microsimulation," *Population Studies* 48 (1994): 413–425.

7. James Lee and Cameron Campbell, *Fate and Fortune in Rural China: Social Organization and Population Behavior in Liaoning, 1774–1873* (Cambridge: Cambridge University Press, 1997).

8. For a discussion, see Patricia Ebrey, *Confucianism and Family Rituals in Imperial China: A Social History of Writing about Rites* (Princeton, N.J.: Princeton University Press, 1991), 29–31.

9. Some Taiwanese scholars use the terms "great" and "small lineage" *(da*

zongzu, xiao zongzu) to describe Taiwanese lineages whose claimed common founding ancestor was a person from the mainland or a person from Taiwan, respectively. Obviously this is a rather different usage.

10. Mao Zedong, *Selected Works of Mao Tse-tung* (Beijing: Foreign Languages Press, 1967), 1:23–59.

11. Zuo Yunpeng, "Citang, zuzhang, zuquan de xingcheng jiqi zuoyong shishuo," *Lishi yanjiu* (1964), 5–6.

12. Xu Yangjie, "Song-Ming yilai de fengjian jiazu zhidu lunshu," *Zhongguo shehui kexue,* no. 4 (1980).

13. Fu Yiling, "Guanyu Zhongguo fengjian shehui houqi jingji fazhan de ruogan wenti de kaocha," *Lishi yanjiu,* no. 4 (1963); reprinted in Fu Yiling, *Ming Qing shehui jingji shi lunwenji* (Beijing: Renmin, 1982).

14. Fu Yiling, "Lun xiangzu shili duiyu Zhongguo fengjian jingji de ganshe," *Xiamen daxue xuebao,* no. 3 (1961); reprinted in Fu Yiling, *Ming Qing shehui jingji shi lunwenji,* 81.

15. Fu Yiling and Yang Guozhen, eds., *Ming–Qing Fujian shehui yu xiangcun jingji* (Xiamen: Xiamen daxue, 1987); Mori Masao, "Weirao xiangzu wenti," *Zhongguo shehui jingji shi yanjiu,* no. 2 (1986): 1–8.

16. Tang Meijun, "Taiwan chuantong de shehui jiegou," in Liu Ningyan, ed., *Taiwan shiji yuanliu* (Taibei: Taiwan sheng wenxian, 1981).

17. Chen Qi'nan, *Taiwan de chuantong Zhongguo shehui* (Taibei: Yunzhen, 1989); Zhuang Yingzhang, *Linpipu—Yige Taiwan shizhen de shehui jingji fazhan shi* (Nangang: Zhongyang yanjiuyuan minzuxue yanjiusuo, 1977).

18. Patricia Ebrey and James Watson, "Introduction," in their *Kinship Organization in Late Imperial China, 1000–1940* (Berkeley: University of California Press, 1986), 1.

19. Maurice Freedman, *Lineage Organization in Southeastern China* (London: Athlone, 1958).

20. See the list of works in Ebrey and Watson, *Kinship Organization,* 2.

21. Joseph Esherick and Mary Backus Rankin, "Introduction," in their *Chinese Local Elites and Patterns of Dominance* (Berkeley: University of California Press, 1990), 11.

22. Ebrey, *Confucianism and Family Rituals in Imperial China* (1991); Kai-wing Chow, *The Rise of Confucian Ritualism in Late Imperial China: Ethics, Classics, and Lineage Discourse* (Stanford, Calif.: Stanford University Press, 1994).

23. James Watson, "Chinese Kinship Reconsidered: Anthropological Perspectives on Historical Research," *China Quarterly* 92 (1982): 594.

24. Myron Cohen, "Lineage Organization in North China," *Journal of Asian Studies* 49, no. 3 (1990): 509–534.

25. Zheng's use of the term "lineage" resembles that of David Faure, who uses the term to refer to "self-professed unilineal descent groups. . . . The focus of the indigenous concepts related to lineage is common descent along the male line, and for my purpose here it is only necessary to note that those people who considered themselves to make up a *zu* or a *fang* would have considered that as an essential bond among themselves. It is not necessary to claim that these people were not related in other ways." David Faure, "The Lineage as a Cultural Invention," *Modern China* 15 (1989): 5.

26. Ebrey and Watson, *Kinship Organization,* 6.

27. He does, however, recognize a distinction between residentially concentrated and residentially dispersed lineages.

28. Morton Fried argued at length against this position in his *The Fabric of Chinese Society* (New York: Praeger, 1953). Hugh Baker's arguments seem quite close to those of Zheng and Fu; *Chinese Family and Kinship* (New York: Columbia University Press, 1979), 164. For more recent considerations of the issue, see Judith Strauch, "Community and Kinship in Southeastern China: The View from the Multilineage Villages of Hong Kong," *Journal of Asian Studies* 43, no. 1 (1983): 21–50, and Steven Sangren, "Traditional Chinese Corporations: Beyond Kinship," *Journal of Asian Studies* 43, no. 3 (1984): 391–414.

29. See the essays in *Modern China* 19, no. 2 (1993); Timothy Brook and B. Michael Frolic, eds., *Civil Society in China* (Armonk, N.Y.: M. E. Sharpe, 1997).

30. See, for example, Hugh Clark, *Community, Trade, and Networks: Southern Fujian from the Third to the Thirteenth Century* (Cambridge: Cambridge University Press, 1991); Eduard Vermeer, ed., *Development and Decline of Fukien Province in the 17th and 18th Centuries* (Leiden: Brill, 1990); Kenneth Dean, *Taoist Ritual and Popular Cults of Southeast China* (Princeton, N.J.: Princeton University Press, 1993). Important Chinese sources on the general history of Fujian include: Tang Wenji, ed., *Fujian gudai jingji shi* (Fuzhou: Fujian jiaoyu, 1995); Zhu Weigan, *Fujian shigao* (Fuzhou: Fujian jiaoyu, 1986); and, on lineage history in particular, Chen Zhiping, *Jin wubai nian Fujian de jiazu shehui yu wenhua* (Shanghai: Sanlian, 1991).

31. Hans Bielenstein, "The Chinese Colonization of Fukien until the End of T'ang," in Søren Egerod and Else Glahn, eds., *Studia Serica Bernhard Karlgren Dedicata* (Copenhagen: Ejnar Munksgaard, 1959).

32. Edward Schafer, *The Empire of Min* (Rutland, Vt.: Charles Tuttle, 1954).

33. Shiba Yoshinobu, *Commerce and Society in Sung China,* trans. Mark Elvin (Ann Arbor) *Michigan Abstracts of Chinese and Japanese Works on Chinese History* 2 (1970); Clark, *Community, Trade, and Networks* (1991).

34. So Kwan-wai, *Japanese Piracy in Ming China during the Sixteenth Century* (East Lansing: Michigan State University Press, 1975).

35. William Skinner, "Presidential Address: The Structure of Chinese History," *Journal of Asian Studies* 44 (1985): 271–292.

36. Ng Chin-keong, *Trade and Society: The Amoy Network on the China Coast, 1683–1735* (Singapore: Singapore University Press, 1983).

37. Evelyn Rawski, *Agricultural Change and the Peasant Economy of South China* (Cambridge, Mass.: Harvard University Press, 1972).

38. Yang Guozhen, "Ming Qing Fujian tudi siren suoyouquan neizai jiegou de yanjiu," in Fu Yiling and Yang Guozhen, eds., *Ming Qing Fujian shehui yu xiangcun jingji* (Xiamen: Xiamen daxue, 1987); *Ming–Qing tudi qiyue wenshu yanjiu* (Beijing: Renmin, 1988).

39. Dean, *Taoist Ritual* (1993).

40. David Faure, *The Structure of Chinese Rural Society: Lineage and Village in the Eastern New Territories, Hong Kong* (Cambridge: Cambridge University Press, 1986); Ebrey, *Confucianism and Family Rituals in Imperial China* (1991).

CHAPTER 1

1. Mao Zedong, "Report of an Investigation into the Peasant Movement in Hunan," in *Selected Works of Mao Tse-tung* (Beijing: Foreign Languages Press, 1967), 1:45.

2. [The body of Zheng's discussion of previous scholarship has been omitted in the translation. Trans.]

3. [On *guoji* adoption, see David Wakefield, *Fenjia: Household Division and Inheritance in Qing and Republican China* (Honolulu: University of Hawai'i Press, 1998), 73. Trans.]

4. [The *lijia* and *baojia* systems were sub-bureaucratic local administrative systems, intended to facilitate the collection of tax and labor services and the maintenance of local order, respectively. The *lijia*, which was established in the early Ming, divided the population into units called *li*, each consisting of one hundred and ten households. Each *li* was further subdivided into ten units called *jia*, each consisting of ten households. Each of the ten *jia* was responsible in a decennial rotation to provide both labor service and material requisitions for the state for one year. The ten wealthiest households in the *li*, measured in terms of land ownership and number of tax-bearing males *(ding)*, were the *jia* heads. Each *jia* head served as *li* head *(lizhang)* in a separate decennial rotation, responsible for overseeing the fulfillment of labor service and other responsibilities. The Ming *baojia* system was based on a Song model and divided the population up for the purposes of community policing and defense. On the two systems, see Martin Heijdra, "The Socio-Economic Development of Rural China during the Ming," in Denis Twitchett and Frederick Mote, eds., *The Ming Dynasty, 1368–1644, Part 2. The Cambridge History of China,* vol. 8 (Cambridge: Cambridge University Press, 1998), 486–489. Trans.]

5. Frederick Engels, *The Origin of the Family, Private Property and the State* (New York: International Publishers, 1942), 5.

6. See Ye Qingkun, "Xinjiapo he Malaya de zaoqi Zhongguo renmin zuzhi, 1819–1911," *Dongnanya yanjiu* 7 (1981).

CHAPTER 2

1. There has been considerable debate on the question of the predominant household structure of the traditional Chinese family. Some scholars argue that the Qin to Sui period was the "high point of the stem family," the Tang to the Qing was the "high point of the lineal family," and since the late Qing the large family has given way to the small family; see Rui Yifu, "Dibian zhong de Zhongguo jiating jiegou," paper presented at the Tenth Conference on Pacific Sciences, Honolulu, 1961. Other scholars suggest that the large family predominated only among the wealthy urban classes: "In the past, some people believed that the large family was the chief form of the family in traditional Chinese society. At least in the rural areas this does not accord with the facts"; see Fei Xiaotong, "Jiating jiegou biandongzhong de laonian shanyang wenti," in *Xiandaihua yu Zhongguo wenhua yanjiuhui lunwen huibian* (Hong Kong: Zhongwen daxue shehui kexue yanjiusuo, 1985). Other scholars believe that the most highly devel-

oped family was normally the "medium" family, in other words, the stem family: "For the past several thousand years it has been the medium family; it continues to be the medium family; it will still be the medium family in the future"; see Lai Zehan and Chen Kuanzheng, "Woguo jiating xingshi de lishi yu renkou tantao," in *Zhongguo shehui xuekan* 5 (1980). These differing interpretations are largely hypothetical and are not based on substantial research. Because of the lack of complete and reliable population records for traditional Chinese society, attempting to make accurate estimates of the relative distribution of the various forms of family structure is extremely problematic. Moreover, because of the development cycle of the family, a static calculation is clearly inadequate.

2. The research of Qu Tongzu has shown that the Tang, Song, Yuan, Ming, and Qing legal codes all considered "descendants living apart and dividing their property while the parents are still alive" to be a crime against filiality. In the Tang and Song, offenders were punished with three years' exile; in the Ming and Qing, with one hundred strokes. See Qu Tongzu, *Zhongguo falü yu Zhongguo shehui* (Shanghai: Shangwu, 1946; reprint, Beijing: Zhonghua, 1981), 16.

3. *Min Shu*, 1629, j. 39.

4. "Qingyuan Heshi shixi," in *(Minnan) Heshi zupu*, MS, Xiamen University.

5. [It is now widely accepted that the term, which literally means "dwarf bandits," encompassed Japanese, Chinese, and perhaps others. See above, pp. 12–13. Trans.]

6. "Quan-Zhang Heshi shijia xingzhuang," in *(Minnan) Heshi zupu*.

7. "He Xunben shixi," in ibid.

8. "Sishizu Ren'an fujun zhuan," in *(Quanzhou) Chenjiang Dingshi zupu*.

9. *Min Shu*, 1629, j. 39.

10. "Tonggong zuxun," in *(Jianyang) Qingyuan Lishi jiapu*.

11. [Where *li* refers to a geographic unit in the subcounty administration subordinate to the canton *(xiang)*, I translate it as subcanton. Where the term refers to a unit in the *lijia* tax and corvee system, I leave it untranslated. See Timothy Brook, "The Spatial Structure of Ming Local Administration," *Late Imperial China* 6 (1985). Trans.]

12. [Literally, "was like drawing a tiger but only achieving the likeness of a dog." Trans.]

13. [Because the tax obligation would have been transferred to the new household registrations of the two sons. Trans.]

14. "Shouba gong yiwen," in *(Chong'an) Yuanshi zongpu*.

15. "Zhou Ziyuan fen sanzi wei sanfang ji," 1392, in *(Jianyang) Zhoushi zongpu*, j. 1.

16. *(Yongchun) Taoyuan Fengshan Kangshi zupu*.

17. "Jiushu hetong zi," in ibid.

18. *(Yongchun) Liushi zupu*.

19. "Jiaxun shier tiao," in *(Tong'an) Lin Xiyuan jiapu*.

20. See Fu Yiling and Chen Zhiping, eds., "Ming–Qing Fujian shehui jingji shiliao zachao 7," *Zhongguo shehui jingji shi yanjiu*, no. 4 (1987).

21. *Min Shu*, 1629, j. 38.

22. "Fengsu lue," in *Haicheng xianzhi*, 1632.

23. Cai Qing, *Cai Wenzhuang gong wenji*, j. 2.

24. [Plot sizes in Fujian were often expressed in terms of the amount of seed that should be planted on them, which seems to be the case here. Trans.]

25. *(Shaowu) Qingqin li benren Tang Lishi zongpu,* j. 10.

26. [The term used is *mingling,* the mulberry wasp that was believed to steal the offspring of other caterpillars. See Ann Waltner, "Kinship between the Lines: The Patriline, the Concubine and the Adopted Son in Late Imperial China," in Mary Jo Maynes et al., eds., *Gender, Kinship, Power: A Comparative and Inter-disciplinary History* (New York: Routledge, 1996). Trans.]

27. "Yishu," Lin surname, 1709; MS, History Department, Fujian Normal University.

28. "Xinding puli," in *(Jinjiang) Hongshan Pengshi zupu.*

29. "Zhizu zhai shifang yishu," 1864; MS, Fujian Provincial Library.

30. Qu Tongzu (1981), p. 5.

31. Chen Zhiping and Zheng Zhenman, "Pucheng xian Dongtou cun wushi tongtang diaocha," in Fu Yiling and Yang Guozhen, eds. (1987).

32. "Jiushu," surname unknown, 1714; MS, History Department, Fujian Normal University.

33. "Fenguan," Fang surname, 1855; reproduction in History Department, Xiamen University.

34. "Lin Yangsu xiansheng xichan jiushu"; MS, Fujian Provincial Library.

35. Ibid.

36. *(Changting) Fanyang Zoushi zupu,* j. 33.

37. "Fenguan," Ouyang surname, 1809; reproduction in History Department, Xiamen University.

38. "Fenguan," Gu surname, 1831; reproduction in History Department, Xiamen University.

39. "Lin Yangsu xiansheng xichan jiushu;" MS, Fujian Provincial Library.

40. "Wen xing zhong xin xu," in *(Chong'an) Yuanshi zongpu,* j. 1.

41. [In other words, they divided their estate from Guangzu, but not from one another. Trans.]

42. *(Yongchun) Rongfang Chenshi zupu.*

43. "Jiushu," in *(Min) Wenshan Huangshi jiapu.* [See Wakefield, *Fenjia* (1998), 232 n. 14, for discussion of the term "retirement estate." Trans.]

44. A number of examples are found in my "Ming Qing Fujian de jiating jiegou jiqi yanbian qushi," *Zhongguo shehui jingji shi yanjiu,* no. 4 (1988).

45. Chen Kongli, "Qingdai Taiwan yimin shehui de tedian: yi *Wensu Lu* wei zhongxin de yanjiu," *Taiwan yanjiu jikan,* no. 2 (1988).

46. Rinji Taiwan kyūkan chōsakai, *Taiwan shihō furoku sankōsho* (Taibei: Rinji Taiwan kyūkan chōsakai, 1909–1911).

47. For examples of such deeds, see *Taiwan shihō furoku sankōsho,* j. 2b, items 26–27, and j. 1b, items 28–35.

48. [If in either case the document involved designating an heir after the death of the proprietor, then the term "entrustment of an orphan" applied, for the heir was considered comparable to an adopted son who was orphaned when the proprietor had died. Trans.]

49. "Tuogu zi," in *Taiwan shihō furoku sankōsho,* j. 1b, pp. 359–360.

50. "Heyuzi," in ibid., j. 1b, pp. 361–362.

51. Ibid., j. 1b, item 63; j. 2b, item 25; j. 1b, item 11; j. 2b, item 12.

52. "Jiushu," in ibid., j. 1b, pp. 335–336, item 11. [The large silver dollar was one of many types of silver dollar in use in the Qing period. Trans.]

53. "Hetong jiushu," in *Taiwan shihō furoku sankōsho*, j. 1b, pp. 397–398, item 32.

54. "Zhujiu fenzi," in ibid., j. 2b, pp. 311–312, item 16.

55. "Jiushu," in ibid., j. 1b, pp. 409–410, item 75.

56. "Zaifen jiushu hetong zi," in ibid., j. 1b, pp. 320–322, item 2.

57. "Fenye jiushu heyue zi," in ibid., j. 1b, pp. 332–333, item 10.

58. "Yizhu jiushu," in ibid., j. 1b, pp. 331–332, item 9.

59. "Jiushu," in ibid., j. 1b, pp. 329–331, item 8.

CHAPTER 3

1. Tang Meijun, "Taiwan chuantong de shehui jiegou," in Liu Ningyan, ed., *Taiwan shiji yuanliu* (Taibei: Taiwan sheng wenxian, 1981).

2. [This refers to the territorial sacrifices to tutelary deities. Trans.]

3. "Fenguan," Ouyang surname; 1809, reproduction in History Department, Xiamen University.

4. "Liangfang jitian ji," 1621, in *(Jianyang) Lujiang Heshi zongpu*, Guangxu ed., j. 3.

5. "Wen xing zhong xin xu," in *(Chong'an) Yuanshi zongpu*, 1883, j. 1.

6. "Fanli," in ibid., j. 1.

7. [The *luo* was a measure of volume roughly equivalent to 0.25 piculs *(dan)*. Trans.]

8. "Wen xing zhong xin xu," in *(Chong'an) Yuanshi zongpu*, 1883, j. 1.

9. Ibid.

10. MS in the Pucheng County Wenhua guan.

11. "Zujie," in *(Pucheng) Jinzhang Yangshi zupu*, j. 1.

12. Chen Shengshao, *Wensu lu* (1842), j. 1.

13. [The solar term beginning around September 8. Trans.]

14. "Xiabiao gong zili sichan tianzhai banji zhangcheng," in *(Shunchang) Xieshi zongpu*, 1902.

15. "Wen xing zhong xin xu," in *(Chong'an) Yuanshi zongpu*, 1883, j. 1.

16. "Xiabiao gong lunliu zhishou banji buji," in *(Shunchang) Xieshi zongpu*, 1902.

17. "Shuyuan chengzhang jitian," in *(Lufeng) Caishi zupu*, 1744, j. 5.

18. "Chenghai Chengqing gong yizi," in *(Jianning) Wangshi zupu*, j. 1.

19. "Qian Chongzheng she zixu," in *(Jianyang) Xikou Yeshi zongpu*, 1919, j. 1. [The academy here refers to an ancestral hall. Trans.]

20. "(Longxi) Chenshi Zhuiyuan tang heyueji," MS, History Department, Xiamen University.

21. [The point here is that, as long as the estate was held corporately, Longyang could not dispose of it. He had to divide it among all those who had rights to it before he could sell his own share. Trans.]

22. "Chengzhai gong xuceng sichan yin," in *(Shunchang) Xieshi zongpu*, 1902.

23. "Jichan," in *(Pucheng) Zhanshi zupu*, 1922, j. 21.

24. "Fu zhenghai zonglan," in *(Xianyou) Zhushi zupu.*

25. *(Shaowu) Xuntan Huangshi zupu,* 1881, j. 15.

26. Ibid.

27. Chen Shengshao, *Wensu lu,* j. 4.

28. *(Fuzhou) Shimei Wushi zupu.*

29. "Zumu shanyue," in *(Jianyang) Lujiang Heshi zongpu,* Guangxu ed., j. 3.

30. *(Pucheng) Liangshi Hexiu zupu,* j. 1.

31. "Citang kao," in *(Chong'an) Wushi jialu.*

32. *(Pucheng) Liangshi Hexiu zupu,* j. 1.

33. "Hekouxu ji," in *(Shunchang) Qinghe Zhangshi jiuxiu zupu.*

34. *(Pucheng) Wangshi jiapu,* 1948.

35. [The text actually reads "retirement estate" because the estate had clearly been set up originally as Grandmother Zhou's pension, but presumably had been converted after her death into an estate to pay the expenses of sacrifice. Trans.]

36. "Qifang yisun yiba Lian'gong ji ru ci yizi" (1903), in *(Pucheng) Wangshi jiapu,* 1948.

37. Ibid.

38. Ibid.

39. Chen Shengshao, *Wensu lu,* j. 5.

40. "Ren Yi liangfang gongchan yin" (1828) in *(Shunchang) Xieshi zongpu,* 1902.

41. "Xiabiao gong beizheng xianhou liang sichan benghuai feiyong gongye zhangcheng," in ibid.

42. *(Fuzhou) Jintang Wangshi zhipu,* Guangxu ed., j. 2.

43. "Xunhai Shishi zuyue," in *(Jinjiang) Xunhai Shishi zupu,* 1715.

44. Ibid.

45. "Cigui-Qianjieci Qikun gong jidian," in *(Pucheng) Donghai Xushi zongpu,* 1946, j. 1.

46. "Shangtong zongci gui," in *(Pucheng) Zhanshi zupu,* 1922, j. 1.

47. "Fanli," in *(Pucheng) Lianhu Zushi zupu,* 1772, j. 1.

48. "Fangui," in *(Fu'ou) Shangyang Chenshi zongpu,* Daoguang ed., j. 1.

49. "Rusi tiaoli," in *(Fuzhou) Sanshan Yeshi cilu,* 1887, j. 4.

50. "Zhici tiaoli," in ibid., j. 4.

51. "Jintang Wangshi zhici guizhi," in *(Fuzhou) Jintang Wangshi zhipu* Guangxu ed., j. 2.

52. "Zhici tiaoli," in *(Fuzhou) Sanshan Yeshi cilu,* 1887, j. 4.

53. "Ruxian gong sichan zhangcheng," in *(Shunchang) Xieshi zongpu,* 1902.

54. "Ti Zhoushi citang ji," in *(Pucheng) Zhoushi zongpu,* 1900, j. 1.

55. Ibid.

56. "Shangyang citang hetong yizi," in *(Shunchang) Xieshi zongpu,* 1902.

57. *(Jianyang) Shulin Xushi chongxiu zupu,* 1886, j. 1.

58. "Tianduan," in ibid.

59. "Shizu qiuji changtian," in *(Wuping) Lishi zongpu,* 1930, j. *mou.*

60. "E zuo na ding jiuxu," in *(Jianyang) Houju Pingshi zupu,* 1846, j. 1. [Obviously, the sacrificial meat in this case was not in fact meat but rice. Trans.]

61. "Cigui," in *(Pucheng) Donghai Xushi zongpu,* 1946, j. 1.

62. "Jichan," in *(Min'ou) Tunshan Zushi zongpu,* compiled 1822, printed 1939, j. 8.

63. See Zhu Yong, *Qingdai zongzu fa yanjiu* (Changsha: Hunan jiaoyu, 1987).

64. "Cigui," in *(Jianyang) Fushi zongpu,* 1910, j. 1.

65. Zheng Zhenman, "Ming–Qing Minbei xiangzu dizhu jingji de fazhan," in Fu Yiling and Yang Guozhen, eds., *Ming Qing Fujian shehui yu xiangcun jingji* (1987).

66. *(Min'ou) Tunshan Zushi zongpu,* compiled 1822, printed 1939.

67. *(Shunchang) Xieshi zongpu,* 1902.

68. "Xunhai Shishi zuyue," in *(Jinjiang) Xunhai Shishi zupu,* 1715.

69. *(Xianyou) Fengxi Xueshi zupu,* Qianlong ed.

70. "Xunhai Shishi zuyue," in *(Jinjiang) Xunhai Shishi zupu,* 1715.

71. *(Nan'an) Liutian Youshi zupu.*

72. *(Hui'an) Longshan Luoshi zupu.*

73. *(Xianyou) Fengxi Xueshi zupu,* Qianlong ed.

74. *(Quanzhou) Guoshi jiapu,* 1930.

75. "Chongxiu zupu queyi" (1451), in *(Jinjiang) Xunhai Shishi zupu,* 1715.

76. "Fulu," in *(Pucheng) Zhanshi zupu,* 1922.

77. "Jichan," in ibid., j. 21.

78. "Zhulin gegong tianshan," in *(Jianyang) Yingchuan Chenshi zongpu,* j. 1.

79. *(Changting) Fanyang Zoushi zupu,* 1947, j. 29.

80. "Shixi," in ibid., j. 1.

81. "Zaji, Dingfu gong citang beiji," in ibid., j. 35.

82. Ibid., j. 29.

83. Ibid.

84. Ibid.

85. "Yiqi shizu chunji chengzhang ji," in *(Liancheng) Tongshi zupu,* 1937, j. 10.

86. "Yiqi ji shizu xu," in ibid., j. 10. [The *tong* is a box for measuring grain, the size of which varied; it tended to be around six pints. Trans.]

87. "Fushu shizu ci yuandeng xu," in ibid.

88. "Shizu ci yiqi tudihui xu," in ibid.

89. "Yiqi ershizu Jingzhai gong chengzhang ji"; "Zengzhi ershizu fen chunqiu peizhangji ji," both in ibid.

90. "Shangjie ci denghui yin," in ibid.

91. "Shenzhai gong ci zhengyue siri baitushe," in ibid.

92. "Shangjie wushizu fenci liezu zhangtian tuce," in ibid.

93. "Bashizu Zilu gong ci qingming she bing tijuan zhugong mingyi," in ibid.

94. "Bashizu Zilu gong ci yicangshe," in ibid.

95. "Lü ci zhengyue shisanri huadeng she," in ibid.

96. "Shisong fang yiqi jitian ji," in ibid.

97. "Yiqi ji shizu xu," in ibid.

98. "Yiqi ershizu Jingzhai gong chengzhang ji," in ibid.

99. "Chongxiu shizu ci yiqi chunqiu jitian"; "Shangjie ci denghui yin"; "Jian (Zilu)ci tijuan mingci," in ibid.

100. *(Ouning) Huangxi Geshi zupu,* 1921, j. 6.

101. Ibid.

102. "Zhulin shanfen ci shu," in *(Jianyang) Chenshi zupu*, 1872, j. 1.

103. "Jichan Zailu dongzhihui yuanyou," in *(Pucheng) Zhanshi zupu*, 1922, j. 21.

104. [Zirong's descendant. Trans.]

105. "Ziyuan gong, Zirong gong liangfang hetong," in *(Wenchuan) Lishi qixiu zupu*, 1947, j. 1.

106. "Jianzhi yinjiang zuci xu," in ibid.

107. "Heyi hetong," in ibid.

108. "Shengci xu," in ibid.

109. "Changjian shengci xu," in ibid.

110. "Cigui," in ibid.

111. "Heyi zi," in ibid.

112. "Sidian ji," in ibid.

113. Ibid.

114. [Zheng's point here is that a residentially dispersed lineage is not simply a collection of residentially concentrated ones. Rather, the dispersed lineage comprises only certain members of the residentially concentrated lineages. The membership of a contractual lineage consists of the people who own shares, and *only* those who own shares. Trans.]

115. Ibid.

116. *Jianyang xianzhi*, 1832, j. 1.

117. "Touzhuang," 1679, by Zhu Chaodu, in *(Jianyang) Ziyangtang Zhushi zongpu*, 1895.

118. "Tongxiang wengao," in ibid.

CHAPTER 4

1. *Chong'anxian xinzhi*, 1942, j. 4.

2. Ibid., j. 4.

3. *(Min'ou) Tunshan Zushi zongpu*, comp. 1822, printed 1939, j. 2. Subsequent unfootnoted citations are all from this source.

4. "Tunshan diyutu yin," in *(Min'ou) Tunshan Zushi zongpu*, j. 1.

5. Ibid.

6. "Jiagui Jiqi Yiding," in ibid.

7. "Jishanci ji," 1822, in ibid.

8. "Jichan," in ibid., j. 8.

9. "Dianlici ji," in ibid., j. 1.

10. "Rongjie gong jichan xu," in ibid., j. 8.

11. "Qianshan Lingyun miao xiangtianji," 1561, in ibid.

12. "Chongli Qianshan miao xiangtianji," 1567, in ibid.

13. "Xinxiu zongpu xu," 1823, in ibid., j. 1.

14. "Xinxiu zongpu xu," 1823, in ibid.

15. "Shideci ji," 1672, in ibid.

16. "Jishanci ji," in ibid.

17. "Guyu jigui," in ibid.

18. "Shideci dongzhi jibu xu," 1784, in ibid.

19. "Dongzhi zhiji tiaoli," in ibid.
20. "Shizu Xixi gong jibu xu," 1808, in ibid.
21. "Dianlici ji," in ibid.
22. "Xinxiu zongpu ji," in ibid.
23. "Chuifan gong, Ye Quan niang, Wu Xi niangma chengzhang xu," 1754, in ibid.
24. "Jigui," in ibid.
25. "Hanfang zhiji Yongning gong xinli dingpu xu," in ibid.
26. "Siwu wenge jibu xu," 1823, in ibid.
27. "Hansi gong jibu xu," in ibid.
28. [It appears that the mill had to be temporarily dismantled to allow lumber to be floated past. Trans.] "Yonggeng gong jichan hetong," in ibid.
29. [Hence the use of the term "so-called," since not all of the income from the estate actually goes to sacrifice. Trans.]
30. "Xinli Li'nan gong jichan xu," in ibid.
31. "Li'nan gong guji buxu," 1735, in ibid.
32. [Because Xiong took an extra turn in the rotation, he was liable for an extra share of the tax and rent obligations. Trans.]
33. "Bingyan gong jibu xu," in ibid.
34. "Yihua gong jitian buxu," in ibid.
35. "Yanzong gong jichan xu," 1862, in ibid.
36. "Cuanhou gong jiang chengzhang zuo shutian yishu," in ibid.
37. "Yinxia gong shudeng hetong," 1783, in ibid.
38. "Jieshi tu," in ibid.
39. "Wutuncun shanmu beiji," 1815, in ibid., j. 8.
40. "Shizu Xixi gong jibu xu," 1860, in ibid.
41. "Tunshan shecang xu," 1907, in ibid.
42. See n. 28 above.
43. Huang Zhenjian, "Xu," in *(Huangxi) Geshi zongpu*, vol. 1.
44. Wei Binggui, "Xu," in ibid., vol. 6.
45. "Shuoming Kuangzhi jitian xiangzi yuanyou," in ibid.
46. "Yizhiwushi zu gonggong chengzhang tiaogui," in ibid. Subsequent unfootnoted citations are from this source.
47. "Liushizu Fotong gong jichan xu," 1835, in ibid.
48. [I.e., in every twelfth year, in which the character *you* is one of those assigned to the year in the hexadecimal numbering system. Trans.]
49. "Xingfang shishi Guoche, shiyishi Mingji jigui," in *(Huangxi) Geshi zongpu*, vol. 1.
50. [In other words, a person who has not yet paid his fees may not register in the name of someone who has died after already paying his. Trans.]
51. "Zhuxiu zupu xu," in *Huangxi Geshi zongpu*, vol. 1.
52. *Jian'an xiangtuzhi*, 1905.
53. "Xiangli tushuo," in *(Min-Yue-Gan) Wuwei Liaoshi zupu*, j. 1. Subsequent unfootnoted citations are from this source.
54. "Bashi zubi Liupo taimu ji xu," in ibid.
55. "Ciyu tushuo," in ibid.

56. "Wuwei Liaoshi xiupu yuanqi," in ibid.

57. "Chongxiu Shifan Hua gong fenmu beiji," in *(Dongjiang) Liaoshi zupu,* j. 1.

58. "Fenmu tushuo," in *(Min-Yue-Gan) Wuwei Liaoshi zupu,* j. 1.

59. "Shanghang cheng Yibentang jilue," in ibid.

60. "Shanghang Yibentang qinqin chengxu," in ibid.

61. [This is an odd usage of *ji,* but the sense is clear from the text. Trans.]

62. "Yongding Tianduan Qimou hu dazongci jicheng xu," 1801, in *(Min-Yue-Gan) Wuwei Liaoshi zupu,* j. 1.

63. "Bayi Liao jiaci xiuzheng quanzheng yin," in ibid.

64. "Minsheng Yulintang hetongzi," 1829, in ibid.

65. *Houguan xian xiangtuzhi,* 1903, j. 6.

66. *Minxian xiangtuzhi,* 1906, j. 2.

67. Ibid., j. 2.

68. Ibid. *Houguan xian xiangtuzhi,* 1903, j. 6.

69. Cai Xiang, "Shangdaoshi Wang Dianyuan shu," in *Cai Zhonghui gong ji,* j. 24.

70. See Chapter 5, part 1, and my "Song yihou Fujian de jizu xiguan yu zongzu zuzhi," *Xiamen Daxue xuebao* (1987).

71. "Huangshi zuci Sijing tang ji," in Kenneth Dean and Zheng Zhengman, *Fujian zongjiao beiming huibian, Xinghua fu fenjuan* (Fuzhou: Fujian Renmin, 1996), 51. The exact date of this inscription is not known. Huang Zhongyuan was a Metropolitan Graduate of 1271. After the fall of the Song he established a school in his native place. His corpus of writings is rich, and he became known as a "famous scholar of the School of Principle." Of the relatives mentioned in the inscription, we know that his younger brothers Zhonggu and Rixin held the offices of Instructor and Superintendent respectively, and his nephews Xianzu and Yuquan served as Commandant-Escort and Clerk. All were gentrymen at the very end of the Song; the hall was probably constructed at around that time.

72. According to another inscription, the founding ancestor of the Huang of Dongli was one Censor Tao, a metropolitan graduate of 758. "Pinshu lianyin tuji," 1443, in ibid., 95.

73. Ibid., 95–96.

74. Song Lian, "Putian Linshi chongjian zongci ji," in *Song Wenxian gong quanji,* j. 12.

75. [The honorifics *chaofeng* and *fujun* are translated here as "Gentleman." Trans.]

76. "Qingjiang Zhoushi zongtiao beiming." This inscription still stands inside the Zhou ancestral hall of Qingjiang, Huangshi, Putian. Dean and Zheng, *Fujian zongjiao beiming huibian,* 107. Weng Shizi was a Metropolitan Graduate of 1442 and served as president of the Board of Revenue. This inscription was erected in 1480.

77. "Yongsitang ji," 1526, in Dean and Zheng, *Fujian zongjiao beiming huibian,* 84.

78. "Jiaxun ershi tiao," in *(Tong'an) Lin Xiyuan jiapu.*

79. Peng Shao, "Baitang Lishi chongxiu xianci bei," in Dean and Zheng, *Fujian zongjiao beiming huibian,* 116.

80. "Lishi chongxiu Dongtunci ji," 1537, in Dean and Zheng, 167. The king of Jiang was a legendary member of the Tang imperial family who had fled to Fujian to avoid persecution by the Empress Wu. Yuxuan was the first ancestor of the Li to settle in Baitang. In the Zhenzong period of the Song, he "moved from Youyang in Nan'an in Quanzhou, searched around, and then settled here."

81. Lin Jun, "Yongsitang ji," 1526, in ibid., 84. [It is clear that by the time this text was written, the term lesser descent line *(xiao zong)* no longer retained its original meaning, but referred simply to a branch or a branch hall of the lineage. Trans.]

82. Ibid.

83. Ibid.

84. Lin Jun, "Linshi zufan bei," 1526, in ibid., 164.

85. Ibid.

86. "Zuyi chongjian citang shu," in *(Puyang) Gongxi Huangshi zongpu.*

87. "Shixi," in *(Nan'an) Wurong Yingshan Hongshi zupu*, 1597.

88. "Taijiang citang ji," in *(Tong'an) Sushi zupu*, 1826.

89. *Haicheng xianzhi*, 1761, j. 21.

90. The incidents are described in chronological order:

1555: Zhendong walled guard fort captured; Haikou town in Fuqing County besieged.

1556: Funing prefectural city, Qinyu fort and Luxia fort besieged.

1557: Fuzhou provincial capital and Lianjiang county seat besieged.

1558: Fuqing county seat, Nan'an county seat, and Zhao'an county seat captured; Fuzhou provincial capital, Quanzhou prefectural seat, Luoyuan county seat, Changle county seat, Hui'an county seat, Tong'an county seat (twice), Tongshanshui fort, Anping city, and Qinyu fort, etc. besieged.

1559: Fu'an county seat, Yongchun county seat, and Yongfu county seat captured. Fuzhou provincial capital, Funing prefectural seat, Quanzhou prefectural seat, Gutian county seat, Changle county seat, Tong'an county seat, Zhangpu county seat, Zheyang fort, etc. besieged.

1560: Anxi county seat, Nanjing county seat, Chongwu battalion fort and Guanyao battalion fort captured. Fuzhou provincial capital, Quanzhou prefectural seat, Lianjiang county seat, Pinghe county seat besieged.

1561: Ningde county seat (twice) and Zhenhai guard fort captured. Fuqing county seat and Tong'an county seat besieged.

1562: Xinghua prefectural seat, Ningde county seat, Zhenghe county seat, Shouning county seat, Yongning guard fort (twice), Guazhong guard fort, and Fuquan battalion fort captured. Zhangpu county seat and Longxi county seat besieged.

1563: Ningde county seat and Pinghai guard fort captured. Xianyou county seat and Xiayong fort in Dehua, etc. besieged.

Zhu Weigan, *Fujian shigao* (Fuzhou: Fujian jiaoyu, 1986), 2:207–210.

91. Lin Run, "Qing xue sanfu shu," in *Yuanzhi tang ji*, cited in Zhu Weigan, *Fujian shigao*, 2:233.

92. Shi Lishou, "Xiupu zaowo zhi," in *(Jinjiang) Linpu tang Shishi zupu,* copy of MS in History Department, Xiamen University.

93. "Citang ji," in *(Xunxi) Huangshi zupu,* j. 2.

94. "Wushizu Junde gong zhuan," in *(Yongchun) Qingyuan Liu Liu shi zupu,* j. 4.

95. "Puyu-Mingtian fang Zhike gong liu ji," in *(Fuzhou) Guoshi zhipu,* j. 10.

96. [I.e., to force them to live up to their agreements. Trans.]

97. "Chongxing jiamiao xu," in *(Xianyou) Qianjiang Zhushi zupu,* j. 1.

98. *(Jin'nan) Caishi zupu,* 1730, j. 1.

99. "Jigong," in ibid., j. 9.

100. "Fuzi shier gong xu," in ibid., j. 10.

101. Zhu Weigan, *Fujian shigao,* 2:250–251.

102. *Zhangpu xianzhi,* 1699, j. 11

103. "Xinjian yuxiao tucheng beiji," 1517, in *(Linghai) Wushi zupu,* j. 3.

104. Gu Yanwu, *Tianxia junguo libing shu,* j. 93.

105. Ibid., j. 95.

106. *Funing fuzhi,* 1762, j. 39.

107. Ibid., j. 43.

108. *Zhangpu xianzhi,* 1699, j. 11.

109. *Tong'an xianzhi,* 1798, j. 9.

110. Ibid.

111. "Yongli liezhuan," in *Changtai xianzhi,* 1750, j. 9.

112. "Zeng Su jun Shifen liangfu que fuchou gai ying wodai xu," 1576, in *(Haicheng) Sushi zupu.*

113. "Qishi zu Xiancan gong Dong gong fang fenzhi zhuan," in *(Quannan) Furong Lishi zupu.*

114. *Zhangpu xianzhi,* 1699, j. 11.

115. See Chen Shengshao, *Wensu lu,* j. 4; *Zhao'an xianzhi,* 1801, j. 3; and my "Qingdai Minnan de xiangzu xiedou yu shehui zuzhi," *Zhongguo shehui jingji shi yanjiu,* no. 3 (1984).

116. Yu Biao, *Pu bian shiji.*

117. Shen Yun, *Zhengshi shimo,* j. 4.

118. *DaQing lichao shilu, Shengzu shilu,* j. 4.

119. Zhu Weigan, *Fujian shigao,* 2:380ff.

120. Du Zhen, *Yue-Min Xun shiji lue,* j. 4–5.

121. Sources such as Haiwai sanren, *Rongcheng jiwen;* Ruan Minxi, *Haishang jianwenlu,* and *Haikou ji,* give this figure. According to Qu Dajun, *Guangdong xinyu,* in Guangdong the coastal evacuation was imposed fifty *li* from the shoreline, but this may refer to the actual situation in Guangdong rather than the policy.

122. Zhu Weigan, *Fujian Shigao,* vol. 2, chap. 25.

123. Haiwai sanren, *Rongcheng jiwen.*

124. Yu Biao, *Pu bian shiji.*

125. *DaQing lichao shilu, Shengzu shilu,* j. 4.

126. [This is a reference to two great forced resettlements of the past. The first was coordinated by Gu Rang in the Han, in response to flooding; the second was the evacuation of South China after an uprising against their Han rulers. Trans.]

127. *Nanchuang caocun*, j. 1.

128. Cited in Zhuang Weiji and Wang Lianmao, *Min-Tai guanxi zupu ziliao xuanji* (Fuzhou: Fujian renmin, 1984), 428.

129. Ibid., 430. The genealogy of a lineage from Haicheng County records: "In 1662, it was strictly prohibited to provide assistance [to Zheng Chenggong]. The court ordered the evacuation of the borders to cut off any communications. All that lay east of Zheng Bridge was abandoned because it was outside the boundary, so the fields of the area became wasteland. The members of the lineage members called out to one another in the marshes. The temple where the spirits rest was completely destroyed by armed cavalrymen" (ibid., 429).

The genealogy of the Chen of Jimei in Tong'an records: "In 1663, we were invaded by a large body of troops. Descendants of the lineage numbering several thousand were scattered beyond their home country. It is not known where they went" (ibid., 428).

According to the Genealogy of the Guo of Panyang in Dongshi in Jinjiang: "In 1660 troops set fires and evacuated the area. Our gates and rooms were filled with weeds; the halls were all ruined. Fathers, sons, and brothers wandered homeless. The genealogy was completely lost" (ibid., 426).

The Genealogy of the Cai of Jin'nan from Putian records: "In 1646 at the time of the Clear and Bright Festival the dynasty changed over. There was constant turmoil at this time. Then, in 1661, the coast was evacuated, and the old home became filled with weeds. After the evacuation, the boundaries were restored, but after the restoration there was another evacuation. In all, this went on for over twenty years. The descendants of the surname were scattered. It was impossible to record people's names, let alone [maintain] the family records." "Xuxiu xu," 1699, in *(Putian) Jin'nan Caishi shipu*, 1730.

130. "Xiupu wenxu," in *(Jinjiang) Xunhai Shishi zupu*, 1715.

131. "Jiangjun danchen teji xiaoyin," in ibid.

132. "Xiupu wenxu," in ibid.

133. "Jiangjun danchen teji xiaoyin," in ibid.

134. Ibid.

135. Shi Shilu, "Jian dazong yixue ji," and Shi Shilun, "Xunhai Shishi zuyue," in ibid.

136. Shi Rentong, "Ti Kun Yiyuan gong xiu zupu xu," in ibid.

137. "Mukao–Jiecao shan shi jin kunsang wen," in ibid.

138. "Sidian Zu'e beiji," in ibid. This inscription is still extant in the Yakou Shi ancestral hall. [Grain Rains *(guyu)* is the solar term that begins on approximately April 20. Trans.]

139. "Mu'en beiji." This inscription is still extant in the Longhu Longwang temple.

140. *Quanzhou Huizu pudie ziliao xuanji* (Quanzhou: Quanzhou Lishi yanjiuhui, Chenkang Huizu weiyuanhui, 1980).

141. See Zheng Zhenman, "Mingdai Chenjiang Dingshi Huizu de zongzu zuzhi yu wenhua guocheng," in *Xiamen daxue xuebao*, 1990; reprinted in *Chenkang Huizu shi yanjiu* (Beijing: Zhongguo shehui kexue, 1991).

142. *Quanzhou Huizu pudie ziliao xuanji*.

143. "Chang er san fang jinzhu heyue," in *Chenjiang Dingshi zupu*.

144. "Chang er san fang jinzhu heyue," in ibid.

145. "Xianwu gong xuxiu xu," in (Putian) *Jin'nan Caishi shipu,* 1730, j. 1.

146. "Tongji disi," in ibid.

147. "Jianzhi Jinpu huxi Yi'anbao, jiamiao, yixue, jitian, xuetian, yitian beiji." This inscription is still extant in Yi'anbao, Huxi, Zhangpu County.

148. "Xiaozong ci bei," 1690. This stone is still extant in the Xihu Huang ancestral hall.

149. "Chongxiu citang heyue," 1688, in *(Xianyou) Qianjiang Zhushi zupu.*

150. "Kangkou Shangwu dizhi," in *(Xianyou) Zhushi zupu.*

151. [The picul *(dan)* here is a measure of weight formally equal to 100 catties of 1 1/3 pounds. Trans.]

152. "Liezhuan," in (Putian) *Jin'nan Caishi shipu,* 1730.

153. "Tongji," in ibid., j. 4.

154. "Hecun Cai gong jiazhuan," in *(Lufeng) Caishi zupu,* 1744, j. 12.

155. *(Quanzhou) Yanzhi Wushi jiapu,* j. 6.

156. Investigations at the time of land reform indicate that the proportion of lineage corporate land in northwestern Fujian was generally greater than half, while in the coast the figures range from 20% to 30%; *Fujian sheng nongcun diaocha* (Fuzhou: Huadong junzheng weiyuanhui, 1951), 110. See Chapter 5, part 3, for more details.

157. Chen Shengshao, *Wensu lu,* j. 4.

158. "Qijiang Huangxiang dazongci bing dahe pudie xu," 1643, in *(Puyang) Gongxi Huangshi zongpu.*

159. "Longsun fang xiupu xu," in *(Quanzhou) Longsun fang Zengshi zupu,* 1933.

160. *Haicheng xianzhi,* 1761, j. 5.

161. *Zhangpu xianzhi,* 1699, j. 20.

162. Ibid.

163. ["Xici zhuan," *xia; Yijing,* see Richard Lynn, trans., *The Classic of Changes: A New Translation of the I Ching as Interpreted by Wang Bi* (New York: Columbia University Press, 1994), 84. Trans.]

164. "Guizong heyue," in *(Anxi) Chenshi zupu.*

165. "Puxu," in ibid.

166. "Shixi," in *(Haicheng) Daguan Yeshi zupu,* 1694, j. 4.

167. Ibid. See Chapter 5, part 1, for details.

168. "Jiupu xu," in *(Haicheng) Daguan Yeshi zupu,* 1694.

169. Chen Shengshao, *Wensu lu,* j. 4.

170. [The sense here is that there is a danger that the participation of people other than Huang Qitai in the registration of Guan Yongmao will be obscured. Trans.]

171. This stone is still extant in the Dongshan Guandi temple.

172. "Fuji," in *(Anxi) Guanshi zupu,* Qianlong ed., j. 9.

173. Ibid.

174. "Gupu," in ibid.

175. "Fanli," in *Wuxing fenpai Qingtian Youshi zongpu,* Republican ed., j. 1.

176. "Chongzheng xianyi jingcheng tang gongbu xiaoyan," in *(Xianyou) Xianxi Huang dazongci gongbu,* 1933.

177. "Jiu gui," in ibid.
178. "Jisi guicheng," in ibid.
179. "Zhengli cichan, chongding gongbu xu," in ibid.
180. Chen Shengshao, *Wensu lu*, j. 3.
181. "Guangzhong dang–Liu shi nuzhe," cited in Zhuang Jifa, *Qingdai Tiandihui yuanliu kao* (Taibei: Guoli gugong bowuyuan, 1981).
182. *Tong'an xianzhi*, 1929, j. 3.
183. Jiang Risheng, *Taiwan waiji*, j. 6, cited in Fu Yiling, *Ming–Qing shehui jingji bianqian lun* (Beijing: Renmin, 1989).
184. "Chongxiu Tianhou miao xu." This inscription is still extant in Jiuzhen, Zhangpu, although the text is no longer completely legible.
185. *Ka-I Hentai*, cited in Chen Qi'nan, *Taiwan de chuantong Zhongguo shehui* (Taibei: Yunzhen, 1989), 20.
186. See *Taiwan sheng tongzhi*, 1961, j. 2; Chen Kongli, *Qingdai Taiwan yimin shehui yanjiu* (Xiamen: Xiamen daxue, 1990).
187. Chen Qi'nan, *Taiwan de chuantong Zhongguo shehui*, 132–133. The data is drawn from Chen Shaoxin and Morton Fried, *Taiwan renkou zhi xingshi fenbu* (Taibei: Meiguo Yazhou xuehui zhongwen yanjiu ziliao zhongxin, 1968), the calculations of which were made on the basis of 25% of the results from the 1956 census.
188. Ibid., 133. Elsewhere (136), Chen gives the following population totals for 1956: Lai of Dacun, 9,644; Zhang of Puxin and Yuanlin, 14,196; Huang of Puxin and Yuanlin, 12,636; Liu of Shetou, 5,432; Zhao of the region between Shetou and Tianzhong, 13,204; Chen of Tianzhong and Ershui, 12,984.
189. For Taiwanese scholarship that has influenced Zheng's ideas, see, for example: Zhuang Yingzhang and Chen Qi'nan, "Xian jieduan Zhongguo shehui jiegou yanjiu de jiantao: Taiwan yanjiu de yixie qishi," in *Shehui ji xingwei kexue yanjiu de Zhongguo hua* (Nangang: Zhongyang yanjiuyuan minzuxue yanjiu-suo, 1982); Zhuang Yingzhang, "Taiwan zongzu zuzhi de xingcheng ji qi tedian," in *Xiandaihua yu Zhongguo wenhua yanjiuhui lunwen huibian* (Hong Kong: Zhongwen daxue shehui kexue yanjiusuo, 1985); Wang Songxing, "Zhuoda liuyu de minzuxue yanjiu," *Minzuxue yanjiusuo jikan* 36 (1973); Wang Songxing, "Lun diyuan yu xueyuan," in Li Yiyuan and Jiao Jian, eds., *Zhongguo de minzu, shehui yu wenhua* (Taibei: Shihuo, 1981); Zhuang Yingzhang, *Linpipu: Yige Taiwan Shizhen de Shehui Jingji Fazhan Shi* (Nangang: Zhongyang yanjiu yuan minzuxue yanjiusuo, 1987); Chen Qi'nan, "Qingdai Taiwan shehui de jiegou bianqian," *Minsu xue yanjiusuo jikan* 49 (1980); Huang Shumin, "Cong zaoqi Dajia diqu de kaituo kan Taiwan Hanren zuzhi de fazhan," in Li Yiyuan and Jiao Jian, eds., *Zhongguo de minzu, shehui yu wenhua* (Taibei: Shihuo, 1981).
190. Rinji Taiwan kyūkan chōsakai, *Taiwan shihō furoku sankōsho*, j. 1b, 284.
191. Ibid.
192. Zhuang Yingzhang and Chen Yundong, "Qingdai Toufen de zongzu yu shehui fazhanshi," *Guoli Taiwan shifan daxue lishi xuebao* 10 (1982). Subsequent references in this section are all drawn from this work.
193. The same is true of other men named. Wen Dianyu was a fourteenth-generation member of the Wen lineage of Meikoubao, Jiaying Prefecture, Guangdong Province. It is not clear when he lived, but it was his descendants in the

sixteenth and seventeenth generation who moved to Taiwan and opened up land for cultivation. Huang Rixin was the second-generation ancestor of the Huang surname of the area of Meixian, Pingyuan, and Zhenping counties, Guangdong Province, who probably lived in the late Yuan or early Ming. His descendants in the fifteenth and sixteenth generations settled in different parts of Taiwan. Luo Deda was the founding ancestor of the Luo of Tiekang, Zhenping County. He lived around the late fourteenth century. His descendants in the twelfth to fifteenth generations moved to Toufen.

194. Chen Qi'nan, *Taiwan de chuantong Zhongguo shehui*, 146, with minor changes.

195. In early 1991, I accompanied Chen Qi'nan in doing fieldwork in Shuyang. We learned that the lineage organization of the Zhao of the area used to be most comprehensive, with sacrificial estates for each generation. The names of several ancestral halls in Shuyang, and the names of the ancestors who received sacrifice in them, corresponded exactly to those of the Zhao in Taiwan.

196. Chen Qi'nan, *Taiwan de chuantong Zhongguo shehui*, 148.

197. These documents were provided by Chen Qi'nan.

198. Rinji Taiwan kyūkan chōsakai, *Taiwan shihō furoku sankōsho*, j. 1b, 278.

199. Huang Zhao, "Shiku yizheng," in *Zhenping xianzhi*, 1876, shows that lineage organization in Zhenping in the Qing period was highly developed.

200. Rinji Taiwan kyūkan chōsakai, *Taiwan shihō furoku sankōsho*, j. 1b, 279–281.

201. Ibid., 281.

202. Ibid., 281–282.

203. [Zheng's point here is that this was an important step in the transformation to a native lineage. Because the tablets of all the collective ancestors of the Tang in Taiwan were found in the hall, descendants had to sacrifice to them, and vest any sacrificial estate in their name, in the hall. Trans.]

204. Zhuang Yingzhang, *Linpipu*, 194.

205. Ibid., 185–190.

206. Rinji Taiwan kyūkan chōsakai, *Taiwan shihō furoku sankōsho; Taiwan gongsi cang guwenshu jicheng*. I thank David Wakefield for providing these documents.

207. *Taiwan gongsi cang guwenshu jicheng*, Document no. 7-7-449.

208. "Jiuzhu yuezi," Ye surname, 1897, in Rinji Taiwan kyūkan chōsakai, *Taiwan shihō furoku sankōsho*, j. 1b, 368.

209. "Zhujiushu yuezi," 1817, in *Taiwan gongsi cang guwenshu jicheng*, Document no. 8-7-644.

210. "Jiushu zi," 1822, in ibid., Document no. 8-7-649.

211. "Jiushu," 1736, in ibid., Document no. 6-7-284.

212. Chen Shengshao wrote, "the wealthy of Taiwan are extremely wealthy, the poor extremely poor. It is very different from the mainland. . . . The wealthy households are called leading families. The greatest have several million [taels]; those of mid-rank have a million, and rich households with several hundred thousand are everywhere" (*Wensu lu*, j. 6).

213. "Jiushu," Han surname, 1793, in Rinji Taiwan kyūkan chōsakai, *Taiwan shihō furoku sankōsho*, j. 1b, 409–410.

214. "Shutian yuezi," Han surname, 1797, in ibid., 411.

215. "Fenguan chanyezi," surname unknown, 1838, in *Taiwan gongsi cang guwenshu jicheng*, Document no. 1-9-830.

216. "Jiushu," surname unknown, 1868, in Rinji Taiwan kyūkan chōsakai, *Taiwan shihō furoku sankōsho*, j. 1b, 329.

217. "Zhujiushu yuezi," surname unknown, 1817, in *Taiwan gongsi cang guwenshu jicheng*, 8-7-644.

218. "Jiushu," He surname, 1866, in Rinji Taiwan kyūkan chōsakai, *Taiwan shihō furoku sankōsho*, j. 1b, 403.

219. "Jiushu," Chen surname, 1879, in ibid., 353.

220. "Jiushu yuezi," Li surname, 1886, in ibid., 327.

221. Dai Yanhui, "Qingdai Taiwan xiangzhuang shehui de kaocha," *Taiwan jingji shi* 10 (1966).

222. Zhuang Yingzhang, *Linpipu*, 195.

223. Cited in ibid., 182. This text was copied from Liu Zhiwan, "Nantou xian fengsuzhi zongjiao biangao," *Nantou wenxian congji* 9 (1961).

224. Zhuang Yingzhang, *Linpipu*, 182.

225. "Zuchang bu," Zhong surname, in Rinji Taiwan kyūkan chōsakai, *Taiwan shihō furoku sankōsho*, j. 1b, 282–283.

Chapter 5

1. Ban Gu, *Bohu tong* 3b:13a. [See Tjan Tjoe Som, trans., *Po Hu T'ung: The Comprehensive Discussions in the White Tiger Hall* (Leiden: Brill, 1949), 2:574. Trans.]

2. "Dazhuan," *Liji*. [See James Legge, trans., *Li Chi, Book of Rites* (Oxford: Oxford University Press, 1885; reprint, New York: University Books, 1967), 2: 66–67. Trans.]

3. On the basic content of the descent-line regulations in different periods, see Qu Tongzu, *Zhongguo falü yu Zhongguo shehui*, sections 1.1 and 3.4.

4. "Wangzhi," *Liji*. [Legge, trans., *Li Chi, Book of Rites*, 1:223. Trans.]

5. "Dazhuan," *Liji*. [Legge, trans., *Li Chi, Book of Rites*, 2:65. Trans.]

6. Ban Gu, *Bohu tong* 3b: 13a. [Tjan, trans., *Po Hu T'ung*, 574. Trans.]

7. See Sha Shenxing et al., *DaMing huidian*, Wanli ed., j. 95.

8. *Qing tongli*, j. 17.

9. See, for example, *DaQing lüli* (1740), j. 8: "The punishment for violating the rule on establishing the son of the principal wife as heir is eighty blows with the bamboo staff. If the principal wife is more than fifty years old and has no son, the eldest son of other wives can be designated as heir. The punishment for violating the rule on establishing the eldest son as heir is the same."

10. "The restriction against gentry and commoners erecting family temples . . . was eliminated in the mid-Ming"; Zuo Yunpeng, "Citang zuzhang zuquan jiqi zuoyong shishuo." Many scholars have accepted this view and have even argued that by the Ming there was no legal restriction on sacrificing to founding ancestors. See, for example, Li Wenzhi, "Mingdai zongzu shi de tixian xingshi ji qi jiceng zhengquan zuoyong," *Zhongguo jingji shi yanjiu*, no. 1 (1988).

11. Cheng Yi, *Yichuan wenji*.

12. Zhu Xi, *Zhuzi jiali*, j. 1. [See Patricia Ebrey, trans., *Chu Hsi's* Family Rituals: *A Twelfth-Century Chinese Manual for the Performance of Cappings, Weddings, Funerals, and Ancestral Rites* (Princeton, N.J.: Princeton University Press, 1991), 5. Trans.]

13. Zhu Xi, *Zhuzi jiali*, j. 4.

14. Ibid., j. 1. [Patricia Ebrey, trans., *Chu Hsi's* Family Rituals, 10–11. Trans.]

15. Shen Han, "Caishi zupu xu," 1705, in *(Jianyang) Lufeng Caishi zupu*, 1916, j. 4.

16. Ibid., j. 1.

17. Peng Shao, "Baishuitang Lishi chongxiu xianci bei," 1489, in *(Putian) Longxi Lishi zongpu*, Qianlong ed., j. 1. This inscription is still extant in the Li ancestral hall of Hanjiang in Putian. The text is also found Dean and Zheng, *Fujian zongjiao beiming huibian* (1996), 116.

18. *Fujian tongzhi*, 1937, j. 21.

19. *Fujian tongzhi*, 1829, j. 55.

20. Chen Shengshao, *Wensu lu*, j. 4.

21. See my "Song yihou Fujian de jizu xisu yu zongzu zuzhi," *Xiamen daxue xuebao*, 1987.

22. Peng Shao, "Baishuitang Lishi chongxiu xianci bei," 1489, in *(Putian) Longxi Lishi zongpu*, Qianlong ed.; Dean and Zheng, *Fujian zongjiao beiming huibian*, 116.

23. *(Fuzhou) Shimei Wushi zupu*.

24. *(Yongchun) Guanshi zupu*, 1902, j. 1.

25. Peng Shao, "Baishuitang Lishi chongxiu xianci bei," 1489, in *(Putian) Longxi Lishi zongpu*, Qianlong ed.; Dean and Zheng, *Fujian zongjiao beiming huibian*, 116.

26. "Chongjian fukou ciyu ji," in *(Yongchun) Taoyuan Huqiao Lishi zupu*, 1943, j. 5.

27. "Yongcun xiangsi tiancu shanpu yuezi," Lin surname, 1835, in Rinji Taiwan kyūkan chōsakai, *Taiwan shihō furoku sankōsho*, j. 1b, 22.

28. "Heyuzi," Zhang surname, 1856, in ibid., j. 1b, 55.

29. "Jiuzhu zi," Chen surname, 1879, in ibid., j. 1b, 24.

30. "Shufen jiuyue gongye zi," Li surname, 1892, in ibid., j. 1b, 13.

31. "Zhushu fuyueju," Chen surname, 1898, in ibid., j. 1b, 47.

32. *Sanshan zhi*, 1182, 44.

33. "Jiagui," in *(Min'ou) Tunshan Zushi zongpu*, j. 1.

34. "Zujie," in *(Pucheng) Liangshi hexiu zupu*, j. 1.

35. "Tiaoyue," in *(Fuzhou) Shimei Wushi zupu*.

36. Ban Gu, *Bohu tong* 3b:13a. [Tjan, trans., *Po Hu T'ung*, 574. Trans.]

37. *(Tong'an) Lin Xiyuan jiapu*.

38. "Huili zongzi jifu zhishu," 1554, in *(Tong'an) Suzhi zupu*, 1701.

39. *(Jianyang) Lufeng Caishi zupu*, 1744, j. 4.

40. From the early Ming to the mid-Qing, officials at various levels in the Fujian administration provided assistance to the Cai lineage to reconstruct ancestral halls and expand sacrificial estates, or granted different sorts of tax exemptions, more than a dozen times. "Lidai aochong dianzhang," in ibid.

41. "Caishi zupu xu," in ibid.

42. "Jiufeng gong ci ji Chongxian shuyuan zhi," in ibid.

43. *(Puyang) Gongxi Huangshi zongpu.*

44. "Wenbu," in *(Fuzhou) Jintang Wangshi zupu.*

45. "Shixi," j. 4, and "Zongtu xu," j. 1, in *(Haicheng) Daguan Yeshi zupu,* 1694.

46. *Min Shu,* 1629, j. 39.

47. "Longtou yijia Zhengshi hujie," in *(Yongchun) Rongfang Zhengshi zupu,* Qing ed.

48. Ibid.

49. "Tonggong zuxun," in *(Jianyang) Qingyuan Lishi zongpu,* 1891, j. 1.

50. See Sha Shenxing et al., *DaMing huidian,* Wanli ed., j. 20.

51. "Fuyi zhi," in *(Yong'an) Xushi zupu,* Republican ed.

52. "Zhike gong li shu junyou," in *(Fuzhou) Guoshi zhipu,* Republican ed., j. 10.

53. Zheng Ji, "Yu Pang Dacan shu," in *Fujian tongzhi,* 1829, j. 49.

54. *Min Shu,* 1629, j. 39.

55. *Fujian tongzhi,* 1829, j. 40.

56. [Many of the early Ming sectors were later combined with neighboring ones, and the resulting amalgamated sector bore the number of both the original sectors. Trans.]

57. "Lu gupu zai," in *(Taoyuan) Fengshan Kangshi zupu,* 1924, j. 1.

58. "Chengdang jiashou zi," in ibid.

59. "Lizhang songtian zi," in ibid.

60. Zheng Ji, "Xin lijia mulu xu," in *Fujian tongzhi,* 1829, j. 40.

61. The first official to try to implement changes to the allocation of service-levy responsibilities in Ming Fujian was Censor Shen Zhuo. In the Zhengde period, he promoted two reforms, known as the 8 percent *(bafen)* method and the combined payments *(gangyin)* method. The former was used to pay for "meeting the demand for tribute goods and other required exactions." It took the form of a supplementary tax of 0.08 taels levied on each picul of tax rice and each *ding* of head tax. The latter was used to meet the expenses of local government. The basic system was to combine the total expenses of the county government into standard and miscellaneous categories and then allocate these to the tax base, according to the formula 60% to the land tax and 40% to the head tax (*Anxi xianzhi,* 1552, j. 1). Later, the taxes collected were insufficient to meet the ever-growing supplementary expenses, and *li* heads were called upon to meet the shortfall in rotation (*Min Shu,* 1629, j. 39). There were various terms for this exaction. In the late Ming, it was repeatedly adjusted, but proved impossible to eliminate and remained in place until the mid-Qing. From the mid-Ming, *lijia* households were also obliged to meet the variable expenses associated with tax collection.

62. *Min Shu,* 1629, j. 39.

63. "Fuyi zhi," in *(Yong'an) Xushi jiapu.*

64. *(Dehua) Shuanghan Sushi zupu,* Qing ed.

65. On the *dadang* supplementary exactions, see pp. 295–302.

66. "Longtou yijia Zhengshi hujie," in *(Yongchun) Rongfang Zhengshi zupu,* Qing ed.

67. "Tingnian, dadang kao," in *(Yongchun) Guanlin Lishi qixiu zupu*, 1927, j. 1. Subsequent unfootnoted citations all come from this source.

68. [The tax assessment on the Li must have been greater than the total tax obligation of the *jia*. So a portion of their tax assessment was transferred to meet the obligations of another *jia*, whose assessments were presumably insufficient to meet its obligations. Trans.]

69. "Jiaxun," in *(Tong'an) Lin Xiyuan jiapu*.

70. The above is drawn from selections from *(Hui'an) Longshan Luoshi zupu*, cited in Fu Yiling and Chen Zhiping, eds., "Ming–Qing Fujian shehui jingji shiliao zachao 7."

71. "Xinding puli," in *(Jinjiang) Hongshan Pengshi zupu*, j. 1.

72. "Bagong ding situ lizhang shi," in *(Fanyang) Zoushi zupu*, j. 34.

73. "Taixuesheng Zou Hefa shouwen," in ibid., j. 34.

74. "Huyizhi yin," in *(Shaowu) Huangshi zupu*, 1881, j. 15.

75. "Ting gong zanshu," 1693, in ibid.

76. Chen Shengshao, *Wensu lu*, j. 4.

77. [I.e., land-tax obligations that had previously been monetized were being demanded in kind, presumably at a higher rate. Trans.]

78. "Huyizhi," in *(Shaowu) Huangshi zupu*, j. 15.

79. *(Yongchun) Guanlin Lishi qixiu zupu*, 1927, j. 1.

80. Ibid.

81. Cheng Rongchun, "Zhi Maxiang tingbing qiuxie shiyou," in his *Dongxuan Andu*.

82. "Hehu shimo," in *Zhangzhou fuzhi*, 1877, j. 14.

83. "Longtou yijia Zhengshi hujie," in *(Yongchun) Rongfang Zhengshi zupu*.

84. Ibid.

85. *(Yongchun) Guanlin Lishi qixiu zupu*, 1927, j. 1.

86. See my "Ming–Qing Minbei xiangzu dizhu jingji de fazhan," in Fu Yiling and Yang Guozhen, eds., *Ming Qing Fujian shehui yu xiangcun jingji* (1987).

87. *Fujian sheng nongcun diaocha* (Fuzhou: Huadong junzheng weiyuanhui, 1951), 110.

88. "Zhou Ziyuan fen sanzi wei sanfang ji," in *(Jianyang) Zhoushi zupu*, 1816, j. 1.

89. "Shouba gong yiwen," in *(Chong'an) Yuanshi zongpu*, j. 1.

90. "Fanli," in *(Jianyang) chongxiu Huang Wensu gong zupu*.

91. Chen Menglai et al., *Gujin tushu jicheng*, j. 1094.

92. "Fulu," in *(Jianyang) Wengshi zongpu*.

93. "Jitian yin," in *(Pucheng) Houshan Caishi zupu*, j. 2.

94. Chen Shengshao, *Wensu lu*, j. 1.

95. "Wen xing zhong xin xu," in *(Chong'an) Yuanshi zongpu*, 1883, j. 2.

96. "Ming Nai, Xiang erzi gengli sitian ji," in *(Pucheng) Lianhu Zushi zupu*, 1772.

97. See my "Qing zhi Minguo Minbei liujian fenguan de fenxi," *Zhongguo shehui jingji shi yanjiu*, no. 3 (1984).

98. "Fenguan," Su surname, 1930.

99. "Gaofeng fengzhi dafu Huatang fujun jishu," in *(Shaowu) Huangshi zupu*, j. 10.

100. "Dengjin gong ji pei Wu ruren hesang muzhiming," in ibid., j. 10.

101. "Taixue Liuwu fujun xingzhuang," in ibid., j. 10.

102. "Sisi zhiyin," in ibid., j. 13.

103. "Xinli Li'nan gong jibu xu," in *(Ouning) Min'ou Tunshan Zushi zongpu,* j. 8.

104. "Jichan," in *(Pucheng) Donghai Xushi zongpu,* 1946, j. 10.

105. "Jichan," in *(Ouning) Min'ou Tunshan Zushi zongpu,* j. 8.

106. Rinji Taiwan kyūkan chōsakai, *Taiwan shihō furoku sankōsho,* j. 1b.

107. "Jiushu," in *(Min) Wenshan Huangshi jiapu,* 1920.

108. "Gongji tang gongchan lunnian gongyue," in ibid.

109. MS History Department, Xiamen University.

110. "Zhulin gegong tianshan," in *(Jianyang) Yingchuan Chenshi zongpu,* j. 1. (See Chapter 3, note 78, for the details of this case.)

111. "Qiyue," in *(Shaowu) Qiaoxi Gutan Heshi zupu.*

112. MS History Department, Xiamen University.

113. *(Ouning) Huangxi Geshi zongpu,* 1921, j. 6.

114. "Jichan," in *(Pucheng) Zhanshi zupu,* 1922, j. 21.

115. Ding Rugong, *Xuwu zhilue,* j. 3.

116. Ibid.

117. MS History Department, Fujian Normal University.

118. MS History Department, Fujian Normal University.

CHAPTER 6

1. See the following essays of mine: "Shilun Minbei xiangzu dizhu jingji de xingtai yu jiegou," *Zhongguo shehui jingji shi yanjiu,* no. 4 (1985); "Qingdai Taiwan de hegu jingying," *Taiwan yanjiu jikan,* no. 3 (1987); "Ming–Qing Fujian yanhai nongtian shuili zhidu yu xiangzu zuzhi," *Zhongguo shehui jingji shi yanjiu,* no. 4 (1987); "Ming–Qing Minbei xiangzu dizhu jingji de fazhan," in Fu Yiling and Yang Guozhen, eds., *Ming Qing Fujian shehui yu xiangcun jingji*; "Qingdai Taiwan xiangzu zuzhi de gongyou jingji," *Taiwan yanjiu jikan,* no. 2 (1988); "Ming yihou Minbei xiangzu tudi de suoyou quan xingtai," *Pinghuai xuekan,* vol. 5 (1989).

2. Fu Yiling, *Ming Qing shehui jingji bianqian lun* (Beijing: Renmin, 1989), 45.

3. [Karl Marx, *The Poverty of Philosophy* (New York: International Publishers, 1963), 147. Trans.]

4. [See Lewis Morgan, *Ancient Society* (1877; reprint, Cambridge, Mass.: Harvard University Press, 1964), 14. Trans.]

5. Fu Yiling, "Zhongguo chuantong shehui: Duoyuan de jiegou," *Zhongguo shehui jingji shi yanjiu,* no. 3 (1988).

List of Characters

bafen 八分
baxian miao 八賢廟
bai tu she 拜圖社
ban 班
bangren menhu 傍人門戶
bao ding 報丁
bao gong 報功
baojia 保甲

celi 冊裡
chan 懺
chaofeng 朝奉
chengbao 城堡
chi 尺
Chongben Tang 崇本堂
Chongwendian 崇文典
ci 祠
cisheng 祠生
cishou 祠首
citang 祠堂

da zongzu 大宗族
dadang 大當
dafu 大夫
dayuan 大元
dazong 大宗
dazongci ji 大宗祠季
dan 石
deye jun 得業軍

Dianli Ci 典禮祠
ding 丁
dingban 頂班
dingzaihui 丁仔會
dongshi 懂事
dou 斗
du 都
dunben 敦本

fang 房
Fangyuan Tang 芳遠堂
fen 分
fenguan 分關
fengjian tudi 封建土地
fu 府
fuhai 附海
fujun 府君
fusi 附祀

gangyin 綱銀
gong 公
gongchan 公產
gong citang 公祠堂
gongfei 公費
gonghui 公會
Gongji Tang gongsi 公積堂公司
gongting 公廳
gongye 公業
gongyouhua 共有化

353

gu 股
gufen 股份
guyu 穀雨
guanding 官丁
guannian 管年
guizong 歸宗
guizong hehu 歸宗合戶
guoji 過繼

hai Ë
heji 合祭
Hengjisuo 亨記所
hetong 合同
hetongshi zongzu 合同式宗族
heyuezi zongzu 合約字宗族
hezhi 合志
hu 戶
huzu 戶族
huahu 花戶
Huang xiang 黃巷
hui 會

ji 季
ji^a 基
ji^b 己
jibu 祭簿
jichan 祭產
jichanbu 祭產簿
jicheng 基澄
jichengshi zongzu 繼承式宗族
jigu 集股
Jishan Ci 繼善祠
jishou 祭首
jisi 繼嗣
jia 家
jia^a 甲
jiamiao 家廟
jiancheng 建澄
jiao 角
jiaozu 醮租
jiazu 家族
Jie ji 捷記
jin 斤/觔
Jingcheng Tang 敬承堂

jingshe 精舍
jiu 鬮
jiuban xinban 舊班新班
jiufenzi zongzu 鬮分字宗族
ju 居
juanshou 捐首
junhu 軍戶
junmiao 均苗
junyao 均搖
junzhuang 軍莊

kai Tai zu 開臺祖
Kaixian Ci 開先祠
kaoshi yusuo 考試寓所
ketian 課田
kendan heyue 墾單合約

li 里
Li 禮
lijia 里甲
lilao 里老
lishi 理事
lizheng 里正
liang 兩
lianghu guizong 糧戶歸宗
liangzhang 糧長
lianshe 聯社
linshui furen 臨水夫人
longxiang hui 龍翔會
Longyishu 隆益樞
luzhu 爐主
luanzong 亂宗
luo 籮

mao 卯
minhu 民戶
ming 名
ming dipai 明嫡派
minglingzi 螟蛉子
mu 畝
Muchuang tang 睦創堂

nazuo 納胙
nüxu jun 女婿軍

pengmin 棚民
pin 品
ping 秤

qian 錢
Qianxiao Ci 謙孝祠
qin 寢
qinqin 親親
qing 頃
Qingming 清明
qingxi 清系

ren 壬
ren[a] 人
rending bu 人丁簿
Rongqian Ci 榮千祠
ruhai 入海
ruMin shizu 入閩始祖

sai 塞
sanchu 散處
shan 贍
shangyi 尚義
shanlao 贍老
shanlao ye 贍老業
Shaocai Tang 紹綵堂
shen 申
shenming hui 神明會
shenzhu qian 神主錢
sheng 升
Shide Ci 世德祠
shizhi 市值
shizu 世族
shizu zhi jiamiao 始祖之家廟
shoushi 首事
shuhang 叔行
shuyuan 書院
shunji gong 順濟宮
shunji miao 順濟廟
si 私
sici 私祠
siding 私丁
Sijing 思敬
sishi 私室

su youlai 溯由來
suo 所

tang 堂
Tangshan zu 唐山祖
teji 特祭
tijuan jiaxue paiwei 題捐家學牌位
timian 體面
tianhou 天后
tiao 桃
tong 桶
tongci heji 同祠合祭
tongxing jun 同姓軍
tu 圖
tucha 圖差
tudigong 土地公
tutou 圖頭
tuzhu 土主
tuzhu hua 土著化
tuofu 托付
tuogu 托孤

Wanshou Gong 萬壽宮
wei 衛
wen 文
wokou 倭寇
Wuwei Tang 武威堂

xiaji 祫祭
xian 獻
xianci 賢祠
xianji 賢籍
xiang 鄉
xiangbing 鄉兵
xiang bugui zhitu 鄉不軌之徒
xiangshen 鄉紳
xiangzhen 鄉鎮
xiangzu 鄉族
xiangzu gongyou di 鄉族共有地
xiangzu gongyou jingji 鄉族共有
    經濟
xiaojia 小甲
xiaojia[a] 小家
xiaozong 小宗

xiaozong shiyu 小宗室宇
xiao zongzu 小宗族
xiewu 廨屋

yamen 衙門
Yangong 宴公
yanglao 養老
yangshan ye 養贍業
yangyuan 洋元
yangzi 養子
Yiben Tang 一本堂
yifushi zongzu 依附式宗族
yitian 義田
yizi 義子
yin 印
yingtang 影堂
yongjing 永敬
Yongsi Tang 永思堂
you 尤
yuan 元
Yuanji dagong 元記大公
Yusen Tang 玉森堂

zaju 雜居
zaifen jiushu 再分鬮書
zhang 長
zhaomu 昭穆
zhen 鎮

zhengchang tian 征嘗田
zhenggu caishi 征穀採實
Zhiben Tang 知本堂
zhong'an 塚庵
zhou 州
Zhoujia xiang 周家巷
Zhu Xi 朱熹
Zhuzi Jiali 朱子家禮
zhuanci 傳祠
zhuiyuan 追遠
Zifu 資福
zihu 子戶
zizhi 自治
zong 宗
zongci 宗祠
zongfa 宗法
zonghu 總戶
zonglao 宗老
zongli 總理
zongsun 宗孫
Zongxiang Ci 宗享祠
zongzi 宗子
zongzu 宗族
zu 族
zucuo 族厝
zugonghui 祖公會
zuzhang 族長
zuo 胙

Bibliography

CHINESE PRIMARY SOURCES

GAZETTEERS

Anxi xianzhi, 1552.
Changtai xianzhi, 1750.
Chong'an xian xinzhi, 1942.
Fujian tongzhi, 1829.
Fujian tongzhi, 1937.
Funing fuzhi, 1762.
Haicheng xianzhi, 1632.
Haicheng xianzhi, 1761.
Houguan xian xiangtuzhi, 1903.
Jian'an xiangtuzhi, 1905.
Jianyang xianzhi, 1832.
Min Shu, 1629.
Minxian xiangtuzhi, 1906.
Sanshan zhi, 1182.
Taiwan tongzhi, 1961.
Tong'an xianzhi, 1798.
Tong'an xianzhi, 1929.
Wufuzi lizhi, 1931.
Zhangpu xianzhi, 1699.
Zhangzhou fuzhi, 1877.
Zhao'an xianzhi, 1801.
Zhenping xianzhi, 1876.

GENEALOGICAL MATERIALS

(Anxi) Chenshi zupu.
(Anxi) Guanshi zupu. Qianlong edition.
(Changting) Fanyang Zoushi zupu. 1947.
(Chenjiang) Dingshi zupu.

(Chong'an) Wushi jiapu. Qing edition.
(Chong'an) Yuanshi zongpu. 1883.
(Dehua) Shuanghan Sushi zupu. Qing edition.
(Dongjiang) Liaoshi zupu.
(Fanyang) Zoushi zupu.
(Fu'ou) Shangyang Chenshi zongpu. Daoguang edition.
(Fuzhou) Guoshi zhipu. Republican edition.
(Fuzhou) Jintang Wangshi zhipu. Guangxu edition.
(Fuzhou) Jintang Wangshi zupu.
(Fuzhou) Sanshan Yeshi cilu. 1887.
(Fuzhou) Shimei Wushi zupu.
*(Haicheng) Daguan Yeshi zupu.*1694.
(Haicheng) Sushi zupu.
(Hui'an) Longshan Luoshi zupu.
(Jianning) Wangshi zupu.
(Jianyang) Chenshi zupu. 1872.
(Jianyang) chongxiu Huang Wensu gong zupu.
(Jianyang) Fushi zongpu. 1910.
(Jianyang) Houju Pingshi zupu. 1846.
(Jianyang) Lufeng Caishi zupu. 1916.
(Jianyang) Lujiang Heshi zongpu. Guangxu edition.
(Jianyang) Qingyuan Lishi jiapu.
(Jianyang) Qingyuan Lishi zongpu. 1891.
(Jianyang) Shulin Xushi chongxiu zupu. 1886.
(Jianyang) Wengshi zongpu.
(Jianyang) Xikou Yeshi zongpu. 1919.
(Jianyang) Yingchuan Chenshi zongpu.
(Jianyang) Zhoushi zongpu.
(Jianyang) Zhoushi zupu. 1816.
(Jianyang) Ziyangtang Zhushi zongpu. 1895.
(Jinjiang) Hongshan Pengshi zupu.
(Jinjiang) Linpu tang Shishi zupu.
(Jinjiang) Xunhai Shishi zupu. 1715.
(Liancheng) Tongshi zupu. 1937.
(Linghai) Wushi zupu.
(Lufeng) Caishi zupu, 1744.
(Min) Wenshan Huangshi jiapu. 1920.
(Minnan) Heshi zupu.
(Min'ou) Tunshan Zushi zongpu. Compiled 1822. Printed 1939.
(Min-Yue-Gan) Wuwei Liaoshi zupu.
(Nan'an) Liutian Youshi zupu.
(Nan'an) Wurong Yingshan Hongshi zupu. 1597.
(Ouning) Huangxi Geshi zongpu. 1921.
(Ouning) Min'ou Tunshan Zushi zongpu.
(Pucheng) Donghai Xushi zongpu. 1946.
(Pucheng) Houshan Caishi zupu.

(Pucheng) Huangshi zupu.
(Pucheng) Jinzhang Yangshi zupu.
(Pucheng) Liangshi hexiu zupu.
(Pucheng) Lianhu Zushi zupu. 1772.
(Pucheng) Wangshi jiapu. 1948.
(Pucheng) Zhanshi zupu. 1922.
(Pucheng) Zhoushi zongpu. 1900.
(Putian) Jin'nan Caishi shipu. 1730.
(Putian) Lishi zongpu.
(Putian) Longxi Lishi zongpu. Qianlong edition.
(Putian) Xunhai Shishi zupu.
(Puyang) Gongxi Huangshi zongpu. 1643.
(Quannan) Furong Lishi zupu.
(Quanzhou) Chenjiang Dingshi zupu.
(Quanzhou) Guoshi jiapu. 1930.
(Quanzhou) Longsun fang Zengshi zupu. 1933.
(Quanzhou) Yanzhi Wushi jiapu.
(Shaowu) Huangshi zupu. 1881.
(Shaowu) Qiaoxi Gutan Heshi zupu.
(Shaowu) Qingqin li benren tang Lishi zongpu.
(Shaowu) Xuntan Huangshi zupu. 1881.
(Shunchang) Qinghe Zhangshi liuxiu zupu.
(Shunchang) Xieshi zongpu. 1902.
(Taoyuan) Fengshan Kangshi zupu. 1924.
(Tong'an) Lin Xiyuan jiapu.
(Tong'an) Sushi zupu. 1701 and 1826.
(Wenchuan) Lishi qixiu zupu. 1947.
(Wuping) Lishi zongpu. 1930.
Wuxing fenpai Qingtian Youshi zongpu. Republican edition.
(Xianyou) Fengxi Xueshi zupu. Qianlong edition.
(Xianyou) Qianjiang Zhushi zupu.
(Xianyou) Xianxi Huang dazongci gongbu. 1933.
(Xianyou) Zhushi zupu.
(Xunxi) Huangshi zupu.
(Yong'an) Xushi jiapu.
(Yong'an) Xushi zupu. Republican edition.
(Yongchun) Guanlin Lishi qixiu zupu. 1927.
(Yongchun) Guanshi zupu. 1902.
(Yongchun) Liushi zupu.
(Yongchun) Qingyuan Liu Liushi zupu.
(Yongchun) Rongfang Chenshi zupu.
(Yongchun) Rongfang Zhengshi zupu. Qing edition.
(Yongchun) Taoyuan Fengshan Kangshi zupu.
(Yongchun) Taoyuan Huqiao Lishi zupu. 1943.
(Yongding) Tianduan Qimou hu dazongci jicheng xu.
Zhengshi shimo.

OTHER PRIMARY SOURCES

Ban Gu. *Bohu tong.*
Cai Qing. *Cai Wenzhuang gong wenji.*
Cai Xiang. *Cai Zhonghui gong ji.*
Chen Menglei et al. *Gujin tushu jicheng.*
Chen Shengshao. *Wensu lu.* 1842.
Cheng Rongchun. *Dongxuan Andu.*
Cheng Yi. *Yichuan wenji.*
DaQing lichao shilu.
DaQing lüli. 1740.
Ding Rugong. *Xuwu zhilue.*
Du Zhen. *Yue-Min xun shiji lue.*
Gu Yanwu. *Tianxia junguo libing shu.*
Haikou ji.
Haiwai sanren. *Rongcheng jiwen.* Vol. 1. Reprint, *Qingshi ziliao*, Beijing, 1980.
Kongzi jiayu. Ed. Wang Su.
Liji.
Nanchuang caocun.
Qing tongli.
Qu Dajun. *Guangdong xinyu.* Reprint, Hong Kong: Zhonghua, 1974.
Ruan Minxi. *Haishang jianwenlu.*
Sha Shenxing et al. *DaMing huidian.* Wanli edition.
Song Lian. *Song Wenxian gong quanji.*
Yu Biao. *Pu bian shiji.* Vol. 1. Reprint, *Qingshi ziliao,* Beijing, 1980.
Zhu Xi. *Zhuzi jiali.*

SECONDARY SOURCES

Baker, Hugh. *Chinese Family and Kinship.* New York: Columbia University Press, 1979.
Berkner, Lutz. "The Stem Family and the Developmental Cycle of the Peasant Household: An Eighteenth-Century Austrian Example." *American Historical Review* 77 (1972): 398–418.
———. "The Use and Misuse of Census Data for the Historical Analysis of Family Structure: A Review of *Household and Family in Past Time.*" *Journal of Interdisciplinary History* 4 (1975): 721–738.
Berkner, Lutz, and Franklin Mendels. "Inheritance Systems, Family Structure, and Demographic Patterns in Western Europe, 1700–1900." In Charles Tilly, ed., *Historical Studies in Changing Fertility.* Princeton, N.J.: Princeton University Press, 1978.
Bielenstein, Hans. "The Chinese Colonization of Fukien until the End of T'ang." In Søren Egerod and Else Glahn, eds., *Studia Serica Bernhard Karlgren Dedicata.* Copenhagen: Ejnar Munksgaard, 1959.
Brook, Timothy. "The Spatial Structure of Ming Local Administration." *Late Imperial China* 6 (1985): 1–55.

Brook, Timothy, and B. Michael Frolic, eds. *Civil Society in China*. Armonk: M. E. Sharpe, 1997.

Chen Kongli. "Qingdai Taiwan yimin shehui de tedian: Yi *Wensu lu* wei zhong-xin de yanjiu." *Taiwan yanjiu jikan*, no. 2 (1988).

———. *Qingdai Taiwan yimin shehui yanjiu*. Xiamen: Xiamen daxue, 1990.

Chen Qi'nan. "Qingdai Taiwan shehui de jiegou bianqian." *Minsu xue yanjiusuo jikan* 49 (1980).

———. *Taiwan de chuantong Zhongguo shehui*. Taibei: Yunzhen, 1989.

Chen Shaoxin and Morton Fried. *Taiwan renkou zhi xingshi fenbu*. Taibei: Meiguo Yazhou xuehui zhongwen yanjiu ziliao zhongxin, 1968.

Chen Zhiping. *Jin wubai nian Fujian de jiazu shehui yu wenhua*. Shanghai: San-lian, 1991.

Chen Zhiping and Zheng Zhenman. "Pucheng xian Dongtou cun wushi tongtang diaocha." In Fu Yiling and Yang Guozhen, eds., *Ming Qing Fujian shehui yu xiangcun jingji*. Xiamen: Xiamen daxue, 1987.

Chow Kai-wing. *The Rise of Confucian Ritualism in Late Imperial China: Ethics, Classics, and Lineage Discourse*. Stanford, Calif.: Stanford University Press, 1994.

Clark, Hugh. *Community, Trade, and Networks: Southern Fujian from the Third to the Thirteenth Century*. Cambridge: Cambridge University Press, 1991.

Cohen, Myron. *House United, House Divided: The Chinese Family in Taiwan*. New York: Columbia University Press, 1976.

———. "Lineage Organization in North China." *Journal of Asian Studies* 49 (1990): 509–534.

Dai Yanhui. "Taiwan de jiazu zhidu yu zuxian jisi tuanti." *Taiwan wenhua lun-cong*, no. 2 (1945).

———. "Qingdai Taiwan xiangzhuang shehui de kaocha." *Taiwan jingji shi* 10 (1966).

Dean, Kenneth. *Taoist Ritual and Popular Cults of Southeast China*. Princeton, N.J.: Princeton University Press, 1993.

Dean, Kenneth, and Zheng Zhenman. *Fujian zongjiao beiming huibian, Xinghua fu fenjuan*. Fuzhou: Fujian renmin, 1996.

Ebrey, Patricia. *Confucianism and Family Rituals in Imperial China: A Social History of Writing about Rites*. Princeton, N.J.: Princeton University Press, 1991.

———, trans. *Chu Hsi's* Family Rituals: *A Twelfth Century Chinese Manual for the Performance of Cappings, Weddings, Funerals, and Ancestral Rites*. Princeton, N.J.: Princeton University Press, 1991.

Ebrey, Patricia, and James Watson. "Introduction." In Patricia Ebrey and James Watson, eds., *Kinship Organization in Late Imperial China, 1000–1940*. Berkeley: University of California Press, 1986.

Engels, Frederick. *The Origin of the Family, Private Property and the State*. New York: International Publishers, 1942.

Esherick, Joseph, and Mary Backus Rankin. "Introduction." In Joseph Esherick and Mary Backus Rankin, *Chinese Local Elites and Patterns of Dominance*. Berkeley: University of California Press, 1990.

Faure, David. *The Structure of Chinese Rural Society: Lineage and Village in the*

Eastern New Territories, Hong Kong. Cambridge: Cambridge University Press, 1986.

———. "The Lineage as a Cultural Invention." *Modern China* 15 (1989): 4–36.

Fei Xiaotong. "Jiating jiegou biandongzhong de laonian shanyang wenti." *Xiandaihua yu Zhongguo wenhua yanjiuhui lunwen huibian.* Hong Kong: Zhongwen daxue shehui kexue yanjiusuo, 1985.

Freedman, Maurice. *Lineage Organization in Southeastern China.* London: Athlone, 1958.

Fried, Morton. *The Fabric of Chinese Society.* New York: Praeger, 1953.

———. "Clans and Lineages: How to Tell Them Apart and Why—with Special Reference to Chinese Society." *Bulletin of the Institute of Ethnology* (1970).

Fu Yiling. "Lun xiangzu shili duiyu Zhongguo fengjian jingji de ganshe." *Xiamen daxue xuebao,* no. 3 (1961). Reprinted in Fu Yiling, *Ming Qing shehui jingji shi lunwenji.* Beijing: Renmin, 1982.

———. "Guanyu Zhongguo fengjian shehui houqi jingji fazhan de ruogan wenti de kaocha." *Lishi yanjiu,* no. 4 (1963). Reprinted in Fu Yiling, *Ming Qing shehui jingji shi lunwenji.* Beijing: Renmin, 1982.

———. "Zhongguo chuantong shehui: Duoyuan de jiegou." *Zhongguo shehui jingji shi yanjiu,* no. 3 (1988).

———. *Ming–Qing shehui jingji bianqian lun.* Beijing: Renmin, 1989.

Fu Yiling and Chen Zhiping, eds. "Ming–Qing Fujian shehui jingji shiliao zachao 7." *Zhongguo shehui jingji shi yanjiu,* no. 4 (1987).

Fu Yiling and Yang Guozhen, eds. *Ming–Qing Fujian shehui yu xiangcun jingji.* Xiamen: Xiamen daxue, 1987.

Fujian sheng nongcun diaocha. Fuzhou: Huadong junzheng weiyuanhui, 1951.

Heijdra, Martin. "The Socio-economic Development of Rural China during the Ming." In Denis Twitchett and Frederick Mote, eds., *Cambridge History of China,* vol. 8. Cambridge: Cambridge University Press, 1998.

Huang Shumin. "Cong zaoqi Dajia diqu de kaituo kan Taiwan Hanren zuzhi de fazhan." In Li Yiyuan and Jiao Jian, eds., *Zhongguo de minzu, shehui yu wenhua.* Taibei: Shihuo, 1981.

Lai Zehan and Chen Kuanzheng. "Woguo jiating xingshi de lishi yu renkou tantao." *Zhongguo shehui xuekan* 5 (1980).

Lang, Olga. *Chinese Family and Society.* New Haven, Conn.: Yale University Press, 1946.

Laslett, Peter. "Introduction." In Peter Laslett, ed., *Household and Family in Past Time.* Cambridge: Cambridge University Press, 1972.

Lee, James, and Cameron Campbell. *Fate and Fortune in Rural China: Social Organization and Population Behavior in Liaoning, 1774–1873.* Cambridge: Cambridge University Press, 1997.

Legge, James, trans. *Li Chi, Book of Rites.* 2 vols. Oxford: Oxford University Press, 1885. Reprint, New York: University Books, 1967.

Li Wenzhi. "Mingdai zongzu zhi de tixian xingshi ji qi jiceng zhengquan zuoyong." *Zhongguo jingji shi yanjiu,* no. 1 (1988).

Liu Ts'ui-jung. "Demographic Constraint and Family Structure in Traditional Chinese Lineages, ca. 1200–1900." In Stevan Harrell, ed., *Chinese Historical Microdemography.* Berkeley: University of California Press, 1995.

Liu Zhiwan. "Nantou xian fengsuzhi zongjiao biangao." *Nantou wenxian congji* 9 (1961).

Lynn, Richard, trans. *The Classic of Changes: A New Translation of the I Ching as Interpreted by Wang Bi.* New York: Columbia University Press, 1994.

Mao Zedong. *Selected Works of Mao Tse-tung.* Beijing: Foreign Languages Press, 1967.

Marx, Karl. *The Poverty of Philosophy.* New York: International Publishers, 1963.

Morgan, Lewis. *Ancient Society.* 1877. Reprint, Cambridge, Mass.: Harvard University Press, 1964.

Mori Masao. "Weirao xiangzu wenti." *Zhongguo shehui jingji shi yanjiu,* no. 2 (1986): 1–8.

Ng Chin-keong. *Trade and Society: The Amoy Network on the China Coast, 1683–1735.* Singapore: Singapore University Press, 1983.

Putian wenshi muke tuoben zhi chugao. Putian: Putian xian wenhua guan, 1963.

Qu Tongzu. *Zhongguo falü yu Zhongguo shehui.* Shanghai: Shangwu, 1946. Reprint, Beijing: Zhonghua, 1981.

Quanzhou Huizu pudie ziliao xuanji. Quanzhou: Quanzhou lishi yanjiuhui, Chenkang Huizu weiyuanhui, 1980.

Rawski, Evelyn. *Agricultural Change and the Peasant Economy of South China.* Cambridge, Mass.: Harvard University Press, 1972.

Rinji Taiwan kyūkan chōsakai. *Taiwan shihō furoku sankōsho.* Taibei: Rinji Taiwan kyūkan chōsakai, 1909–1911.

Rui Yifu. "Dibian zhong de Zhongguo jiating jiegou." Paper presented at the Tenth Conference on Pacific Sciences, Honolulu, 1961.

Sangren, Steven. "Traditional Chinese Corporations: Beyond Kinship." *Journal of Asian Studies* 43 (1984): 391–414.

Schafer, Edward. *The Empire of Min.* Rutland, Vt.: Charles Tuttle, 1954.

Shiba Yoshinobu. *Commerce and Society in Sung China.* Trans. Mark Elvin. (Ann Arbor) *Michigan Abstracts of Chinese and Japanese Works on Chinese History* 2 (1970).

Skinner, William. "Presidential Address: The Structure of Chinese History." *Journal of Asian Studies* 44 (1985): 271–292.

So Kwan-wai. *Japanese Piracy in Ming China during the Sixteenth Century.* East Lansing: Michigan State University Press, 1975.

Strauch, Judith. "Community and Kinship in Southeastern China: The View from the Multilineage Villages of Hong Kong." *Journal of Asian Studies* 43 (1983): 21–50.

Taiwan gongsi cang guwenshu jicheng. Nangang: Zhongyang yanjiu yuan, 1977–1984.

Tang Meijun. "Taiwan chuantong de shehui jiegou." In Liu Ningyan, ed., *Taiwan shiji yuanliu.* Taibei: Taiwan sheng wenxian, 1981.

Tang Wenji, ed. *Fujian gudai jingji shi.* Fuzhou: Fujian jiaoyu, 1995.

Tjan Tjoe Som, trans. *Po Hu T'ung: The Comprehensive Discussions in the White Tiger Hall.* Leiden: Brill, 1949.

Vermeer, Eduard, ed. *Development and Decline of Fukien Province in the 17th and 18th Centuries.* Leiden: Brill, 1990.

Wakefield, David. *Fenjia: Household Division and Inheritance in Qing and Republican China.* Honolulu: University of Hawai'i Press, 1998.

Waltner, Ann. "Kinship between the Lines: The Patriline, the Concubine and the Adopted Son in Late Imperial China." In Mary Jo Maynes et al., eds. *Gender, Kinship, Power: A Comparative and Interdisciplinary History.* New York: Routledge, 1996.

Wang Songxing. "Lun diyuan yu xueyuan." In Li Yiyuan and Jiao Jian, eds., *Zhongguo de minzu, shehui yu wenhua.* Taibei: Shihuo, 1981.

———. "Zhuoda liuyu de minzu xue yanjiu." *Minzuxue yanjiusuo jikan* 36 (1973).

Watson, James. "Chinese Kinship Reconsidered: Anthropological Perspectives on Historical Research." *China Quarterly* 92 (1982): 586–622.

Wolf, Arthur. "Family Life and the Life Cycle in Rural China." In Robert Netting, Richard Wilk, and Eric Arnould, eds., *Households: Comparative and Historical Studies of the Domestic Group.* Berkeley: University of California Press, 1984.

———. "Chinese Family Size: A Myth Revitalized." In Hsieh Jih-chang and Chuang Ying-chang, eds., *The Chinese Family and Its Ritual Behaviour.* Nangang: Institute of Ethnology, Academia Sinica, 1985.

Xu Yangjie. "Song–Ming yilai de fengjian jiazu zhidu lunshu." *Zhongguo shehui kexue,* no. 4 (1980).

Yang Guozhen. "Ming Qing Fujian tudi siren suoyouquan neizai jiegou de yanjiu." In Fu Yiling and Yang Guozhen, eds., *Ming Qing Fujian shehui yu xiangcun jingji.* Xiamen: Xiamen daxue, 1987.

———. *Ming–Qing tudi qiyue wenshu yanjiu.* Beijing: Renmin, 1988.

Ye Qingkun. "Xinjiapo he Malaya de zaoqi Zhongguo renmin zuzhi, 1819–1911." *Dongnanya yanjiu* 7 (1981).

Zhao Zhongwei. "Demographic Conditions and Multi-generation Households in Chinese History: Results from Genealogical Research and Microsimulation." *Population Studies* 48 (1994): 413–425.

Zheng Zhenman. "Qingdai Minnan de xiangzu xiedou yu shehui zuzhi." *Zhongguo shehui jingji shi yanjiu,* no. 3 (1984).

———. "Qing zhi Minguo Minbei liujian fenguan de fenxi." *Zhongguo shehui jingji shi yanjiu,* no. 3 (1984).

———. "Shilun Minbei xiangzu dizhu jingji de xingtai yu jiegou." *Zhongguo shehui jingji shi yanjiu,* no. 4 (1985).

———. "Ming–Qing Fujian yanhai nongtian shuili zhidu yu xiangzu zuzhi." *Zhongguo shehui jingji shi yanjiu,* no. 4 (1987).

———. "Ming–Qing Minbei xiangzu dizhu jingji de fazhan." In Fu Yiling and Yang Guozhen, eds., *Ming Qing Fujian shehui yu xiangcun jingji.* Xiamen: Xiamen daxue, 1987.

———. "Qingdai Taiwan de hegu jingying." *Taiwan yanjiu jikan,* no. 3 (1987).

———. "Song yihou Fujian de jizu xisu yu zongzu zuzhi." *Xiamen daxue xuebao,* 1987.

———. "Ming Qing Fujian de jiating jiegou jiqi yanbian qushi." *Zhongguo shehui jingji shi yanjiu,* no. 4 (1988).

———. "Qingdai Taiwan xiangzu zuzhi de gongyou jingji." *Taiwan yanjiu jikan,* no. 2 (1988).

———. "Ming yihou Minbei xiangzu tudi de suoyou quan xingtai." In *Pinghuai xuekan,* no. 5 (1989).

———. "Mingdai Chenjiang Dingshi Huizu de zongzu zuzhi yu wenhua guocheng." In *Xiamen daxue xuebao,* 1990. Reprinted in *Chenkang Huizu shi yanjiu.* Beijing: Zhongguo shehui kexue, 1991.

Zhu Weigan. *Fujian shigao.* Fuzhou: Fujian jiaoyu, 1986.

Zhu Yong. *Qingdai zongzu fa yanjiu.* Changsha: Hunan jiaoyu, 1987.

Zhuang Jifa. *Qingdai Tiandihui yuanliu kao.* Taibei: Guoli gugong bowuyuan, 1981.

Zhuang Weiji and Wang Lianmao. *Min-Tai guanxi zupu ziliao xuanji.* Fuzhou: Fujian renmin, 1984.

Zhuang Yingzhang, *Linpipu: Yige Taiwan shizhen de shehui jingji fazhan shi.* Nangang: Zhongyang yanjiuyuan minzuxue yanjiusuo, 1977.

Zhuang Yingzhang and Chen Qi'nan. "Xian jieduan Zhongguo shehui jiegou yanjiu de jiantao: Taiwan yanjiu de yixie qishi." In Zhuang Yingzhang and Chen Qi'nan, eds., *Shehui ji xingwei kexue yanjiu de Zhongguohua.* Nangang: Zhongyang yanjiuyuan minzuxue yanjiusuo, 1982.

Zhuang Yingzhang and Chen Qi'nan, eds. *Shehui ji xingwei kexue yanjiu de Zhongguo hua.* Nangang: Zhongyang yanjiuyuan minzuxue yanjiusuo, 1982.

Zhuang Yingzhang and Chen Yundong. "Qingdai Toufen de zongzu yu shehui fazhanshi." *Guoli Taiwan shifan daxue lishi xuebao* 10 (1982).

Zhuang Yingzhang. "Taiwan zongzu zuzhi de xingcheng ji qi tedian." In *Xiandaihua yu Zhongguo wenhua yanjiuhui lunwen huibian.* Hong Kong: Zhongwen daxue shehui kexue yanjiusuo, 1985.

Zuo Yunpeng. "Citang, zuzhang, zuquan de xingcheng jiqi zuoyong shishu." *Lishi yanjiu,* 1964.

Index

adoption, 14, 22, 25, 55, 75, 300–301, 334nn. 26, 48; and commercial development, 38; consequences for household structure, 38–41; in control-subordination lineage, 119–120; designated heir, 40, 51–52, 58–60; in inheritance lineage, 75–77, 262–263; legal regulations on, 76; lineage regulations on, 40, 120

ancestors, invented, 232, 285. *See also* First Ancestor of the Surname to Migrate to Fujian; First Ancestor to Settle

ancestral graves, 80, 92–93, 132, 176–177, 277–278. *See also* ancestral sacrifice; lineage corporate property

ancestral hall (*citang*), 14, 113, 137, 192–196, 270–271; in coastal Fujian, 192–202; in contractual lineage, 204–205; distinction between private and public, 150, 170, 198–199; in early Ming, 200; gentry and, 194–197; in northwestern Fujian, 146, 150–154, 175–185; ownership rights of, 133–140, 176–185; regulations concerning, 197, 269–270; in residentially dispersed lineage, 175–185, 236–238; from Song to Ming, 194; in Taiwan, 252–257; as tool of social control, 201–202

ancestral home (*zucuo*), 192, 194, 274–277

ancestral sacrifice, 72, 90–92, 177–178; accompanying (*fusi*), 78, 85, 107; ancient principles of, 6, 91, 93, 269–271; attitudes to, 284–285; to distant generations, 272–273; to founding ancestor, 91, 197; at graves, 75, 81–83, 85, 93, 147, 155–157, 277–278; increasing scale in Ming, 197; and inheritance, 66–67, 90–92; in northwestern Fujian, 146. *See also* ancestral hall; ancestral home; ancestral tablets; lineage corporate property

ancestral societies (*zugonghui*), 248

ancestral tablets, 90, 107–109, 138–140, 153, 195; fees to install, 63, 112, 152–153, 177–184, 238, 254

Anhui, 186

Anxi County, 236–237

Ban Gu, 268

baojia, 23, 332n. 4

Berkner, Lutz, 3

Bohu tong (Comprehensive Discussions in the White Tiger Hall), 268

bond-servants, 38, 300–301

Book of Rites (*Liji*), 6, 46, 269, 280

bottom-soil rent. *See* multiple land-ownership

Buddhist rituals, 148

Cai lineage of Jianyang, 84–85, 271–272, 282–284, 286; official support for, 348n. 40

Cai lineage of Pucheng, 312–313

Cai lineage of Putian, 220–221, 225–227

Cai Xiang, 191, 207

Campbell, Cameron, 4

Changtai County, 210

Changting County, 301. *See also* Zou lineage of Changting

ABOUT THE AUTHOR

Zheng Zhenman is one of the leading social historians of late imperial China. He is professor of history at Xiamen University.

ABOUT THE TRANSLATOR

Michael Szonyi is assistant professor of modern Chinese history at the University of Toronto.